Keto Air Fryer Cookbook

1000 Quick & Flavorful Low-Carb Recipes to Air Fry, Bake, Grill and Roast for Boosting Energy and Keeping Healthy (2022 Edition)

Sara S. Nelson

Table of Content

Chapter 4 Beef, Pork, and Lamb 31

Chapter 5 Poultry 58

Chapter 6 Fish and Seafood 82

Chapter 7 Vegetarian Mains 106

Chapter 8 Side Dishes 125

Chapter 9 Appetizers and Snacks 142

Chapter 10 Desserts 163

INTRODUCTION

If you've already used an air fryer prior, you'll probably know that it is a revolutionary cooking apparatus that can make you live better and save your time. But even so, what is special about this piece of the appliance?

Air fryers have what it takes to replace microwave, oven dehydrator, deep fryer while preparing some of the most delicious meals you've ever tasted in a shorter time. If you have a very busy schedule and you still plan to cook some healthy meals for your family, then air fryers are your best bet.

They can also be useful with our overall commitment and success to the ketogenic diet scheme. Long-term triumph on the keto diet scheme is attributable to how you easily prepare your meals. And that is why we recommend air fryers for your ketogenic diet journey to help you prepare your meals, especially on days when you are very busy and need all the time in the world.

Throughout this cookbook, you'll learn all you need to know about some ketogenic diet air fryer recipes, why you should use air fryers in the preparation of your diets, and some of the basics of being successful with the keto diet scheme. Let's cook!

Chapter 1 The Keto Diet 101

What is Ketogenic Diet?

Practically all known diets, to varying degrees, concentrate on either lowering the levels of calories or just manipulating the rate of the intake of one of the three important macronutrients (proteins, fats, or carbohydrates) to get the same results.

Ketogenic diets are a group of special diets that have a very high concentration of fats but with a very low carbohydrate concentration. The term "ketogenic" typically means the increased production of ketone bodies caused by the high rate of lipolysis (the breakdown of fats). Ketones are acid byproducts formed during the intermediate breakdown of "fat" into "fatty acids" by the liver.

Today, ketogenic diet advocates firmly believe that carbohydrates, especially those with a high glycemic index, are some of the major factors why several people add weight.

Carbohydrate foods are usually digested to produce glucose, a simple form of sugar that is generally considered the body's preferred energy source because it is fast-burning energy that is readily available after a meal.

Even though the human body can digest glycogen and fats to produce energy for its use, it prefers to get it from carbohydrates because it is an easy route.

Ketogenic diets are designed to "force" the body to use up its endogenous glucose stores and then make it switch to the fat stores as the main energy-generating equivalent for the body.

Although the ketogenic diet is known for its rapid weight loss advantage, especially in the early stages of the diet practice, weight loss is surely a moderate and tedious process.

How Does Ketogenic Diet Work?

To know how the ketogenic diet works, it is important to know the physiology behind it. The type of change that the body undergoes when it is undergoing ketogenesis is known as ketosis. The term "Ketosis" often causes skepticism or even fear in those who try as much as possible to decide if it is a good thing. Below is an easy insight into what ketosis means.

KETO DIET: HIGHER FAT

GLUCOSE LEVELS FALL   LIPASE RELEASES STORED TRIGLYCERIDES   FATTY ACIDS TRAVEL TO THE LIVER   LIVER PRODUCES KETONES

ENERGY

Ketosis simply denotes that the body has stopped using carbohydrates as its source of fuel and then switches to fat almost exclusively as its alternative energy source.

But then it can get a little more complex than that. Ketosis starts when there are low levels of carbohydrates (specifically, glucose) in the blood to replenish the endogenous glycogen stores in the liver.

What then is this glycogen? Glycogen can simply be seen as long and branched chains of glucose molecules joined end-to-end in a certain manner to confer the right chemical integrity to it. The liver produces glycogen from carbohydrates as a fast-food source for the body after a carbohydrate-rich meal.

A lack of carbohydrates means that the body needs an alternative food source to compensate for the enormous amount of energy required in its daily processes. So then the body makes use of its fat stores, especially fatty acids.

The liver breaks down these fats into compounds which are ultimately converted to ketone bodies through series of chemical reactions that are highly specialized for that process.

When the liver then discharges these ketone bodies into the bloodstream to utilize as energy, this is ketosis in its simplest definition.

When you eat carbohydrates rich foods, your body uses them for energy generation and converts the undigested ones into fat making use of insulin.

What this means is that carbohydrates are not stored in your body, except those stored in your liver as glycogen molecules.

If you do not replenish the carbohydrates in your blood after using them, your body will eventually use the fats you consume with your food and the fats stored in the body as fuel. Ketosis usually begins at about 48 hours after the last carbohydrate meal.

Keto Macros

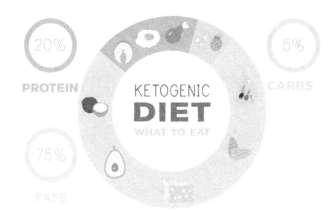

The most common macros nutrient ratio for keto diets is 25% protein, 5% carbohydrates, and 70% fats. In certain cases, some nutritionists and dieticians will recommend that you increase the fat percentage to about 75% and decrease that of protein to about 20%.

Also, you can check another substitute for the average keto diet: the cyclic ketogenic diet. This type of diet is advised for individuals who are trying to decrease their fat mass and increase their muscle mass. While observing this diet, you will have to control your food intake to the standard ketogenic diet for about five to six days, and then one to two days of raised carbohydrates consumption. What this diet attempts to do is to restore your blood glucose level.

Steps to Getting your Macro Right

1. Determine your exact calorie need (Cal/day)

Here's how to calculate it for men and women.

- Men

10 x weight (kilogram) + 6.25 x height (cm) - 5 x age (y) + 5

- Women

10 x weight (kilogram) + 6.25 x height (cm) - 5 x age (y) - 161

Then multiply your result by an activity factor.

- Resting: x 1.2

- Slightly active: x 1,375

- Moderately active: x 1.55

- Very active: x 1.725

- Extra active: x 1.9

The result gives you your total daily energy expenditure.

2. Decide on the ideal distribution of your macronutrients

Typical macronutrient recommendations are as follows:

- Carbohydrates: 45 to 65% of total calories

- Fat: 20 to 35% of total calories

- Protein: 10 to 35% of the total number of calories

A person who follows a ketogenic diet would need a lot more fat and fewer carbohydrates, while an endurance athlete might need a higher carbohydrate intake.

3. Follow your macros and your caloric intake

There are many user-friendly tools specifically designed to simplify tracking macros.

Many applications have a barcode reader that automatically enters a portion of a scanned food into your macro log.

You can also write macros manually in a physical log. The method depends on your individual preferences.

4. Counting example

Here is an example of calculating macronutrients for a 2000 calorie diet consisting of 40% carbohydrate, 30% protein, and 30% fat.

* *Carbohydrates:*

- 4 calories per gram

- 40% of 2,000 calories = 800 calories of carbohydrate per day

- Total grams of carbohydrate allowed per day = 800/4 = 200 grams

* *Protein:*

- 4 calories per gram

- 30% of 2,000 Cal = 600 Cal of protein per day

- Total protein allowed gram/day = 600/4 = 150 grams

* *Fats:*

- 9 calories per gram
- 30% of 2,000 Cal = 600 Cal of protein/day
- Total fat allowed (gram/day) = 600/9 = 67 grams

Keto Foods to Eat and Avoid

Foods to Eat on a Keto Diet

Foods Not to Eat on a Keto Diet

Keto-Friendly Foods to Eat

When you are sticking to the ketogenic diet scheme, there are some foods should constitute your diet and some that you should avoid.

Examples of keto-centric foods are:

- **Eggs:** Organic and pastured eggs.
- **Poultry:** Turkey and chicken.
- **Fatty fish:** Mackerel, herring, and wild-caught salmon.
- **Meat:** Pork, venison, grass-fed beef, bison, and organ meats.
- **Full-fat dairy:** Cream, butter, and yogurt.
- **Full-fat cheese:** Brie, mozzarella, cheddar, cream cheese, and goat cheese.
- **Seeds and nuts:** Almonds, macadamia nuts, pumpkin seeds, walnuts, flaxseeds, and peanuts.
- **Nut butter:** Cashew butter, almond, and natural peanut.
- **Healthy fats:** Avocado oil, olive oil, coconut oil, sesame oil, and coconut butter.
- **Avocados:** You can add whole avocados to almost any snack or meal.
- **Non-starchy vegetables:** Tomatoes, broccoli, greens, peppers, and mushrooms.
- **Condiments:** Vinegar, pepper, salt, spices, fresh herbs, and lemon juice.

Foods to Stay Away From

When you are observing the ketogenic diet, there are some foods that you need to stay away from. These are generally foods that are rich in carbohydrates. Below are some of the foods that you should avoid to get the most in your ketogenic diet commitments.

- **Baked Foods and Bread:** Whole-wheat bread, white bread, cookies, crackers, rolls, and doughnuts.
- **Sugary and Sweets Foods:** Ice cream, sugar, maple syrup, candy, coconut sugar, and agave syrup.
- **Sweetened Beverages:** Juice, soda, sports drinks, and sweetened teas.
- **Pasta:** Noodles and spaghetti.
- **Grain products and Grains:** Rice, wheat, tortillas, breakfast cereals, and oats.
- **Starchy vegetables:** Sweet potatoes, potatoes, corn, butternut squash, pumpkin, and peas.
- **Legumes and Beans:** Chickpeas, black beans, kidney beans, and lentils.
- **Fruit:** Grapes, citrus, pineapples, and bananas.
- **High-carb Sauces:** Dipping sauces, sugar-rich salad dressings, and Barbecue sauce.
- **Some Alcoholic Beverages:** Sugar-rich mixed beverages and beer.

Even though it is not advisable to consume carbohydrate-rich foods when you are on the ketogenic diet scheme, fruits with low-glycemic values like berries may be taken in restricted amounts if you are sticking to a keto-centric macronutrient range.

Steps to Keto Success

1. Know the Right Amount of Macronutrients You Need

Knowing the exact amount of fat, carbs, and protein that you need during a ketogenic diet exercise is the most important step that you need to take when drafting the perfect ketogenic diet menu.

2. Understand Your Exact Macro Requirements

You also need the precise macro requirements that will help you enter the state of ketosis and help you regulate your energy levels as it supports your body fitness objectives. Like we discussed earlier, a macro calculator will help you approximate your nutritional portion. For example, to calculate the percentage of your macros, divide the calorie values by the value of the micronutrients you consume daily and multiply by 100%.

Example of Keto Macros Calculation:

- Your carbs requirement is (80g/1800g) x 100% = 5%
- Your protein requirement (600g/1800g) x 100% = 33%
- Your fats requirement (1,120g/1800g) x 100% = 62%

Hence, the total amount of calories should sum up to 100% (5% + 33 %+ 62% = 100).

3. Pick the Best Keto-Centric Foods

When you've ascertained your macro objectives, then get busy selecting some of the best ketogenic-centric foods that match your macros.

4. Know Your Servings

When you completely come to terms with the number of carbs, fat, and protein that you need to consume, then the next thing to do is to know the serving amount that is right for you. Becoming a master in this can take a bit of practice and time, but one good way to learning this is to carefully track the food amount that you eat every day.

Guidelines for Setting a Keto Meal Plan

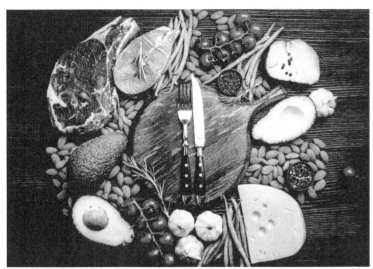

As noted before, certain individuals need to decrease the levels of their carbs intake if they must enter the state of ketosis.

Adapting to a ketogenic diet scheme can sometimes be overpowering, but it does not have to be hard.

You should concentrate on decreasing your carbohydrate consumption while raising the levels of your protein and fat intake of your snacks and meals. You must limit your intake of carb if you must enter a state of ketosis.

While it is true that some people can enter the ketosis state by just consuming twenty grams of carbohydrates a day, some others may need higher to achieve the same feat.

The general rule is that you'll achieve ketosis faster if you lower your carbs intake. Thus, committing to eating carbs-rich foods would make you lose weight faster if you are practicing the ketogenic regimen.

A healthy keto diet should comprise about 10-30% protein, 75% fat, and no greater than 20 to 50 grams or 5%of carbohydrates per day.

Focus on low-carb, high-fat foods like meats, eggs, low-carb vegetables, and dairy, in addition to sugar-free beverages. Ensure that you limit your consumption of unhealthy fats and highly processed foods.

Even though a lot of keto-based foods are centered on animal products, the scheme has a lot of vegetarian alternatives that you can settle for too.

If you are sticking to a more accommodating ketogenic diet scheme, including small carbohydrate veggies in your dinner or one cup of berries for breakfast will raise the number of carbohydrates in your ketogenic meal plan.

Chapter 2 Air Fryer for Keto

Air fryers are a very helpful and popular cooking appliance that you can use to prepare different air fryer-based ketogenic recipes. And with their fantastic cooking ability, air fryers can also make your dishes more tasteful.

Also, the process of air frying is super easy, quick, and convenient. It is important to note that the process does not supernaturally make carbohydrates vanish. It can only provide different recipe types that are low carbohydrates and keto.

With an air fryer, you can reduce the amount of oil that you use in the preparation of the recipes and make cooking time shorter. This implies that you can browse recipes that are keto-friendly and low in carbohydrate content.

Keto air fryer recipes include meals consumed at different times, such as dinner, lunch, breakfast, and some other indulgent keto desserts.

Why Air Fryer for Keto?

- **Prepare Keto-Based Diets with Minimal Efforts**

With an air fryer, you can prepare certain kinds of ketogenic diets in less than an hour. Some of these recipes even take a much lower time to prepare.

- **Prepare Nice Hard-Boiled Eggs with Ease**

It is indeed a fun fact to know that you don't need to hard-boiled for preparing hard-boiled eggs with air fryers. Just position the eggs inside the air fryer space and have the timer set for 260°F and sixteen minutes.

- **Prepare Keto Breaded Crispy Snacks**

Air fryers are helpful to those who prepare keto breaded crispy snacks. For example, you can prepare super simple air-fried crunchy pickles with an air fryer by making beading from crushed pork rinds and grated Parmesan cheese.

- **Quick Keto Snacks**

One satisfying and easy idea for quick keto snacks is to prepare wrapped salami mozzarella cheese sticks with air fryers.

Slice the cheese sticks to one-third of its size. Coat each of them with a salami piece and keep them in place using a toothpick. Put it inside an air fryer and allow it to cook at 360°F Fahrenheit for six minutes.

- ## Make Meats Juicy and Delicious

The application of air fryers for use in cooking keto-based meals is far beyond snacks and fries.

You can prepare wonderful burgers with this powerful kitchen appliance. Also, you can cook mid-sized patties at 350° for about ten minutes, or just when they've reached the preferred doneness.

- ## Prepare Fantastic Keto Fries for Your Burger

You probably do not know that jicama is an amazing substitute for potatoes in preparing keto French fries? You can toss these jicama fries inside your air fryer and set the temperature to 400°F and cook for twenty minutes. The experience is worthy of your trial.

- ## Make Keto-Centric Vegetable Crisps

With air fryers, you can easily prepare Brussels sprouts that will be tender inside and crispy outside without cooking for eternity. Ten minutes is sufficient to prepare for this amazing and tasteful meal.

- ## Prepare Mess-Free Bacon

The duration of cooking will differ contingently on how thick the bacon is, but you can prepare crispy, traditional bacon at 390°F in just eight minutes. If the bacon is thick, then the duration of cooling can last up to eleven minutes or more if you want your bacon to be very crispy.

Some other reasons why an air fryer is a great option for you!

- Unlike other difficult cooking options, the ease of using of air fryers is one of its strong points.
- Cleaning this kitchen apparatus is very easy. Plus air fryers are portable so that you can convey them to different places without breaking a sweat.
- You can conveniently remove the air fryer's basket to see if food is done cooking and then just place it back in to cook longer if desired.
- As noted earlier, the duration of cooking is faster when the device is an air fryer. It cooks faster than most traditional ovens out there!
- Cook time is also the literal meaning and you don't have to waste extra time preheating the cooking apparatus or waiting for the device to attain the desired pressure, as in the case of pressure cookers.
- The temperature of the kitchen will be cooler if you are using an air fryer. This is unlike the case of conventional ovens which heighten your kitchen's temperature.

Air Fryer Cooking Tips

* ## Have Your Air Fryer Preheated

If you bring an air fryer that does not come with preheat settings, then set it to your preferred temperature and let it work for some three minutes before putting your food inside.

* ## Utilize Oil on Certain Foods

There are some types of foods that you can make crisp using oil. Some others do not require oil to achieve the same results.

* Lubricate the Air Fryer Basket

Take a little time and lubricate the basket of your air fryer. Get this done even the food you are preparing does not need oil. This helps prevent the food from becoming non-sticky.

* Use Aerosol Spray Cans

Using an aerosol spray can can keep food from sticking on the air fryer basket, and thus reduce the burden of cleaning it.

* Do Not Choke the Air Fryer Basket

If you desire that your fried meals become crispy, then you must keep the basket relatively free. Don't stuff it with too many things. If you do, you risk preventing whatever you are preparing from browning and crisping. If you don't want this to occur, then prepare your meal in different batches or buy a larger air fryer.

* Shake the Basket

When you are preparing smaller food like French fries, chicken wings, it makes sense that you frequently shake the air fryer basket for some minutes to make sure the cooking is even.

* Spray Midway While Cooking

Foods that are coated need to be sprayed. And, don't forget to spray dry flour patches that will occur midway while air frying your foods.

* Put Water at the Bottom

If you are preparing a greasy meal with your air fryer, do not be astonished if you discover that some white smoke is coming out of the apparatus. All you need to do to address this is to put a small amount of water at the bottom of your device's basket.

* Be Cautious of Petite-Sized Items

All air fryers feature a very effective fan fixed atop them. This fan makes some items with lighter weight to be swept up by the fan and this can be very dangerous.

* Regulate the Temperature for Particular Foods

Sometimes, it can be appealing to crank the temperature of your air fryer to its maximum so that it can work faster, but you need to take great care because certain foods can quickly dry out.

One great rule that works the magic is to regulate the time and heat to the time required for the preparation of the meal you are preparing. If you regulate the temperature below 350°F for twenty minutes in your oven, but for your air fryer, you can decrease the temperature to about 320°F and cook the meal for sixteen minutes.

* Buy a Good Thermometer

You must acquire a quick-read thermometer for your air fryer particularly in the preparation of certain kinds of meats, such as pork, chicken, and steak.

Air Fryer Pantry List for Keto

And so it is time to go for another round of crazy shopping, but you are wondering what you need to settle after you've decided to stick to the ketogenic regimen.

It may seem like rocket science to some, especially when they think about the different keto-based ingredients that they need to buy, but with a few instructions, they can know what is exactly needed.

While some of the inclusions of this list can easily be gotten from shops in the neighborhood, some others may need dedicated search and online ordering if you must use them.

It would be great if you can visit any grocery store around you to know what appeared air-fryer-worthy. Don't limit yourself to the normal suspects and try some unanticipated grocery stuff.

When you do, you will almost always notice that the results will be by-and-large a resounding, fun-filled, and sometimes astonishing success.

Just as you would expect, different products have different duration, and you may need some patience and a handful of trials to do it the right way. Air fryers are somewhat forgiving, so that you may not likely save a severe situation if you did not do the right thing. If needed, deliberately make mistakes on the part of less time than more time until you arrive at your meal choice.

Before then, you need to know what you need for your keto air fryer pantry list. If you go shopping, you should buy the following items:

- **Portable Protein Sources**

  * Canned tuna   * Canned salmon   * Hard-boiled eggs   * Pepperoni
  * Beef meat sticks   * Cheese   * Salami   * Pork rinds
  * Canned sardines   * Smoked oysters   * Jerky

- **Healthy Keto Fat Sources**

  * Coconut oil   * Avocado oil   * Extra Virgin Olive Oil   * Grass-fed butter ghee

- **Keto Snacks**

  * Pecans   * Pili nuts   * Pumpkin seeds
  * Almonds   * Unsweetened peanut butter   * Avocado
  * Walnuts   * Nutzo   * Cheese crisps
  * Macadamia nuts   * Unsweetened almond butter   * Lily's Chocolate bars
  * Unsweetened coconut butter * Sunflower seeds   * Olives single servings

- **Keto Baking Essentials**

* Coconut unsweetened, shredded
* Almond flour
* Cacao butter
* Coconut flour
* Ground Flaxseed
* Chia seeds
* Sesame flour
* Unsweetened Cocoa powder
* Pork rind breadcrumbs
* Baking powder

* Pink Himalayan sea salt
* Bone broth
* Baking soda
* Gelatin
* Cream of tartar
* Apple extract
* Xanthan gum
* Caramel extract
* Almond extract
* Maple extract
* Lemon extract

* Vanilla stevia
* Vanilla extract
* Clear stevia
* Swerve confectioners
* Swerve granular
* Swerve brown sugar
* Sugar-Free Chocolate chips
* Monk fruit sweetener
* Whey protein powder
* 85% dark chocolate
* Egg white protein powder

- **Other Pantry Condiments**

* No Sugar Added Ketchup
* Dressings

* Mustard
* Mayo

* No Sugar added Tomato sauce
* Lakanto maple syrup

Air Fryer Accessory

There are many quick keto-based air fryer foods to prepare with the assistance of some good air fryer accessories. You can fully indulge in many of these foods that you never imagined could be air-fried. Take your cooking to the next level. But before then, get busy buying some of these air fryer accessories.

- Silicone Trivet
- Tortilla Stand for Crispy Tacos
- Cupcake cups or silicon muffin
- Silicone Tongs
- Deep Baking Pans: Cake pans or barrel pans
- Skewers and rack
- Silicone pots
- Shallow Baking Pans or "pizza pan"
- Larger Size Air Fryer
- Parchment sheets

Chapter 3 Breakfast

Toast Pavlova

Prep time: 15 minutes | Cook time: 60 minutes | Serves 4

3 large egg whites
¼ teaspoon cream of tartar
¾ cup Swerve confectioners-style sweetener
1 teaspoon ground cinnamon
1 teaspoon maple extract

Toppings:
½ cup heavy cream
3 tablespoons Swerve confectioners-style sweetener, plus more for garnish
Fresh strawberries (optional)

1. Preheat the air fryer to 275°F. Thoroughly grease a 7-inch pie pan with butter or coconut oil. Place a large bowl in the refrigerator to chill.
2. In a small bowl, combine the egg whites and cream of tartar. Using a hand mixer, beat until soft peaks form. Turn the mixer to low and slowly sprinkle in the sweetener while mixing until completely incorporated. Add the cinnamon and maple extract and beat on medium-high until the peaks become stiff.
3. Spoon the mixture into the greased pie pan, then smooth it across the bottom, up the sides, and onto the rim of the pie pan to form a shell. Cook in the air fryer for 1 hour, then turn off the air fryer and let the shell stand in the air fryer for another 20 minutes. Once the shell has set, transfer it to the refrigerator to chill for 20 minutes or the freezer to chill for 10 minutes.
4. While the shell sets and chills, make the topping: Remove the large bowl from the refrigerator and place the heavy cream in it. Whip with a hand mixer on high until soft peaks form. Add the sweetener and beat until medium peaks form. Taste and adjust the sweetness to your liking.
5. Place the chilled shell on a serving platter and spoon on the cream topping. Top with the strawberries, if desired, and garnish with powdered sweetener. Slice and serve.
6. If you won't be eating the pavlova right away, store the shell and topping in separate airtight containers in the refrigerator for up to 3 days.

Per Serving

calories: 115 | fat: 11g | protein: 3g | carbs: 2g | net carbs: 1.7g | fiber: 0.3g

Broccoli Frittata

Prep time: 15 minutes | Cook time: 12 minutes | Serves 4

6 large eggs
¼ cup heavy whipping cream
½ cup chopped broccoli

¼ cup chopped yellow onion
¼ cup chopped green bell pepper

1. In a large bowl, whisk eggs and heavy whipping cream. Mix in broccoli, onion, and bell pepper.
2. Pour into a 6-inch round oven-safe baking dish. Place baking dish into the air fryer basket.
3. Adjust the temperature to 350°F (180ºC) and set the timer for 12 minutes.
4. Eggs should be firm and cooked fully when the frittata is done. Serve warm.

Per Serving

calories: 168 | fat: 11g | protein: 10g | carbs: 3g | net carbs: 2g | fiber: 1g

Cheese Soufflés

Prep time: 15 minutes | Cook time: 12 minutes | Serves 4

3 large eggs, whites and yolks separated
¼ teaspoon cream of tartar

½ cup shredded sharp Cheddar cheese
3 ounces (85 g) cream cheese, softened

1. In a large bowl, beat egg whites together with cream of tartar until soft peaks form, for about 2 minutes.
2. In a separate medium bowl, beat egg yolks, Cheddar, and cream cheese together until frothy, for about 1 minute. Add egg yolk mixture to whites, gently folding until combined.
3. Pour mixture evenly into four 4-inch ramekins greased with cooking spray. Place ramekins into air fryer basket. Adjust the temperature to 350°F (180ºC) and set the timer for 12 minutes. Eggs will be browned on the top and firm in the center when done. Serve warm.

Per Serving

calories: 183 | fat: 14g | protein: 9g | carbs: 1g | net carbs: 1g | fiber: 0g

Keto Breakfast Quiche

Prep time: 10 minutes | Cook time: 60 minutes | Serves 8

Crust:
Cooking spray
1¼ cups blanched almond flour
1¼ cups grated Parmesan or Gouda cheese
¼ teaspoon fine sea salt
1 large egg, beaten
Filling:
½ cup chicken or beef broth (or vegetable broth for vegetarian)

1 cup shredded Swiss cheese
4 ounces cream cheese
1 tablespoon unsalted butter, melted
4 large eggs, beaten
⅓ cup minced leeks or sliced green onions
¾ teaspoon fine sea salt
⅛ teaspoon cayenne pepper
Chopped green onions, for garnish

1. Preheat the air fryer to 325°F. Grease a 6-inch pie pan. Spray two large pieces of parchment paper with avocado oil and set them on the countertop.
2. Make the crust: In a medium-sized bowl, combine the flour, cheese, and salt and mix well. Add the egg and mix until the dough is well combined and stiff.
3. Place the dough in the center of one of the greased pieces of parchment. Top with the other piece of parchment. Using a rolling pin, roll out the dough into a circle about 1/16 inch thick.
4. Press the pie crust into the prepared pie pan. Place it in the air fryer and bake for 12 minutes, or until it starts to lightly brown.
5. While the crust bakes, make the filling: In a large bowl, combine the broth, Swiss cheese, cream cheese, and butter. Stir in the eggs, leeks, salt, and cayenne pepper. When the crust is ready, pour the mixture into the crust.
6. Place the quiche in the air fryer and bake for 15 minutes. Turn the heat down to 300°F and bake for an additional 30 minutes, or until a knife inserted 1 inch from the edge comes out clean. You may have to cover the edges of the crust with foil to prevent burning.
7. Allow the quiche to cool for 10 minutes before garnishing it with chopped green onions and cutting it into wedges.
8. Store leftovers in an airtight container in the refrigerator for up to 4 days or in the freezer for up to a month. Reheat in a preheated 350°F air fryer for a few minutes, until warmed through.

Per Serving
calories: 333 | fat: 26g | protein: 20g | carbs: 6g | net carbs: 4g | fiber: 2g

Golden Biscuits

Prep time: 15 minutes | Cook time: 13 minutes | Serves 8

2 cups blanched almond flour
½ cup Swerve confectioners-style sweetener
1 teaspoon baking powder
½ teaspoon fine sea salt
¼ cup plus 2 tablespoons (¾ stick) very cold unsalted butter

¼ cup unsweetened, unflavored almond milk
1 large egg
1 teaspoon vanilla extract
3 teaspoons ground cinnamon
Glaze:
½ cup Swerve confectioners-style sweetener
¼ cup heavy cream

1. Preheat the air fryer to 350°F (180°C). Line a pie pan that fits into your air fryer with parchment paper.
2. In a medium-sized bowl, mix together the almond flour, sweetener (if powdered, do not add liquid sweetener), baking powder, and salt. Cut the butter into ½-inch squares, and then use a hand mixer to work the butter into the dry ingredients. When you are done, the mixture should still have chunks of butter.
3. In a small bowl, whisk together the almond milk, egg, and vanilla extract (if using liquid sweetener, add it as well) until blended. Using a fork, stir the wet ingredients into the dry ingredients until large clumps form. Add the cinnamon and use your hands to swirl it into the dough.
4. Form the dough into sixteen 1-inch balls and place them on the prepared pan, spacing them about ½-inch apart. (If you're using a smaller air fryer, work in batches if necessary.) Bake in the air fryer until golden, for 10 to 13 minutes. Remove from the air fryer and let it cool on the pan for at least 5 minutes.
5. While the biscuits bake, make the glaze: Place the powdered sweetener in a small bowl and slowly stir in the heavy cream with a fork.
6. When the biscuits have cooled somewhat, dip the tops into the glaze, allow it to dry a bit, and then dip again for a thick glaze.
7. Serve warm or at room temperature. Store unglazed biscuits in an airtight container in the refrigerator for up to 3 days or in the freezer for up to a month. Reheat in a preheated 350°F (180°C) air fryer for 5 minutes, or until warmed through, and dip in the glaze as instructed above.

Per Serving
calories: 546 | fat: 51g | protein: 14g | carbs: 13g | net carbs: 7g | fiber: 6g

Cheesy Danish

Prep time: 15 minutes | Cook time: 20 minutes | Serves 6

Pastry:
3 large eggs
¼ teaspoon cream of tartar
¼ cup vanilla-flavored egg white protein powder
¼ cup Swerve confectioners-style sweetener
3 tablespoons full-fat sour cream
1 teaspoon vanilla extract
Filling:
4 ounces (113 g) cream cheese, softened
2 large egg yolks (from above)
¼ cup Swerve confectioners-style sweetener
1 teaspoon vanilla extract
¼ teaspoon ground cinnamon
Drizzle:
1 ounce (28 g) cream cheese, softened
1 tablespoon Swerve confectioners-style sweetener
1 tablespoon unsweetened, unflavored almond milk

1. Preheat the air fryer to 300°F (150ºC). Spray a casserole dish that will fit in your air fryer with avocado oil.
2. Make the pastry: Separate the eggs, putting all the whites in a large bowl, one yolk in a medium-sized bowl, and two yolks in a small bowl. Beat all the egg yolks and set aside.
3. Add the cream of tartar to the egg whites. Whip the whites with a hand mixer until very stiff, then turn the hand mixer's setting to low and slowly add the protein powder while mixing. Mix until only just combined, if you mix too long, the whites will fall. Set aside.
4. To the egg yolk in the medium-sized bowl, add the sweetener, sour cream, and vanilla extract. Mix well. Slowly pour the yolk mixture into the egg whites and gently combine. Dollop 6 equal-sized mounds of batter into the casserole dish. Use the back of a large spoon to make an indentation on the top of each mound. Set aside.
5. Make the filling: Place the cream cheese in a small bowl and stir to break it up. Add the 2 remaining egg yolks, the sweetener, vanilla extract, and cinnamon and stir until well combined. Divide the filling among the mounds of batter, pouring it into the indentations on the tops.
6. Place the Danish in the air fryer and bake for about 20 minutes, or until golden brown.
7. While the Danish bake, make the drizzle: In a small bowl, stir the cream cheese to break it up. Stir in the sweetener and almond milk. Place the mixture in a piping bag or a small resealable plastic bag with one corner snipped off. After the Danish have cooled, pipe the drizzle over the Danish.
8. Store leftovers in airtight container in the fridge for up to 4 days.

Per Serving
calories: 160 | fat: 12g | protein: 8g | carbs: 2g | net carbs: 1g | fiber: 1g

Meat Patties with Tzatziki

Prep time: 10 minutes | Cook time: 20 minutes | Serves 16

Patties:
2 pounds (907 g) ground lamb or beef
½ cup diced red onions
¼ cup sliced black olives
2 tablespoons tomato purée
1 teaspoon dried oregano leaves
1 teaspoon Greek seasoning
2 cloves garlic, minced
1 teaspoon fine sea salt
Tzatziki:
1 cup full-fat sour cream
1 small cucumber, chopped
½ teaspoon fine sea salt
½ teaspoon garlic powder
¼ teaspoon dried dill weed
For Garnish/Serving:
½ cup crumbled feta cheese (about 2 ounces)
Diced red onions
Sliced black olives
Sliced cucumbers

1. Preheat the air fryer to 350°F (180ºC).
2. Place the ground lamb, onions, olives, tomato purée, oregano, Greek seasoning, garlic, and salt in a large bowl. Mix well to combine the ingredients.
3. Using your hands, form the mixture into sixteen 3-inch patties. Place about 5 of the patties in the air fryer and fry for 20 minutes, flipping halfway through. Remove the patties and place them on a serving platter. Repeat with the remaining patties.
4. While the patties cook, make the tzatziki: Place all the ingredients in a small bowl and stir well. Cover and store in the fridge until ready to serve. Garnish with ground black pepper before serving.
5. Serve the patties with a dollop of tzatziki, a sprinkle of crumbled feta cheese, diced red onions, sliced black olives, and sliced cucumbers.
6. Store leftovers in an airtight container in the refrigerator for up to 5 days or in the freezer for up to a month. Reheat the patties in a preheated 390°F (199ºC) air fryer for a few minutes, until warmed through.

Per Serving
calories: 396 | fat: 31g | protein: 23g | carbs: 4g | net carbs: 3g | fiber: 1g

Pork Sausage and Cream Cheese Biscuit

Prep time: 20 minutes | Cook time: 30 minutes | Serves 4

Filling:
10 ounces (283 g) bulk pork sausage, crumbled
¼ cup minced onions
2 cloves garlic, minced
½ teaspoon fine sea salt
½ teaspoon ground black pepper
1 (8-ounce / 227-g) package cream cheese, softened
¾ cup beef or chicken broth

Biscuits:
3 large egg whites
¾ cup blanched almond flour
1 teaspoon baking powder
¼ teaspoon fine sea salt
2½ tablespoons very cold unsalted butter, cut into ¼-inch pieces
Fresh thyme leaves, for garnish

1. Preheat the air fryer to 400°F (205ºC).
2. Place the sausage, onions, and garlic in a 7-inch pie pan. Using your hands, break up the sausage into small pieces and spread it evenly throughout the pie pan. Season with the salt and pepper. Place the pan in the air fryer and cook for 5 minutes.
3. While the sausage cooks, place the cream cheese and broth in a food processor or blender and purée until smooth.
4. Remove the pork from the air fryer and use a fork or metal spatula to crumble it more. Pour the cream cheese mixture into the sausage and stir to combine. Set aside.
5. Make the biscuits: Place the egg whites in a medium-sized mixing bowl or the bowl of a stand mixer and whip with a hand mixer or stand mixer until stiff peaks form.
6. In a separate medium-sized bowl, whisk together the almond flour, baking powder, and salt, then cut in the butter. When you are done, the mixture should still have chunks of butter. Gently fold the flour mixture into the egg whites with a rubber spatula.
7. Use a large spoon or ice cream scoop to scoop the dough into 4 equal-sized biscuits, making sure the butter is evenly distributed. Place the biscuits on top of the sausage and cook in the air fryer for 5 minutes, then turn the heat down to 325°F (163ºC) and cook for another 17 to 20 minutes, until the biscuits are golden brown. Serve garnished with fresh thyme leaves.
8. Store leftovers in an airtight container in the refrigerator for up to 3 days. Reheat in a preheated 350°F (180ºC) air fryer for 5 minutes, or until warmed through.

Per Serving
calories: 623 | fat: 55g | protein: 23g | carbs: 8g | net carbs: 5g | fiber: 3g

Mozzarella Almond Bagels

Prep time: 15 minutes | Cook time: 14 minutes | Serves 6

1¾ cups shredded Mozzarella cheese or goat cheese
2 tablespoons unsalted butter or coconut oil
1 large egg, beaten
1 tablespoon apple cider vinegar

1 cup blanched almond flour
1 tablespoon baking powder
⅛ teaspoon fine sea salt
1½ teaspoons everything bagel seasoning

1. Make the dough: Put the Mozzarella and butter in a large microwave-safe bowl and microwave for 1 to 2 minutes, until the cheese is entirely melted. Stir well. Add the egg and vinegar. Using a hand mixer on medium, combine well. Add the almond flour, baking powder, and salt and, using the mixer, combine well.
2. Lay a piece of parchment paper on the countertop and place the dough on it. Knead it for about 3 minutes. The dough should be a little sticky but pliable. (If the dough is too sticky, chill it in the refrigerator for an hour or overnight.)
3. Preheat the air fryer to 350°F (180ºC). Spray a baking sheet or pie pan that will fit into your air fryer with avocado oil.
4. Divide the dough into 6 equal portions. Roll 1 portion into a log that is 6 inches long and about ½-inch thick. Form the log into a circle and seal the edges together, making a bagel shape. Repeat with the remaining portions of dough, making 6 bagels.
5. Place the bagels on the greased baking sheet. Spray the bagels with avocado oil and top with everything bagel seasoning, pressing the seasoning into the dough with your hands.
6. Place the bagels in the air fryer and cook for 14 minutes, or until cooked through and golden brown, flipping after 6 minutes.
7. Remove the bagels from the air fryer and allow them to cool slightly before slicing them in half and serving. Store leftovers in an airtight container in the fridge for up to 4 days or in the freezer for up to a month.

Per Serving
calories: 224 | fat: 19g | protein: 12g | carbs: 4g | net carbs: 2g | fiber: 2g

Mushroom with Tomato

Prep time: 15 minutes | Cook time: 14 minutes | Serves 2

1 tablespoon olive oil
2 cloves garlic, minced
¼ teaspoon dried thyme
2 portobello mushrooms, stems removed and gills scraped out
2 Roma tomatoes, halved lengthwise

Salt and freshly ground black pepper
2 large eggs
2 tablespoons grated Pecorino Romano cheese
1 tablespoon chopped fresh parsley, for garnish

1. Preheat the air fryer to 400°F (205ºC).
2. In a small bowl, combine the olive oil, garlic, and thyme. Brush the mixture over the mushrooms and tomatoes until thoroughly coated. Season to taste with salt and freshly ground black pepper.
3. Arrange the vegetables, cut side up and put in the air fryer basket. Crack an egg into the center of each mushroom and sprinkle with cheese. Air fry for 10 to 14 minutes until the vegetables are tender and the whites are firm. When cool enough to handle, coarsely chop the tomatoes and place on top of the eggs. Scatter parsley on top just before serving.

Per Serving

calories: 255 | fat: 20g | protein: 11g | carbs: 10g | net carbs: 7g | fiber: 3g

Cauliflower with Avocado

Prep time: 15 minutes | Cook time: 8 minutes | Serves 2

1 (12-ounce / 340-g) steamer bag cauliflower
1 large egg
½ cup shredded Mozzarella cheese

1 ripe medium avocado
½ teaspoon garlic powder
¼ teaspoon ground black pepper

1. Cook cauliflower according to package instructions. Remove from bag and place into cheesecloth or clean towel to remove excess moisture.
2. Place cauliflower into a large bowl and mix the egg and Mozzarella. Cut a piece of parchment to fit your air fryer basket. Separate the cauliflower mixture into two, and place it on the parchment in two mounds. Press out the cauliflower mounds into a ¼-inch-thick rectangle. Place the parchment into the air fryer basket.
3. Adjust the temperature to 400°F (205ºC) and set the timer for 8 minutes.

4. Flip the cauliflower halfway through the cooking time.
5. When the timer beeps, remove the parchment and allow the cauliflower to cool for 5 minutes.
6. Cut open the avocado and remove the pit. Scoop out the inside, place it in a medium bowl, and mash it with garlic powder and pepper. Spread onto the cauliflower. Serve immediately.

Per Serving

calories: 278 | fat: 15g | protein: 14g | carbs: 16g | net carbs: 8g | fiber: 8g

Sausage Eggs with Smoky Mustard Sauce

Prep time: 20 minutes | Cook time: 12 minutes | Serves 8

1 pound (454 g) pork sausage
8 soft-boiled or hard-boiled eggs, peeled
1 large egg
2 tablespoons milk
1 cup crushed pork rinds

Smoky Mustard Sauce:
¼ cup mayonnaise
2 tablespoons sour cream
1 tablespoon Dijon mustard
1 teaspoon chipotle hot sauce

1. Preheat the air fryer to 390°F (199ºC).
2. Divide the sausage into 8 portions. Take each portion of sausage, pat it down into a patty, and place 1 egg in the middle, gently wrapping the sausage around the egg until the egg is completely covered. (Wet your hands slightly if you find the sausage to be too sticky.) Repeat with the remaining eggs and sausage.
3. In a small shallow bowl, whisk the egg and milk until frothy. In another shallow bowl, place the crushed pork rinds. Working one at a time, dip a sausage-wrapped egg into the beaten egg and then into the pork rinds, gently rolling to coat evenly. Repeat with the remaining sausage-wrapped eggs.
4. Arrange the eggs in a single layer in the air fryer basket, and lightly spray with olive oil. Air fry for 10 to 12 minutes, pausing halfway through the baking time to turn the eggs, until the eggs are hot and the sausage is cooked through.
5. To make the sauce: In a small bowl, combine the mayonnaise, sour cream, Dijon, and hot sauce. Whisk until thoroughly combined. Serve with the Scotch eggs.

Per Serving

calories: 340 | fat: 28g | protein: 22g | carbs: 1g | net carbs: 1g | fiber: 0g

Fluffy Pancakes with Cream Cheese

Prep time: 10 minutes | Cook time: 5 minutes | Serves 3

½ cup coconut flour
1 teaspoon baking powder
¼ teaspoon salt
2 tablespoons erythritol
½ teaspoon cinnamon
1 teaspoon red paste food color
1 egg
½ cup milk
1 teaspoon vanilla
Topping:
2 ounces (57 g) cream cheese, softened
2 tablespoons butter, softened
¾ cup powdered swerve

1. Mix the coconut flour, baking powder, salt, erythritol, cinnamon, red paste food color in a large bowl.
2. Gradually add the egg, milk and vanilla, whisking continuously, until well combined. Let it stand for 20 minutes.
3. Spritz the Air Fryer baking pan with cooking spray. Pour the batter into the pan using a measuring cup.
4. Cook at 230ºF for 4 to 5 minutes or until golden brown. Repeat with the remaining batter.
5. Meanwhile, make your topping by mixing the ingredients until creamy and fluffy. Decorate your pancakes with topping. Bon appétit!

Per Serving
calories: 315 | fat: 31g | protein: 6g | carbs: 5g | net carbs: 3g | fiber: 2g

Duo-Cheese Roll

Prep time: 10 minutes | Cook time: 20 minutes | Makes 12 rolls

2½ cups shredded Mozzarella cheese
2 ounces (57 g) cream cheese, softened
1 cup blanched finely ground almond flour
½ teaspoon vanilla extract
½ cup erythritol
1 tablespoon ground cinnamon

1. In a large microwave-safe bowl, combine Mozzarella cheese, cream cheese, and flour. Microwave the mixture on high 90 seconds until cheese is melted.
2. Add vanilla extract and erythritol, and mix for 2 minutes until a dough forms.
3. Once the dough is cool enough to work with your hands, for about 2 minutes, spread it out into a 12-inch × 4-inch rectangle on ungreased parchment paper. Evenly sprinkle dough with cinnamon.
4. Starting at the long side of the dough, roll lengthwise to form a log. Slice the log into twelve even pieces.
5. Divide rolls between two ungreased 6-inch round nonstick baking dishes. Place one dish into air fryer basket. Adjust the temperature to 375°F (190ºC) and set the timer for 10 minutes.
6. Cinnamon rolls will be done when golden around the edges and mostly firm. Repeat with second dish. Allow the rolls to cool in dishes for 10 minutes before serving.

Per Serving
calories: 145 | fat: 10g | protein: 8g | carbs: 10g | net carbs: 9g | fiber: 1g

Bacon-and-Eggs Avocado

Prep time: 5 minutes | Cook time: 17 minutes | Serves 1

1 large egg
1 avocado, halved, peeled, and pitted
2 slices bacon
Fresh parsley, for serving (optional)
Sea salt flakes, for garnish (optional)

1. Spray the air fryer basket with avocado oil. Preheat the air fryer to 320°F (160ºC). Fill a small bowl with cool water.
2. Soft-boil the egg: Place the egg in the air fryer basket. Cook for 6 minutes for a soft yolk or 7 minutes for a cooked yolk. Transfer the egg to the bowl of cool water and let it sit for 2 minutes. Peel and set aside.
3. Use a spoon to carve out extra space in the center of the avocado halves until the cavities are big enough to fit the soft-boiled egg. Place the soft-boiled egg in the center of one half of the avocado and replace the other half of the avocado on top, so the avocado appears whole on the outside.
4. Starting at one end of the avocado, wrap the bacon around the avocado to completely cover it. Use toothpicks to hold the bacon in place.
5. Place the bacon-wrapped avocado in the air fryer basket and cook for 5 minutes. Flip the avocado over and cook for another 5 minutes, or until the bacon is cooked to your liking. Serve on a bed of fresh parsley, if desired, and sprinkle with salt flakes, if desired.
6. Best served fresh. Store extras in an airtight container in the fridge for up to 4 days. Reheat in a preheated 320ºF (160ºC) air fryer for 4 minutes, or until heated through.

Per Serving
calories: 535 | fat: 46g | protein: 18g | carbs: 18g | net carbs: 4g | fiber: 14g

Simple Ham and Pepper Omelet

Prep time: 5 minutes | Cook time: 8 minutes | Serves 1

2 large eggs
¼ cup unsweetened, unflavored almond milk
¼ teaspoon fine sea salt
⅛ teaspoon ground black pepper
¼ cup diced ham (omit for vegetarian)
¼ cup diced green and red bell peppers

2 tablespoons diced green onions, plus more for garnish
¼ cup shredded Cheddar cheese (about 1 ounce / 28g) (omit for dairy-free)
Quartered cherry tomatoes, for serving (optional)

1. Preheat the air fryer to 350°F (180ºC). Grease a 6 by 3 inch cake pan and set aside.
2. In a small bowl, use a fork to whisk together the eggs, almond milk, salt, and pepper. Add the ham, bell peppers, and green onions. Pour the mixture into the greased pan. Add the cheese on top (if using).
3. Place the pan in the basket of the air fryer. Cook for 8 minutes, or until the eggs are cooked to your liking.
4. Loosen the omelet from the sides of the pan with a spatula and place it on a serving plate. Garnish with green onions and serve with cherry tomatoes, if desired. Best served fresh.

Per Serving

calories: 476 | fat: 32g | protein: 41g | carbs: 3g | net carbs: 2g | fiber: 1g

Bacon Calzones

Prep time: 15 minutes | Cook time: 12 minutes | Serves 4

2 large eggs
1 cup blanched finely ground almond flour
2 cups shredded Mozzarella cheese

2 ounces (57 g) cream cheese, softened and broken into small pieces
4 slices cooked sugar-free bacon, crumbled

1. Beat eggs in a small bowl. Pour into a medium nonstick skillet over medium heat and scramble. Set aside.
2. In a large microwave-safe bowl, mix flour and Mozzarella. Add cream cheese to bowl.
3. Place bowl in microwave and cook 45 seconds on high to melt cheese, then stir with a fork until a soft dough ball forms.
4. Cut a piece of parchment to fit air fryer basket. Separate the dough into two sections and press each

out into an 8-inch round.
5. On half of each dough round, place half of the scrambled eggs and crumbled bacon. Fold the other side of the dough over and press to seal the edges.
6. Place calzones on ungreased parchment and into air fryer basket. Adjust the temperature to 350°F (180ºC) and set the timer for 12 minutes, turning calzones halfway through cooking. Crust will be golden and firm when done.
7. Let the calzones cool on a cooking rack 5 minutes before serving.

Per Serving

calories: 477 | fat: 35g | protein: 28g | carbs: 10g | net carbs: 7g | fiber: 3g

Sausage with Peppers

Prep time: 15 minutes | Cook time: 15 minutes | Serves 4

½ pound (227 g) spicy ground pork breakfast sausage
4 large eggs
4 ounces (113 g) full-fat cream cheese, softened
¼ cup canned diced

tomatoes and green chiles, drained
4 large poblano peppers
8 tablespoons shredded pepper jack cheese
½ cup full-fat sour cream

1. In a medium skillet over medium heat, crumble and brown the ground sausage until no pink remains. Remove sausage and drain the fat from the pan. Crack eggs into the pan, scramble, and cook until no longer runny.
2. Place the cooked sausage in a large bowl and fold in cream cheese. Mix in diced tomatoes and chiles. Gently fold in eggs.
3. Cut a 4-inch–5-inch slit in the top of each poblano, removing the seeds and white membrane with a small knife. Separate the filling into four servings and spoon carefully into each pepper. Top each with 2 tablespoons pepper jack cheese.
4. Place each pepper into the air fryer basket.
5. Adjust the temperature to 350°F (180ºC) and set the timer for 15 minutes.
6. Peppers will be soft and cheese will be browned when ready. Serve immediately with sour cream on top.

Per Serving

calories: 489 | fat: 35g | protein: 23g | carbs: 13g | net carbs: 9g | fiber: 4g

Pecan and Almond Granola

Prep time: 10 minutes | Cook time: 5 minutes | Serves 6

2 cups pecans, chopped
1 cup unsweetened coconut flakes
1 cup almond slivers
⅓ cup sunflower seeds
¼ cup golden flaxseed
¼ cup low-carb, sugar-

free chocolate chips
¼ cup granular erythritol
2 tablespoons unsalted butter
1 teaspoon ground cinnamon

1. In a large bowl, mix all ingredients.
2. Place the mixture into a 4-cup round baking dish. Place dish into the air fryer basket.
3. Adjust the temperature to 320°F (160°C) and set the timer for 5 minutes.
4. Allow it to cool completely before serving.

Per Serving

calories: 617 | fat: 55g | protein: 11g | carbs: 32g | net carbs: 21g | fiber: 11g

Cheese and Bacon Quiche

Prep time: 5 minutes | Cook time: 12 minutes | Serves 2

3 large eggs
2 tablespoons heavy whipping cream
¼ teaspoon salt

4 slices cooked sugar-free bacon, crumbled
½ cup shredded mild Cheddar cheese

1. In a large bowl, whisk eggs, cream, and salt together until combined. Mix the bacon and Cheddar.
2. Pour mixture evenly into two ungreased 4-inch ramekins. Place into air fryer basket. Adjust the temperature to 320°F (160°C) and set the timer for 12 minutes. Quiche will be fluffy and set in the middle when done.
3. Let the quiche cool in ramekins 5 minutes. Serve warm.

Per Serving

calories: 380 | fat: 28g | protein: 24g | carbs: 2g | net carbs: 2g | fiber: 0g

Broccoli and Mushroom Frittata

Prep time: 15 minutes | Cook time: 20 minutes | Serves 2

1 tablespoon olive oil
1½ cups broccoli florets, finely chopped
½ cup sliced brown mushrooms
¼ cup finely chopped

onion
½ teaspoon salt
¼ teaspoon freshly ground black pepper
6 eggs
¼ cup Parmesan cheese

1. In an 8-inch nonstick cake pan, combine the olive oil, broccoli, mushrooms, onion, salt, and pepper. Stir until the vegetables are thoroughly coated with oil. Place the cake pan in the air fryer basket and set the air fryer to 400°F (205°C). Air fry for 5 minutes until the vegetables soften.
2. Meanwhile, in a medium bowl, whisk the eggs and Parmesan until thoroughly combined. Pour the egg mixture into the pan and shake gently to distribute the vegetables. Air fry for another 15 minutes until the eggs are set.
3. Remove from the air fryer and let them sit for 5 minutes to cool slightly. Use a silicone spatula to gently lift the frittata onto a plate before serving.

Per Serving

calories: 360 | fat: 25g | protein: 25g | carbs: 10g | net carbs: 8g | fiber: 2g

Ham with Avocado

Prep time: 5 minutes | Cook time: 10 minutes | Serves 2

1 large Hass avocado, halved and pitted
2 thin slices ham
2 large eggs
2 tablespoons chopped green onions, plus more for garnish

½ teaspoon fine sea salt
¼ teaspoon ground black pepper
¼ cup shredded Cheddar cheese (omit for dairy-free)

1. Preheat the air fryer to 400°F (205°C).
2. Place a slice of ham into the cavity of each avocado half. Crack an egg on top of the ham, then sprinkle on the green onions, salt, and pepper.
3. Place the avocado halves in the air fryer cut side up and cook for 10 minutes, or until the egg is cooked to your desired doneness. Top with the cheese (if using) and cook for 30 seconds or more, or until the cheese is melted. Garnish with chopped green onions.
4. Best served fresh. Store extras in an airtight container in the fridge for up to 4 days. Reheat in a preheated 350°F (180°C) air fryer for a few minutes, until warmed through.

Per Serving

calories: 307 | fat: 24g | protein: 14g | carbs: 10g | net carbs: 3g | fiber: 7g

Cheese Soufflés, page 14

Pound Cake, page 27

Fluffy Pancakes with Cream Cheese, page 19

Egg Breakfast Ramekin, page 25

Spinach and Tomato Egg

Prep time: 10 minutes | Cook time: 15 minutes | Serves 4

2 cups 100% liquid egg whites
3 tablespoons salted butter, melted
¼ teaspoon salt
¼ teaspoon onion powder
½ medium Roma tomato, cored and diced
½ cup chopped fresh spinach leaves

1. In a large bowl, whisk egg whites with butter, salt, and onion powder. Stir in tomato and spinach, then pour evenly into four 4-inch ramekins greased with cooking spray.
2. Place ramekins into air fryer basket. Adjust the temperature to 300°F (150ºC) and set the timer for 15 minutes. Eggs will be fully cooked and firm in the center when done. Serve warm.

Per Serving

calories: 146 | fat: 8g | protein: 14g | carbs: 1g | net carbs: 1g | fiber: 0g

Blueberry Muffin

Prep time: 5 minutes | Cook time: 15 minutes | Makes 6 muffins

1½ cups blanched finely ground almond flour
½ cup granular erythritol
4 tablespoons salted butter, melted
2 large eggs, whisked
2 teaspoons baking powder
⅓cup fresh blueberries, chopped

1. In a large bowl, combine all ingredients. Evenly pour batter into six silicone muffin cups greased with cooking spray.
2. Place muffin cups into air fryer basket. Adjust the temperature to 320°F (160ºC) and set the timer for 15 minutes. Muffins should be golden brown when done.
3. Let the muffins cool in cups 15 minutes to avoid crumbling. Serve warm.

Per Serving

calories:269 | fat: 24g | protein: 8g | carbs: 23g | net carbs: 20g | fiber: 3g

Turkey Sausage with Tabasco Sauce

Prep time: 15 minutes | Cook time: 20 minutes | Serves 8

1½ pounds (680g) 85% lean ground turkey
3 cloves garlic, finely chopped
¼ onion, grated
1 teaspoon Tabasco sauce
1 teaspoon Creole seasoning
1 teaspoon dried thyme
½ teaspoon paprika
½ teaspoon cayenne

1. Preheat the air fryer to 370°F (188ºC).
2. In a large bowl, combine the turkey, garlic, onion, Tabasco, Creole seasoning, thyme, paprika, and cayenne. Mix with clean hands until thoroughly combined. Shape into 16 patties, about ½-inch thick. (Wet your hands slightly if you find the sausage too sticky to handle.)
3. Working in batches if necessary, arrange the patties in a single layer in the air fryer basket. Pausing halfway through the cooking time to flip the patties, air fry for 15 to 20 minutes until a thermometer inserted into the thickest portion registers 165°F (74ºC).

Per Serving

calories: 170 | fat: 11g | protein: 16g | carbs: 1g | net carbs: 1g | fiber: 0g

Cream Cauliflower with Cheese

Prep time: 15 minutes | Cook time: 20 minutes | Serves 4

6 large eggs
¼ cup heavy whipping cream
1½ cups chopped cauliflower
1 cup shredded medium Cheddar cheese
1 medium avocado, peeled and pitted
8 tablespoons full-fat sour cream
2 scallions, sliced on the bias
12 slices sugar-free bacon, cooked and crumbled

1. In a medium bowl, whisk eggs and cream together. Pour into a 4-cup round baking dish.
2. Add cauliflower and mix, then top with Cheddar. Place dish into the air fryer basket.
3. Adjust the temperature to 320°F (160ºC) and set the timer for 20 minutes.
4. When completely cooked, eggs will be firm and cheese will be browned. Slice into four pieces.
5. Slice avocado and divide evenly among pieces. Top each piece with 2 tablespoons sour cream, sliced scallions, and crumbled bacon.

Per Serving

calories: 512 | fat: 38g | protein: 27g | carbs: 8g | net carbs: 5g | fiber: 3g

Breakfast Almond Cake

Prep time: 10 minutes | Cook time: 7 minutes | Serves 4

½ cup blanched finely ground almond flour
¼ cup powdered erythritol
½ teaspoon baking powder
2 tablespoons unsalted butter, softened

1 large egg
½ teaspoon unflavored gelatin
½ teaspoon vanilla extract
½ teaspoon ground cinnamon

1. In a large bowl, mix almond flour, erythritol, and baking powder. Add butter, egg, gelatin, vanilla, and cinnamon. Pour into 6-inch round baking pan.
2. Place pan into the air fryer basket.
3. Adjust the temperature to 300°F (150ºC) and set the timer for 7 minutes.
4. When the cake is completely cooked, a toothpick will come out clean. Cut cake into four and serve.

Per Serving

calories: 153 | fat: 13g | protein: 5g | carbs: 13g | net carbs: 11g | fiber: 2g

Bacon Lettuce Wraps

Prep time: 20 minutes | Cook time: 13 minutes | Serves 4

8 ounces (227 g) (about 12 slices) reduced-sodium bacon
8 tablespoons mayonnaise

8 large romaine lettuce leaves
4 Roma tomatoes, sliced
Salt and freshly ground black pepper

1. Arrange the bacon in a single layer in the air fryer basket. (It's OK if the bacon sits a bit on the sides.) Set the air fryer to 350°F (180ºC) and cook for 10 minutes. Check for crispiness and cook for 2 to 3 minutes longer if needed. Cook in batches, if necessary, and drain the grease in between batches.
2. Spread 1 tablespoon of mayonnaise on each of the lettuce leaves and top with the tomatoes and cooked bacon. Season to taste with salt and freshly ground black pepper. Roll the lettuce leaves as you would a burrito, securing with a toothpick if desired.

Per Serving

calories: 370 | fat: 34g | protein: 11g | carbs: 7g | net carbs: 4g | fiber: 3g

Spaghetti Squash Patties

Prep time: 15 minutes | Cook time: 8 minutes | Serves 4

2 cups cooked spaghetti squash
2 tablespoons unsalted butter, softened
1 large egg
¼ cup blanched finely

ground almond flour
2 stalks green onion, sliced
½ teaspoon garlic powder
1 teaspoon dried parsley

1. Remove excess moisture from the squash using a cheesecloth or kitchen towel.
2. Mix all ingredients in a large bowl. Form into four patties.
3. Cut a piece of parchment to fit your air fryer basket. Place each patty on the parchment and place into the air fryer basket.
4. Adjust the temperature to 400°F (205ºC) and set the timer for 8 minutes.
5. Flip the patties halfway through the cooking time. Serve warm.

Per Serving

calories: 131 | fat: 10g | protein: 4g | carbs: 7g | net carbs: 5g | fiber: 2g

Ham Egg

Prep time: 10 minutes | Cook time: 15 minutes | Serves 4

4 medium green bell peppers, tops removed, seeded
1 tablespoon coconut oil
3 ounces (85 g) chopped cooked no-sugar-added ham

¼ cup peeled and chopped white onion
4 large eggs
½ teaspoon salt
1 cup shredded mild Cheddar cheese

1. Place peppers upright into ungreased air fryer basket. Drizzle each pepper with coconut oil. Divide ham and onion evenly among peppers.
2. In a medium bowl, whisk eggs, then sprinkle with salt. Pour mixture evenly into each pepper. Top each with ¼ cup Cheddar.
3. Adjust the temperature to 320°F (160ºC) and set the timer for 15 minutes. Peppers will be tender and eggs will be firm when done.
4. Serve warm on four medium plates.

Per Serving

calories: 281 | fat: 18g | protein: 18g | carbs: 8g | net carbs: 6g | fiber: 2g

Gold Muffin

Prep time: 5 minutes | Cook time: 15 minutes | Makes 6 muffins

1 cup blanched finely ground almond flour
¼ cup granular erythritol
2 tablespoons salted butter, melted

1 large egg, whisked
2 teaspoons baking powder
1 teaspoon ground allspice

1. In a large bowl, combine all ingredients. Evenly pour batter into six silicone muffin cups greased with cooking spray.
2. Place muffin cups into air fryer basket. Adjust the temperature to 320°F (160ºC) and set the timer for 15 minutes. Cooked muffins should be golden brown.
3. Let the muffins cool in cups 15 minutes to avoid crumbling. Serve warm.

Per Serving

calories: 160 | fat: 14g | protein: 5g | carbs: 20g | net carbs: 18g | fiber: 2g

Egg Breakfast Ramekin

Prep time: 5 minutes | Cook time: 8 minutes | Serves 2

2 teaspoons unsalted butter, for greasing the ramekins
4 large eggs
2 teaspoons chopped fresh thyme
½ teaspoon fine sea salt
¼ teaspoon ground black

pepper
2 tablespoons heavy cream
3 tablespoons finely grated Parmesan cheese
Fresh thyme leaves, for garnish (optional)

1. Preheat the air fryer to 400°F (205ºC). Grease two 4-ounce (113-g) ramekins with the butter.
2. Crack 2 eggs into each ramekin and divide the thyme, salt, and pepper between the ramekins. Pour 1 tablespoon of the heavy cream into each ramekin. Sprinkle each ramekin with 1½ tablespoons of the Parmesan cheese.
3. Place the ramekins in the air fryer and cook for 8 minutes for soft-cooked yolks (longer if you desire a harder yolk).
4. Garnish with a sprinkle of ground black pepper and thyme leaves, if desired. Best served fresh.

Per Serving

calories: 331 | fat: 29g | protein: 16g | carbs: 2g | net carbs: 1g | fiber: 1g

Chocolate Chip Muffin

Prep time: 5 minutes | Cook time: 15 minutes | Makes 6 muffins

1½ cups blanched finely ground almond flour
⅓ cup granular brown erythritol
4 tablespoons salted butter, melted

2 large eggs, whisked
1 tablespoon baking powder
½ cup low-carb chocolate chips

1. In a large bowl, combine all ingredients. Evenly pour batter into six silicone muffin cups greased with cooking spray.
2. Place muffin cups into air fryer basket. Adjust the temperature to 320°F (160ºC) and set the timer for 15 minutes. Muffins will be golden brown when done.
3. Let the muffins cool in cups for 15 minutes to avoid crumbling. Serve warm.

Per Serving

calories: 329 | fat: 29g | protein: 10g | carbs: 28g | net carbs: 20g | fiber: 8g

Cauliflower Hash Browns

Prep time: 20 minutes | Cook time: 12 minutes | Serves 4

1 (12-ounce / 340-g) steamer bag cauliflower
1 large egg

1 cup shredded sharp Cheddar cheese

1. Place the bag in microwave and cook according to package instructions. Allow it to cool completely and put cauliflower into a cheesecloth or kitchen towel and squeeze to remove excess moisture.
2. Mash cauliflower with a fork and add egg and cheese.
3. Cut a piece of parchment to fit your air fryer basket. Take ¼ of the mixture and form it into a hash brown patty shape. Place it onto the parchment and into the air fryer basket, working in batches if necessary.
4. Adjust the temperature to 400°F (205ºC) and set the timer for 12 minutes.
5. Flip the hash browns halfway through the cooking time. When completely cooked, they will be golden brown. Serve immediately.

Per Serving

calories: 153 | fat: 9g | protein: 10g | carbs: 5g | net carbs: 3g | fiber: 2g

Pepperoni Egg

Prep time: 5 minutes | Cook time: 10 minutes | Serves 2

1 cup shredded Mozzarella cheese
7 slices pepperoni, chopped
1 large egg, whisked
¼ teaspoon dried

oregano
¼ teaspoon dried parsley
¼ teaspoon garlic powder
¼ teaspoon salt

1. Place Mozzarella in a single layer on the bottom of an ungreased 6-inch round nonstick baking dish. Scatter pepperoni over cheese, then pour egg evenly around baking dish.
2. Sprinkle with the remaining ingredients and place into air fryer basket. Adjust the temperature to 330°F (166ºC) and set the timer for 10 minutes. When cheese is brown and egg is set, dish will be done.
3. Let it cool in dish 5 minutes before serving.

Per Serving
calories: 241 | fat: 15g | protein: 19g | carbs: 4g | net carbs: 4g | fiber: 0g

Breakfast Sammies

Prep time: 15 minutes | Cook time: 20 minutes | Serves 5

Biscuits:
6 large egg whites
2 cups blanched almond flour, plus more if needed
1½ teaspoons baking powder
½ teaspoon fine sea salt
¼ cup (½ stick) very cold unsalted butter, cut into ¼-inch pieces

Eggs:
5 large eggs
½ teaspoon fine sea salt
¼ teaspoon ground black pepper
5 (1-ounce / 28-g) slices Cheddar cheese (omit for dairy-free)
10 thin slices ham

1. Spray the air fryer basket with avocado oil. Preheat the air fryer to 350°F (180ºC). Grease two 6-inch pie pans or two baking pans that will fit inside your air fryer.
2. Make the biscuits: In a medium-sized bowl, whip the egg whites with a hand mixer until very stiff. Set aside.
3. In a separate medium-sized bowl, stir together the almond flour, baking powder, and salt until well combined. Cut in the butter. Gently fold the flour mixture into the egg whites with a rubber spatula. If the dough is too wet to form into mounds, add a few tablespoons of almond flour until the dough holds

together well.
4. Using a large spoon, divide the dough into 5 equal portions and drop them about 1-inch apart on one of the greased pie pans. (If you're using a smaller air fryer, work in batches if necessary.) Place the pan in the air fryer and cook for 11 to 14 minutes, until the biscuits are golden brown. Remove from the air fryer and set aside to cool.
5. Make the eggs: Set the air fryer to 375°F (190ºC). Crack the eggs into the remaining greased pie pan and sprinkle with the salt and pepper. Place the eggs in the air fryer to cook for 5 minutes, or until they are cooked to your liking.
6. Open the air fryer and top each egg yolk with a slice of cheese (if using). Cook for another minute, or until the cheese is melted.
7. Once the biscuits are cool, slice them in half lengthwise. Place 1 cooked egg topped with cheese and 2 slices of ham in each biscuit.
8. Store leftover biscuits, eggs, and ham in separate airtight containers in the fridge for up to 3 days. Reheat the biscuits and eggs on a baking sheet in a preheated 350°F (180ºC) air fryer for 5 minutes, or until warmed through.

Per Serving
calories: 585 | fat: 46g | protein: 36g | carbs: 11g | net carbs: 6g | fiber: 5g

Bacon Cheese Pizza

Prep time: 5 minutes | Cook time: 10 minutes | Serves 2

1 cup shredded Mozzarella cheese
1 ounce (28 g) cream cheese, broken into small pieces
4 slices cooked sugar-

free bacon, chopped
¼ cup chopped pickled jalapeños
1 large egg, whisked
¼ teaspoon salt

1. Place Mozzarella in a single layer on the bottom of an ungreased 6-inch round nonstick baking dish. Scatter cream cheese pieces, bacon, and jalapeños over Mozzarella, then pour egg evenly around baking dish.
2. Sprinkle with salt and place into air fryer basket. Adjust the temperature to 330°F (166ºC) and set the timer for 10 minutes. When cheese is brown and egg is set, pizza will be done.
3. Let it cool on a large plate 5 minutes before serving.

Per Serving
calories: 361 | fat: 24g | protein: 26g | carbs: 5g | net carbs: 5g | fiber: 0g

Egg with Cheddar

Prep time: 5 minutes | Cook time: 15 minutes | Serves 2

4 large eggs
2 tablespoons unsalted butter, melted

½ cup shredded sharp Cheddar cheese

1. Crack eggs into 2-cup round baking dish and whisk. Place dish into the air fryer basket.
2. Adjust the temperature to 400°F (205ºC) and set the timer for 10 minutes.
3. After 5 minutes, stir the eggs and add the butter and cheese. Cook for 3 more minutes and stir again.
4. Allow the eggs to finish cooking for an additional 2 minutes or remove if they are to your desired liking.
5. Use a fork to fluff. Serve warm.

Per Serving
calories: 359 | fat: 27g | protein: 20g | carbs: 1g | net carbs: 1g | fiber: 0g

Parmesan and Pepperoni Breakfast Pizza

Prep time: 5 minutes | Cook time: 8 minutes | Serves 1

2 large eggs
¼ cup unsweetened, unflavored almond milk
¼ teaspoon fine sea salt
⅛ teaspoon ground black pepper
¼ cup diced onions
¼ cup shredded

Parmesan cheese (omit for dairy-free)
6 pepperoni slices (omit for vegetarian)
¼ teaspoon dried oregano leaves
¼ cup pizza sauce, warmed, for serving

1. Preheat the air fryer to 350°F. Grease a 6 by 3-inch cake pan.
2. In a small bowl, use a fork to whisk together the eggs, almond milk, salt, and pepper. Add the onions and stir to mix. Pour the mixture into the greased pan. Top with the cheese (if using), pepperoni slices (if using), and oregano.
3. Place the pan in the air fryer and cook for 8 minutes, or until the eggs are cooked to your liking.
4. Loosen the eggs from the sides of the pan with a spatula and place them on a serving plate. Drizzle the pizza sauce on top. Best served fresh.

Per Serving
calories: 357 | fat: 25g | protein: 24g | carbs: 9g | net carbs: 7g | fiber: 2g

Duo-Cheese Sausage Meatball

Prep time: 10 minutes | Cook time: 15 minutes | Serves 18 meatballs

1 pound (454 g) ground pork breakfast sausage
½ teaspoon salt
¼ teaspoon ground black pepper

½ cup shredded sharp Cheddar cheese
1 ounce (28 g) cream cheese, softened
1 large egg, whisked

1. Combine all ingredients in a large bowl. Form mixture into eighteen 1-inch meatballs.
2. Place meatballs into ungreased air fryer basket. Adjust the temperature to 400°F and set the timer for 15 minutes, shaking basket three times during cooking. Meatballs will be browned on the outside and have an internal temperature of at least 145°F (63ºC) when completely cooked. Serve warm.

Per Serving
calories: 288 | fat: 24g | protein: 11g | carbs: 1g | net carbs: 1g | fiber: 0g

Pound Cake

Prep time: 10 minutes | Cook time: 30 minutes | Serves 8

1 stick butter, at room temperature
1 cup Swerve
4 eggs
1½ cups coconut flour
½ teaspoon baking powder
½ teaspoon baking soda

¼ teaspoon salt
A pinch of freshly grated nutmeg
A pinch of ground star anise
½ cup buttermilk
1 teaspoon vanilla essence

1. Begin by preheating your Air Fryer to 320ºF. Spritz the bottom and sides of a baking pan with cooking spray.
2. Beat the butter and swerve with a hand mixer until creamy. Then, fold in the eggs, one at a time, and mix well until fluffy.
3. Stir in the flour along with the remaining ingredients. Mix to combine well. Scrape the batter into the prepared baking pan.
4. Bake for 15 minutes, rotate the pan and bake an additional 15 minutes, until the top of the cake springs back when gently pressed with your fingers. Bon appétit!

Per Serving
calories: 193 | fat: 19g | protein: 4g | carbs: 3g | net carbs: 2g | fiber: 1g

Bell Pepper and Ham Omelet

Prep time: 5 minutes | Cook time: 15 minutes | Serves 2

3 large eggs
1 tablespoon salted butter, melted
¼ cup seeded and chopped green bell pepper
2 tablespoons peeled and chopped yellow onion
¼ cup chopped cooked no-sugar-added ham
¼ teaspoon salt
¼ teaspoon ground black pepper

1. Crack eggs into an ungreased 6-inch round nonstick baking dish. Mix in butter, bell pepper, onion, ham, salt, and black pepper.
2. Place dish into air fryer basket. Adjust the temperature to 320°F (160ºC) and set the timer for 15 minutes. The eggs will be fully cooked and firm in the middle when done.
3. Slice in half and serve warm on two medium plates.

Per Serving

calories: 201 | fat: 14g | protein: 13g | carbs: 3g | net carbs: 2g | fiber: 1g

Mexican Shakshuka

Prep time: 5 minutes | Cook time: 6 minutes | Serves 1

½ cup salsa
2 large eggs, room temperature
½ teaspoon fine sea salt
¼ teaspoon smoked paprika
⅛ teaspoon ground cumin
For Garnish:
2 tablespoons cilantro leaves

1. Preheat the air fryer to 400°F.
2. Place the salsa in a 6-inch pie pan or a casserole dish that will fit into your air fryer. Crack the eggs into the salsa and sprinkle them with the salt, paprika, and cumin.
3. Place the pan in the air fryer and cook for 6 minutes, or until the egg whites are set and the yolks are cooked to your liking.
4. Remove from the air fryer and garnish with the cilantro before serving.
5. Best served fresh.

Per Serving

calories: 258 | fat: 17g | protein: 14g | carbs: 11g | net carbs: 7g | fiber: 4g

Orange Galettes

Prep time: 10 minutes | Cook time: 5 minutes | Serves 6

1 cup almond meal
½ cup coconut flour
3 eggs
⅓ cup milk
2 tablespoons monk fruit
2 teaspoons grated lemon peel
⅓ teaspoon ground nutmeg, preferably freshly ground
1½ teaspoons baking powder
3 tablespoons orange juice
A pinch of turmeric

1. Grab two mixing bowls. Combine dry ingredients in the first bowl.
2. In the second bowl, combine all wet ingredients. Add wet mixture to the dry mixture and mix until smooth and uniform.
3. Air-fry for 4 to 5 minutes at 345ºF. Work in batches. Dust with confectioners' swerve if desired. Bon appétit!

Per Serving

calories: 177 | fat: 14g | protein: 7g | carbs: 7g | net carbs: 4g | fiber: 3g

Turkey Sausage and Avocado Burger

Prep time: 5 minutes | Cook time: 15 minutes | Serves 4

1 pound (454 g) ground turkey breakfast sausage
½ teaspoon salt
¼ teaspoon ground black pepper
¼ cup seeded and chopped green bell pepper
2 tablespoons mayonnaise
1 medium avocado, peeled, pitted, and sliced

1. In a large bowl, mix sausage with salt, black pepper, bell pepper, and mayonnaise. Form meat into four patties.
2. Place patties into ungreased air fryer basket. Adjust the temperature to 370°F and set the timer for 15 minutes, turning patties halfway through cooking. Burgers will be done when dark brown and they have an internal temperature of at least 165°F (74ºC).
3. Serve burgers topped with avocado slices on four medium plates.

Per Serving

calories: 276 | fat: 17g | protein: 22g | carbs: 4g | net carbs: 1g | fiber: 3g

Spinach Omelet

Prep time: 5 minutes | Cook time: 12 minutes | Serves 2

4 large eggs
1½ cups chopped fresh spinach leaves
2 tablespoons peeled and chopped yellow onion

2 tablespoons salted butter, melted
½ cup shredded mild Cheddar cheese
¼ teaspoon salt

1. In an ungreased 6-inch round nonstick baking dish, whisk eggs. Stir in spinach, onion, butter, Cheddar, and salt.
2. Place dish into air fryer basket. Adjust the temperature to 320°F (160ºC) and set the timer for 12 minutes. Omelet will be done when browned on the top and firm in the middle.
3. Slice in half and serve warm on two medium plates.

Per Serving

calories: 368 | fat: 28g | protein: 20g | carbs: 3g | net carbs:2g | fiber: 1g

Sausage Egg Cup

Prep time: 10 minutes | Cook time: 15 minutes | Serves 6

12 ounces (340 g) ground pork breakfast sausage
6 large eggs
½ teaspoon salt

¼ teaspoon ground black pepper
½ teaspoon crushed red pepper flakes

1. Place sausage in six 4-inch ramekins (about 2 ounces, 57 g per ramekin) greased with cooking oil. Press sausage down to cover bottom and about ½-inch up the sides of ramekins. Crack one egg into each ramekin and sprinkle evenly with salt, black pepper, and red pepper flakes.
2. Place ramekins into air fryer basket. Adjust the temperature to 350°F (180ºC) and set the timer for 15 minutes. Egg cups will be done when sausage is fully cooked to at least 145°F (63ºC) and the egg is firm. Serve warm.

Per Serving

calories: 267 | fat: 21g | protein: 14g | carbs: 1g | net carbs: 1g | fiber: 0g

Lemony Cake

Prep time: 10 minutes | Cook time: 14 minutes | Serves 6

1 cup blanched finely ground almond flour
½ cup powdered erythritol
½ teaspoon baking powder
¼ cup unsalted butter, melted
¼ cup unsweetened almond milk

2 large eggs
1 teaspoon vanilla extract
1 medium lemon
1 teaspoon poppy seeds

1. In a large bowl, mix almond flour, erythritol, baking powder, butter, almond milk, eggs, and vanilla.
2. Slice the lemon in half and squeeze the juice into a small bowl, then add to the batter.
3. Using a fine grater, zest the lemon and add 1 tablespoon of zest to the batter and stir. Add poppy seeds to batter.
4. Pour batter into nonstick 6-inch round cake pan. Place pan into the air fryer basket.
5. Adjust the temperature to 300°F (150ºC) and set the timer for 14 minutes.
6. When fully cooked, a toothpick inserted in center will come out mostly clean. The cake will finish cooking and firm up as it cools. Serve at room temperature.

Per Serving

calories: 204 | fat: 18g | protein: 6g | carbs: 17g | net carbs: 15g | fiber: 2g

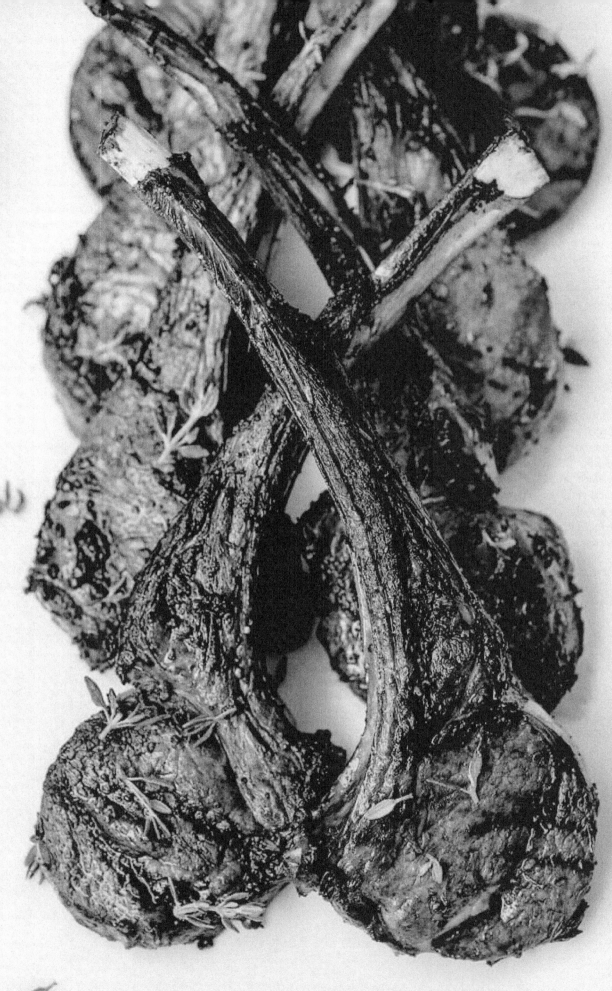

Chapter 4 Beef, Pork, and Lamb

Pork with Lime Sauce

Prep time: 10 minutes | Cook time: 15 minutes | Serves 4

Marinade:
½ cup lime juice
Grated zest of 1 lime
2 teaspoons stevia glycerite
3 cloves garlic, minced
1½ teaspoons fine sea salt
1 teaspoon chili powder, or more for more heat
1 teaspoon smoked paprika
1 pound (454 g) pork tenderloin
Avocado Lime Sauce:

1 medium-sized ripe avocado, roughly chopped
½ cup full-fat sour cream
Grated zest of 1 lime
Juice of 1 lime
2 cloves garlic, roughly chopped
½ teaspoon fine sea salt
¼ teaspoon ground black pepper
Chopped fresh cilantro leaves, for garnish
Lime slices, for serving
Pico de gallo, for serving

1. In a medium-sized casserole dish, stir together all the marinade ingredients until well combined. Add the tenderloin and coat it well in the marinade. Cover and place in the fridge to marinate for 2 hours or overnight.
2. Spray the air fryer basket with avocado oil. Preheat the air fryer to 400°F (205ºC).
3. Remove the pork from the marinade and place it in the air fryer basket. Cook for 13 to 15 minutes, until the internal temperature of the pork is 145°F (63ºC), flipping after 7 minutes. Remove the pork from the air fryer and place it on a cutting board. Allow it to rest for 8 to 10 minutes, then cut it into ½-inch-thick slices.
4. While the pork cooks, make the avocado lime sauce: Place all the sauce ingredients in a food processor and purée until smooth. Taste and adjust the seasoning to your liking.
5. Place the pork slices on a serving platter and spoon the avocado lime sauce on top. Garnish with cilantro leaves and serve with lime slices and pico de gallo.
6. Store leftovers in an airtight container in the fridge for up to 4 days. Reheat in a preheated 400°F (205ºC) air fryer for 5 minutes, or until heated through.

Per Serving
calories: 326 | fat: 19g | protein: 26g | carbs: 15g | net carbs: 9g | fiber: 6g

Blue Cheese Sirloin Steak with Spinach

Prep time: 15 minutes | Cook time: 22 minutes | Serves 4

2 tablespoons balsamic vinegar
2 tablespoons red wine vinegar
1 tablespoon Dijon mustard
1 tablespoon Swerve
1 teaspoon minced garlic
Sea salt and freshly ground black pepper, to taste
¾ cup extra-virgin olive

oil
1 pound (454 g) boneless sirloin steak
Avocado oil spray
1 small red onion, cut into ¼-inch-thick rounds
6 ounces (170 g) baby spinach
½ cup cherry tomatoes, halved
3 ounces (85 g) blue cheese, crumbled

1. In a blender, combine the balsamic vinegar, red wine vinegar, Dijon mustard, Swerve, and garlic. Season with salt and pepper and process until smooth. With the blender running, drizzle in the olive oil. Process until well combined. Transfer to a jar with a tight-fitting lid, and refrigerate until ready to serve (it will keep for up to 2 weeks).
2. Season the steak with salt and pepper and let sit at room temperature for at least 45 minutes, time permitting.
3. Set the air fryer to 400°F (205ºC). Spray the steak with oil and place it in the air fryer basket. Cook for 6 minutes. Flip the steak and spray it with more oil. Cook for 6 minutes or more for medium-rare or until the steak is done to your liking.
4. Transfer the steak to a plate, tent with a piece of aluminum foil, and allow it to rest.
5. Spray the onion slices with oil and place them in the air fryer basket. Cook at 400°F (205ºC) for 5 minutes. Flip the onion slices and spray them with more oil. Cook for 5 minutes or more.
6. Slice the steak diagonally into thin strips. Place the spinach, cherry tomatoes, onion slices, and steak in a large bowl. Toss with the desired amount of dressing. Sprinkle with crumbled blue cheese and serve.

Per Serving
calories: 670 | fat: 53g | protein: 41g | carbs: 9g | net carbs: 7g | fiber: 2g

Italian Sausage and Pepper Casserole

Prep time: 10 minutes | Cook time: 15 minutes | Serves 4

1 pound (454 g) Italian sausage	1 teaspoon dried oregano
2 Italian peppers, seeded and sliced	¼ teaspoon black pepper
1 cup mushrooms, sliced	¼ teaspoon cayenne pepper
1 shallot, sliced	Sea salt, to taste
4 cloves garlic	2 tablespoons Dijon mustard
1 teaspoon dried basil	1 cup chicken broth

1. Toss all ingredients in a lightly greased baking pan. Make sure the sausages and vegetables are coated with the oil and seasonings.
2. Bake in the preheated Air Fryer at 380ºF for 15 minutes.
3. Divide between individual bowls and serve warm. Bon appétit!

Per Serving
calories: 508 | fat: 40g | protein: 3g | carbs: 35g | net carbs: 31g | fiber: 4g

Beef Poppers

Prep time: 15 minutes | Cook time: 15 minutes | Serves 4

8 medium jalapeño peppers, stemmed, halved, and seeded	beef (85% lean)
	1 teaspoon fine sea salt
1 (8-ounce / 227-g) package cream cheese, softened	½ teaspoon ground black pepper
	8 slices thin-cut bacon
2 pounds (907 g) ground	Fresh cilantro leaves, for garnish

1. Spray the air fryer basket with avocado oil. Preheat the air fryer to 400°F.
2. Stuff each jalapeño half with a few tablespoons of cream cheese. Place the halves back together again to form 8 jalapeños.
3. Season the ground beef with the salt and pepper and mix with your hands to incorporate. Flatten about ¼ pound of ground beef in the palm of your hand and place a stuffed jalapeño in the center. Fold the beef around the jalapeño, forming an egg shape. Wrap the beef-covered jalapeño with a slice of bacon and secure it with a toothpick.
4. Place the jalapeños in the air fryer basket, leaving space between them (if you're using a smaller air fryer, work in batches if necessary), and cook for 15 minutes, or until the beef is cooked through and the bacon is crispy. Garnish with cilantro before serving.
5. Store leftovers in an airtight container in the fridge for 3 days or in the freezer for up to a month. Reheat in a preheated 350°F air fryer for 4 minutes, or until heated through and the bacon is crispy.

Per Serving
calories: 679 | fat: 53g | protein: 42g | carbs: 3g | net carbs: 2g | fiber: 1g

Swiss Burgers with Mushroom

Prep time: 5 minutes | Cook time: 15 minutes | Serves 2

2 large portobello mushrooms	paprika
1 teaspoon fine sea salt, divided	2 (¼-pound / 113-g) hamburger patties, ½ inch thick
¼ teaspoon garlic powder	2 slices Swiss cheese (omit for dairy-free)
¼ teaspoon ground black pepper	Condiments of choice, such as Ranch Dressing, prepared yellow mustard, for serving
¼ teaspoon onion powder	
¼ teaspoon smoked	

1. Preheat the air fryer to 360°F.
2. Clean the portobello mushrooms and remove the stems. Spray the mushrooms on all sides with avocado oil and season them with ½ teaspoon of the salt. Place the mushrooms in the air fryer basket and cook for 7 to 8 minutes, until fork-tender and soft to the touch.
3. While the mushrooms cook, in a small bowl mix together the remaining ½ teaspoon of salt, the garlic powder, pepper, onion powder, and paprika. Sprinkle the hamburger patties with the seasoning mixture.
4. When the mushrooms are done cooking, remove them from the air fryer and place them on a serving platter with the cap side down.
5. Place the hamburger patties in the air fryer and cook for 7 minutes, or until the internal temperature reaches 145°F for a medium-done burger. Place a slice of Swiss cheese on each patty and cook for another minute to melt the cheese.
6. Place the burgers on top of the mushrooms and drizzle with condiments of your choice. Best served fresh.

Per Serving
calories: 345 | fat: 23g | protein: 30g | carbs: 5g | net carbs: 4g | fiber: 1g

Beef Steak Shallots

Prep time: 5 minutes | Cook time: 18 to 20 minutes | Serves 6

1½ pounds (680g) beef tenderloin steaks
Sea salt, Freshly ground black pepper, to taste
4 medium shallots
1 teaspoon olive oil or avocado oil

1. Season both sides of the steaks with salt and pepper, and let them sit at room temperature for 45 minutes.
2. Set the air fryer to 400°F (205ºC) and let it preheat for 5 minutes.
3. Working in batches if necessary, place the steaks in the air fryer basket in a single layer and cook for 5 minutes. Flip and cook for 5 minutes longer, until an instant-read thermometer inserted in the center of the steaks registers 120°F (49ºC) for medium-rare (or as desired). Remove the steaks and tent with aluminum foil to rest.
4. Set the air fryer to 300°F (150ºC). In a medium bowl, toss the shallots with the oil. Place the shallots in the basket and cook for 5 minutes, then give them a toss and cook for 3 to 5 minutes or more, until crispy and golden brown.
5. Place the steaks on serving plates and arrange the shallots on top.

Per Serving
calories: 186 | fat: 5g | protein: 30g | carbs: 5g | net carbs: 5g | fiber: 0g

Lettuce Wrapped Fajita Meatball

Prep time: 10 minutes | Cook time: 10 minutes | Serves 4

1 pound (454 g) ground beef (85% lean)
½ cup salsa, plus more for serving if desired
¼ cup chopped onions
¼ cup diced green or red bell peppers
1 large egg, beaten
1 teaspoon fine sea salt
½ teaspoon chili powder
½ teaspoon ground cumin
1 clove garlic, minced
For Serving (Optional):
8 leaves Boston lettuce
Pico de gallo or salsa
Lime slices

1. Spray the air fryer basket with avocado oil. Preheat the air fryer to 350°F.
2. In a large bowl, mix together all the ingredients until well combined.
3. Shape the meat mixture into eight 1-inch balls. Place the meatballs in the air fryer basket, leaving a little

space between them. Cook for 10 minutes, or until cooked through and no longer pink inside and the internal temperature reaches 145°F.
4. Serve each meatball on a lettuce leaf, topped with pico de gallo or salsa, if desired. Serve with lime slices if desired.
5. Store leftovers in an airtight container in the fridge for 3 days or in the freezer for up to a month. Reheat in a preheated 350°F air fryer for 4 minutes, or until heated through.

Per Serving
calories: 272 | fat: 18g | protein: 23g | carbs: 3g | net carbs: 2.5g | fiber: 0.5g

Ribs with Chimichurri Sauce

Prep time: 15 minutes | Cook time: 13 minutes | Serves 4

1 pound (454 g) boneless short ribs
1½ teaspoons sea salt, divided
½ teaspoon freshly ground black pepper, divided
½ cup fresh parsley leaves
½ cup fresh cilantro leaves
1 teaspoon minced garlic
1 tablespoon freshly squeezed lemon juice
½ teaspoon ground cumin
¼ teaspoon red pepper flakes
2 tablespoons extra-virgin olive oil
Avocado oil spray

1. Pat the short ribs dry with paper towels. Sprinkle the ribs all over with 1 teaspoon salt and ¼ teaspoon black pepper. Let it sit at room temperature for 45 minutes.
2. Meanwhile, place the parsley, cilantro, garlic, lemon juice, cumin, red pepper flakes, the remaining ½ teaspoon salt, and the remaining ¼ teaspoon black pepper in a blender or food processor. With the blender running, slowly drizzle in the olive oil. Blend for about 1 minute, until the mixture is smooth and well combined.
3. Set the air fryer to 400°F (205ºC). Spray both sides of the ribs with oil. Place in the basket and cook for 8 minutes. Flip and cook for another 5 minutes, until an instant-read thermometer reads 125°F (52ºC) for medium-rare (or to your desired doneness).
4. Allow the meat to rest for 5 to 10 minutes, then slice. Serve warm with the chimichurri sauce.

Per Serving
calories: 329 | fat: 24g | protein: 21g | carbs: 7g | net carbs: 6g | fiber: 1g

Japanese Rump Steak

Prep time: 15 minutes | Cook time: 13 minutes | Serves 4

½ head broccoli, broken into florets
⅓ cup keto teriyaki marinade
Fine sea salt and ground black pepper, to taste
½ pound (227 g) rump steak
2 red capsicums, sliced
1½ teaspoons sesame oil

1. Add rump roast and teriyaki marinade to a mixing dish, stir to coat. Let it marinate for about 40 minutes.
2. Then, roast in the preheated Air Fryer for 13 minutes at 395ºF. Stir halfway through cooking time.
3. Meanwhile, sauté the broccoli in the hot sesame oil along with sliced capsicum, cook until tender and season with salt and pepper to savor.
4. Place the prepared rump steak on a serving platter and serve garnished with sautéed broccoli. Bon appétit!

Per Serving
calories: 220 | fat: 12g | protein: 20g | carbs: 8g | net carbs: 7g | fiber: 1g

Crispy Pork Chop with Parmesan

Prep time: 15 minutes | Cook time: 9 to 14 minutes | Serves 4

2 large eggs
½ cup finely grated Parmesan cheese
½ cup finely ground blanched almond flour
1 teaspoon paprika
½ teaspoon dried oregano
½ teaspoon garlic powder
Salt, Freshly ground black pepper, to taste
1¼ pounds (567g) (1-inch-thick) boneless pork chops
Avocado oil spray

1. Beat the eggs in a shallow bowl. In a separate bowl, combine the Parmesan cheese, almond flour, paprika, oregano, garlic powder, and salt and pepper to taste.
2. Dip the pork chops into the eggs, then coat them with the Parmesan mixture, gently pressing the coating onto the meat. Spray the breaded pork chops with oil.
3. Set the air fryer to 400°F. Place the pork chops in the air fryer basket in a single layer, working in batches if necessary. Cook for 6 minutes. Flip the chops and spray them with more oil. Cook for another 3 to 8

minutes, until an instant-read thermometer reads 145°F (63ºC).
4. Allow the pork chops to rest for at least 5 minutes, and then serve.

Per Serving
calories: 351 | fat: 20g | protein: 38g | carbs: 4g | net carbs: 2g | fiber: 2g

Herbed Lamb Chops with Parmesan

Prep time: 10 minutes | Cook time: 5 minutes | Serves 2

1 large egg
2 cloves garlic, minced
¼ cup pork dust
¼ cup powdered Parmesan cheese
1 tablespoon chopped fresh oregano leaves
1 tablespoon chopped fresh rosemary leaves
1 teaspoon chopped fresh thyme leaves
½ teaspoon ground black pepper
4 (1-inch-thick) lamb chops
For Garnish/Serving (Optional):
Sprigs of fresh oregano
Sprigs of fresh rosemary
Sprigs of fresh thyme
Lavender flowers
Lemon slices

1. Spray the air fryer basket with avocado oil. Preheat the air fryer to 400°F.
2. Beat the egg in a shallow bowl, add the garlic, and stir well to combine. In another shallow bowl, mix together the pork dust, Parmesan, herbs, and pepper.
3. One at a time, dip the lamb chops into the egg mixture, shake off the excess egg, and then dredge them in the Parmesan mixture. Use your hands to coat the chops well in the Parmesan mixture and form a nice crust on all sides, if necessary, dip the chops again in both the egg and the Parmesan mixture.
4. Place the lamb chops in the air fryer basket, leaving space between them, and cook for 5 minutes, or until the internal temperature reaches 145°F for medium doneness. Allow them to rest for 10 minutes before serving.
5. Garnish with sprigs of oregano, rosemary, and thyme, and lavender flowers, if desired. Serve with lemon slices, if desired.
6. Best served fresh. Store leftovers in an airtight container in the fridge for up to 4 days. Serve chilled over a salad, or reheat in a 350°F air fryer for 3 minutes, or until heated through.

Per Serving
calories: 790 | fat: 60g | protein: 57g | carbs: 2g | net carbs: 1.6g | fiber: 0.4g

Balsamic London Broil

Prep time: 30 minutes | Cook time: 8 to 10 minutes | Serves 8

2 pounds (907 g) London broil
3 large garlic cloves, minced
3 tablespoons balsamic vinegar
3 tablespoons whole-grain mustard
2 tablespoons olive oil
Sea salt and ground black pepper, to taste
½ teaspoon dried hot red pepper flakes

1. Score both sides of the cleaned London broil.
2. Thoroughly combine the remaining ingredients, massage this mixture into the meat to coat it on all sides. Let it marinate for at least 3 hours.
3. Set the Air Fryer to cook at 400ºF (205ºC), Then cook the London broil for 15 minutes. Flip it over and cook another 10 to 12 minutes. Bon appétit!

Per Serving
calories: 257 | fat: 9g | protein: 41g | carbs: 1g | net carbs: 0g | fiber: 1g

Ritzy Meatloaf with Swedish Sauce

Prep time: 10 minutes | Cook time: 35 minutes | Serves 8

1½ pounds (680 g) ground beef (85% lean)
¼ pound (113 g) ground pork
1 large egg (omit for egg-free)
½ cup minced onions
¼ cup tomato sauce
2 tablespoons dry mustard
2 cloves garlic, minced
2 teaspoons fine sea salt
1 teaspoon ground black pepper, plus more for garnish
Sauce:
½ cup (1 stick) unsalted butter
½ cup shredded Swiss or mild Cheddar cheese
2 ounces (57 g) cream cheese (¼ cup), softened
⅓ cup beef broth
⅛ teaspoon ground nutmeg
Halved cherry tomatoes, for serving (optional)

1. Preheat the air fryer to 390°F.
2. In a large bowl, combine the ground beef, ground pork, egg, onions, tomato sauce, dry mustard, garlic, salt, and pepper. Using your hands, mix until well combined.
3. Place the meatloaf mixture in a 9 by 5-inch loaf pan and place it in the air fryer. Cook for 35 minutes, or until cooked through and the internal temperature reaches 145°F. Check the meatloaf after 25 minutes, if it's getting too brown on the top, cover it loosely with foil to prevent burning.
4. While the meatloaf cooks, make the sauce: Heat the butter in a saucepan over medium-high heat until it sizzles and brown flecks appear, stirring constantly to keep the butter from burning. Turn the heat down to low and whisk in the Swiss cheese, cream cheese, broth, and nutmeg. Simmer for at least 10 minutes. The longer it simmers, the more the flavors open up.
5. When the meatloaf is done, transfer it to a serving tray and pour the sauce over it. Garnish with ground black pepper and serve with cherry tomatoes, if desired. Allow the meatloaf to rest for 10 minutes before slicing so it doesn't crumble apart.
6. Store leftovers in an airtight container in the fridge for 3 days or in the freezer for up to a month. Reheat in a preheated 350°F air fryer for 4 minutes, or until heated through.

Per Serving
calories: 395 | fat: 32g | protein: 23g | carbs: 3g | net carbs: 2g | fiber: 1g

Zucchini and Ham Casserole

Prep time: 15 minutes | Cook time: 26 minutes | Serves 4

2 tablespoons butter, melted
1 zucchini, diced
1 bell pepper, seeded and sliced
1 red chili pepper, seeded and minced
1 medium-sized leek, sliced
¾ pound (340 g) ham, cooked and diced
5 eggs
1 teaspoon cayenne pepper
Sea salt, to taste
½ teaspoon ground black pepper
1 tablespoon fresh cilantro, chopped

1. Start by preheating the Air Fryer to 380ºF. Grease the sides and bottom of a baking pan with the melted butter.
2. Place the zucchini, peppers, leeks and ham in the baking pan. Bake in the preheated Air Fryer for 6 minutes.
3. Crack the eggs on top of ham and vegetables, season with the cayenne pepper, salt, and black pepper. Bake for a further 20 minutes or until the whites are completely set.
4. Garnish with fresh cilantro and serve. Bon appétit!

Per Serving
calories: 325 | fat: 21g | protein: 7g | carbs: 28g | net carbs: 26g | fiber: 2g

Pork Twist with Bolognese Sauce

Prep time: 10 minutes | Cook time: 15 minutes | Serves 4

1 teaspoon kosher salt
⅓ teaspoon cayenne pepper
1½ pounds (680 g) ground pork
⅓ cup tomato paste
3 cloves garlic, minced
½ medium-sized white onion, peeled and

chopped
⅓ tablespoon fresh cilantro, chopped
½ tablespoon extra-virgin olive oil
⅓ teaspoon freshly cracked black pepper
½ teaspoon grated fresh ginger

1. Begin by preheating your Air Fryer to 395ºF.
2. Then, thoroughly combine all the ingredients until the mixture is uniform.
3. Transfer the meat mixture to the Air Fryer baking dish and cook for about 14 minutes. Serve with zucchini noodles and enjoy.

Per Serving
calories: 490 | fat: 37g | protein: 29g | carbs: 6g | net carbs: 5g | fiber: 1g

Buttery Strip Steak

Prep time: 7 minutes | Cook time: 12 minutes | Serves 6

½ cup (1 stick) unsalted butter, at room temperature
1 cup finely grated Parmesan cheese
¼ cup finely ground

blanched almond flour
1½ pounds (680g) New York strip steak
Sea salt, freshly ground black pepper, to taste

1. Place the butter, Parmesan cheese, and almond flour in a food processor. Process until smooth. Transfer to a sheet of parchment paper and form into a log. Wrap tightly in plastic wrap. Freeze for 45 minutes or refrigerate for at least 4 hours.
2. While the butter is chilling, season the steak liberally with salt and pepper. Let the steak rest at room temperature for about 45 minutes.
3. Place the grill pan or basket in your air fryer, set it to 400°F (205ºC), and let it preheat for 5 minutes.
4. Working in batches, if necessary, place the steak on the grill pan and cook for 4 minutes. Flip and cook for 3 minutes or more, until the steak is brown on both sides.
5. Remove the steak from the air fryer and arrange an equal amount of the Parmesan butter on top of each

steak. Return the steak to the air fryer and continue cooking for another 5 minutes, until an instant-read thermometer reads 120°F (49ºC) for medium-rare and the crust is golden brown (or to your desired doneness).
6. Transfer the cooked steak to a plate, let it rest for 10 minutes before serving.

Per Serving
calories: 463 | fat: 37g | protein: 33g | carbs: 2g | net carbs: 1g | fiber: 1g

Reuben Beef Fritters with Sauerkraut

Prep time: 10 minutes | Cook time: 16 minutes | Serves 6

2 cups finely diced cooked corned beef
1 (8-ounce / 227-g) package cream cheese, softened
½ cup finely shredded Swiss cheese
¼ cup sauerkraut
1 cup pork dust or powdered Parmesan

cheese
Chopped fresh thyme, for garnish
Thousand Island Dipping Sauce, for serving (optional, omit for egg-free)
Cornichons, for serving (optional)

1. Spray the air fryer basket with avocado oil. Preheat the air fryer to 390°F.
2. In a large bowl, mix together the corned beef, cream cheese, Swiss cheese, and sauerkraut until well combined. Form the corned beef mixture into twelve 1½-inch balls.
3. Place the pork dust in a shallow bowl. Roll the corned beef balls in the pork dust and use your hands to form it into a thick crust around each ball.
4. Place 6 balls in the air fryer basket, spaced about ½ inch apart, and cook for 8 minutes, or until golden brown and crispy. Allow them to cool a bit before lifting them out of the air fryer (the fritters are very soft when the cheese is melted, they're easier to handle once the cheese has hardened a bit). Repeat with the remaining fritters.
5. Garnish with chopped fresh thyme and serve with the dipping sauce and cornichons, if desired. Store leftovers in an airtight container in the fridge for 3 days or in the freezer for up to a month. Reheat in a preheated 350°F air fryer for 4 minutes, or until heated through.

Per Serving
calories: 527 | fat: 50g | protein: 18g | carbs: 2g | net carbs: 1.9g | fiber: 0.1g

Aromatic Pork Loin Roast

Prep time: 55 minutes | Cook time: 55 minutes | Serves 6

1½ pounds (680g) boneless pork loin roast, washed
1 teaspoon mustard seeds
1 teaspoon garlic powder
1 teaspoon porcini powder
1 teaspoon shallot powder
¾ teaspoon sea salt flakes
1 teaspoon red pepper flakes, crushed
2 dried sprigs thyme, crushed
2 tablespoons lime juice

1. Firstly, score the meat using a small knife, make sure to not cut too deep.
2. In a small-sized mixing dish, combine all seasonings in the order listed above, mix to combine well.
3. Massage the spice mix into the pork meat to evenly distribute. Drizzle with lemon juice.
4. Then, set your Air Fryer to cook at 360ºF (182ºC). Place the pork in the Air Fryer basket, roast for 25 to 30 minutes. Pause the machine, check for doneness and cook for 25 minutes or more.

Per Serving
calories: 278 | fat: 16g | protein: 31g | carbs: 2g | net carbs: 1g | fiber: 1g

Air Fried Flank Steak

Prep time: 5 minutes | Cook time: 8 to 10 minutes | Serves 6

½ cup avocado oil
¼ cup coconut aminos
1 shallot, minced
1 tablespoon minced garlic
2 tablespoons chopped fresh oregano, or 2 teaspoons dried
1½ teaspoons sea salt
1 teaspoon freshly ground black pepper
¼ teaspoon red pepper flakes
2 pounds (907 g) flank steak

1. In a blender, combine the avocado oil, coconut aminos, shallot, garlic, oregano, salt, black pepper, and red pepper flakes. Process until smooth.
2. Place the steak in a zip-top plastic bag or shallow dish with the marinade. Seal the bag or cover the dish and marinate in the refrigerator for at least 2 hours or overnight.
3. Remove the steak from the bag and discard the marinade.
4. Set the air fryer to 400°F (205ºC). Place the steak in the air fryer basket (if needed, cut into sections and work in batches). Cook for 4 to 6 minutes, flip the steak, and cook for another 4 minutes or until the internal temperature reaches 120°F (49ºC) in the thickest part for medium-rare (or as desired).

Per Serving
calories: 304 | fat: 23g | protein: 16g | carbs: 4g | net carbs: 3g | fiber: 1g

Pork Belly with Onion Sauce

Prep time: 10 minutes | Cook time: 17 minutes | Serves 4

1 pound (454 g) unsalted pork belly
2 teaspoons Chinese five-spice powder
Sauce:
1 tablespoon coconut oil
1 (1-inch) piece fresh ginger, peeled and grated
2 cloves garlic, minced
½ cup beef or chicken broth
¼ to ½ cup Swerve confectioners-style sweetener
3 tablespoons wheat-free tamari, or ½ cup coconut aminos
1 green onion, sliced, plus more for garnish

1. Spray the air fryer basket with avocado oil. Preheat the air fryer to 400°F (205ºC).
2. Cut the pork belly into ½-inch-thick slices and season well on all sides with the five-spice powder. Place the slices in a single layer in the air fryer basket (if you're using a smaller air fryer, work in batches if necessary) and cook for 8 minutes, or until cooked to your liking, flipping halfway through.
3. While the pork belly cooks, make the sauce: Heat the coconut oil in a small saucepan over medium heat. Add the ginger and garlic and sauté for 1 minute, or until fragrant. Add the broth, sweetener, and tamari and simmer for 10 to 15 minutes, until thickened. Add the green onion and cook for another minute, until the green onion is softened. Taste and adjust the seasoning to your liking.
4. Transfer the pork belly to a large bowl. Pour the sauce over the pork belly and coat well. Place the pork belly slices on a serving platter and garnish with sliced green onions.
5. Best served fresh. Store leftovers in an airtight container in the fridge for up to 4 days. Reheat in a preheated 400°F (205ºC) air fryer for 3 minutes, or until heated through.

Per Serving
calories: 365 | fat: 32g | protein: 19g | carbs: 2g | net carbs: 1g | fiber: 1g

Sausage and Beef Meatloaf

Prep time: 15 minutes | Cook time: 25 minutes | Serves 4

¾ pound (340 g) ground chuck
¼ pound (113 g) ground pork sausage
1 cup shallot, finely chopped
2 eggs, well beaten
3 tablespoons plain milk
1 tablespoon oyster sauce
1 teaspoon porcini mushrooms
½ teaspoon cumin powder
1 teaspoon garlic paste
1 tablespoon fresh parsley
Seasoned salt and crushed red pepper flakes, to taste
1 cup Parmesan cheese, grated

1. Simply place all ingredients in a large-sized mixing dish, mix until everything is thoroughly combined.
2. Press the meatloaf mixture into the Air Fryer baking dish, set your Air Fryer to cook at 360ºF for 25 minutes. Press the power button and cook until heated through.
3. Check for doneness and serve with your favorite wine!

Per Serving
calories: 206 | fat: 8g | protein: 18g | carbs: 16g | net carbs: 15g | fiber: 1g

Lush Spiced Ribeye Steak

Prep time: 20 minutes | Cook time: 15 minutes | Serves 3

1½ pounds (680g) ribeye, bone-in
1 tablespoon butter, room temperature
Salt, to taste
½ teaspoon crushed black pepper
½ teaspoon dried dill
½ teaspoon cayenne pepper
½ teaspoon garlic powder
½ teaspoon onion powder
1 teaspoon ground coriander
3 tablespoons mayonnaise
1 teaspoon garlic, minced

1. Start by preheating your Air Fryer to 400ºF (205ºC).
2. Pat dry the ribeye and rub it with softened butter on all sides. Sprinkle with seasonings and transfer to the cooking basket.
3. Cook in the preheated Air Fryer for 15 minutes, flipping them halfway through the cooking time.
4. In the meantime, simply mix the mayonnaise with garlic and place in the refrigerator until ready to serve. Bon appétit!

Per Serving
calories: 437 | fat: 24g | protein: 51g | carbs: 2g | net carbs: 1g | fiber: 1g

Steak with Mushroom Onion Gravy

Prep time: 10 minutes | Cook time: 33 minutes | Serves 2

Mushroom Onion Gravy:
¾ cup sliced button mushrooms
¼ cup thinly sliced onions
¼ cup unsalted butter, melted
½ teaspoon fine sea salt
¼ cup beef broth
Steaks:
½ pound (227 g) ground beef (85% lean)
¼ cup minced onions, or ½ teaspoon onion powder
2 tablespoons tomato paste
1 tablespoon dry mustard
1 clove garlic, minced, or ¼ teaspoon garlic powder
½ teaspoon fine sea salt
¼ teaspoon ground black pepper, plus more for garnish if desired
Chopped fresh thyme leaves, for garnish (optional)

1. Preheat the air fryer to 390°F.
2. Make the gravy: Place the mushrooms and onions in a casserole dish that will fit in your air fryer. Pour the melted butter over them and stir to coat, then season with the salt. Place the dish in the air fryer and cook for 5 minutes, stir, then cook for another 3 minutes, or until the onions are soft and the mushrooms are browning. Add the broth and cook for another 10 minutes.
3. While the gravy is cooking, prepare the steaks: In a large bowl, mix together the ground beef, onions, tomato paste, dry mustard, garlic, salt, and pepper until well combined. Form the mixture into 2 oval-shaped patties.
4. Place the patties on top of the mushroom gravy. Cook for 10 minutes, gently flip the patties, then cook for another 2 to 5 minutes, until the beef is cooked through and the internal temperature reaches 145°F.
5. Transfer the steaks to a serving platter and pour the gravy over them. Garnish with ground black pepper and chopped fresh thyme, if desired. Store leftovers in an airtight container in the fridge for 3 days or in the freezer for up to a month. Reheat in a preheated 350°F air fryer for 4 minutes, or until heated through.

Per Serving
calories: 588 | fat: 44g | protein: 33g | carbs: 11g | net carbs: 8g | fiber: 3g

Pork Meatballs with Worcester Sauce

Prep time: 20 minutes | Cook time: 15 minutes | Serves 4

1 pound (454 g) ground pork	1 tablespoon coconut aminos
1 cup scallions, finely chopped	1 teaspoon turmeric powder
2 cloves garlic, finely minced	½ teaspoon freshly grated ginger root
1½ tablespoons Worcester sauce	1 small sliced red chili, for garnish

1. Mix all of the above ingredients, apart from the red chili. Knead with your hands to ensure an even mixture.
2. Roll into equal balls and transfer them to the Air Fryer cooking basket.
3. Set the timer for 15 minutes and push the power button. Air-fry at 350ºF (180ºC). Sprinkle with sliced red chili, serve immediately with your favorite sauce for dipping. Enjoy!

Per Serving
calories: 506 | fat: 42g | protein: 24g | carbs: 7g | net carbs: 5g | fiber: 2g

Beef Sausage and Veg Mélange

Prep time: 15 minutes | Cook time: 40 minutes | Serves 2

1 tablespoon lard, melted	pepper
1 shallot, chopped	4 beef good quality sausages, thinly sliced
1 bell pepper, chopped	
2 red chilies, finely chopped	2 teaspoons smoked paprika
1 teaspoon ginger-garlic paste	1 cup beef bone broth
Sea salt, to taste	½ cup tomato puree
¼ teaspoon ground black	2 handfuls spring greens, shredded

1. Melt the lard in a Dutch oven over medium-high flame, sauté the shallots and peppers about 4 minutes or until fragrant.
2. Add the ginger-garlic paste and cook for an additional minute. Season with salt and black pepper and transfer to a lightly greased baking pan.
3. Then, brown the sausages, stirring occasionally, working in batches. Add to the baking pan.
4. Add the smoked paprika, broth, and tomato puree. Lower the pan onto the Air Fryer basket. Bake at 325ºF for 30 minutes.

5. Stir in the spring greens and cook for 5 minutes or more or until they wilt. Serve over the hot rice if desired. Bon appétit!

Per Serving
calories: 565 | fat: 47g | protein: 21g | carbs: 14g | net carbs: 13g | fiber: 1g

Skirt Steak Carne Asada

Prep time: 5 minutes | Cook time: 8 minutes | Serves 4

Marinade:	1 teaspoon stevia glycerite
1 cup fresh cilantro leaves and stems, plus more for garnish if desired	2 teaspoons ancho chili powder
1 jalapeño pepper, seeded and diced	2 teaspoons fine sea salt
½ cup lime juice	1 teaspoon coriander seeds
2 tablespoons avocado oil	1 teaspoon cumin seeds
2 tablespoons coconut vinegar or apple cider vinegar	1 pound (454 g) skirt steak, cut into 4 equal portions
2 teaspoons orange extract	**For Serving (Optional):** Chopped avocado Lime slices Sliced radishes

1. Make the marinade: Place all the ingredients for the marinade in a blender and puree until smooth.
2. Place the steak in a shallow dish and pour the marinade over it, making sure the meat is covered completely. Cover and place in the fridge for 2 hours or overnight.
3. Spray the air fryer basket with avocado oil. Preheat the air fryer to 400°F.
4. Remove the steak from the marinade and place it in the air fryer basket in one layer. Cook for 8 minutes, or until the internal temperature is 145°F, do not overcook or it will become tough.
5. Remove the steak from the air fryer and place it on a cutting board to rest for 10 minutes before slicing it against the grain. Garnish with cilantro, if desired, and serve with chopped avocado, lime slices, and/or sliced radishes, if desired.
6. Store the leftovers in an airtight container in the fridge for 3 days or in the freezer for up to a month. Reheat in a preheated 350°F air fryer for 4 minutes, or until heated through.

Per Serving
calories: 263 | fat: 17g | protein: 24g | carbs: 4g | net carbs: 3g | fiber: 1g

Bacon-Wrapped Hot Dogs with Mayo Sauce

Prep time: 10 minutes | Cook time: 10 minutes | Serves 5

10 thin slices of bacon	¼ cup mayo
5 pork hot dogs, halved	4 tablespoons ketchup, low-carb
1 teaspoon cayenne pepper	1 teaspoon rice vinegar
Sauce:	1 teaspoon chili powder

1. Lay the slices of bacon on your working surface. Place a hot dog on one end of each slice, sprinkle with cayenne pepper and roll them over.
2. Cook in the preheated Air Fryer at 390ºF for 10 to 12 minutes.
3. Whisk all ingredients for the sauce in a mixing bowl and store in your refrigerator, covered, until ready to serve.
4. Serve bacon-wrapped hot dogs with the sauce on the side. Enjoy!

Per Serving

calories: 297 | fat: 26g | protein: 7g | carbs: 9g | net carbs: 8g | fiber: 1g

Bacon-Wrapped Cheese Pork

Prep time: 10 minutes | Cook time: 20 minutes | Serves 4

4 (1-inch-thick) boneless pork chops	g) packages Boursin cheese
2 (5.2-ounce / 147	8 slices thin-cut bacon

1. Spray the air fryer basket with avocado oil. Preheat the air fryer to 400°F (205ºC).
2. Place one of the chops on a cutting board. With a sharp knife held parallel to the cutting board, make a 1-inch-wide incision on the top edge of the chop. Carefully cut into the chop to form a large pocket, leaving a ½-inch border along the sides and bottom. Repeat with the other 3 chops.
3. Snip the corner of a large resealable plastic bag to form a ¾-inch hole. Place the Boursin cheese in the bag and pipe the cheese into the pockets in the chops, dividing the cheese evenly among them.
4. Wrap 2 slices of bacon around each chop and secure the ends with toothpicks. Place the bacon-wrapped chops in the air fryer basket and cook for 10 minutes, then flip the chops and cook for another 8 to 10 minutes, until the bacon is crisp, the chops are cooked through, and the internal temperature

reaches 145°F (63ºC).

5. Store the leftovers in an airtight container in the refrigerator for up to 3 days. Reheat in a preheated 400°F (205ºC) air fryer for 5 minutes, or until warmed through.

Per Serving

calories: 578 | fat: 45g | protein: 37g | carbs: 16g | net carbs: 15g | fiber: 1g

Stuffed Beef Tenderloin

Prep time: 10 minutes | Cook time: 10 minutes | Serves 4

1½ pounds (680 g) venison or beef tenderloin, pounded to ¼ inch thick	¼ cup finely chopped onions
3 teaspoons fine sea salt	2 cloves garlic, minced
1 teaspoon ground black pepper	**For Garnish/Serving (Optional):**
2 ounces (57 g) creamy goat cheese	Prepared yellow mustard
½ cup crumbled feta cheese	Halved cherry tomatoes
	Extra-virgin olive oil
	Sprigs of fresh rosemary
	Lavender flowers

1. Spray the air fryer basket with avocado oil. Preheat the air fryer to 400°F.
2. Season the tenderloin on all sides with the salt and pepper.
3. In a medium-sized mixing bowl, combine the goat cheese, feta, onions, and garlic. Place the mixture in the center of the tenderloin. Starting at the end closest to you, tightly roll the tenderloin like a jelly roll. Tie the rolled tenderloin tightly with kitchen twine.
4. Place the meat in the air fryer basket and cook for 5 minutes. Flip the meat over and cook for another 5 minutes, or until the internal temperature reaches 135°F for medium-rare.
5. To serve, smear a line of prepared yellow mustard on a platter, then place the meat next to it and add halved cherry tomatoes on the side, if desired. Drizzle with olive oil and garnish with rosemary sprigs and lavender flowers, if desired.
6. Best served fresh. Store leftovers in an airtight container in the fridge for 3 days. Reheat in a preheated 350°F air fryer for 4 minutes, or until heated through.

Per Serving

calories: 415 | fat: 16g | protein: 62g | carbs: 4g | net carbs: 3.7g | fiber: 0.3g

Beef and Mushroom Burger

Prep time: 10 minutes | Cook time: 21 to 23 minutes | Serves 4

1 pound (454 g) ground beef, formed into 4 patties
Sea salt, freshly ground black pepper, to taste
1 cup thinly sliced onion
8 ounces (227 g) mushrooms, sliced
1 tablespoon avocado oil
2 ounces (57 g) Gruyère cheese, shredded (about ½ cup)

1. Season the patties on both sides with salt and pepper.
2. Set the air fryer to 375°F (190ºC). Place the patties in the basket and cook for 3 minutes. Flip and cook for another 2 minutes. Remove the burgers and set aside.
3. Place the onion and mushrooms in a medium bowl. Add the avocado oil and salt and pepper to taste, toss well.
4. Place the onion and mushrooms in the air fryer basket. Cook for 15 minutes, stirring occasionally.
5. Spoon the onions and mushrooms over the patties. Top with the cheese. Place the patties back in the air fryer basket and cook for another 1 to 3 minutes, until the cheese melts and an instant-read thermometer reads 160°F (71ºC). Remove and let them rest. The temperature will rise to 165°F (74ºC), yielding a perfect medium-well burger.

Per Serving

calories: 470 | fat: 38g | protein: 25g | carbs: 5g | net carbs: 4g | fiber: 1g

Pork Cutlets with Red Wine

Prep time: 20 minutes | Cook time: 15 minutes | Serves 2

1 cup water
1 cup red wine
1 tablespoon sea salt
2 pork cutlets
¼ cup almond meal
¼ cup flaxseed meal
½ teaspoon baking powder
1 teaspoon shallot powder
½ teaspoon porcini powder
Sea salt and ground black pepper, to taste
1 egg
¼ cup yogurt
1 teaspoon brown mustard
⅓ cup Parmesan cheese, grated

1. In a large ceramic dish, combine the water, wine and salt. Add the pork cutlets and put for 1 hour in the refrigerator.

2. In a shallow bowl, mix the almond meal, flaxseed meal, baking powder, shallot powder, porcini powder, salt, and ground pepper. In another bowl, whisk the eggs with yogurt and mustard.
3. In a third bowl, place the grated Parmesan cheese.
4. Dip the pork cutlets in the seasoned flour mixture and toss evenly, then, in the egg mixture. Finally, roll them over the grated Parmesan cheese.
5. Spritz the bottom of the cooking basket with cooking oil. Add the breaded pork cutlets and cook at 395ºF (202ºC) and for 10 minutes.
6. Flip and cook for 5 minutes or more on the other side. Serve warm.

Per Serving

calories: 450 | fat: 26g | protein: 41g | carbs: 9g | net carbs: 7g | fiber: 2g

Flank Steak with Lettuce and Cucumber

Prep time: 15 minutes | Cook time: 8 to 10 minutes | Serves 4

1 pound (454 g) flank steak
1 teaspoon garlic powder
1 teaspoon ground cumin
½ teaspoon sea salt
½ teaspoon freshly ground black pepper
5 ounces (142 g) shredded romaine lettuce
½ cup crumbled feta
cheese
½ cup peeled and diced cucumber
⅓ cup sliced red onion
¼ cup seeded and diced tomato
2 tablespoons pitted and sliced black olives
Tzatziki Sauce, for serving

1. Pat the steak dry with paper towels. In a small bowl, combine the garlic powder, cumin, salt, and pepper. Sprinkle this mixture all over the steak, and allow the steak to rest at room temperature for 45 minutes.
2. Preheat the air fryer to 400°F (205ºC). Place the steak in the air fryer basket and cook for 4 minutes. Flip the steak and cook 4 to 6 minutes or more, until an instant-read thermometer reads 120°F (49ºC) at the thickest point for medium-rare (or as desired). Remove the steak from the air fryer and let it rest for 5 minutes.
3. Divide the romaine among plates. Top with the feta, cucumber, red onion, tomato, and olives.
4. Thinly slice the steak diagonally. Add the steak to the plates and drizzle with tzatziki sauce before serving.

Per Serving

calories: 244 | fat: 12g | protein: 28g | carbs: 5g | net carbs: 4g | fiber: 1g

Herbed Filet Mignon

Prep time: 20 minutes | Cook time: 13 minutes | Serves 4

1 pound (454 g) filet mignon
Sea salt and ground black pepper, to taste
½ teaspoon cayenne pepper
1 teaspoon dried basil
1 teaspoon dried

rosemary
1 teaspoon dried thyme
1 tablespoon sesame oil
1 small-sized egg, well-whisked
½ cup Parmesan cheese, grated

1. Season the filet mignon with salt, black pepper, cayenne pepper, basil, rosemary, and thyme. Brush with sesame oil.
2. Put the egg in a shallow plate. Now, place the Parmesan cheese in another plate.
3. Coat the filet mignon with the egg, then, lay it into the Parmesan cheese. Set your Air Fryer to cook at 360ºF (182ºC).
4. Cook for 10 to 13 minutes or until golden. Serve with mixed salad leaves and enjoy!

Per Serving

calories: 315 | fat: 20g | protein: 30g | carbs: 4g | net carbs: 3g | fiber: 1g

Beef Chuck with Brussels Sprouts

Prep time: 30 minutes | Cook time: 25 minutes | Serves 4

1 pound (454 g) beef chuck shoulder steak
2 tablespoons olive oil
1 tablespoon red wine vinegar
1 teaspoon fine sea salt
½ teaspoon ground black pepper
1 teaspoon smoked paprika

1 teaspoon onion powder
½ teaspoon garlic powder
½ pound (227g) Brussels sprouts, cleaned and halved
½ teaspoon fennel seeds
1 teaspoon dried basil
1 teaspoon dried sage

1. Firstly, marinate the beef with olive oil, wine vinegar, salt, black pepper, paprika, onion powder, and garlic powder. Rub the marinade into the meat and let it stay for at least for 3 hours.
2. Air fry at 390ºF (199ºC) for 10 minutes. Pause the machine and add the prepared Brussels sprouts, sprinkle them with fennel seeds, basil, and sage.
3. Turn the machine to 380ºF (193ºC), press the power button and cook for 5 more minutes. Pause the

machine, stir and cook for further 10 minutes.
4. Next, remove the meat from the cooking basket and cook the vegetables a few minutes or more if needed and according to your taste. Serve with your favorite mayo sauce.

Per Serving

calories: 272 | fat: 14g | protein: 26g | carbs: 6g | net carbs: 3g | fiber: 3g

Blue Cheese Hamburgers

Prep time: 5 minutes | Cook time: 10 minutes | Serves 2

½ teaspoon fine sea salt
¼ teaspoon ground black pepper
¼ teaspoon garlic powder
¼ teaspoon onion powder
¼ teaspoon smoked paprika
2 (¼-pound / 113-g)

hamburger patties, ½ inch thick
½ cup crumbled blue cheese (omit for dairy-free)
2 Hamburger Buns
2 tablespoons mayonnaise
6 red onion slices
2 Boston lettuce leaves

1. Spray the air fryer basket with avocado oil. Preheat the air fryer to 360°F.
2. In a small bowl, combine the salt, pepper, and seasonings. Season the patties well on both sides with the seasoning mixture.
3. Place the patties in the air fryer basket and cook for 7 minutes, or until the internal temperature reaches 145°F for a medium-done burger. Place the blue cheese on top of the patties and cook for another minute to melt the cheese. Remove the burgers from the air fryer and allow them to rest for 5 minutes.
4. Slice the buns in half and smear 2 halves with a tablespoon of mayo each. Increase the heat to 400°F and place the buns in the air fryer basket cut side up. Toast the buns for 1 to 2 minutes, until golden brown.
5. Remove the buns from the air fryer and place them on a serving plate. Place the burgers on the buns and top each burger with 3 red onion slices and a lettuce leaf.
6. Best served fresh. Store leftover patties in an airtight container in the fridge for 3 days or in the freezer for up to a month. Reheat in a preheated 350°F air fryer for 4 minutes, or until heated through.

Per Serving

calories: 237 | fat: 20g | protein: 11g | carbs: 3g | net carbs: 2g | fiber: 1g

Herbed Top Chuck

Prep time: 15 minutes | Cook time: 50 minutes | Serves 3

1½ pounds (680g) top chuck
2 teaspoons olive oil
1 tablespoon Dijon mustard
Sea salt and ground

black pepper, to taste
1 teaspoon dried marjoram
1 teaspoon dried thyme
½ teaspoon fennel seeds

1. Start by preheating your Air Fryer to 380ºF (193ºC)
2. Add all ingredients in a Ziploc bag, shake to mix well. Next, spritz the bottom of the Air Fryer basket with cooking spray.
3. Place the beef in the cooking basket and cook for 50 minutes, turning every 10 to 15 minutes.
4. Let it rest for 5 to 7 minutes before slicing and serving. Enjoy!

Per Serving

calories: 406 | fat: 24g | protein: 44g | carbs: 2 g | net carbs:1g | fiber: 1g

Mushroom Sausage Biscuit

Prep time: 15 minutes | Cook time: 34 minutes | Serves 4

Filling:
1 pound (454 g) ground Italian sausage
1 cup sliced mushrooms
1 teaspoon fine sea salt
2 cups no-sugar-added marinara sauce
Biscuits:
3 large egg whites
¾ cup blanched almond

flour
1 teaspoon baking powder
¼ teaspoon fine sea salt
2½ tablespoons very cold unsalted butter, cut into ¼-inch pieces
Fresh basil leaves, for garnish

1. Preheat the air fryer to 400°F (205ºC).
2. Place the sausage in a 7-inch pie pan (or a pan that fits into your air fryer). Use your hands to break up the sausage and spread it evenly on the bottom of the pan. Place the pan in the air fryer and cook for 5 minutes.
3. Remove the pan from the air fryer and use a fork or metal spatula to crumble the sausage more. Season the mushrooms with the salt and add them to the pie pan. Stir to combine the mushrooms and sausage, then return the pan to the air fryer and cook for 4 minutes, or until the mushrooms are soft and the sausage is cooked through.

4. Remove the pan from the air fryer. Add the marinara sauce and stir well. Set aside.
5. Make the biscuits: Place the egg whites in a large mixing bowl or the bowl of a stand mixer. Using a hand mixer or stand mixer, whip the egg whites until stiff peaks form.
6. In a medium-sized bowl, whisk together the almond flour, baking powder, and salt, then cut in the butter. Gently fold the flour mixture into the egg whites with a rubber spatula.
7. Using a large spoon or ice cream scoop, spoon one-quarter of the dough on top of the sausage mixture, making sure the butter stays in separate clumps. Repeat with the remaining dough, spacing the biscuits about 1-inch apart.
8. Place the pan in the air fryer and cook for 5 minutes, then lower the heat to 325°F (163ºC) and cook for another 15 to 20 minutes, until the biscuits are golden brown. Serve garnished with fresh basil leaves.
9. Store leftovers in an airtight container in the refrigerator for up to 3 days. Reheat in a preheated 350°F (180ºC) air fryer for 5 minutes, or until warmed through.

Per Serving

calories: 588 | fat: 48g | protein: 28g | carbs: 9g | net carbs: 6g | fiber: 3g

Walliser Schnitzel

Prep time: 10 minutes | Cook time: 15 minutes | Serves 2

⅓ tablespoon cider vinegar
⅓ teaspoon ground black pepper
1 teaspoon garlic salt
½ teaspoon mustard

½ heaping tablespoon fresh parsley
½ cup pork rinds
2 eggs, beaten
½ teaspoon fennel seed
2 pork schnitzel, halved

1. Blitz the vinegar, black pepper, garlic salt, mustard, fennel seeds, fresh parsley and pork rinds in your food processor until uniform and smooth.
2. Dump the blended mixture into a shallow bowl. Add the beaten egg to another shallow bowl.
3. Coat the pork schnitzel with the beaten egg, then, dredge them in the herb mixture.
4. Cook in the preheated Air Fryer at 355ºF for about 14 minutes. Bon appétit!

Per Serving

calories: 495 | fat: 34g | protein: 42g | carbs: 2g | net carbs: 1.6g | fiber: 0.4g

Skirt Steak Carne Asada, page 39

Steak with Mushroom Onion Gravy, page 38

Reuben Beef Fritters with Sauerkraut, page 36

Bacon-Wrapped Hot Dogs with Mayo Sauce, page 40

Garlicky Beef Flank Steak with Sour Cream

Prep time: 13 minutes | Cook time: 7 minutes | Serves 2

⅓ cup sour cream
½ cup green onion, chopped
1 tablespoon mayonnaise
3 cloves garlic, smashed
1 pound (454 g) beef

flank steak, trimmed and cubed
2 tablespoons fresh sage, minced
½ teaspoon salt
⅓ teaspoon black pepper, or to taste

1. Season your meat with salt and pepper, arrange beef cubes on the bottom of a baking dish that fits in your air fryer.
2. Stir in green onions and garlic, air-fry for about 7 minutes at 385ºF (196ºC).
3. Once your beef starts to tender, add the cream, mayonnaise, and sage, air-fry an additional 8 minutes. Bon appétit!

Per Serving

calories: 428 | fat: 20g | protein: 50g | carbs: 7g | net carbs: 6g | fiber: 1g

Greek Pork with Tzatziki Sauce

Prep time:55 minutes | Cook time: 50 minutes | Serves 4

Greek Pork:
2 pounds (907 g) pork sirloin roast
Salt and black pepper, to taste
1 teaspoon smoked paprika
½ teaspoon mustard seeds
½ teaspoon celery seeds
1 teaspoon fennel seeds
1 teaspoon Ancho chili powder
1 teaspoon turmeric powder
½ teaspoon ground ginger

2 tablespoons olive oil
2 cloves garlic, finely chopped
Tzatziki:
½ cucumber, finely chopped and squeezed
1 cup full-fat Greek yogurt
1 garlic clove, minced
1 tablespoon extra virgin olive oil
1 teaspoon balsamic vinegar
1 teaspoon minced fresh dill
A pinch of salt

1. Toss all ingredients for Greek pork in a large mixing bowl. Toss until the meat is well coated.
2. Cook in the preheated Air Fryer at 360ºF (182ºC) for 30 minutes, turn over and cook for another 20

minutes.
3. Meanwhile, prepare the tzatziki by mixing all the tzatziki ingredients. Place in your refrigerator until ready to use.
4. Serve the pork sirloin roast with the chilled tzatziki on the side. Enjoy!

Per Serving

calories: 560 | fat: 30g | protein: 64g | carbs: 5g | net carbs: 3g | fiber: 2g

Steak with Bell Pepper

Prep time: 15 minutes | Cook time: 20 to 23 minutes | Serves 6

¼ cup avocado oil
¼ cup freshly squeezed lime juice
2 teaspoons minced garlic
1 tablespoon chili powder
½ teaspoon ground cumin
Sea salt, Freshly ground black pepper, to taste

1 pound (454 g) top sirloin steak
1 red bell pepper, cored, seeded, and cut into ½-inch slices
1 green bell pepper, cored, seeded, and cut into ½-inch slices
1 large onion, sliced

1. In a small bowl or blender, combine the avocado oil, lime juice, garlic, chili powder, cumin, and salt and pepper to taste.
2. Place the sliced steak in a zip-top bag or shallow dish. Place the bell peppers and onion in a separate zip-top bag or dish. Pour half the marinade over the steak and the other half over the vegetables. Seal both bags and let the steak and vegetables marinate in the refrigerator for at least 1 hour or up to 4 hours.
3. Line the air fryer basket with an air fryer liner or aluminum foil. Remove the vegetables from their bag or dish and shake off any excess marinade. Set the air fryer to 400°F (205ºC). Place the vegetables in the air fryer basket and cook for 13 minutes.
4. Remove the steak from its bag or dish and shake off any excess marinade. Place the steak on top of the vegetables in the air fryer, and cook for 7 to 10 minutes or until an instant-read thermometer reads 120°F (49ºC) for medium-rare (or cook to your desired doneness).
5. Serve with desired fixings, such as keto tortillas, lettuce, sour cream, avocado slices, shredded Cheddar cheese, and cilantro.

Per Serving

calories: 229 | fat: 14g | protein: 17g | carbs: 7g | net carbs: 5g | fiber: 2g

Baked Sauerkraut with Sausage

Prep time: 35 minutes | Cook time: 16 minutes | Serves 4

4 pork sausages, smoked
2 tablespoons olive oil
2 garlic cloves, minced
1 pound (454 g) sauerkraut
1 teaspoon cayenne pepper
½ teaspoon black peppercorns
2 bay leaves

1. Start by preheating your Air Fryer to 360ºF (182ºC).
2. Prick holes into the sausages using a fork and transfer them to the cooking basket. Cook approximately 14 minutes, shaking the basket a couple of times. Set aside.
3. Now, heat the olive oil in a baking pan at 380ºF (193ºC). Add the garlic and cook for 1 minute. Immediately stir in the sauerkraut, cayenne pepper, peppercorns, and bay leaves.
4. Let it cook for 15 minutes, stirring every 5 minutes. Serve in individual bowls with warm sausages on the side!

Per Serving

calories: 453 | fat: 42g | protein: 17g | carbs: 6g | net carbs: 3g | fiber: 3g

Pork Kebab with Yogurt Sauce

Prep time: 25 minutes | Cook time: 12 minutes | Serves 4

2 teaspoons olive oil
½ pound (227g) ground pork
½ pound (227g) ground beef
1 egg, whisked
Sea salt and ground black pepper, to taste
1 teaspoon paprika
2 garlic cloves, minced
1 teaspoon dried marjoram
1 teaspoon mustard
seeds
½ teaspoon celery seeds
Yogurt Sauce:
2 tablespoons olive oil
2 tablespoons fresh lemon juice
Sea salt, to taste
¼ teaspoon red pepper flakes, crushed
½ cup full-fat yogurt
1 teaspoon dried dill weed

1. Spritz the sides and bottom of the cooking basket with 2 teaspoons of olive oil.
2. In a mixing dish, thoroughly combine the ground pork, beef, egg, salt, black pepper, paprika, garlic, marjoram, mustard seeds, and celery seeds.
3. Form the mixture into kebabs and transfer them to the greased cooking basket. Cook at 365ºF (185ºC)

for 11 to 12 minutes, turning them over once or twice.
4. In the meantime, mix all the sauce ingredients and place in the refrigerator until ready to serve. Serve the pork kebabs with the yogurt sauce on the side. Enjoy!

Per Serving

calories: 407 | fat: 29g | protein: 33g | carbs: 4g | net carbs: 3g | fiber: 1g

Zucchini Noodle with Beef Meatball

Prep time: 15 minutes | Cook time: 11 to 13 minutes | Serves 6

1 pound (454 g) ground beef
1½ teaspoons sea salt, plus more for seasoning
1 large egg, beaten
1 teaspoon gelatin
¾ cup Parmesan cheese
2 teaspoons minced garlic
1 teaspoon Italian
seasoning
Freshly ground black pepper, to taste
Avocado oil spray
Keto-friendly marinara sauce, for serving
6 ounces (170 g) zucchini noodles, made using a spiralizer or store-bought

1. Place the ground beef in a large bowl, and season with the salt.
2. Place the egg in a separate bowl and sprinkle with the gelatin. Allow it to sit for 5 minutes.
3. Stir the gelatin mixture, then pour it over the ground beef. Add the Parmesan, garlic, and Italian seasoning. Season with salt and pepper.
4. Form the mixture into 1½-inch meatballs and place them on a plate, cover with plastic wrap and refrigerate for at least 1 hour or overnight.
5. Spray the meatballs with oil. Set the air fryer to 400°F (205ºC) and arrange the meatballs in a single layer in the air fryer basket. Cook for 4 minutes. Flip the meatballs and spray them with more oil. Cook for 4 minutes or more, until an instant-read thermometer reads 160°F (71ºC). Transfer the meatballs to a plate and allow them to rest.
6. While the meatballs are resting, heat the marinara in a saucepan on the stove over medium heat.
7. Place the zucchini noodles in the air fryer, and cook at 400°F (205ºC) for 3 to 5 minutes.
8. To serve, place the zucchini noodles in serving bowls. Top with meatballs and warm marinara.

Per Serving

calories: 312 | fat: 25g | protein: 20g | carbs: 2g | net carbs: 1g | fiber: 1g

Rosemary Beef Roast

Prep time: 5 minutes | Cook time: 30 to 35 minutes | Serves 8

1 (2-pound / 907-g) top round beef roast, tied with kitchen string Sea salt, Freshly ground black pepper, to taste	2 teaspoons minced garlic 2 tablespoons finely chopped fresh rosemary ¼ cup avocado oil

1. Season the roast generously with salt and pepper.
2. In a small bowl, whisk together the garlic, rosemary, and avocado oil. Rub this all over the roast. Cover loosely with aluminum foil or plastic wrap and refrigerate for at least 12 hours or up to 2 days.
3. Remove the roast from the refrigerator and allow to sit at room temperature for about 1 hour.
4. Set the air fryer to 325°F (163ºC). Place the roast in the air fryer basket and cook for 15 minutes. Flip the roast and cook for 15 to 20 minutes or more, until the meat is browned and an instant-read thermometer reads 120°F (49ºC) at the thickest part (for medium-rare).
5. Transfer the meat to a cutting board, and let it rest for 15 minutes before thinly slicing and serving.

Per Serving
calories: 213 | fat: 10g | protein: 25g | carbs: 2g | net carbs: 1g | fiber: 1g

Simple Air Fried New York Strip

Prep time: 5 minutes | Cook time: 10 minutes | Serves 6

½ cup olive oil 2 tablespoons minced garlic Sea salt, freshly ground black pepper, to taste	1½ pounds (680g) New York strip or top sirloin steak Unsalted butter, for serving (optional)

1. In a bowl or blender, combine the olive oil, garlic, and salt and pepper to taste.
2. Place the steak in a shallow bowl or zip-top bag. Pour the marinade over the meat, seal, and marinate in the refrigerator for at least 1 hour and up to 24 hours.
3. Place a grill pan or basket in the air fryer, set it to 400°F (205ºC), and let it preheat for 5 minutes.
4. Place the steak on the grill pan in a single layer, working in batches if necessary, and cook for 5 minutes. Flip the steak and cook for another 5 minutes, until an instant-read thermometer reads 120°F (49ºC) for medium-rare (or cook to your desired doneness).
5. Transfer the steak to a plate, and let rest for 10 minutes before serving. If desired, top the steaks with a pat of butter while they rest.

Per Serving
calories: 386 | fat: 32g | protein: 25g | carbs: 1g | net carbs: 1g | fiber: 0g

Pork Cheese Casserole

Prep time: 50 minutes | Cook time: 30 minutes | Serves 4

2 chili peppers 1 red bell pepper 2 tablespoons olive oil 1 large-sized shallot, chopped 1 pound (454 g) ground pork 2 garlic cloves, minced 2 ripe tomatoes, puréed 1 teaspoon dried marjoram ½ teaspoon mustard seeds ½ teaspoon celery seeds	1 teaspoon Mexican oregano 1 tablespoon fish sauce 2 tablespoons fresh coriander, chopped Salt and ground black pepper, to taste 2 cups water 1 tablespoon chicken bouillon granules 2 tablespoons sherry wine 1 cup Mexican cheese blend

1. Roast the peppers in the preheated Air Fryer at 395ºF (202ºC) for 10 minutes, flipping them halfway through cook time.
2. Let them steam for 10 minutes, then, peel the skin and discard the stems and seeds. Slice the peppers into halves.
3. Heat the olive oil in a baking pan at 380ºF (193ºC) for 2 minutes, add the shallots and cook for 4 minutes. Add the ground pork and garlic, cook for a further 4 to 5 minutes.
4. After that, stir in the tomatoes, marjoram, mustard seeds, celery seeds, oregano, fish sauce, coriander, salt, and pepper. Add a layer of sliced peppers to the baking pan.
5. Mix the water with the chicken bouillon granules and sherry wine. Add the mixture to the baking pan.
6. Cook in the preheated Air Fryer at 395ºF (202ºC) for 10 minutes. Top with cheese and bake an additional 5 minutes until the cheese has melted. Serve immediately.

Per Serving
calories: 505 | fat: 39g | protein: 28g | carbs: 10g | net carbs: 8g | fiber: 2g

Steak with Horseradish Cream

Prep time: 5 minutes | Cook time: 10 minutes | Serves 8

2 pounds (907 g) rib eye steaks
Sea salt, Freshly ground black pepper, to taste
Unsalted butter, for serving
1 cup sour cream
⅓ cup heavy (whipping) cream
4 tablespoons prepared horseradish
1 teaspoon Dijon mustard
1 teaspoon apple cider vinegar
¼ teaspoon Swerve, to taste

1. Pat the steaks dry. Season with salt and pepper and let sit at room temperature for about 45 minutes.
2. Place the grill pan in the air fryer and set the air fryer to 400°F (205°C). Let it preheat for 5 minutes.
3. Working in batches, place the steaks in a single layer on the grill pan and cook for 5 minutes. Flip the steaks and cook for 5 minutes or more, until an instant-read thermometer reads 120°F (49°C) (or to your desired doneness).
4. Transfer the steaks to a plate and top each with a pat of butter. Tent with foil and let it rest for 10 minutes.
5. Combine the sour cream, heavy cream, horseradish, Dijon mustard, vinegar, and Swerve in a bowl. Stir until smooth.
6. Serve the steaks with the horseradish cream.

Per Serving
calories: 322 | fat: 22g | protein: 23g | carbs: 6g | net carbs: 5g | fiber: 1g

Lime Sirloin Steak with Red Wine

Prep time: 20 minutes | Cook time: 14 minutes | Serves 4

1½ pounds (680g) sirloin steak
¼ cup red wine
¼ cup fresh lime juice
1 teaspoon garlic powder
1 teaspoon shallot powder
1 teaspoon celery seeds
1 teaspoon mustard
seeds
Coarse sea salt and ground black pepper, to taste
1 teaspoon red pepper flakes
2 eggs, lightly whisked
1 cup Parmesan cheese
1 teaspoon paprika

1. Place the steak, red wine, lime juice, garlic powder, shallot powder, celery seeds, mustard seeds, salt, black pepper, and red pepper in a large ceramic bowl, let it marinate for 3 hours.
2. Tenderize the cube steak by pounding with a mallet,

cut into 1-inch strips.
3. In a shallow bowl, whisk the eggs. In another bowl, mix the Parmesan cheese and paprika.
4. Dip the beef pieces into the whisked eggs and coat on all sides. Now, dredge the beef pieces in the Parmesan mixture.
5. Cook at 400ºF (205ºC) for 14 minutes, flipping halfway through the cooking time.
6. Meanwhile, make the sauce by heating the reserved marinade in a saucepan over medium heat, let it simmer until thoroughly warmed. Serve the steak fingers with the sauce on the side. Enjoy!

Per Serving
calories: 475 | fat: 26g | protein: 45g | carbs: 8g | net carbs: 7g | fiber: 1g

Lime Marinated Lamb Chop

Prep time: 5 minutes | Cook time: 5 minutes | Serves 2

4 (1-inch-thick) lamb chops
Sprigs of fresh mint, for garnish (optional)
Lime slices, for serving (optional)
Marinade:
2 teaspoons grated lime zest
½ cup lime juice
¼ cup avocado oil
¼ cup chopped fresh mint leaves
4 cloves garlic, roughly chopped
2 teaspoons fine sea salt
½ teaspoon ground black pepper

1. Make the marinade: Place all the ingredients for the marinade in a food processor or blender and purée until mostly smooth with a few small chunks. Transfer half of the marinade to a shallow dish and set the other half aside for serving. Add the lamb to the shallow dish, cover, and place in the refrigerator to marinate for at least 2 hours or overnight.
2. Spray the air fryer basket with avocado oil. Preheat the air fryer to 390°F (199ºC).
3. Remove the chops from the marinade and place them in the air fryer basket. Cook for 5 minutes, or until the internal temperature reaches 145°F for medium doneness.
4. Allow the chops to rest for 10 minutes before serving with the rest of the marinade as a sauce. Garnish with fresh mint leaves and serve with lime slices, if desired. Best served fresh.

Per Serving
calories: 692 | fat: 53g | protein: 48g | carbs: 2g | net carbs: 1g | fiber: 1g

Double-Cheese Sausage Balls

Prep time: 10 minutes | Cook time: 10 minutes | Serves 12

1¾ cups finely ground blanched almond flour
1 tablespoon baking powder
½ teaspoon sea salt
¼ teaspoon freshly ground black pepper
¼ teaspoon cayenne pepper
1 pound (454 g) fresh pork sausage, casings removed, crumbled
8 ounces (227 g) Cheddar cheese, shredded
8 ounces (227 g) cream cheese, at room temperature, cut into chunks

1. In a large mixing bowl, combine the almond flour, baking powder, salt, black pepper, and cayenne pepper.
2. Add the sausage, Cheddar cheese, and cream cheese. Stir to combine, and then, using clean hands, mix until all of the ingredients are well incorporated.
3. Form the mixture into 1½-inch balls.
4. Set the air fryer to 350°F (180°C). Arrange the sausage balls in a single layer in the air fryer basket, working in batches if necessary. Cook for 5 minutes. Flip the sausage balls and cook for 5 minutes or more.

Per Serving
calories: 386 | fat: 27g | protein: 16g | carbs: 5g | net carbs: 3g | fiber: 2g

Flank Steak with Baby Spinach

Prep time: 10 minutes | Cook time: 14 minutes | Serves 6

1 pound (454 g) flank steak
1 tablespoon avocado oil
½ teaspoon sea salt
½ teaspoon garlic powder
¼ teaspoon freshly ground black pepper
2 ounces (57 g) goat cheese, crumbled
1 cup baby spinach, chopped

1. Place the steak in a large zip-top bag or between two pieces of plastic wrap. Using a meat mallet or heavy-bottomed skillet, pound the steak to an even ¼-inch thickness.
2. Brush both sides of the steak with the avocado oil.
3. Mix the salt, garlic powder, and pepper in a small dish. Sprinkle this mixture over both sides of the steak.
4. Sprinkle the goat cheese over top, and top that with the spinach.
5. Starting at one of the long sides, roll the steak up tightly. Tie the rolled steak with kitchen string at 3-inch intervals.
6. Set the air fryer to 400°F (205°C). Place the steak roll-up in the air fryer basket. Cook for 7 minutes. Flip the steak and cook for an additional 7 minutes, until an instant-read thermometer reads 120°F (49°C) for medium-rare (adjust the cooking time for your desired doneness).

Per Serving
calories: 165 | fat: 9g | protein: 18g | carbs: 1g | net carbs: 0g | fiber: 1g

Pork Butt with Coriander-Garlic Sauce

Prep time: 15 minutes | Cook time: 30 minutes | Serves 4

1 pound (454 g) pork butt, cut into pieces 2-inches long
1 teaspoon golden flaxseed meal
1 egg white, well whisked
Salt and ground black pepper, to taste
1 tablespoon olive oil
1 tablespoon coconut aminos
1 teaspoon lemon juice, preferably freshly squeezed
For the Coriander-Garlic Sauce:
3 garlic cloves, peeled
⅓ cup fresh parsley leaves
⅓ cup fresh coriander leaves
½ tablespoon salt
1 teaspoon lemon juice
⅓ cup extra-virgin olive oil

1. Combine the pork strips with the flaxseed meal, egg white, salt, pepper, olive oil, coconut aminos, and lemon juice. Cover and refrigerate for 30 to 45 minutes.
2. After that, spritz the pork strips with a nonstick cooking spray.
3. Set your Air Fryer to cook at 380°F. Press the power button and air-fry for 15 minutes, pause the machine, shake the basket and cook for 15 more minutes.
4. Meanwhile, puree the garlic in a food processor until finely minced. Now, puree the parsley, coriander, salt, and lemon juice. With the machine running, carefully pour in the olive oil.
5. Serve the pork with well-chilled sauce with and enjoy!

Per Serving
calories: 422 | fat: 31g | protein: 31g | carbs: 3g | net carbs: 2g | fiber: 1g

Onion Pork Kebabs

Prep time: 22 minutes | Cook time: 18 minutes | Serves 3

2 tablespoons tomato purée
½ fresh serrano, minced
⅓ teaspoon paprika
1 pound (454 g) pork, ground
½ cup green onions, finely chopped
3 cloves garlic, peeled and finely minced
1 teaspoon ground black pepper, or more to taste
1 teaspoon salt, or more to taste

1. Thoroughly combine all ingredients in a mixing dish. Then, form your mixture into sausage shapes.
2. Cook for 18 minutes at 355ºF (181ºC). Mound salad on a serving platter, top with air-fried kebabs and serve warm. Bon appétit!

Per Serving

calories: 413 | fat: 32g | protein: 26g | carbs: 3g | net carbs: 2g | fiber: 1g

Pork Chops with Vermouth

Prep time: 22 minutes | Cook time: 18 minutes | Serves 6

2 tablespoons vermouth
6 center-cut loin pork chops
½ tablespoon fresh basil, minced
⅓ teaspoon freshly ground black pepper, or more to taste
2 tablespoons whole grain mustard
1 teaspoon fine kosher salt

1. Toss pork chops with other ingredients until they are well coated on both sides.
2. Air-fry your chops for 18 minutes at 405ºF (207ºC), turning once or twice.
3. Mound your favorite salad on a serving plate, top with pork chops and enjoy.

Per Serving

calories: 393 | fat: 15g | protein: 56g | carbs: 3g | net carbs: 2g | fiber: 1g

Red Wine Rib

Prep time: 20 minutes | Cook time: 10 minutes | Serves 4

1½ pounds (680g) short ribs
1 cup red wine
1 lemon, juiced
1 teaspoon fresh ginger, grated
1 teaspoon salt
1 teaspoon black pepper
1 teaspoon paprika
1 teaspoon chipotle chili powder
1 cup keto tomato paste
1 teaspoon garlic powder
1 teaspoon cumin

1. In a ceramic bowl, place the beef ribs, wine, lemon juice, ginger, salt, black pepper, paprika, and chipotle chili powder. Cover and let it marinate for 3 hours in the refrigerator.
2. Discard the marinade and add the short ribs to the Air Fryer basket. Cook in the preheated Air fry at 380ºF (193ºC) for 10 minutes, turning them over halfway through the cooking time.
3. In the meantime, heat the saucepan over medium heat, add the reserved marinade and stir in the tomato paste, garlic powder, and cumin. Cook until the sauce has thickened slightly.
4. Pour the sauce over the warm ribs and serve immediately. Bon appétit!

Per Serving

calories: 397 | fat: 15g | protein: 35g | carbs: 5g | net carbs: 4g | fiber: 1g

Pork and Beef Casserole

Prep time: 20 minutes | Cook time: 10 minutes | Serves 4

1 pound (454 g) lean ground pork
½ pound (227g) ground beef
¼ cup tomato purée
Sea salt and ground black pepper, to taste
1 teaspoon smoked paprika
½ teaspoon dried oregano
1 teaspoon dried basil
1 teaspoon dried rosemary
2 eggs
1 cup Cottage cheese, crumbled, at room temperature
½ cup Cotija cheese, shredded

1. Lightly grease a casserole dish with a nonstick cooking oil. Add the ground meat to the bottom of your casserole dish.
2. Add the tomato purée. Sprinkle with salt, black pepper, paprika, oregano, basil, and rosemary.
3. In a mixing bowl, whisk the egg with cheese. Place on top of the ground meat mixture. Place a piece of foil on top.
4. Bake in the preheated Air Fryer at 350ºF (180ºC) for 10 minutes, remove the foil and cook for an additional 6 minutes. Bon appétit!

Per Serving

calories: 449 | fat: 23g | protein: 54g | carbs: 5g | net carbs: 4g | fiber: 1g

Herbed Beef Steaks

Prep time: 20 minutes | Cook time: 20 minutes | Serves 4

2 tablespoons coconut aminos
3 heaping tablespoons fresh chives
2 tablespoons olive oil
3 tablespoons dry white wine
4 small-sized beef steaks
2 teaspoons smoked
cayenne pepper
½ teaspoon dried basil
½ teaspoon dried rosemary
1 teaspoon freshly ground black pepper
1 teaspoon sea salt, or more to taste

1. Firstly, coat the steaks with the cayenne pepper, black pepper, salt, basil, and rosemary.
2. Drizzle the steaks with olive oil, white wine, and coconut aminos.
3. Finally, roast in an Air Fryer basket for 20 minutes at 335ºF (168ºC). Serve garnished with fresh chives. Bon appétit!

Per Serving
calories: 445 | fat: 23g | protein: 51g | carbs: 11g | net carbs: 10g | fiber: 1g

Skirt Steak with Rice Vinegar

Prep time: 20 minutes | Cook time: 12 minutes | Serves 5

2 pounds (907 g) skirt steak
2 tablespoons keto tomato paste
1 tablespoon olive oil
1 tablespoon coconut aminos
¼ cup rice vinegar
1 tablespoon fish sauce
Sea salt, to taste
½ teaspoon dried dill
½ teaspoon dried rosemary
¼ teaspoon black pepper, freshly cracked

1. Place all ingredients in a large ceramic dish, let it marinate for 3 hours in your refrigerator.
2. Coat the sides and bottom of the Air Fryer with cooking spray.
3. Add your steak to the cooking basket, reserve the marinade. Cook the skirt steak in the preheated Air Fryer at 400ºF (205ºC) for 12 minutes, turning over a couple of times, basting with the reserved marinade.
4. Bon appétit!

Per Serving
calories: 401 | fat: 21g | protein: 51g | carbs: 2g | net carbs: 1g | fiber: 1g

Italian Sausage Link

Prep time: 10 minutes | Cook time: 24 minutes | Serves 4

1 bell pepper (any color), sliced
1 medium onion, sliced
1 tablespoon avocado oil
1 teaspoon Italian
seasoning
Sea salt, Freshly ground black pepper, to taste
1 pound (454 g) Italian sausage links

1. Place the bell pepper and onion in a medium bowl, and toss with the avocado oil, Italian seasoning, and salt and pepper to taste.
2. Set the air fryer to 400°F (205ºC). Put the vegetables in the air fryer basket and cook for 12 minutes.
3. Push the vegetables to the side of the basket and arrange the sausage links in the bottom of the basket in a single layer. Spoon the vegetables over the sausages. Cook for 12 minutes, tossing halfway through, until an instant-read thermometer inserted into the sausage reads 160°F (71ºC).

Per Serving
calories: 339 | fat: 27g | protein: 17g | carbs: 5g | net carbs: 4g | fiber: 1g

Roast Beef with Jalapeño Peppers

Prep time: 20 minutes | Cook time: 45 minutes | Serves 8

2 pounds (907 g) roast beef, at room temperature
2 tablespoons extra-virgin olive oil
1 teaspoon sea salt flakes
1 teaspoon black pepper,
preferably freshly ground
1 teaspoon smoked paprika
A few dashes of liquid smoke
2 jalapeño peppers, thinly sliced

1. Start by preheating the Air Fryer to 330ºF (166ºC).
2. Then, pat the roast dry using kitchen towels. Rub with extra-virgin olive oil and all seasonings along with liquid smoke.
3. Roast for 30 minutes in the preheated Air Fryer, then, pause the machine and turn the roast over, roast for additional 15 minutes.
4. Check for doneness using a meat thermometer and serve sprinkled with sliced jalapeños. Bon appétit!

Per Serving
calories: 167 | fat: 5g | protein: 26g | carbs: 2g | net carbs: 1g | fiber: 1g

Herbed Pork Tenderloin

Prep time: 20 minutes | Cook time: 17 minutes | Serves 4

1 pound (454 g) pork tenderloin
4-5 garlic cloves, peeled and halved
1 teaspoon kosher salt
⅓ teaspoon ground black pepper
1 teaspoon dried basil
½ teaspoon dried oregano
½ teaspoon dried rosemary
½ teaspoon dried marjoram
2 tablespoons cooking wine

1. Rub the pork with garlic halves, add the seasoning and drizzle with the cooking wine. Then, cut slits completely through pork tenderloin. Tuck the remaining garlic into the slits.
2. Wrap the pork tenderloin with foil, let it marinate overnight.
3. Roast at 360ºF (182ºC) for 15 to 17 minutes. Serve warm.

Per Serving

calories: 168 | fat: 4g | protein: 30g | carbs: 2g | net carbs: 1g | fiber: 1g

Italian Pork Top Loin

Prep time: 50 minutes | Cook time: 16 minutes | Serves 3

1 teaspoon Celtic sea salt
½ teaspoon black pepper, freshly cracked
¼ cup red wine
2 tablespoons mustard
2 garlic cloves, minced
1 pound (454 g) pork top loin
1 tablespoon Italian herb seasoning blend

1. In a ceramic bowl, mix the salt, black pepper, red wine, mustard, and garlic. Add the pork top loin and let it marinate for at least 30 minutes.
2. Spritz the sides and bottom of the cooking basket with a nonstick cooking spray.
3. Place the pork top loin in the basket, sprinkle with the Italian herb seasoning blend.
4. Cook the pork tenderloin at 370ºF (188ºC) for 10 minutes. Flip halfway through, spraying with cooking oil and cook for 5 to 6 minutes. Serve immediately.

Per Serving

calories: 300 | fat: 9g | protein: 34g | carbs: 2g | net carbs: 1g | fiber: 1g

Loin Steak with Mayo

Prep time: 20 minutes | Cook time: 15 minutes | Serves 4

1 cup mayonnaise
1 tablespoon fresh rosemary, finely chopped
2 tablespoons Worcestershire sauce
Sea salt, to taste
½ teaspoon ground black
pepper
1 teaspoon smoked paprika
1 teaspoon garlic, minced
1½ pounds (680g) short loin steak

1. Combine the mayonnaise, rosemary, Worcestershire sauce, salt, pepper, paprika, and garlic, mix to combine well.
2. Now, brush the mayonnaise mixture over both sides of the steak. Lower the steak onto the grill pan.
3. Grill in the preheated Air Fryer at 390ºF (199ºC) for 8 minutes. Turn the steaks over and grill for an additional 7 minutes.
4. Check for doneness with a meat thermometer. Serve warm and enjoy!

Per Serving

calories: 620 | fat: 50g | protein: 40g | carbs: 3g | net carbs: 2g | fiber: 1g

Lemony Beef Steak

Prep time: 25 minutes | Cook time: 18 minutes | Serves 2

1 pound (454 g) beef steaks
4 tablespoons white wine
2 teaspoons crushed coriander seeds
½ teaspoon fennel seeds
⅓ cup beef broth
2 tablespoons lemon zest, grated
2 tablespoons olive oil
½ lemon, cut into wedges
Salt flakes and freshly ground black pepper, to taste

1. Heat the oil in a saucepan over a moderate flame. Then, cook the garlic for 1 minute, or until just fragrant.
2. Remove the pan from the heat, add the beef broth, wine, lemon zest, coriander seeds, fennel, salt flakes, and freshly ground black. Pour the mixture into a baking dish.
3. Add beef steaks to the baking dish, toss to coat well. Now, tuck the lemon wedges among the beef steaks.
4. Bake for 18 minutes at 335ºF (168ºC). Serve warm.

Per Serving

calories: 447 | fat: 27g | protein: 48g | carbs: 3g | net carbs: 2g | fiber: 1g

Monterey-Jack Cheeseburgers

Prep time: 5 minutes | Cook time: 11 minutes | Serves 4

1½ pounds (680 g) ground chuck
1 envelope onion soup mix
Kosher salt and freshly
ground black pepper, to taste
1 teaspoon paprika
4 slices Monterey-Jack cheese

1. In a mixing dish, thoroughly combine ground chuck, onion soup mix, salt, black pepper, and paprika.
2. Then, set your Air Fryer to cook at 385ºF. Shape the mixture into 4 patties. Air-fry them for 10 minutes.
3. Next step, place the slices of cheese on the top of the warm burgers. Air-fry for one minute more.
4. Serve with mustard and pickled salad of choice. Bon appétit!

Per Serving

calories: 271 | fat: 13g | protein: 15g | carbs: 22g | net carbs: 21g | fiber: 1g

Beef Parboiled Sausage

Prep time: 35 minutes | Cook time: 30 minutes | Serves 4

2 teaspoons olive oil
2 bell peppers, sliced
1 green bell pepper, sliced
1 serrano pepper, sliced
1 shallot, sliced
Sea salt and pepper, to taste
½ teaspoon dried thyme
1 teaspoon dried rosemary
½ teaspoon mustard seeds
1 teaspoon fennel seeds
2 pounds (907 g) thin beef parboiled sausage

1. Brush the sides and bottom of the cooking basket with 1 teaspoon of olive oil. Add the peppers and shallot to the cooking basket.
2. Toss them with the spices and cook at 390ºF (199ºC) for 15 minutes, shaking the basket occasionally. Reserve.
3. Turn the temperature to 380ºF (193ºC)
4. Then, add the remaining 1 teaspoon of oil. Once hot, add the sausage and cook in the preheated Air Frye for 15 minutes, flipping them halfway through the cooking time.
5. Serve with reserved pepper mixture. Bon appétit!

Per Serving

calories: 563 | fat: 41g | protein: 35g | carbs: 11g | net carbs: 10g | fiber: 1g

Herbed Porterhouse Steak

Prep time: 20 minutes | Cook time: 14 minutes | Serves 2

1 pound (454 g) porterhouse steak, cut meat from bones in 2 pieces
½ teaspoon ground black pepper
1 teaspoon cayenne pepper
½ teaspoon salt
1 teaspoon garlic powder
½ teaspoon dried thyme
½ teaspoon dried marjoram
1 teaspoon Dijon mustard
1 tablespoon butter, melted

1. Sprinkle the porterhouse steak with all the seasonings.
2. Spread the mustard and butter evenly over the meat.
3. Cook in the preheated Air Fryer at 390ºF (199ºC) for 12 to 14 minutes.
4. Taste for doneness with a meat thermometer and serve immediately.

Per Serving

calories: 402 | fat: 14g | protein: 67g | carbs: 2g | net carbs: 1g | fiber: 1g

Roasted Pork Belly with Bell Peppers

Prep time: 20 minutes | Cook time: 30 minutes | Serves 6

1½ pounds (680g) pork belly
2 bell peppers, sliced
2 cloves garlic, finely minced
4 green onions, quartered, white and green parts
¼ cup cooking wine
Kosher salt and ground black pepper, to taste
1 teaspoon cayenne pepper
1 tablespoon coriander
1 teaspoon celery seeds

1. Blanch the pork belly in boiling water for approximately 15 minutes. Then, cut it into chunks.
2. Arrange the pork chunks, bell peppers, garlic, and green onions in the Air Fryer basket. Drizzle everything with cooking wine of your choice.
3. Sprinkle with salt, black pepper, cayenne pepper, fresh coriander, and celery seeds. Toss to coat well.
4. Roast in the preheated Air Fryer at 330º(166ºC) F for 30 minutes.
5. Serve on individual serving plates. Bon appétit!

Per Serving

calories: 589 | fat: 60g | protein: 12g | carbs: 3g | net carbs: 2g | fiber: 1g

Miso Flank Steak

Prep time: 10 minutes | Cook time: 12 minutes | Serves 4

1¼ pounds (567 g) flank steak
1½ tablespoons sake
1 tablespoon brown miso paste
2 garlic cloves, pressed
1 tablespoon olive oil

1. Place all the ingredients in a sealable food bag, shake until completely coated and place in your refrigerator for at least 1 hour.
2. Then, spritz the steak with a non-stick cooking spray, make sure to coat on all sides. Place the steak in the Air Fryer baking pan.
3. Set your Air Fryer to cook at 400ºF. Roast for 12 minutes, flipping twice. Serve immediately.

Per Serving

calories: 367 | fat: 15g | protein: 49g | carbs: 6g | net carbs: 5g | fiber: 1g

Beef Burger

Prep time: 20 minutes | Cook time: 12 minutes | Serves 4

1¼ pounds (567g) lean ground beef
1 tablespoon coconut aminos
1 teaspoon Dijon mustard
A few dashes of liquid smoke
1 teaspoon shallot powder
1 clove garlic, minced
½ teaspoon cumin powder
¼ cup scallions, minced
⅓ teaspoon sea salt flakes
⅓ teaspoon freshly cracked mixed peppercorns
1 teaspoon celery seeds
1 teaspoon parsley flakes

1. Mix all of the above ingredients in a bowl, knead until everything is well incorporated.
2. Shape the mixture into four patties. Next, make a shallow dip in the center of each patty to prevent them puffing up during air-frying.
3. Spritz the patties on all sides using a non-stick cooking spray. Cook for approximately 12 minutes at 360ºF (182ºC).
4. Check for doneness – an instant read thermometer should read 160ºF (71ºC). Bon appétit!

Per Serving

calories: 425 | fat: 25g | protein: 38g | carbs: 10g | net carbs: 8g | fiber: 2g

Pork Meatballs

Prep time: 15 minutes | Cook time: 7 minutes | Serves 3

1 pound (454 g) ground pork
1 tablespoon coconut aminos
1 teaspoon garlic, minced
2 tablespoons spring onions, finely chopped
½ cup pork rinds
½ cup Parmesan cheese, preferably freshly grated

1. Combine the ground pork, coconut aminos, garlic, and spring onions in a mixing dish. Mix until everything is well incorporated.
2. Form the mixture into small meatballs.
3. In a shallow bowl, mix the pork rinds and grated Parmesan cheese. Roll the meatballs over the Parmesan mixture.
4. Cook at 380ºF (193ºC) for 3 minutes, shake the basket and cook for an additional 4 minutes or until meatballs are browned on all sides. Bon appétit!

Per Serving

calories: 539 | fat: 43g | protein: 32g | carbs: 3g | net carbs: 2g | fiber: 1g

Sausage and Pork Meatball

Prep time: 20 minutes | Cook time: 10 minutes | Serves 4

1 pound (454 g) pork sausage meat
1 shallot, finely chopped
2 garlic cloves, finely minced
½ teaspoon fine sea salt
¼ teaspoon ground black pepper, or more to taste
¾ teaspoon paprika
½ cup Parmesan cheese, preferably freshly grated
½ jar no-sugar-added marinara sauce

1. Mix all of the above ingredients, except the marinara sauce, in a large-sized dish, until everything is well incorporated.
2. Shape into meatballs. Air-fry them at 360ºF (182ºC) for 10 minutes, pause the Air Fryer, shake them up and cook for additional 6 minutes or until the balls are no longer pink in the middle.
3. Meanwhile, heat the marinara sauce over a medium flame. Serve the pork sausage meatballs with marinara sauce. Bon appétit!

Per Serving

calories: 409 | fat: 33g | protein: 17g | carbs: 7g | net carbs: 6g | fiber: 1g

Pork Tenderloin with Ricotta

Prep time: 25 minutes | Cook time: 22 minutes | Serves 4

2 tablespoons olive oil
2 pounds (907 g) pork tenderloin, cut into serving-size pieces
1 teaspoon coarse sea salt
½ teaspoon freshly
ground pepper
¼ teaspoon chili powder
1 teaspoon dried marjoram
1 tablespoon mustard
1 cup Ricotta cheese
1½ cups chicken broth

1. Start by preheating your Air Fryer to 350ºF (180ºC).
2. Heat the olive oil in a pan over medium-high heat. Once hot, cook the pork for 6 to 7 minutes, flipping it to ensure even cooking.
3. Arrange the pork in a lightly greased casserole dish. Season with salt, black pepper, chili powder, and marjoram.
4. In a mixing dish, thoroughly combine the mustard, cheese, and chicken broth. Pour the mixture over the pork chops in the casserole dish.
5. Bake for another 15 minutes or until bubbly and heated through. Bon appétit!

Per Serving
calories: 433 | fat: 20g | protein: 56g | carbs: 3g | net carbs: 2g | fiber: 1g

Easy Smoked Beef Burgers

Prep time: 10 minutes | Cook time: 12 minutes | Serves 4

1¼ pounds (567 g) lean ground beef
1 tablespoon soy sauce
1 teaspoon Dijon mustard
A few dashes of liquid smoke
1 teaspoon shallot powder
1 clove garlic, minced
½ teaspoon cumin
powder
¼ cup scallions, minced
⅓ teaspoon sea salt flakes
⅓ teaspoon freshly cracked mixed peppercorns
1 teaspoon celery seeds
1 teaspoon parsley flakes

1. Mix all of the above ingredients in a bowl, knead until everything is well incorporated.
2. Shape the mixture into four patties. Next, make a shallow dip in the center of each patty to prevent them puffing up during air-frying.
3. Spritz the patties on all sides using a non-stick cooking spray. Cook for approximately 12 minutes at 360ºF.

4. Check for doneness – an instant read thermometer should read 160ºF. Bon appétit!

Per Serving
calories: 425 | fat: 26g | protein: 38g | carbs: 10g | net carbs: 8g | fiber: 2g

Mixed Greens with Bacon

Prep time: 10 minutes | Cook time: 7 minutes | Serves 2

7 ounces (198 g) mixed greens
8 thick slices pork bacon
2 shallots, peeled and diced
Nonstick cooking spray

1. Begin by preheating the air fryer to 345ºF (174ºC).
2. Now, add the shallot and bacon to the Air Fryer cooking basket, set the timer for 2 minutes. Spritz with a nonstick cooking spray.
3. After that, pause the Air Fryer, throw in the mixed greens, give it a good stir and cook for an additional 5 minutes. Serve warm.

Per Serving
calories: 259 | fat: 16g | protein: 19g | carbs: 10g | net carbs: 5g | fiber: 5g

Air Fried Beef Steak

Prep time: 16 minutes | Cook time: 10 minutes | Serves 4

⅓ cup almond flour
2 eggs
2 teaspoons caraway seeds
4 beef steaks
2 teaspoons garlic
powder
1 tablespoon melted butter
Fine sea salt and cayenne pepper, to taste

1. Generously coat steaks with garlic powder, caraway seeds, salt, and cayenne pepper.
2. In a mixing dish, thoroughly combine melted butter with seasoned crumbs. In another bowl, beat the eggs until they're well whisked.
3. First, coat steaks with the beaten egg, then, coat beef steaks with the buttered crumb mixture.
4. Place the steaks in the Air Fryer cooking basket, cook for 10 minutes at 355ºF (181ºC). Bon appétit!

Per Serving
calories: 474 | fat: 22g | protein: 55g | carbs: 9g | net carbs: 8g | fiber: 1g

Beef Sausage with Tomato Bowl

Prep time: 35 minutes | Cook time: 20 minutes | Serves 4

4 bell peppers	4 spring onions
2 tablespoons olive oil	4 beef sausages
2 medium-sized tomatoes, halved	1 tablespoon mustard

1. Start by preheating your Air Fryer to 400ºF (205ºC).
2. Add the bell peppers to the cooking basket. Drizzle 1 tablespoon of olive oil all over the bell peppers.
3. Cook for 5 minutes. Turn the temperature down to 350ºF (180ºC). Add the tomatoes and spring onions to the cooking basket and cook for an additional 10 minutes.
4. Reserve your vegetables.
5. Then, add the sausages to the cooking basket. Drizzle with the remaining tablespoon of olive oil.
6. Cook in the preheated Air Fryer at 380ºF (193ºC) for 15 minutes, flipping them halfway through the cooking time.
7. Serve sausages with the air-fried vegetables and mustard, serve.

Per Serving
calories: 490 | fat: 42g | protein: 19g | carbs: 9g | net carbs: 7g | fiber: 2g

Creamy Beef Sirloin Steak

Prep time: 20 minutes | Cook time: 15 minutes | Serves 4

1¼ pounds (567g) beef sirloin steak, cut into small-sized strips	2 cloves garlic, crushed
¼ cup balsamic vinegar	1 teaspoon cayenne pepper
1 tablespoon brown mustard	Sea salt flakes and crushed red pepper, to taste
1 tablespoon butter	1 cup sour cream
1 cup beef broth	2½ tablespoons keto tomato paste
1 cup leek, chopped	

1. Place the beef along with the balsamic vinegar and the mustard in a mixing dish, cover and marinate in your refrigerator for about 1 hour.
2. Butter the inside of a baking dish and put the beef into the dish.
3. Add the broth, leeks and garlic. Cook at 380º(193ºC) for 8 minutes. Pause the machine and add the cayenne pepper, salt, red pepper, sour cream and tomato paste, cook for additional 7 minutes.

4. Bon appétit!

Per Serving
calories: 418 | fat: 25g | protein: 33g | carbs: 9g | net carbs: 8g | fiber: 1g

Chuck and Arugula Kebab

Prep time: 30 minutes | Cook time: 25 minutes | Serves 4

½ cup leeks, chopped	sumac
2 garlic cloves, smashed	3 saffron threads
2 pounds (907 g) ground chuck	2 tablespoons loosely packed fresh continental parsley leaves
Salt, to taste	
¼ teaspoon ground black pepper, or more to taste	4 tablespoons tahini sauce
1 teaspoon cayenne pepper	4 ounces (113 g) baby arugula
½ teaspoon ground	1 tomato, cut into slices

1. In a bowl, mix the chopped leeks, garlic, ground chuck, and spices, knead with your hands until everything is well incorporated.
2. Now, mound the beef mixture around a wooden skewer into a pointed-ended sausage.
3. Cook in the preheated Air Fryer at 360ºF (182ºC) for 25 minutes.
4. Serve your kebab with the tahini sauce baby arugula and tomato. Enjoy!

Per Serving
calories: 354 | fat: 15g | protein: 49g | carbs: 6g | net carbs: 4g | fiber: 2g

Chapter 5 Poultry

Chicken with Peanuts

Prep time: 10 minutes | Cook time: 15 minutes | Serves 4

1½ pounds (680 g) chicken tenderloins
2 tablespoons peanut oil
½ cup Parmesan cheese, grated
Sea salt and ground black pepper, to taste
½ teaspoon garlic powder
1 teaspoon red pepper flakes
2 tablespoons peanuts, roasted and roughly chopped

1. Start by preheating your Air Fryer to 360ºF.
2. Brush the chicken tenderloins with peanut oil on all sides.
3. In a mixing bowl, thoroughly combine grated Parmesan cheese, salt, black pepper, garlic powder, and red pepper flakes. Dredge the chicken in the breading, shaking off any residual coating.
4. Lay the chicken tenderloins into the cooking basket. Cook for 12 to 13 minutes or until it is no longer pink in the center. Work in batches, an instant-read thermometer should read at least 165ºF.
5. Serve garnished with roasted peanuts. Bon appétit!

Per Serving
calories: 280 | fat: 19g | protein: 3g | carbs: 22g | net carbs: 21g | fiber: 1g

Glazed Turkey Tenderloins with Pickles

Prep time: 15 minutes | Cook time: 50 minutes | Serves 4

1 pound (454 g) turkey tenderloins
1 tablespoon Dijon-style mustard
1 tablespoon olive oil
Sea salt and ground black pepper, to taste
1 teaspoon Italian
seasoning mix
1 cup turkey stock
½ teaspoon xanthan gum
4 tablespoons tomato ketchup
4 tablespoons mayonnaise
4 pickles, sliced

1. Rub the turkey tenderloins with the mustard and olive oil. Season with salt, black pepper, and Italian seasoning mix.

2. Cook the turkey tenderloins at 350ºF for 30 minutes, flipping them over halfway through. Let them rest for 5 to 7 minutes before slicing.
3. For the gravy, in a saucepan, place the drippings from the roasted turkey. Add in turkey stock and bring to a boil.
4. Stir in xanthan gum and whisk to combine. Let it simmer another 5 to 10 minutes until starting to thicken. Gravy will thicken more as it cools.
5. Serve turkey tenderloins with gravy, tomato ketchup, mayonnaise, and pickles. Serve and enjoy!

Per Serving
calories: 276 | fat: 16g | protein: 3g | carbs: 15g | net carbs: 13g | fiber: 2g

Chicken Thighs with Creamy Rosemary Sauce

Prep time: 15 minutes | Cook time: 18 minutes | Serves 4

½ cup full-fat sour cream
1 teaspoon ground cinnamon
½ teaspoon whole grain mustard
1½ tablespoons mayonnaise
1 pound (454 g) chicken thighs, boneless, skinless, and cut into
pieces
1½ tablespoons olive oil
2 heaping tablespoons fresh rosemary, minced
½ cup white wine
3 cloves garlic, minced
½ teaspoon smoked paprika
Salt and freshly cracked black pepper, to taste

1. Firstly, in a mixing dish, combine chicken thighs with olive oil and white wine, stir to coat.
2. After that, throw in the garlic, smoked paprika, ground cinnamon, salt, and black pepper, cover and refrigerate for 1 to 3 hours.
3. Set the Air Fryer to cook at 375ºF. Roast the chicken thighs for 18 minutes, turning halfway through and working in batches.
4. To make the sauce, combine the sour cream, whole grain mustard, mayonnaise and rosemary. Serve the turkey with the mustard/rosemary sauce and enjoy!

Per Serving
calories: 362 | fat: 28g | protein: 8g | carbs: 17g | net carbs: 16g | fiber: 1g

Cheese Loaded Turkey Meatloaf

Prep time: 15 minutes | Cook time: 47 minutes | Serves 6

2 pounds (907 g) turkey mince
½ cup scallions, finely chopped
2 garlic cloves, finely minced
1 teaspoon dried thyme
½ teaspoon dried basil
¾ cup Colby cheese, shredded

1 tablespoon tamari sauce
Salt and black pepper, to your liking
¼ cup roasted red pepper tomato sauce
¾ tablespoons olive oil
1 medium-sized egg, well beaten

1. In a nonstick skillet, that is preheated over a moderate heat, sauté the turkey mince, scallions, garlic, thyme, and basil until just tender and fragrant.
2. Then set your Air Fryer to cook at 360 degrees. Combine sautéed mixture with the cheese and tamari sauce, then form the mixture into a loaf shape.
3. Mix the remaining items and pour them over the meatloaf. Cook in the Air Fryer baking pan for 45 to 47 minutes. Eat warm.

Per Serving
calories: 324 | fat: 19g | protein: 16g | carbs: 33g | net carbs: 32g | fiber: 1g

Turkey and Bacon Burgers

Prep time: 15 minutes | Cook time: 26 minutes | Serves 4

2 tablespoons vermouth
2 strips Canadian bacon, sliced
1 pound (454 g) ground turkey
½ shallot, minced
2 garlic cloves, minced
2 tablespoons fish sauce
Sea salt and ground black pepper, to taste

1 teaspoon red pepper flakes
4 tablespoons tomato ketchup
4 tablespoons mayonnaise
4 (1-ounce / 28-g) slices Cheddar cheese
4 lettuce leaves

1. Start by preheating your Air Fryer to 400ºF. Brush the Canadian bacon with the vermouth.
2. Cook for 3 minutes. Flip the bacon over and cook for an additional 3 minutes.
3. Then, thoroughly combine the ground turkey, shallots, garlic, fish sauce, salt, black pepper, and red pepper. Form the meat mixture into 4 burger patties.
4. Bake in the preheated Air Fryer at 370ºF for 10 minutes. Flip them over and cook another for 10 minutes.
5. Serve turkey burgers with the ketchup, mayonnaise, bacon, cheese and lettuce, serve immediately.

Per Serving
calories: 308 | fat: 16g | protein: 4g | carbs: 17g | net carbs: 16g | fiber: 1g

Sausage and Eggs with Keto Rolls

Prep time: 20 minutes | Cook time: 35 minutes | Serves 6

1 teaspoon dried dill weed
1 teaspoon mustard seeds
6 turkey sausages
3 bell peppers, seeded and thinly sliced
6 medium-sized eggs
½ teaspoon fennel seeds
1 teaspoon sea salt
⅓ teaspoon freshly cracked pink peppercorns

Keto Rolls:
½ cup ricotta cheese, crumbled
1 cup part skim Mozzarella cheese, shredded
1 egg
½ cup coconut flour
½ cup almond flour
1 teaspoon baking soda
2 tablespoons plain whey protein isolate

1. Set your Air Fryer to cook at 325ºF. Cook the sausages and bell peppers in the Air Fryer cooking basket for 8 minutes.
2. Crack the eggs into the ramekins, sprinkle them with salt, dill weed, mustard seeds, fennel seeds, and cracked peppercorns. Cook for an additional 12 minutes at 395ºF.
3. To make the keto rolls, microwave the cheese for 1 minute 30 seconds, stirring twice. Add the cheese to the bowl of a food processor and blend well. Fold in the egg and mix again.
4. Add in the flour, baking soda, and plain whey protein isolate, blend again. Scrape the batter onto the center of a lightly greased cling film.
5. Form the dough into a disk and transfer to your freezer to cool, cut into 6 pieces and transfer to a parchment-lined baking pan (make sure to grease your hands).
6. Bake in the preheated oven at 400ºF for about 14 minutes.
7. Serve eggs and sausages on keto rolls and enjoy!

Per Serving
calories: 494 | fat: 30g | protein: 5g | carbs: 19g | net carbs: 18.9g | fiber: 0.1g

Lemon Chicken

Prep time: 20 minutes | Cook time: 7 to 10 minutes | Serves 4

1 pound (454 g) boneless, skinless chicken breasts or thighs	1 teaspoon chopped fresh oregano
2 tablespoons avocado oil	½ teaspoon garlic powder
1 tablespoon freshly squeezed lemon juice	Sea salt
	Freshly ground black pepper

1. Place the chicken in a zip-top bag or between two pieces of plastic wrap. Using a meat mallet or a heavy skillet, pound the chicken until it is very thin, about ¼ -inch thick.
2. In a small bowl, combine the avocado oil, lemon juice, oregano, garlic powder, salt, and pepper. Place the chicken in a shallow dish and pour the marinade over it. Toss to coat all the chicken, and let it rest at room temperature for 10 to 15 minutes.
3. Set the air fryer to 400°F (205ºC). Place the chicken in a single layer in the air fryer basket and cook for 5 minutes. Flip and cook for another 2 to 5 minutes, until an instant-read thermometer reads 160°F (71ºC). Allow it to rest for 5 minutes before serving.

Per Serving
calories: 178 | fat: 10g | protein: 23g | carbs: 2g | net carbs: 1g | fiber: 1g

Chicken-Wrapped Bacon and Spinach

Prep time: 15 minutes | Cook time: 20 minutes | Serves 4

3 tablespoons pine nuts	Salt and freshly ground black pepper
¾ cup frozen spinach, thawed and squeezed dry	4 small boneless, skinless chicken breast halves (about 1½ pounds / 680g)
⅓ cup ricotta cheese	
2 tablespoons grated Parmesan cheese	8 slices bacon
3 cloves garlic, minced	

1. Place the pine nuts in a small pan and set in the air fryer basket. Set the air fryer to 400°F (205ºC) and air fry for 2 to 3 minutes until toasted. Remove the pine nuts to a mixing bowl and continue preheating the air fryer.
2. In a large bowl, combine the spinach, ricotta, Parmesan, and garlic. Season to taste with salt and pepper and stir well until thoroughly combined.

3. Using a sharp knife, cut into the chicken breasts, slicing them across and opening them up like a book, but be careful not to cut them all the way through. Sprinkle the chicken with salt and pepper.
4. Spoon equal amounts of the spinach mixture into the chicken, then fold the top of the chicken breast back over the top of the stuffing. Wrap each chicken breast with 2 slices of bacon.
5. Working in batches if necessary, air fry the chicken for 18 to 20 minutes until the bacon is crisp and a thermometer inserted into the thickest part of the chicken registers 165°F (74ºC).

Per Serving
calories: 440 | fat: 20g | protein: 63g | carbs: 4g | net carbs: 3g | fiber: 1g

Turkey Drumsticks with Hoisin Sauce

Prep time: 15 minutes | Cook time: 40 minutes | Serves 4

2 pounds (907 g) turkey drumsticks	Salt and ground black pepper, to your liking
2 tablespoons balsamic vinegar	2 ½ tablespoons butter, melted
2 tablespoons dry white wine	**For the Hoisin Sauce:**
1 tablespoon sesame oil	2 tablespoons hoisin sauce
1 sprig rosemary, chopped	1 tablespoon mustard

1. Add the turkey drumsticks to a mixing dish, add the vinegar, wine, sesame oil, and rosemary. Let them marinate for 3 hours.
2. Then, preheat the Air Fryer to 350ºF.
3. Season the turkey drumsticks with salt and black pepper, spread the melted butter over the surface of drumsticks.
4. Cook turkey drumsticks at 350ºF for 30 to 35 minutes, working in batches. Turn the drumsticks over a few times during the cooking.
5. While the turkey drumsticks are roasting, prepare the Hoisin sauce by mixing the ingredients. After that, drizzle the turkey with the sauce mixture, roast for a further 5 minutes.
6. Let it rest for about 10 minutes before carving and serving. Bon appétit!

Per Serving
calories: 469 | fat: 26g | protein: 10g | carbs: 20g | net carbs: 19g | fiber: 1g

Turkey Thighs with Lush Vegetables

Prep time: 20 minutes | Cook time: 45 minutes | Serves 4

1 red onion, cut into wedges
1 carrot, trimmed and sliced
1 celery stalk, trimmed and sliced
1 cup Brussels sprouts, trimmed and halved
1 cup roasted vegetable broth
1 tablespoon apple cider vinegar
4 turkey thighs
½ teaspoon mixed peppercorns, freshly cracked
1 teaspoon fine sea salt
1 teaspoon cayenne pepper
1 teaspoon onion powder
½ teaspoon garlic powder
⅓ teaspoon mustard seeds

1. Take a baking dish that easily fits into your device, place the vegetables on the bottom of the baking dish and pour in roasted vegetable broth.
2. In a large-sized mixing dish, place the remaining ingredients, let them marinate for about 30 minutes. Lay them on the top of the vegetables.
3. Roast at 330ºF for 40 to 45 minutes. Bon appétit!

Per Serving
calories: 393 | fat: 21g | protein: 16g | carbs: 36g | net carbs: 35g | fiber: 1g

Aromatic Chicken Thighs

Prep time: 20 minutes | Cook time: 15 minutes | Serves 4

¼ cup full-fat Greek yogurt
½ teaspoon cayenne pepper
½ teaspoon ground cinnamon
½ teaspoon ground black pepper
1 teaspoon kosher salt
1 teaspoon ground cumin
1 tablespoon juiced lime
1 tablespoon avocado oil
1 teaspoon smoked paprika
1 tablespoon keto tomato paste
1 tablespoon minced garlic
pound (454 g) chicken thighs, boneless & skinless

1. Using a large mixing bowl, add in the tomato paste, garlic, oil, juiced lime, cumin, salt, black pepper, cinnamon, paprika, cayenne pepper, yogurt and mix until combined.
2. Add the chicken pieces into the mixing bowl and toss until combined, then set aside to marinate for an hour.

3. Arrange the marinated chicken in the fryer basket then cook for 10 minutes at 370°F (188ºC).
4. Flip the chicken over and cook for an additional 5 minutes.
5. Serve and enjoy as desired.

Per Serving
calories: 298 | fat: 23g | protein: 20g | carbs: 4g | net carbs: 3g | fiber: 1g

Chicken Bacon Salad with Avocado-Lime Dressing

Prep time: 15 minutes | Cook time: 8 minutes | Serves 4

8 slices reduced-sodium bacon
8 chicken breast tenders (about 1½ pounds / 680g)
8 cups chopped romaine lettuce
1 cup cherry tomatoes, halved
¼ red onion, thinly sliced
2 hard-boiled eggs, peeled and sliced
Avocado-Lime Dressing:
½ cup plain Greek yogurt
¼ cup milk
½ avocado
Juice of ½ lime
3 scallions, coarsely chopped
1 clove garlic
2 tablespoons fresh cilantro
⅛ teaspoon ground cumin
Salt and freshly ground black pepper

1. Preheat the air fryer to 400°F (205ºC).
2. Wrap a piece of bacon around each piece of chicken and secure with a toothpick. Working in batches if necessary, arrange the bacon-wrapped chicken in a single layer in the air fryer basket. Air fry for 8 minutes until the bacon is browned and a thermometer inserted into the thickest piece of chicken register 165°F (74ºC). Let it cool for a few minutes, then slice into bite-size pieces.
3. To make the dressing: In a blender or food processor, combine the yogurt, milk, avocado, lime juice, scallions, garlic, cilantro, and cumin. purée until smooth. Season to taste with salt and freshly ground pepper.
4. To assemble the salad, in a large bowl, combine the lettuce, tomatoes, and onion. Drizzle the dressing over the vegetables and toss gently until thoroughly combined. Arrange the chicken and eggs on top just before serving.

Per Serving
calories: 425 | fat: 18g | protein: 52g | carbs: 11g | net carbs: 7g | fiber: 4g

Nacho Chicken Burgers

Prep time: 15 minutes | Cook time: 15 minutes | Serves 4

1 palmful dried basil
⅓ cup Parmesan cheese, grated
2 teaspoons dried marjoram
⅓ teaspoon ancho chili powder
2 teaspoons dried parsley flakes
½ teaspoon onion powder
Toppings, to serve

⅓ teaspoon porcini powder
1 teaspoon sea salt flakes
1 pound (454 g) chicken meat, ground
2 teaspoons cumin powder
⅓ teaspoon red pepper flakes, crushed
1 teaspoon freshly cracked black pepper

1. Generously grease an Air Fryer cooking basket with a thin layer of vegetable oil.
2. In a mixing dish, combine chicken meat with all seasonings. Shape into 4 patties and coat them with grated Parmesan cheese.
3. Cook chicken burgers in the preheated Air Fryer for 15 minutes at 345ºF, working in batches, flipping them once.
4. Serve with toppings of choice. Bon appétit!

Per Serving

calories: 234 | fat: 12g | protein: 6g | carbs: 12g | net carbs: 11g | fiber: 1g

Chicken with Cauliflower and Italian Parsley

Prep time: 15 minutes | Cook time: 28 minutes | Serves 6

2 handful fresh Italian parsley, roughly chopped
½ cup fresh chopped chives
2 sprigs thyme
6 chicken drumsticks
1½ small-sized heads cauliflower, broken into large-sized florets
2 teaspoons mustard powder
⅓ teaspoon porcini powder

1 ½ teaspoons berbere spice
⅓ teaspoon sweet paprika
½ teaspoon shallot powder
1 teaspoon granulated garlic
1 teaspoon freshly cracked pink peppercorns
½ teaspoon sea salt

1. Simply combine all items for the berbere spice rub mix. After that, coat the chicken drumsticks with this rub mix on all sides. Transfer them to the baking dish.
2. Now, lower the cauliflower onto the chicken drumsticks. Add thyme, chives and Italian parsley and spritz everything with a pan spray. Transfer the baking dish to the preheated Air Fryer.
3. Next step, set the timer for 28 minutes, roast at 355ºF (181ºC), turning occasionally. Bon appétit!

Per Serving

calories: 234 | fat: 12g | protein: 2g | carbs: 9g | net carbs: 7g | fiber: 2g

Broccoli Cheese Chicken

Prep time: 10 minutes | Cook time: 19 to 24 minutes | Serves 6

1 tablespoon avocado oil
¼ cup chopped onion
½ cup finely chopped broccoli
4 ounces (113 g) cream cheese, at room temperature
2 ounces (57 g) Cheddar cheese, shredded
1 teaspoon garlic powder
½ teaspoon sea salt, plus

additional for seasoning, divided
¼ freshly ground black pepper, plus additional for seasoning, divided
2 pounds (907 g) boneless, skinless chicken breasts
1 teaspoon smoked paprika

1. Heat a medium skillet over medium-high heat and pour in the avocado oil. Add the onion and broccoli and cook, stirring occasionally, for 5 to 8 minutes, until the onion is tender.
2. Transfer to a large bowl and stir in the cream cheese, Cheddar cheese, and garlic powder, and season to taste with salt and pepper.
3. Hold a sharp knife parallel to the chicken breast and cut a long pocket into one side. Stuff the chicken pockets with the broccoli mixture, using toothpicks to secure the pockets around the filling.
4. In a small dish, combine the paprika, ½ teaspoon salt, and ¼ teaspoon pepper. Sprinkle this over the outside of the chicken.
5. Set the air fryer to 400°F (205ºC). Place the chicken in a single layer in the air fryer basket, cooking in batches if necessary, and cook for 14 to 16 minutes, until an instant-read thermometer reads 160°F (71ºC). Place the chicken on a plate and tent a piece of aluminum foil over the chicken. Allow it to rest for 5 to 10 minutes before serving.

Per Serving

calories: 277 | fat: 15g | protein: 35g | carbs: 3g | net carbs: 2g | fiber: 1g

Duck with Candy Onion

Prep time: 15 minutes | Cook time: 25 minutes | Serves 4

1½ pounds (680 g) duck breasts, skin removed
1 teaspoon kosher salt
½ teaspoon cayenne pepper
⅓ teaspoon black pepper
½ teaspoon smoked paprika
1 tablespoon Thai red curry paste
1 cup candy onions, halved
¼ small pack coriander, chopped

1. Place the duck breasts between 2 sheets of foil, then, use a rolling pin to bash the duck until they are 1-inch thick.
2. Preheat your Air Fryer to 395ºF.
3. Rub the duck breasts with salt, cayenne pepper, black pepper, paprika, and red curry paste. Place the duck breast in the cooking basket.
4. Cook for 11 to 12 minutes. Top with candy onions and cook for another 10 to 11 minutes.
5. Serve garnished with coriander and enjoy!

Per Serving
calories: 362 | fat: 19g | protein: 2g | carbs: 24g | net carbs: 21g | fiber: 3g

Spiced Chicken Thighs

Prep time: 15 minutes | Cook time: 20 minutes | Serves 6

2 teaspoons ground coriander
1 teaspoon ground allspice
1 teaspoon cayenne pepper
1 teaspoon ground ginger
1 teaspoon salt
1 teaspoon dried thyme
½ teaspoon ground cinnamon
½ teaspoon ground nutmeg
2 pounds (907 g) boneless chicken thighs, skin on
2 tablespoons olive oil

1. In a small bowl, combine the coriander, allspice, cayenne, ginger, salt, thyme, cinnamon, and nutmeg. Stir until thoroughly combined.
2. Place the chicken in a 9 × 13-inch baking dish and use paper towels to pat dry. Thoroughly coat both sides of the chicken with the spice mixture. Cover and refrigerate for at least 2 hours, preferably overnight.
3. Preheat the air fryer to 360°F (182ºC).
4. Working in batches if necessary, arrange the chicken in a single layer in the air fryer basket and lightly coat with the olive oil. Pausing halfway through the cooking time to flip the chicken, air fry for 15 to 20 minutes, until a thermometer inserted into the thickest part registers 165°F (74ºC).

Per Serving
calories: 223 | fat: 11g | protein: 30g | carbs: 1g | net carbs: 1g | fiber: 0g

Rosemary Chicken Breast with Olives

Prep time: 15 minutes | Cook time: 25 minutes | Serves 4

4 small boneless, skinless chicken breast halves (about 1½ pounds / 680g)
Salt and freshly ground black pepper
4 ounces (113 g) goat cheese
6 pitted Kalamata olives, coarsely chopped
Zest of ½ lemon
1 teaspoon minced fresh rosemary
½ cup almond meal
¼ cup balsamic vinegar
6 tablespoons unsalted butter

1. Preheat the air fryer to 360°F (182ºC).
2. With a boning knife, cut a wide pocket into the thickest part of each chicken breast half, taking care not to cut all the way through. Season the chicken evenly on both sides with salt and freshly ground black pepper.
3. In a small bowl, mix the cheese, olives, lemon zest, and rosemary. Stuff the pockets with the cheese mixture and secure with toothpicks.
4. Place the almond meal in a shallow bowl and dredge the chicken, shaking off the excess. Coat lightly with olive oil spray.
5. Working in batches if necessary, arrange the chicken breasts in a single layer in the air fryer basket. Pausing halfway through the cooking time to flip the chicken, air fry for 20 to 25 minutes, until a thermometer inserted into the thickest part registers 165°F (74ºC).
6. While the chicken is baking, prepare the sauce. In a small pan over medium heat, simmer the balsamic vinegar until thick and syrupy, about 5 minutes. Set aside until the chicken is done. When ready to serve, warm the sauce over medium heat and whisk in the butter, 1 tablespoon at a time, until melted and smooth. Season to taste with salt and pepper.
7. Serve the chicken breasts with the sauce drizzled on top.

Per Serving
calories: 510 | fat: 32g | protein: 50g | carbs: 7g | net carbs: 7g | fiber: 0g

Zucchini and Sausage Casserole

Prep time: 50 minutes | Cook time: 16 minutes | Serves 4

8 ounces (227 g) zucchini, spiralized
1 pound (454 g) smoked chicken sausage, sliced
1 tomato, puréed
½ cup Asiago cheese, shredded

1 tablespoon Italian seasoning mix
3 tablespoons Romano cheese, grated
1 tablespoon fresh basil leaves, chiffonade

1. Salt the zucchini and let it stand for 30 minutes, pat it dry with kitchen towels.
2. Then, spritz a baking pan with cooking spray, add the zucchini to the pan. Stir in the chicken sausage, tomato purée, Asiago cheese, and Italian seasoning mix.
3. Bake in the preheated Air Fryer at 325ºF (163ºC) for 11 minutes.
4. Top with the grated Romano cheese. Turn the temperature to 390ºF (199ºC) and cook for an additional 5 minutes or until everything is thoroughly heated and the cheese is melted.
5. Garnish with fresh basil leaves. Bon appétit!

Per Serving
calories: 300 | fat: 17g | protein: 5g | carbs: 9g | net carbs: 7g | fiber: 2g

Parmesan Turkey Meatball with Pepper

Prep time: 10 minutes | Cook time: 10 minutes | Serves 4

1 red bell pepper, seeded and coarsely chopped
2 cloves garlic, coarsely chopped
¼ cup chopped fresh parsley
1½ pounds (680g) 85%

lean ground turkey
1 egg, lightly beaten
½ cup grated Parmesan cheese
1 teaspoon salt
½ teaspoon freshly ground black pepper

1. Preheat the air fryer to 400°F (205ºC).
2. In a food processor fitted with a metal blade, combine the bell pepper, garlic, and parsley. Pulse until finely chopped. Transfer the vegetables to a large mixing bowl.
3. Add the turkey, egg, Parmesan, salt, and black pepper. Mix gently until thoroughly combined. Shape the mixture into 1¼-inch meatballs.
4. Working in batches if necessary, arrange the

meatballs in a single layer in the air fryer basket, coat lightly with olive oil spray. Pausing halfway through the cooking time to shake the basket, air fry for 7 to 10 minutes, until lightly browned and a thermometer inserted into the center of a meatball registers 165°F (74ºC).

Per Serving
calories: 410 | fat: 27g | protein: 38g | carbs: 4g | net carbs: 3g | fiber: 1g

Almond Chicken with Marinara Sauce

Prep time: 15 minutes | Cook time: 20 minutes | Serves 4

2 large skinless chicken breasts (about 1¼ pounds / 567g)
Salt and freshly ground black pepper
½ cup almond meal
½ cup grated Parmesan cheese
2 teaspoons Italian

seasoning
1 egg, lightly beaten
1 tablespoon olive oil
1 cup no-sugar-added marinara sauce
4 slices Mozzarella cheese or ½ cup shredded Mozzarella

1. Preheat the air fryer to 360°F (182ºC).
2. Slice the chicken breasts in half horizontally to create 4 thinner chicken breasts. Working with one piece at a time, place the chicken between two pieces of parchment paper and pound with a meat mallet or rolling pin to flatten to an even thickness. Season both sides with salt and freshly ground black pepper.
3. In a large shallow bowl, combine the almond meal, Parmesan, and Italian seasoning, stir until thoroughly combined. Place the egg in another large shallow bowl.
4. Dip the chicken in the egg, followed by the almond meal mixture, pressing the mixture firmly into the chicken to create an even coating.
5. Working in batches if necessary, arrange the chicken breasts in a single layer in the air fryer basket and coat both sides lightly with olive oil. Pausing halfway through the cooking time to flip the chicken, air fry for 15 minutes, or until a thermometer inserted into the thickest part registers 165°F (74ºC).
6. Spoon the marinara sauce over each piece of chicken and top with the Mozzarella cheese. Air fry for an additional 3 to 5 minutes until the cheese is melted.

Per Serving
calories: 460 | fat: 16g | protein: 65g | carbs: 11g | net carbs: 9g | fiber: 2g

Chicken Legs with Turnip

Prep time: 30 minutes | Cook time: 25 minutes | Serves 3

1 pound (454 g) chicken legs
1 teaspoon Himalayan salt
1 teaspoon paprika
½ teaspoon ground black pepper
1 teaspoon butter, melted
1 turnip, trimmed and sliced

1. Spritz the sides and bottom of the cooking basket with a nonstick cooking spray.
2. Season the chicken legs with salt, paprika, and ground black pepper.
3. Cook at 370ºF (188ºC) for 10 minutes. Increase the temperature to 380ºF (193ºC).
4. Drizzle turnip slices with melted butter and transfer them to the cooking basket with the chicken. Cook the turnips and chicken for 15 minutes or more, flipping them halfway through the cooking time.
5. As for the chicken, an instant-read thermometer should read at least 165ºF (74ºC).
6. Serve and enjoy!

Per Serving
calories: 207 | fat: 7g | protein: 29g | carbs: 3g | net carbs: 2g | fiber: 1g

Chicken with Asiago Cheese

Prep time: 10 minutes | Cook time: 10 minutes | Serves 4

2 ounces (57 g) Asiago cheese, cut into sticks
⅓ cup keto tomato paste
½ teaspoon garlic paste
2 chicken breasts, cut in half lengthwise
½ cup green onions, chopped
1 tablespoon chili sauce
½ cup roasted vegetable stock
1 tablespoon sesame oil
1 teaspoon salt
2 teaspoons unsweetened cocoa
½ teaspoon sweet paprika, or more to taste

1. Sprinkle chicken breasts with the salt and sweet paprika, drizzle with chili sauce. Now, place a stick of Asiago cheese in the middle of each chicken breast.
2. Then, tie the whole thing using a kitchen string, give a drizzle of sesame oil.
3. Transfer the stuffed chicken to the cooking basket. Add the other ingredients and toss to coat the chicken.
4. Afterward, cook for about 11 minutes at 395ºF (202ºC). Serve the chicken on two serving plates, garnish with fresh or pickled salad and serve immediately. Bon appétit!

Per Serving
calories: 390 | fat: 12g | protein: 2g | carbs: 8g | net carbs: 7g | fiber: 1g

Buttery Chicken

Prep time:25 minutes | Cook time: 14 to 18 minutes | Serves 8

½ cup (1 stick) unsalted butter, at room temperature
1 teaspoon minced garlic
2 tablespoons chopped fresh parsley
½ teaspoon freshly ground black pepper
2 pounds (907 g) boneless, skinless
chicken breasts
Sea salt
¾ cup finely ground blanched almond flour
¾ cup grated Parmesan cheese
⅛ teaspoon cayenne pepper
2 large eggs
Avocado oil spray

1. In a medium bowl, combine the butter, garlic, parsley, and black pepper. Form the mixture into a log and wrap it tightly with parchment paper or plastic wrap. Refrigerate for at least 2 hours, until firm.
2. Place the chicken breasts in a zip-top bag or between two pieces of plastic wrap. Pound the chicken with a meat mallet or heavy skillet to an even ¼-inch thickness.
3. Place a pat of butter in the center of each chicken breast and wrap the chicken tightly around the butter from the long side, tucking in the short sides as you go. Secure with toothpicks. Season the outside of the chicken with salt. Wrap the stuffed chicken tightly with plastic wrap and refrigerate for at least 2 hours or overnight.
4. In a shallow bowl, combine the almond flour, Parmesan cheese, and cayenne pepper.
5. In another shallow bowl, beat the eggs.
6. Dip each piece of chicken in the eggs, then coat it in the almond flour mixture, using your fingers to press the breading gently into the chicken.
7. Set the air fryer to 350°F (180ºC). Spray the chicken with oil and place it in a single layer in the air fryer basket, working in batches if necessary. Cook for 8 minutes. Flip the chicken, then spray it again with oil. Cook for 6 to 10 minutes, until an instant-read thermometer reads 165°F (74ºC).

Per Serving
calories: 333 | fat: 23g | protein: 31g | carbs: 3g | net carbs: 2g | fiber: 1g

Chicken Thighs with Montreal Chicken Seasoning

Prep time: 15 minutes | Cook time: 25 minutes | Serves 4

1 tablespoon olive oil
Juice of ½ lime
1 tablespoon coconut aminos
1½ teaspoons Montreal

chicken seasoning
8 bone-in chicken thighs, skin on
2 tablespoons chopped fresh cilantro

1. In a gallon-size resealable bag, combine the olive oil, lime juice, coconut aminos, and chicken seasoning. Add the chicken thighs, seal the bag, and massage the bag to ensure the chicken is thoroughly coated. Refrigerate for at least 2 hours, preferably overnight.
2. Preheat the air fryer to 400°F (205ºC).
3. Remove the chicken from the marinade (discard the marinade) and arrange in a single layer in the air fryer basket. Pausing halfway through the cooking time to flip the chicken, air fry for 20 to 25 minutes, until a thermometer inserted into the thickest part registers 165°F (74ºC).
4. Transfer the chicken to a serving platter and top with the cilantro before serving.

Per Serving
calories: 335 | fat: 22g | protein: 31g | carbs: 0g | net carbs: 0g | fiber: 0g

Chicken Wing with Piri Piri Sauce

Prep time: 1 hour 30 minutes | Cook time: 30 minutes | Serves 6

12 chicken wings
1½ ounces (43 g) butter, melted
1 teaspoon onion powder
½ teaspoon cumin powder
1 teaspoon garlic paste
For the Sauce:
2 ounces (57 g) piri piri

peppers, stemmed and chopped
1 tablespoon pimiento, seeded and minced
1 garlic clove, chopped
2 tablespoons fresh lemon juice
⅓ teaspoon sea salt
½ teaspoon tarragon

1. Steam the chicken wings using a steamer basket that is placed over a saucepan with boiling water, reduce the heat.
2. Now, steam the wings for 10 minutes over a moderate heat. Toss the wings with butter, onion powder, cumin powder, and garlic paste.
3. Let the chicken wings cool to room temperature. Then, refrigerate them for 45 to 50 minutes.
4. Roast in the preheated Air Fryer at 330ºF (166ºC) for 25 to 30 minutes, make sure to flip them halfway through.
5. While the chicken wings are cooking, prepare the sauce by mixing all of the sauce ingredients in a food processor. Toss the wings with prepared piri piri Sauce and serve.

Per Serving
calories: 517 | fat: 21g | protein: 4g | carbs: 12g | net carbs: 11g | fiber: 1g

Broccoli and Chicken Casserole

Prep time: 15 minutes | Cook time: 25 minutes | Serves 4

½ pound (227g) broccoli, chopped into florets
2 cups shredded cooked chicken
4 ounces (113 g) cream cheese
⅓ cup heavy cream
1½ teaspoons Dijon mustard

½ teaspoon garlic powder
Salt and freshly ground black pepper
2 tablespoons chopped fresh basil
1 cup shredded Cheddar cheese

1. Preheat the air fryer to 390°F (199ºC). Lightly coat a 6-cup casserole dish that will fit in air fryer, such an 8-inch round pan, with olive oil and set aside.
2. Place the broccoli in a large glass bowl with 1 tablespoon of water and cover with a microwavable plate. Microwave on high for 2 to 3 minutes until the broccoli is bright green but not mushy. Drain if necessary and add to another large bowl along with the shredded chicken.
3. In the same glass bowl used to microwave the broccoli, combine the cream cheese and cream. Microwave for 30 seconds to 1 minute on high and stir until smooth. Add the mustard and garlic powder and season to taste with salt and freshly ground black pepper. Whisk until the sauce is smooth.
4. Pour the warm sauce over the broccoli and chicken mixture and then add the basil. Using a silicone spatula, gently fold the mixture until thoroughly combined.
5. Transfer the chicken mixture to the prepared casserole dish and top with the cheese. Air fry for 20 to 25 minutes until warmed through and the cheese has browned.

Per Serving
calories: 430 | fat: 32g | protein: 29g | carbs: 6g | net carbs: 5g | fiber: 1g

Super Poultry Meal with Leek

Prep time: 40 minutes | Cook time: 36 minutes | Serves 4

½ medium-sized leek, chopped
½ red onion, chopped
2 garlic cloves, minced
1 jalapeño pepper, seeded and minced
1 bell pepper, seeded and chopped
2 tablespoons olive oil
1 pound (454 g) ground turkey, 85% lean 15% fat
2 cups tomato purée
2 cups chicken stock
½ teaspoon black peppercorns
Salt, to taste
1 teaspoon chili powder
1 teaspoon mustard seeds
1 teaspoon ground cumin

1. Start by preheating your Air Fryer to 365ºF (185ºC).
2. Place the leeks, onion, garlic and peppers in a baking pan, drizzle olive oil evenly over the top. Cook for 4 to 6 minutes.
3. Add the ground turkey. Cook for 6 minutes or more or until the meat is no longer pink.
4. Now, add the tomato purée, 1 cup of chicken stock, black peppercorns, salt, chili powder, mustard seeds, and cumin to the baking pan. Cook for 24 minutes, stirring every 7 to 10 minutes.
5. Bon appétit!

Per Serving

calories: 271 | fat: 15g | protein: 6g | carbs: 11g | net carbs: 10g | fiber: 1g

Air Fried Lemon Chicken Drumsticks

Prep time: 5 minutes | Cook time: 25 minutes | Serves 4

¼ cup juiced lemon
½ teaspoon cayenne pepper
½ teaspoon coriander seeds
½ teaspoon whole black peppercorns
1 teaspoon turmeric
1 teaspoon kosher salt
1 teaspoon cumin seeds
1 teaspoon parsley, dried
1 teaspoon oregano, dried
1½ pounds (680g) chicken drumsticks
2 tablespoons coconut oil

1. Using a high speed blender, add in the peppercorns, kosher salt, cayenne pepper, coriander seeds, parsley, oregano, cumin, turmeric and blend together until smooth.
2. Transfer the blended spices into a mixing bowl, then add in the oil, juiced lemon and incorporate together.
3. Add in the drumsticks then toss to coat and allow to marinate for an hour.
4. Arrange the drumsticks in the fryer basket with the skin side up and air fry for 15 minutes at 390°F (199ºC).
5. Flip the chicken drumstick over then fry for an extra 10 minutes.
6. Serve and enjoy as desired.

Per Serving

calories: 253 | fat: 17g | protein: 20g | carbs: 2g | net carbs: 1g | fiber: 1g

Chicken Nuggets with Monk Dip

Prep time: 10 minutes | Cook time: 12 minutes | Serves 4

⅛ teaspoon sea salt
¼ cup coconut flour
½ teaspoon ground ginger
1 teaspoon sesame oil
pound (454-g) chicken breast, boneless & skinless
4 large egg whites
6 tablespoons toasted sesame seeds
nonstick cooking oil spray

For the dip:
½ teaspoon monk fruit
½ teaspoon ground ginger
1 tablespoon water
1 teaspoon sriracha
2 teaspoons rice vinegar
2 tablespoons almond butter
4 teaspoons coconut aminos

1. Chop the chicken breast into 1-inch nuggets then pat dry and place in a medium sized mixing bowl.
2. Pour in the sesame oil, salt and massage into the chicken nuggets.
3. Pour the ground ginger and coconut flour into a large ziploc bag then add in the coated chicken nuggets and shake around to coat.
4. Transfer the chicken nuggets into a bowl filled with the egg whites and toss around until covered in the whites.
5. Shake off excess white from the nuggets then cover with the sesame seeds.
6. Heat the fryer up 400°F (205ºC) for 10 minutes then coat the basket with oil and add in the covered chicken nuggets and fry for 6 minutes.
7. Flip the chicken nuggets over and cook until crispy for 6 extra minutes.
8. In the meantime, combine all the sauce ingredients together until mixed.
9. Serve the fried nuggets along with the sauce and enjoy as desired.

Per Serving

calories: 293 | fat: 14g | protein: 33g | carbs: 8g | net carbs: 6g | fiber: 2g

Garlicky Hen with Fish Sauce

Prep time: 20 minutes | Cook time: 20 minutes | Serves 4

¼ cup fish sauce
1 teaspoon turmeric
1 tablespoon coconut aminos
1 chopped jalapeño peppers
1 cup chopped cilantro leaves
2 tablespoons stevia
2 teaspoons ground

coriander
2 tablespoons lemongrass paste
2 halved whole cornish game hens, with the giblets removed
8 minced garlic cloves
Salt and black pepper, to taste

1. Using a high speed blender, add in the turmeric, salt, coriander, pepper, lemongrass paste, sugar, garlic, cilantro, fish sauce and incorporate together.
2. Add in the broiler chicken and toss together until fully coated with the mixture then set aside to marinate for an hour.
3. Transfer the marinated broiler into the fryer basket and air fry for 10 minutes at 400°F (205ºC).
4. Flip the broiler over then cook for an extra 10 minutes.
5. Serve and enjoy as desired.

Per Serving
calories: 222 | fat: 9g | protein: 14g | carbs: 4g | net carbs: 3g | fiber: 1g

Chicken Breast with Cilantro and Lime

Prep time: 10 minutes | Cook time: 15 minutes | Serves 4

For the Chicken:
1 teaspoon turmeric
1 diced large onion
1 tablespoon avocado oil
1 teaspoon garam masala
1 teaspoon smoked paprika
1 teaspoon ground fennel seeds
pound (454-g) chicken breast, boneless &

skinless
2 teaspoons minced ginger
2 teaspoons minced garlic cloves
nonstick cooking oil spray
salt & cayenne pepper, to taste
To Top:
¼ cup chopped cilantro
2 teaspoons juiced lime

1. Make slight piercing all over the chicken breast then set aside.
2. Using a large mixing bowl add in all the remaining

ingredients and combine together.
3. Add the pierced chicken breast into the bowl then set aside for an hour to marinate.
4. Transfer the marinated chicken and veggies into the fryer basket then coat with the cooking oil spray.
5. Cook for 15 minutes at 360°F (182ºC) then serve and enjoy with a garnish of cilantro topped with the juiced lime.

Per Serving
calories: 305 | fat: 23g | protein: 19g | carbs: 6g | net carbs: 5g | fiber: 1g

Spicy Chicken Roll-Up with Monterey Jack

Prep time: 10 minutes | Cook time: 14 to 17 minutes | Serves 8

2 pounds (907 g) boneless, skinless chicken breasts or thighs
1 teaspoon chili powder
½ teaspoon smoked paprika
½ teaspoon ground cumin
Sea salt

Freshly ground black pepper
6 ounces (170 g) Monterey Jack cheese, shredded
4 ounces (113 g) canned diced green chiles
Avocado oil spray

1. Place the chicken in a large zip-top bag or between two pieces of plastic wrap. Using a meat mallet or heavy skillet, pound the chicken until it is about ¼ -inch thick.
2. In a small bowl, combine the chili powder, smoked paprika, cumin, and salt and pepper to taste. Sprinkle both sides of the chicken with the seasonings.
3. Sprinkle the chicken with the Monterey Jack cheese, then the diced green chiles.
4. Roll up each piece of chicken from the long side, tucking in the ends as you go. Secure the roll-up with a toothpick.
5. Set the air fryer to 350°F (180ºC). Spray the outside of the chicken with avocado oil. Place the chicken in a single layer in the basket, working in batches if necessary, and cook for 7 minutes. Flip and cook for another 7 to 10 minutes, until an instant-read thermometer reads 160°F (71ºC).
6. Remove the chicken from the air fryer and allow it to rest for about 5 minutes before serving.

Per Serving
calories: 192 | fat: 9g | protein: 28g | carbs: 2g | net carbs: 1g | fiber: 1g

Mayo-Dijon Chicken

Prep time: 5 minutes | Cook time: 13 to 16 minutes | Serves 6

½ cup sugar-free mayonnaise
1 tablespoon Dijon mustard
1 tablespoon freshly squeezed lemon juice (optional)
1 tablespoon coconut aminos
1 teaspoon Italian seasoning
1 teaspoon sea salt
½ teaspoon freshly ground black pepper
¼ teaspoon cayenne pepper
1½ pounds (680g) boneless, skinless chicken breasts or thighs

1. In a small bowl, combine the mayonnaise, mustard, lemon juice (if using), coconut aminos, Italian seasoning, salt, black pepper, and cayenne pepper.
2. Place the chicken in a shallow dish or large zip-top plastic bag. Add the marinade, making sure all the pieces are coated. Cover and refrigerate for at least 30 minutes or up to 4 hours.
3. Set the air fryer to 400°F (205ºC). Arrange the chicken in a single layer in the air fryer basket, working in batches if necessary. Cook for 7 minutes. Flip the chicken and continue cooking for 6 to 9 minutes or more, until an instant-read thermometer reads 160°F (71ºC).

Per Serving
calories: 236 | fat: 17g | protein: 23g | carbs: 2g | net carbs: 1g | fiber: 1g

Chicken with Lettuce

Prep time: 15 minutes | Cook time: 14 minutes | Serves 4

1 pound (454 g) chicken breast tenders, chopped into bite-size pieces
½ onion, thinly sliced
½ red bell pepper, seeded and thinly sliced
½ green bell pepper, seeded and thinly sliced
1 tablespoon olive oil
1 tablespoon fajita seasoning
1 teaspoon kosher salt
Juice of ½ lime
8 large lettuce leaves
1 cup prepared guacamole

1. Preheat the air fryer to 400°F (205ºC).
2. In a large bowl, combine the chicken, onion, and peppers. Drizzle with the olive oil and toss until thoroughly coated. Add the fajita seasoning and salt and toss again.
3. Working in batches if necessary, arrange the chicken and vegetables in a single layer in the air fryer basket. Pausing halfway through the cooking time to shake the basket, air fry for 14 minutes, or until the vegetables are tender and a thermometer inserted into the thickest piece of chicken registers 165°F (74ºC).
4. Transfer the mixture to a serving platter and drizzle with the fresh lime juice. Serve with the lettuce leaves and top with the guacamole.

Per Serving
calories: 330 | fat: 22g | protein: 25g | carbs: 8g | net carbs: 3g | fiber: 5g

Chicken Croquettes with Creole Sauce

Prep time: 10 minutes | Cook time: 10 minutes | Serves 4

2 cups shredded cooked chicken
½ cup shredded Cheddar cheese
2 eggs
¼ cup finely chopped onion
¼ cup almond meal
1 tablespoon poultry seasoning
Olive oil

Creole Sauce:
¼ cup mayonnaise
¼ cup sour cream
1½ teaspoons Dijon mustard
1½ teaspoons fresh lemon juice
½ teaspoon garlic powder
½ teaspoon Creole seasoning

1. In a large bowl, combine the chicken, Cheddar, eggs, onion, almond meal, and poultry seasoning. Stir gently until thoroughly combined. Cover and refrigerate for 30 minutes.
2. Meanwhile, to make the Creole sauce: In a small bowl, whisk together the mayonnaise, sour cream, Dijon mustard, lemon juice, garlic powder, and Creole seasoning until thoroughly combined. Cover and refrigerate until ready to serve.
3. Preheat the air fryer to 400°F (205ºC). Divide the chicken mixture into 8 portions and shape into patties.
4. Working in batches if necessary, arrange the patties in a single layer in the air fryer basket and coat both sides lightly with olive oil. Pausing halfway through the cooking time to flip the patties, air fry for 10 minutes, or until lightly browned and the cheese is melted. Serve with the Creole sauce.

Per Serving
calories: 380 | fat: 28g | protein: 29g | carbs: 4g | net carbs: 4g | fiber: 0g

Chicken Thighs with Creamy Rosemary Sauce, page 58

Ranch Chicken Wings, page 75

Spiced Chicken Thighs, page 63

Lemon Chicken, page 60

Chicken with Secret Spice Rub

Prep time: 15 minutes | Cook time: 30 minutes | Serves 4

1 (4-pound / 1.8 kg) chicken, giblets removed
½ onion, quartered
1 tablespoon olive oil
Secret Spice Rub:
2 teaspoons salt
1 teaspoon paprika
½ teaspoon onion powder
½ teaspoon garlic powder
½ teaspoon dried thyme
½ teaspoon freshly ground black pepper
¼ teaspoon cayenne

1. Preheat the air fryer to 350°F (180ºC).
2. Use paper towels to blot the chicken dry. Stuff the chicken with the onion. Rub the chicken with the oil.
3. To make the spice rub: In a small bowl, combine the salt, paprika, onion powder, garlic powder, thyme, black pepper, and cayenne, stir until thoroughly combined. Sprinkle the chicken with the spice rub until thoroughly coated.
4. Place the chicken breast side down in the air fryer basket. Air fry the chicken for 30 minutes. Use tongs to carefully flip the chicken over and air fry for an additional 30 minutes, or until the temperature of a thermometer inserted into the thickest part of the chicken registers 165°F (74ºC).
5. Let the chicken rest for 10 minutes. Discard the onion and serve.

Per Serving
calories: 500 | fat: 27g | protein: 61g | carbs: 2g | net carbs: 0g | fiber: 2g

Duo-Cheese Chicken with Jalapeños

Prep time: 10 minutes | Cook time: 14 to 17 minutes | Serves 8

2 pounds (907 g) boneless, skinless chicken breasts or thighs
Sea salt
Freshly ground black pepper
8 ounces (227 g) cream cheese, at room temperature
4 ounces (113 g) Cheddar cheese, shredded
2 jalapeños, seeded and diced
1 teaspoon minced garlic
Avocado oil spray

1. Place the chicken in a large zip-top bag or between two pieces of plastic wrap. Using a meat mallet or heavy skillet, pound the chicken until it is about ¼-inch thick. Season both sides of the chicken with salt and pepper.
2. In a medium bowl, combine the cream cheese, Cheddar cheese, jalapeños, and garlic. Divide the mixture among the chicken pieces. Roll up each piece from the long side, tucking in the ends as you go. Secure with toothpicks.
3. Set the air fryer to 350°F (180ºC). Spray the outside of the chicken with oil. Place the chicken in a single layer in the air fryer basket, working in batches if necessary, and cook for 7 minutes. Flip the chicken and cook for another 7 to 10 minutes, until an instant-read thermometer reads 160°F (71ºC).

Per Serving
calories: 264 | fat: 17g | protein: 28g | carbs: 2g | net carbs: 1g | fiber: 1g

Chicken Kebabs

Prep time: 15 minutes | Cook time: 20 minutes | Serves 5

¼ diced red onion
½ diced zucchini
½ diced red pepper
½ diced green pepper
½ diced yellow pepper
1 teaspoon BBQ seasoning
1 tablespoon chicken seasoning
2 tablespoons coconut aminos
5 grape tomatoes
16 ounces (454 g) 1-inch cubed chicken breasts
Salt & pepper, to taste
Nonstick cooking oil spray

1. Pat dry the chicken breasts then combine the BBQ seasoning, chicken seasoning, salt, pepper and coconut aminos together.
2. Generously coat the chicken cubes with the mixture then set aside to marinate for about an hour.
3. Sew the marinated chicken cubes onto the wooden skewers.
4. Alternatively layer the chicken cubes with onions, zucchini, pepper and top each skewer with a grape tomato.
5. Spray the layered skewers with the cooking oil then line the fryer basket with parchment paper and fit in a small grill rack.
6. Place the skewers on the grill rack then air fry at 350°F (180ºC) for 10 minutes.
7. Flip the skewers over and fry for an additional 10 minutes.
8. Allow the chicken to cool for a bit then serve and enjoy with any sauce of choice.

Per Serving
calories: 255 | fat: 12g | protein: 25g | carbs: 6g | net carbs: 5g | fiber: 1g

Traditional Kung Pao Chicken

Prep time: 15 minutes | Cook time: 20 minutes | Serves 4

1½ pounds (680 g) chicken breast, halved
1 tablespoon lemon juice
2 tablespoons mirin
¼ cup milk
2 tablespoons soy sauce
1 tablespoon olive oil
1 teaspoon ginger, peeled and grated
2 garlic cloves, minced
½ teaspoon salt
½ teaspoon Szechuan pepper
½ teaspoon xanthan gum

1. In a large ceramic dish, place the chicken, lemon juice, mirin, milk, soy sauce, olive oil, ginger, and garlic. Let it marinate for 30 minutes in your refrigerator.
2. Spritz the sides and bottom of the cooking basket with a nonstick cooking spray. Arrange the chicken in the cooking basket and cook at 370ºF for 10 minutes.
3. Turn over the chicken, baste with the reserved marinade and cook for 4 minutes longer. Taste for doneness, season with salt and pepper, and reserve.
4. Add the marinade to the preheated skillet over medium heat, add in xanthan gum. Let it cook for 5 to 6 minutes until the sauce thickens.
5. Spoon the sauce over the reserved chicken and serve immediately.

Per Serving
calories: 358 | fat: 21g | protein: 37g | carbs: 4g | net carbs: 3g | fiber: 1g

Gingery Parmesan Chicken with Bacon

Prep time: 10 minutes | Cook time: 13 minutes | Serves 2

4 rashers smoked bacon
2 chicken fillets
½ teaspoon coarse sea salt
¼ teaspoon black pepper, preferably freshly ground
1 teaspoon garlic, minced
1 (2-inch) piece ginger,
peeled and minced
1 teaspoon black mustard seeds
1 teaspoon mild curry powder
½ cup coconut milk
½ cup Parmesan cheese, grated

1. Start by preheating your Air Fryer to 400ºF (205ºC). Add the smoked bacon and cook in the preheated Air Fryer for 5 to 7 minutes. Reserve.
2. In a mixing bowl, place the chicken fillets, salt, black pepper, garlic, ginger, mustard seeds, curry powder,

and milk. Let it marinate in your refrigerator for about 30 minutes.
3. In another bowl, place the grated Parmesan cheese.
4. Dredge the chicken fillets through the Parmesan mixture and transfer them to the cooking basket. Reduce the temperature to 380ºF (193ºC) and cook the chicken for 6 minutes.
5. Turn them over and cook for a further 6 minutes. Repeat the process until you have run out of ingredients.
6. Serve with reserved bacon. Enjoy!

Per Serving
calories: 612 | fat: 44g | protein: 16g | carbs: 38g | net carbs: 37g | fiber: 1g

Lemony Chicken Thighs with Greek Yogurt

Prep time: 10 minutes | Cook time: 20 minutes | Serves 6

¼ cup plain Greek yogurt
2 cloves garlic, minced
1 tablespoon grated fresh ginger
½ teaspoon ground cayenne
½ teaspoon ground turmeric
½ teaspoon garam masala
1 teaspoon ground cumin
1 teaspoon salt
2 pounds (907 g) boneless chicken thighs, skin on
2 tablespoons chopped fresh cilantro
1 lemon, cut into 6 wedges
½ sweet onion, sliced

1. In a small bowl, combine the yogurt, garlic, ginger, cayenne, turmeric, garam masala, cumin, and salt. Whisk until thoroughly combined.
2. Transfer the yogurt mixture to a large resealable bag. Add the chicken, seal the bag, and massage the bag to ensure chicken is evenly coated. Refrigerate for 1 hour (or up to 8 hours).
3. Preheat the air fryer to 360°F (182ºC).
4. Remove the chicken from the marinade (discard the marinade) and arrange in a single layer in the air fryer basket. Pausing halfway through the cooking time to flip the chicken, air fry for 15 to 20 minutes, until a thermometer inserted into the thickest part registers 165°F (74ºC).
5. Transfer the chicken to a serving platter. Top with the cilantro and serve with the lemon wedges and sliced onion.

Per Serving
calories: 350 | fat: 22g | protein: 35g | carbs: 1g | net carbs: 1g | fiber: 0g

Chicken with Bacon and Tomato

Prep time: 25 minutes | Cook time: 10 minutes | Serves 4

4 medium-sized skin-on chicken drumsticks
1½ teaspoons herbs de Provence
Salt and pepper, to taste
1 tablespoon rice vinegar
2 tablespoons olive oil
2 garlic cloves, crushed
12 ounces (340 g) crushed canned tomatoes
1 small-size leek, thinly sliced
2 slices smoked bacon, chopped

1. Sprinkle the chicken drumsticks with herbs de Provence, salt and pepper, then, drizzle them with rice vinegar and olive oil.
2. Cook in the baking pan at 360ºF (182ºC) for 8 to 10 minutes.
3. Pause the Air Fryer, stir in the remaining ingredients and continue to cook for 15 minutes longer, make sure to check them periodically. Bon appétit!

Per Serving

calories: 296 | fat: 13g | protein: 34g | carbs: 7g | net carbs: 5g | fiber: 2g

Chicken with Keto Vegetables

Prep time: 25 minutes | Cook time: 22 minutes | Serves 4

3 eggs, whisked
½ teaspoon dried marjoram
⅓ cup Fontina cheese, grated
1 teaspoon sea salt
⅓ teaspoon red pepper flakes, crushed
2 cups leftover keto vegetables
½ red onion, thinly sliced
2 cups cooked chicken, shredded or chopped
3 cloves garlic, finely minced

1. Simply mix all of the above ingredients, except for cheese, with a wide spatula.
2. Scrape the mixture into a previously greased baking dish.
3. Set your Air Fryer to cook at 365ºF (185ºC) for 22 minutes. Air-fry until everything is bubbling. Serve warm topped with grated Fontina cheese. Bon appétit!

Per Serving

calories: 361 | fat: 29g | protein: 1g | carbs: 24g | net carbs: 23g | fiber: 1g

Turkey Sliders with Chive Mayonnaise

Prep time: 15 minutes | Cook time: 15 minutes | Serves 6

For the Turkey Sliders:
¾ pound (340 g) turkey mince
¼ cup pickled jalapeno, chopped
1 tablespoon oyster sauce
1-2 cloves garlic, minced
1 tablespoon chopped fresh cilantro
2 tablespoons chopped scallions
Sea salt and ground black pepper, to savor
For the Chive Mayo:
1 cup mayonnaise
1 tablespoon chives
1 teaspoon salt
Zest of 1 lime

1. In a mixing bowl, thoroughly combine all ingredients for the turkey patties.
2. Mold the mixture into 6 even-sized slider patties. Then, air-fry them at 365ºF for 15 minutes.
3. Meanwhile, make the Chive Mayonnaise by mixing the rest of the above ingredients. Serve warm.

Per Serving

calories: 252 | fat: 16g | protein: 7g | carbs: 30g | net carbs: 29g | fiber: 1g

Turkey Meatballs with Pecorino Romano

Prep time: 15 minutes | Cook time: 7 minutes | Serves 6

1 pound (454 g) ground turkey
1 tablespoon fresh mint leaves, finely chopped
1 teaspoon onion powder
1½ teaspoons garlic paste
1 teaspoon crushed red pepper flakes
¼ cup melted butter
¾ teaspoon fine sea salt
¼ cup grated Pecorino Romano

1. Simply place all of the above ingredients into the mixing dish, mix until everything is well incorporated.
2. Use an ice cream scoop to shape the meat into golf ball sized meatballs.
3. Air fry the meatballs at 380ºF for approximately 7 minutes, work in batches, shaking them to ensure evenness of cooking.
4. Serve with a simple tomato sauce garnished with fresh basil leaves. Bon appétit!

Per Serving

calories: 241 | fat: 18g | protein: 8g | carbs: 21g | net carbs: 20g | fiber: 1g

Pizza Chicken with Pepperoni

Prep time: 5 minutes | Cook time: 15 minutes | Serves 4

4 small-sized chicken breasts, boneless and skinless
¼ cup pizza sauce
½ cup Colby cheese, shredded
16 slices pepperoni
Salt and pepper, to savor
1½ tablespoons olive oil
1½ tablespoons dried oregano

1. Carefully flatten out the chicken breast using a rolling pin.
2. Divide the ingredients among four chicken fillets. Roll the chicken fillets with the stuffing and seal them using a small skewer or two toothpicks.
3. Roast in the preheated Air Fryer grill pan for 13 to 15 minutes at 370ºF. Bon appétit!

Per Serving
calories: 561 | fat: 38g | protein: 9g | carbs: 22g | net carbs: 21g | fiber: 1g

Lemon-Crusted Turkey

Prep time: 1 hour | Cook time: 58 minutes | Serves 4

2 tablespoons olive oil
2 pounds (907 g) turkey breasts, bone-in skin-on
Coarse sea salt and ground black pepper, to
taste
1 teaspoon fresh basil leaves, chopped
2 tablespoons lemon zest, grated

1. Rub olive oil on all sides of the turkey breasts, sprinkle with salt, pepper, basil, and lemon zest.
2. Place the turkey breasts skin side up on a parchment-lined cooking basket.
3. Cook in the preheated Air Fryer at 330ºF (166ºC) for 30 minutes. Now, turn them over and cook for an additional 28 minutes.
4. Serve with lemon wedges, if desired. Bon appétit!

Per Serving
calories: 416 | fat: 22g | protein: 49g | carbs: 0g | net carbs: 0g | fiber: 0g

White Wine Chicken Breast

Prep time: 30 minutes | Cook time: 28 minutes | Serves 4

½ teaspoon grated fresh ginger
⅓ cup coconut milk
½ teaspoon sea salt flakes
3 medium-sized boneless chicken breasts, cut into small pieces
1½ tablespoons sesame
oil
3 green garlic stalks, finely chopped
½ cup dry white wine
½ teaspoon fresh thyme leaves, minced
⅓ teaspoon freshly cracked black pepper

1. Warm the sesame oil in a deep sauté pan over a moderate heat. Then, sauté the green garlic until just fragrant.
2. Remove the pan from the heat and pour in the coconut milk and the white wine. After that, add the thyme, sea salt, fresh ginger, and freshly cracked black pepper. Scrape this mixture into a baking dish.
3. Stir in the chicken chunks.
4. Cook in the preheated Air Fryer for 28 minutes at 335ºF (168ºC). Serve on individual plates and eat warm.

Per Serving
calories: 471 | fat: 28g | protein: 12g | carbs: 31g | net carbs: 31g | fiber: 0g

Turkey with Tabasco Sauce

Prep time: 15 minutes | Cook time: 22 minutes | Serves 6

1½ pounds (680g) ground turkey
6 whole eggs, well beaten
⅓ teaspoon smoked paprika
2 egg whites, beaten
Tabasco sauce, for
drizzling
2 tablespoons sesame oil
2 leeks, chopped
3 cloves garlic, finely minced
1 teaspoon ground black pepper
½ teaspoon sea salt

1. Warm the oil in a pan over moderate heat, then, sweat the leeks and garlic until tender, stir periodically.
2. Next, grease 6 oven safe ramekins with pan spray. Divide the sautéed mixture among six ramekins.
3. In a bowl, beat the eggs and egg whites using a wire whisk. Stir in the smoked paprika, salt and black pepper, whisk until everything is thoroughly combined. Divide the egg mixture among the ramekins.
4. Air-fry approximately 22 minutes at 345ºF (174ºC). Drizzle Tabasco sauce over each portion and serve.

Per Serving
calories: 298 | fat: 15g | protein: 6g | carbs: 25g | net carbs: 24g | fiber: 1g

Turkey and Pork Meatballs with Manchego

Prep time: 10 minutes | Cook time: 7 minutes | Serves 4

1 pound (454 g) ground turkey
½ pound (227 g) ground pork
1 egg, well beaten
1 teaspoon dried basil
1 teaspoon dried rosemary
¼ cup Manchego cheese, grated
2 tablespoons yellow onions, finely chopped
1 teaspoon fresh garlic, finely chopped
Sea salt and ground black pepper, to taste

1. In a mixing bowl, combine all the ingredients until everything is well incorporated.
2. Shape the mixture into 1-inch balls.
3. Cook the meatballs in the preheated Air Fryer at 380º for 7 minutes. Shake halfway through the cooking time. Work in batches.
4. Serve with your favorite pasta. Bon appétit!

Per Serving

calories: 386 | fat: 24g | protein: 15g | carbs: 31g | net carbs: 30g | fiber: 1g

Turkey Kabobs

Prep time: 15 minutes | Cook time: 10 minutes | Serves 8

1 cup Parmesan cheese, grated
1½ cups of water
14 ounces (397 g) ground turkey
2 small eggs, beaten
1 teaspoon ground ginger
2½ tablespoons olive oil
1 cup chopped fresh
parsley
2 tablespoons almond meal
¾ teaspoon salt
1 heaping teaspoon fresh rosemary, finely chopped
½ teaspoon ground allspice

1. Mix all of the above ingredients in a bowl. Knead the mixture with your hands.
2. Then, take small portions and gently roll them into balls.
3. Now, preheat your Air Fryer to 380ºF (193ºC). Air fry for 8 to 10 minutes in the Air Fryer basket. Serve on a serving platter with skewers and eat with your favorite dipping sauce.

Per Serving

calories: 185 | fat: 13g | protein: 14g | carbs: 3g | net carbs: 2g | fiber: 1g

Rosemary Chicken Drumettes with Almond Meal

Prep time: 15 minutes | Cook time: 22 minutes | Serves 3

⅓ cup almond meal
½ teaspoon ground white pepper
1 teaspoon seasoning salt
1 teaspoon garlic paste
1 teaspoon rosemary
1 whole egg plus 1 egg white
6 chicken drumettes
1 heaping tablespoon fresh chives, chopped

1. Start by preheating your Air Fryer to 390º (199ºC).
2. Mix the almond meal with white pepper, salt, garlic paste, and rosemary in a small-sized bowl.
3. In another bowl, beat the eggs until frothy.
4. Dip the chicken into the flour mixture, then into the beaten eggs, coat with the flour mixture one more time.
5. Cook the chicken drumettes for 22 minutes. Serve warm, garnished with chives.

Per Serving

calories: 319 | fat: 11g | protein: 4g | carbs: 22g | net carbs: 21g | fiber: 1g

Ranch Chicken Wings

Prep time: 10 minutes | Cook time: 11 minutes | Serves 3

¼ cup almond meal
¼ cup flaxseed meal
2 tablespoons butter, melted
6 tablespoons Parmesan cheese, preferably
freshly grated
1 tablespoon Ranch seasoning mix
2 tablespoons oyster sauce
6 chicken wings, bone-in

1. Start by preheating your Air Fryer to 370ºF.
2. In a resealable bag, place the almond meal, flaxseed meal, butter, Parmesan, Ranch seasoning mix, and oyster sauce. Add the chicken wings and shake to coat on all sides.
3. Arrange the chicken wings in the Air Fryer basket. Spritz the chicken wings with a nonstick cooking spray.
4. Cook for 11 minutes. Turn them over and cook for an additional 11 minutes. Serve warm with your favorite dipping sauce, if desired. Enjoy!

Per Serving

calories: 285 | fat: 20g | protein: 14g | carbs: 27g | net carbs: 26g | fiber: 1g

Chili Chicken Sliders with Scallions

Prep time: 15 minutes | Cook time: 18 minutes | Serves 4

⅓ teaspoon paprika
⅓ cup scallions, peeled and chopped
3 cloves garlic, peeled and minced
1 teaspoon ground black pepper, or to taste
½ teaspoon fresh basil, minced
1½ cups chicken, minced
1½ tablespoons coconut aminos
½ teaspoon grated fresh ginger
½ tablespoon chili sauce
1 teaspoon salt

1. Thoroughly combine all ingredients in a mixing dish. Then, form into 4 patties.
2. Cook in the preheated Air Fryer for 18 minutes at 355ºF.
3. Garnish with toppings of choice. Bon appétit!

Per Serving
calories: 366 | fat: 10g | protein: 12g | carbs: 35g | net carbs: 34g | fiber: 1g

Cheesy and Spicy Turkey Meatloaf

Prep time: 20 minutes | Cook time: 50 minutes | Serves 6

2 pounds (907 g) turkey breasts, ground
½ pound (227 g) Cheddar cheese, cubed
½ cup turkey stock
⅓ teaspoon hot paprika
3 eggs, lightly beaten
1½ tablespoon olive oil
2 cloves garlic, pressed
1½ teaspoons dried
rosemary
½ cup yellow onion, chopped
⅓ cup ground almonds
½ teaspoon black pepper
A few dashes of Tabasco sauce
1 teaspoon seasoned salt
½ cup tomato sauce

1. Heat the olive oil in a medium-sized saucepan that is placed over a moderate flame, now, sauté the onions, garlic, and dried rosemary until just tender, or for about 3 to 4 minutes.
2. In the meantime, set the Air Fryer to cook at 385ºF.
3. Place all the ingredients, minus the tomato sauce, in a mixing dish together with the sautéed mixture, thoroughly mix to combine.
4. Shape into meatloaf and top with the tomato sauce. Air-fry for 47 minutes. Bon appétit!

Per Serving
calories: 455 | fat: 26g | protein: 46g | carbs: 8g | net carbs: 7g | fiber: 1g

Chicken Breasts with Lime

Prep time: 10 minutes | Cook time: 26 minutes | Serves 4

½ teaspoon stone-ground mustard
½ teaspoon minced fresh oregano
⅓ cup freshly squeezed lime juice
2 small-sized chicken breasts, skin-on
1 teaspoon kosher salt
1teaspoon freshly cracked mixed peppercorns

1. Preheat your Air Fryer to 345ºF.
2. Toss all of the above ingredients in a medium-sized mixing dish, allow it to marinate overnight.
3. Cook in the preheated Air Fryer for 26 minutes. Bon appétit!

Per Serving
calories: 255 | fat: 14g | protein: 8g | carbs: 12g | net carbs: 11g | fiber: 1g

Turkey with Gravy

Prep time: 50 minutes | Cook time: 20 minutes | Serves 6

2 teaspoons butter, softened
1 teaspoon dried sage
2 sprigs rosemary, chopped
1 teaspoon salt
¼ teaspoon freshly ground black pepper, or
more to taste
1 whole turkey breast
2 tablespoons turkey broth
2 tablespoons whole-grain mustard
1 tablespoon butter

1. Start by preheating your Air Fryer to 360ºF (182ºC).
2. To make the rub, combine 2 tablespoons of butter, sage, rosemary, salt, and pepper, mix well to combine and spread it evenly over the surface of the turkey breast.
3. Roast for 20 minutes in an Air Fryer cooking basket. Flip the turkey breast over and cook for a further 15 to 16 minutes. Now, flip it back over and roast for 12 minutes or more.
4. While the turkey is roasting, whisk the other ingredients in a saucepan. After that, spread the gravy all over the turkey breast.
5. Let the turkey rest for a few minutes before carving. Bon appétit!

Per Serving
calories: 384 | fat: 8g | protein: 131g | carbs: 2g | net carbs: 1g | fiber: 1g

Chicken with Brussels Sprouts

Prep time: 30 minutes | Cook time: 35 minutes | Serves 2

2 chicken legs
½ teaspoon paprika
½ teaspoon kosher salt
½ teaspoon black pepper
½ pound (227g) Brussels sprouts
1 teaspoon dill, fresh or dried

1. Start by preheating your Air Fryer to 370ºF (188ºC).
2. Now, season your chicken with paprika, salt, and pepper. Transfer the chicken legs to the cooking basket. Cook for 10 minutes.
3. Flip the chicken legs and cook for an additional 10 minutes. Reserve.
4. Add the Brussels sprouts to the cooking basket, sprinkle with dill. Cook at 380ºF (193ºC) for 15 minutes, shaking the basket halfway through.
5. Serve with the reserved chicken legs. Bon appétit!

Per Serving

calories: 365 | fat: 20g | protein: 14g | carbs: 25g | net carbs: 21g | fiber: 4g

Herbed Turkey Breasts with Mustard

Prep time: 1 hour | Cook time: 53 minutes | Serves 4

½ teaspoon dried thyme
1½ pounds (680g) turkey breasts
½ teaspoon dried sage
3 whole star anise
1½ tablespoons olive oil
1½ tablespoons hot mustard
1 teaspoon smoked cayenne pepper
1 teaspoon fine sea salt

1. Set your Air Fryer to cook at 365ºF (185ºC).
2. Brush the turkey breast with olive oil and sprinkle with seasonings.
3. Cook at 365ºF (185ºC) for 45 minutes, turning twice. Now, pause the machine and spread the cooked breast with the hot mustard.
4. Air-fry for 6 to 8 more minutes. Let it rest before slicing and serving. Bon appétit!

Per Serving

calories: 321 | fat: 17g | protein: 3g | carbs: 21g | net carbs: 20g | fiber: 1g

Turkey Sausage with Cauliflower

Prep time: 45 minutes | Cook time: 28 minutes | Serves 4

1 pound (454 g) ground turkey
1 teaspoon garlic pepper
1 teaspoon garlic powder
⅓ teaspoon dried oregano
½ teaspoon salt
⅓ cup onions, chopped
½ head cauliflower, broken into florets
⅓ teaspoon dried basil
½ teaspoon dried thyme, chopped

1. In a mixing bowl, thoroughly combine the ground turkey, garlic pepper, garlic powder, oregano, salt, and onion, stir well to combine. Spritz a nonstick skillet with pan spray, form the mixture into 4 sausages.
2. Then, cook the sausage over medium heat until they are no longer pink, for approximately 12 minutes.
3. Arrange the cauliflower florets at the bottom of a baking dish. Sprinkle with thyme and basil, spritz with pan spray. Top with the turkey sausages.
4. Roast for 28 minutes at 375ºF (190ºC), turning once halfway through. Eat warm.

Per Serving

calories: 289 | fat: 25g | protein: 11g | carbs: 3g | net carbs: 2g | fiber: 1g

Simple Turkey Breast

Prep time: 5 minutes | Cook time: 45 to 55 minutes | Serves 10

1 tablespoon sea salt
1 teaspoon paprika
1 teaspoon onion powder
1 teaspoon garlic powder
½ teaspoon freshly
ground black pepper
4 pounds (1.8 kg) bone-in, skin-on turkey breast
2 tablespoons unsalted butter, melted

1. In a small bowl, combine the salt, paprika, onion powder, garlic powder, and pepper.
2. Sprinkle the seasonings all over the turkey. Brush the turkey with some of the melted butter.
3. Set the air fryer to 350°F (180ºC). Place the turkey in the air fryer basket, skin-side down, and cook for 25 minutes.
4. Flip the turkey and brush it with the remaining butter. Continue cooking for another 20 to 30 minutes, until an instant-read thermometer reads 160°F.
5. Remove the turkey breast from the air fryer. Tent a piece of aluminum foil over the turkey, and allow it to rest for about 5 minutes before serving.

Per Serving

calories: 278 | fat: 14g | protein: 34g | carbs: 2g | net carbs: 1g | fiber: 1g

Chicken Sausage with Nestled Eggs and Pepper

Prep time: 10 minutes | Cook time: 17 minutes | Serves 6

6 eggs
2 bell peppers, seeded and sliced
1 teaspoon dried oregano
1 teaspoon hot paprika
1 teaspoon freshly

cracked black pepper
6 chicken sausages
1 teaspoon sea salt
1½ shallots, cut into wedges
1 teaspoon dried basil

1. Take four ramekins and divide chicken sausages, shallot, and bell pepper among those ramekins. Cook at 315ºF for about 12 minutes.
2. Now, crack an egg into each ramekin. Sprinkle the eggs with hot paprika, basil, oregano, salt, and cracked black pepper. Cook for 5 more minutes at 405ºF.
3. Bon appétit!

Per Serving
calories: 211 | fat: 15g | protein: 15g | carbs: 26g | net carbs: 25g | fiber: 1g

Nutty Turkey Breast

Prep time: 15 minutes | Cook time: 28 minutes | Serves 2

1½ tablespoons coconut aminos
½ tablespoon xanthan gum
2 bay leaves
⅓ cup dry sherry
1½ tablespoons chopped walnuts
1 teaspoon shallot powder

1 pound (454 g) turkey breasts, sliced
1 teaspoon garlic powder
2 teaspoons olive oil
½ teaspoon onion salt
½ teaspoon red pepper flakes, crushed
1 teaspoon ground black pepper

1. Begin by preheating your Air Fryer to 395ºF. Place all ingredients, minus chopped walnuts, in a mixing bowl and let them marinate for at least 1 hour.
2. After that, cook the marinated turkey breast for approximately 23 minutes or until heated through.
3. Pause the machine, scatter chopped walnuts over the top and air-fry for an additional 5 minutes. Bon appétit!

Per Serving
calories: 395 | fat: 20g | protein: 12g | carbs: 31g | net carbs: 30g | fiber: 1g

Easy Turkey Drumsticks

Prep time: 25 minutes | Cook time: 23 minutes | Serves 2

1 tablespoon red curry paste
½ teaspoon cayenne pepper
1½ tablespoons minced ginger

2 turkey drumsticks
¼ cup coconut milk
1 teaspoon kosher salt, or more to taste
⅓ teaspoon ground pepper, to more to taste

1. First of all, place turkey drumsticks with all ingredients in your refrigerator, let it marinate overnight.
2. Cook turkey drumsticks at 380ºF (193ºC) for 23 minutes, make sure to flip them over at half-time. Serve with the salad on the side.

Per Serving
calories: 298 | fat: 16g | protein: 12g | carbs: 25g | net carbs: 22g | fiber: 3g

Turkey with Mustard Sauce

Prep time: 13 minutes | Cook time: 18 minutes | Serves 4

½ teaspoon cumin powder
2 pounds (907 g) turkey breasts, quartered
2 cloves garlic, smashed
½ teaspoon hot paprika
2 tablespoons melted butter
1 teaspoon fine sea salt

Freshly cracked mixed peppercorns, to taste
Fresh juice of 1 lemon
For the Mustard Sauce:
1½ tablespoons mayonnaise
1½ cups Greek yogurt
½ tablespoon yellow mustard

1. Grab a medium-sized mixing dish and combine together the garlic and melted butter, rub this mixture evenly over the surface of the turkey.
2. Add the cumin powder, followed by paprika, salt, peppercorns, and lemon juice. Place in your refrigerator for at least 55 minutes.
3. Set your Air Fryer to cook at 375ºF (190ºC). Roast the turkey for 18 minutes, turning halfway through, roast in batches.
4. In the meantime, make the mustard sauce by mixing all ingredients for the sauce. Serve warm roasted turkey with the mustard sauce. Bon appétit!

Per Serving
calories: 471 | fat: 23g | protein: 16g | carbs: 34g | net carbs: 33g | fiber: 1g

Turkey Wings Marinated with White Wine

Prep time: 10 minutes | Cook time: 28 minutes | Serves 4

1 teaspoon freshly cracked pink peppercorns
1½ pounds (680 g) turkey wings, cut into smaller pieces

2 teaspoons garlic powder
⅓ cup white wine
½ teaspoon garlic salt
½ tablespoon coriander, ground

1. Toss all of the above ingredients in a mixing dish. Let it marinate for at least 3 hours.
2. Air-fry turkey wings for 28 minutes at 355ºF. Bon appétit!

Per Serving

calories: 346 | fat: 20g | protein: 35g | carbs: 2g | net carbs: 1.9g | fiber: 0.1g

Ham Chicken with Cheese

Prep time: 15 minutes | Cook time: 25 minutes | Serves 4

¼ cup unsalted butter, softened
4 ounces (113 g) cream cheese, softened
1½ teaspoons Dijon mustard
2 tablespoons white wine vinegar

¼ cup water
2 cups shredded cooked chicken
¼ pound (113 g) ham, chopped
4 ounces (113 g) sliced Swiss or Provolone cheese

1. Preheat the air fryer to 380°F (193ºC). Lightly coat a 6-cup casserole dish that will fit in the air fryer, such as an 8-inch round pan, with olive oil and set aside.
2. In a large bowl and using an electric mixer, combine the butter, cream cheese, Dijon mustard, and vinegar. With the motor running on low speed, slowly add the water and beat until smooth. Set aside.
3. Arrange an even layer of chicken in the bottom of the prepared pan, followed by the ham. Spread the butter and cream cheese mixture on top of the ham, followed by the cheese slices on the top layer. Air fry for 20 to 25 minutes until warmed through and the cheese has browned.

Per Serving

calories: 480 | fat: 36g | protein: 34g | carbs: 4g | net carbs: 4g | fiber: 0g

Bacon-Wrapped Turkey with Asiago

Prep time: 20 minutes | Cook time: 13 minutes | Serves 12

1½ small-sized turkey breast, chop into 12 pieces
12 thin slices Asiago cheese

Paprika, to taste
Fine sea salt and ground black pepper, to taste
12 rashers bacon

1. Lay out the bacon rashers, place 1 slice of Asiago cheese on each bacon piece.
2. Top with turkey, season with paprika, salt, and pepper, and roll them up, secure with a cocktail stick.
3. Air-fry at 365ºF (185ºC) for 13 minutes. Bon appétit!

Per Serving

calories: 568 | fat: 34g | protein: 5g | carbs: 30g | net carbs: 29g | fiber: 1g

Herbed Chicken Leg

Prep time: 5 minutes | Cook time: 23 to 27 minutes | Serves 6

½ cup avocado oil
2 teaspoons smoked paprika
1 teaspoon sea salt
1 teaspoon garlic powder
½ teaspoon dried rosemary

½ teaspoon dried thyme
½ teaspoon freshly ground black pepper
2 pounds (907 g) bone-in, skin-on chicken leg quarters

1. In a blender or small bowl, combine the avocado oil, smoked paprika, salt, garlic powder, rosemary, thyme, and black pepper.
2. Place the chicken in a shallow dish or large zip-top bag. Pour the marinade over the chicken, making sure all the legs are coated. Cover and marinate for at least 2 hours or overnight.
3. Place the chicken in a single layer in the air fryer basket, working in batches if necessary. Set the air fryer to 400°F (205ºC) and cook for 15 minutes. Flip the chicken legs, then reduce the temperature to 350°F (180ºC). Cook for 8 to 12 minutes or more, until an instant-read thermometer reads 160°F (71ºC) when inserted into the thickest piece of chicken.
4. Allow them to rest for 5 to 10 minutes before serving.

Per Serving

calories: 569 | fat: 53g | protein: 23g | carbs: 2g | net carbs: 1g | fiber: 1g

Rosemary Chicken Sausage with Dijon Sauce

Prep time: 5 minutes | Cook time: 15 minutes | Serves 4

4 chicken sausages
¼ cup mayonnaise
2 tablespoons Dijon mustard

1 tablespoon balsamic vinegar
½ teaspoon dried rosemary

1. Arrange the sausages on the grill pan and transfer it to the preheated Air Fryer.
2. Grill the sausages at 350ºF for approximately 13 minutes. Turn them halfway through cooking.
3. Meanwhile, prepare the sauce by mixing the remaining ingredients with a wire whisk. Serve the warm sausages with chilled Dijon sauce. Enjoy!

Per Serving

calories: 575 | fat: 52g | protein: 8g | carbs: 33g | net carbs: 32g | fiber: 1g

---

Rosemary Turkey Roast

Prep time: 50 minutes | Cook time: 45 minutes | Serves 6

2½ pounds (1.1kg) turkey breasts
1 tablespoon fresh rosemary, chopped
1 teaspoon sea salt

½ teaspoon ground black pepper
1 onion, chopped
1 celery stalk, chopped

1. Start by preheating your Air Fryer to 360ºF (182ºC). Spritz the sides and bottom of the cooking basket with a nonstick cooking spray.
2. Place the turkey in the cooking basket. Add the rosemary, salt, and black pepper. Cook for 30 minutes in the preheated Air Fryer.
3. Add the onion and celery and cook for an additional 15 minutes. Bon appétit!

Per Serving

calories: 316 | fat: 14g | protein: 41g | carbs: 2g | net carbs: 1g | fiber: 1g

---

Roasted Chicken Leg with Leeks

Prep time: 20 minutes | Cook time: 18 minutes | Serves 6

2 leeks, sliced
2 large-sized tomatoes, chopped
3 cloves garlic, minced
½ teaspoon dried oregano

6 chicken legs, boneless and skinless
½ teaspoon smoked cayenne pepper
2 tablespoons olive oil
A freshly ground nutmeg

1. In a mixing dish, thoroughly combine all ingredients, minus the leeks. Place in the refrigerator and let it marinate overnight.
2. Lay the leeks onto the bottom of an Air Fryer cooking basket. Top with the chicken legs.
3. Roast chicken legs at 375ºF (190ºC) for 18 minutes, turning halfway through. Serve with hoisin sauce.

Per Serving

calories: 390 | fat: 15g | protein: 12g | carbs: 7g | net carbs: 6g | fiber: 1g

Chapter 6 Fish and Seafood

Cauliflower and Shrimp Casserole

Prep time: 10 minutes | Cook time: 22 minutes | Serves 4

1 pound (454 g) shrimp cleaned and deveined	2 bell peppers, sliced
2 cups cauliflower, cut into florets	1 shallot, sliced
	2 tablespoons sesame oil
	1 cup tomato paste

1. Start by preheating your Air Fryer to 360ºF. Spritz the baking pan with cooking spray.
2. Now, arrange the shrimp and vegetables in the baking pan. Then, drizzle the sesame oil over the vegetables. Pour the tomato paste over the vegetables.
3. Cook for 10 minutes in the preheated Air Fryer. Stir with a large spoon and cook for a further 12 minutes. Serve warm.

Per Serving

calories: 209 | fat: 7g | protein: 3g | carbs: 16g | net carbs: 14g | fiber: 2g

Cauliflower and White Fish Cakes

Prep time: 10 minutes | Cook time: 13 minutes | Serves 4

½ pound (227 g) cauliflower florets	minced
½ teaspoon English mustard	2 tablespoons sour cream
2 tablespoons butter, room temperature	2 ½ cups cooked white fish
½ tablespoon cilantro,	Salt and freshly cracked black pepper, to savor

1. Boil the cauliflower until tender. Then, purée the cauliflower in your blender. Transfer to a mixing dish.
2. Now, stir in the fish, cilantro, salt, and black pepper.
3. Add the sour cream, English mustard, and butter, mix until everything's well incorporated. Using your hands, shape into patties.
4. Place in the refrigerator for about 2 hours. Cook for 13 minutes at 395ºF. Serve with some extra English mustard.

Per Serving

calories: 285 | fat: 15g | protein: 31g | carbs: 4g | net carbs: 3g | fiber: 1g

Sardinas Fritas

Prep time: 10 minutes | Cook time: 13 minutes | Serves 4

1½ pounds (680 g) sardines, cleaned and rinsed	1 tablespoon Italian seasoning mix
Salt and ground black pepper, to savor	1 tablespoon lemon juice
	1 tablespoon soy sauce
	2 tablespoons olive oil

1. Firstly, pat the sardines dry with a kitchen towel. Add salt, black pepper, Italian seasoning mix, lemon juice, soy sauce, and olive oil, marinate them for 30 minutes.
2. Air-fry the sardines at 350ºF for approximately 5 minutes. Increase the temperature to 385ºF and air-fry them for further 7 to 8 minutes.
3. Then, place the sardines in a nice serving platter. Bon appétit!

Per Serving

calories: 437 | fat: 26g | protein: 43g | carbs: 4g | net carbs: 3g | fiber: 1g

White Fish Fillets with Parmesan

Prep time: 15 minutes | Cook time: 12 minutes | Serves 4

1 cup Parmesan, grated	4 white fish fillets
1 teaspoon garlic powder	Salt and ground black pepper, to taste
½ teaspoon shallot powder	Fresh Italian parsley, to serve
1 egg, well whisked	

1. Place the Parmesan cheese in a shallow bowl.
2. In another bowl, combine the garlic powder, shallot powder, and the beaten egg.
3. Generously season the fish fillets with salt and pepper. Dip each fillet into the beaten egg.
4. Then, roll the fillets over the Parmesan mixture. Set your Air Fryer to cook at 370ºF. Air-fry for 10 to 12 minutes.
5. Serve garnished with fresh parsley and enjoy!

Per Serving

calories: 297 | fat: 8g | protein: 38g | carbs: 5g | net carbs: 4g | fiber: 1g

Herbed Tuna with Parmesan

Prep time: 20 minutes | Cook time: 17 minutes | Serves 4

1 tablespoon butter, melted
1 medium-sized leek, thinly sliced
1 tablespoon chicken stock
1 tablespoon dry white wine
1 pound (454 g) tuna
½ teaspoon red pepper flakes, crushed
Sea salt and ground black pepper, to taste
½ teaspoon dried rosemary
½ teaspoon dried basil
½ teaspoon dried thyme
2 small ripe tomatoes, puréed
1 cup Parmesan cheese, grated

1. Melt ½ tablespoon of butter in a sauté pan over medium-high heat. Now, cook the leek and garlic until tender and aromatic. Add the stock and wine to deglaze the pan.
2. Preheat your Air Fryer to 370ºF (188ºC).
3. Grease a casserole dish with the remaining ½ tablespoon of melted butter. Place the fish in the casserole dish. Add the seasonings. Top with the sautéed leek mixture.
4. Add the tomato purée. Cook for 10 minutes in the preheated Air Fryer. Top with grated Parmesan cheese, cook for an additional 7 minutes until the crumbs are golden. Bon appétit!

Per Serving
calories: 313 | fat: 15g | protein: 34g | carbs: 8g | net carbs: 7g | fiber: 1g

Buttery Scallops

Prep time: 5 minutes | Cook time: 15 minutes | Serves 4

1 pound (454 g) large sea scallops
Sea salt, freshly ground black pepper, to taste
Avocado oil spray
¼ cup (4 tablespoons)
unsalted butter
1 tablespoon freshly squeezed lemon juice
1 teaspoon minced garlic
¼ teaspoon red pepper flakes

1. If your scallops still have the adductor muscles attached, remove them. Pat the scallops dry with a paper towel.
2. Season the scallops with salt and pepper, then place them on a plate and refrigerate for 15 minutes.
3. Spray the air fryer basket with oil, and arrange the scallops in a single layer. Spray the top of the scallops

with oil.
4. Set the air fryer to 350°F (180ºC) and cook for 6 minutes. Flip the scallops and cook for 6 minutes or more, until an instant-read thermometer reads 145° F (63ºC).
5. While the scallops cook, place the butter, lemon juice, garlic, and red pepper flakes in a small ramekin.
6. When the scallops have finished cooking, remove them from the air fryer. Place the ramekin in the air fryer and cook until the butter melts, for about 3 minutes. Stir.
7. Toss the scallops with the warm butter and serve.

Per Serving
calories: 203 | fat: 12g | protein: 19g | carbs: 3g | net carbs: 3g | fiber: 0g

Snapper with Almond Sauce

Prep time: 15 minutes | Cook time: 15 minutes | Serves 4

4 skin-on snapper fillets
Sea salt and ground pepper, to taste
½ cup Parmesan cheese, grated
2 tablespoons fresh cilantro, chopped
½ cup coconut flour
2 tablespoons flaxseed meal
2 medium-sized eggs
For the Almond sauce:
¼ cup almonds
2 garlic cloves, pressed
1 cup tomato paste
1 teaspoon dried dill weed
½ teaspoon salt
¼ teaspoon freshly ground mixed peppercorns
¼ cup olive oil

1. Season fish fillets with sea salt and pepper.
2. In a shallow plate, thoroughly combine the Parmesan cheese and fresh chopped cilantro.
3. In another shallow plate, whisk the eggs until frothy. Place the coconut flour and flaxseed meal in a third plate.
4. Dip the fish fillets in the flour, then in the egg, afterward, coat them with the Parmesan mixture. Set the Air Fryer to cook at 390ºF, air fry for 14 to 16 minutes or until crisp.
5. To make the sauce, chop the almonds in a food processor. Add the remaining sauce ingredients, but not the olive oil.
6. Blitz for 30 seconds, then, slowly and gradually pour in the oil, process until smooth and even. Serve the sauce with the prepared snapper fillets. Bon appétit!

Per Serving
calories: 491 | fat: 38g | protein: 29g | carbs: 8g | net carbs: 5g | fiber: 3g

Cauliflower and Sole Fritters

Prep time: 15 minutes | Cook time: 24 minutes | Serves 2

½ pound (227 g) sole fillets
½ pound (227 g) mashed cauliflower
1 egg, well beaten
½ cup red onion, chopped
2 garlic cloves, minced
2 tablespoons fresh parsley, chopped
1 bell pepper, finely chopped
½ teaspoon scotch bonnet pepper, minced
1 tablespoon olive oil
1 tablespoon coconut aminos
½ teaspoon paprika
Salt and white pepper, to taste

1. Start by preheating your Air Fryer to 395ºF. Spritz the sides and bottom of the cooking basket with cooking spray.
2. Cook the sole fillets in the preheated Air Fryer for 10 minutes, flipping them halfway through the cooking time.
3. In a mixing bowl, mash the sole fillets into flakes. Stir in the remaining ingredients. Shape the fish mixture into patties.
4. Bake in the preheated Air Fryer at 390ºF for 14 minutes, flipping them halfway through the cooking time. Bon appétit!

Per Serving
calories: 322 | fat: 14g | protein: 22g | carbs: 27g | net carbs: 23g | fiber: 4g

Swordfish Skewers with Cherry Tomato

Prep time: 10 minutes | Cook time: 6 to 8 minutes | Serves 4

1 pound (454 g) filleted swordfish
¼ cup avocado oil
2 tablespoons freshly squeezed lemon juice
1 tablespoon minced fresh parsley
2 teaspoons Dijon mustard
Sea salt, freshly ground black pepper, to taste
3 ounces (85 g) cherry tomatoes

1. Cut the fish into 1½-inch chunks, picking out any remaining bones.
2. In a large bowl, whisk together the oil, lemon juice, parsley, and Dijon mustard. Season to taste with salt and pepper. Add the fish and toss to coat the pieces. Cover and marinate the fish chunks in the refrigerator for 30 minutes.
3. Remove the fish from the marinade. Thread the fish and cherry tomatoes on 4 skewers, alternating as you go.
4. Set the air fryer to 400°F (205ºC). Place the skewers in the air fryer basket and cook for 3 minutes. Flip the skewers and cook for 3 to 5 minutes longer, until the fish is cooked through and an instant-read thermometer reads 140°F (60ºC).

Per Serving
calories: 315 | fat: 20g | protein: 29g | carbs: 2g | net carbs: 1g | fiber: 1g

Crab Cake

Prep time: 10 minutes | Cook time: 14 minutes | Serves 4

Avocado oil spray
⅓ cup red onion, diced
¼ cup red bell pepper, diced
8 ounces (227 g) lump crab meat, picked over for shells
3 tablespoons finely ground blanched almond flour
1 large egg, beaten
1 tablespoon sugar-free
mayonnaise
2 teaspoons Dijon mustard
⅛ teaspoon cayenne pepper
Sea salt, freshly ground black pepper, to taste
Elevated Tartar Sauce, for serving
Lemon wedges, for serving

1. Spray an air fryer–friendly baking pan with oil. Put the onion and red bell pepper in the pan and give them a quick spray with oil. Place the pan in the air fryer basket. Set the air fryer to 400°F (205ºC) and cook the vegetables for 7 minutes, until tender.
2. Transfer the vegetables to a large bowl. Add the crab meat, almond flour, egg, mayonnaise, mustard, and cayenne pepper and season with salt and pepper. Stir until the mixture is well combined.
3. Form the mixture into four 1-inch-thick cakes. Cover with plastic wrap and refrigerate for 1 hour.
4. Place the crab cakes in a single layer in the air fryer basket and spray them with oil.
5. Cook for 4 minutes. Flip the crab cakes and spray with more oil. Cook for 3 minutes or more, until the internal temperature of the crab cakes reaches 155°F (68ºC).
6. Serve with tartar sauce and a squeeze of fresh lemon juice.

Per Serving
calories: 121 | fat: 8g | protein: 11g | carbs: 3g | net carbs: 2g | fiber: 1g

Salmon with Lemon

Prep time: 50 minutes | Cook time: 10 minutes | Serves 4

1½ pounds (680g) salmon steak
½ teaspoon grated lemon zest
Freshly cracked mixed peppercorns, to taste
⅓ cup lemon juice
Fresh chopped chives, for garnish
½ cup dry white wine
½ teaspoon fresh cilantro, chopped
Fine sea salt, to taste

1. To prepare the marinade, place all ingredients, except for salmon steak and chives, in a deep pan. Bring to a boil over medium-high flame until it has reduced by half. Allow it to cool down.
2. After that, allow salmon steak to marinate in the refrigerator for approximately 40 minutes. Discard the marinade and transfer the fish steak to the preheated Air Fryer.
3. Air-fry at 400ºF (205ºC) for 9 to10 minutes. To finish, brush hot fish steaks with the reserved marinade, garnish with fresh chopped chives, and serve right away!

Per Serving
calories: 304 | fat: 15g | protein: 38g | carbs: 2g | net carbs: 1g | fiber: 1g

Coconut Shrimp

Prep time: 15 minutes | Cook time: 17 minutes | Serves 4

¾ cup unsweetened shredded coconut
¾ cup coconut flour
1 teaspoon garlic powder
¼ teaspoon cayenne pepper
Sea salt, freshly ground
black pepper, to taste
2 large eggs
1 pound (454 g) fresh extra-large or jumbo shrimp, peeled and deveined
Avocado oil spray

1. In a medium bowl, combine the shredded coconut, coconut flour, garlic powder, and cayenne pepper. Season to taste with salt and pepper.
2. In a small bowl, beat the eggs.
3. Pat the shrimp dry with paper towels. Dip each shrimp in the eggs and then the coconut mixture. Gently press the coating to the shrimp to help it adhere.
4. Set the air fryer to 400°F (205ºC). Spray the shrimp with oil and place them in a single layer in the air fryer basket, working in batches if necessary.

5. Cook the shrimp for 9 minutes, then flip and spray them with more oil. Cook for 8 minutes or more, until the center of the shrimp is opaque and cooked through.

Per Serving
calories: 362 | fat: 17g | protein: 35g | carbs: 20g | net carbs: 9g | fiber: 11g

Shrimp with Romaine

Prep time: 10 minutes | Cook time: 4 to 6 minutes | Serves 4

12 ounces (340 g) fresh large shrimp, peeled and deveined
1 tablespoon plus 1 teaspoon freshly squeezed lemon juice, divided
4 tablespoons olive oil or avocado oil, divided
2 garlic cloves, minced, divided
¼ teaspoon sea salt, plus additional to season the marinade
¼ teaspoon freshly ground black pepper, plus additional to season the marinade
⅓ cup sugar-free mayonnaise
2 tablespoons freshly grated Parmesan cheese
1 teaspoon Dijon mustard
1 tinned anchovy, mashed
12 ounces (340 g) romaine hearts, torn

1. Place the shrimp in a large bowl. Add 1 tablespoon of lemon juice, 1 tablespoon of olive oil, and 1 minced garlic clove. Season with salt and pepper. Toss well and refrigerate for 15 minutes.
2. While the shrimp marinates, make the dressing: In a blender, combine the mayonnaise, Parmesan cheese, Dijon mustard, the remaining 1 teaspoon of lemon juice, the anchovy, the remaining minced garlic clove, ¼ teaspoon of salt, and ¼ teaspoon of pepper. Process until smooth. With the blender running, slowly stream in the remaining 3 tablespoons of oil. Transfer the mixture to a jar, seal and refrigerate until ready to serve.
3. Remove the shrimp from its marinade and place it in the air fryer basket in a single layer. Set the air fryer to 400°F (205ºC) and cook for 2 minutes. Flip the shrimp and cook for 2 to 4 minutes or more, until the flesh turns opaque.
4. Place the romaine in a large bowl and toss with the desired amount of dressing. Top with the shrimp and serve immediately.

Per Serving
calories: 329 | fat: 30g | protein: 16g | carbs: 4g | net carbs: 2g | fiber: 2g

Lemony Snapper

Prep time: 5 minutes | Cook time: 7 minutes | Serves 4

1 pound (454 g) snapper, grouper, or salmon fillets
Sea salt, freshly ground black pepper, to taste
1 tablespoon avocado oil
¼ cup sour cream
¼ cup sugar-free mayonnaise (homemade, here, or store-bought)
2 tablespoons fresh dill, chopped, plus more for garnish
1 tablespoon freshly squeezed lemon juice
½ teaspoon grated lemon zest

1. Pat the fish dry with paper towels and season well with salt and pepper. Brush with the avocado oil.
2. Set the air fryer to 400°F (205ºC). Place the fillets in the air fryer basket and cook for 1 minute.
3. Lower the air fryer temperature to 325°F and continue cooking for 5 minutes. Flip the fish and cook for 1 minute more or until an instant-read thermometer reads 145°F (63ºC). (If using salmon, cook it to 125°F (52ºC) for medium-rare.)
4. While the fish is cooking, make the sauce by combining the sour cream, mayonnaise, dill, lemon juice, and lemon zest in a medium bowl. Season with salt and pepper and stir until combined. Refrigerate until ready to serve.
5. Serve the fish with the sauce, garnished with the remaining dill.

Per Serving

calories: 304 | fat: 19g | protein: 30g | carbs: 2g | net carbs: 2g | fiber: 0g

Golden Cod with Mayo

Prep time: 10 minutes | Cook time: 9 minutes | Serves 4

1 pound (454 g) cod fillets
1½ cups finely ground blanched almond flour
2 teaspoons Old Bay seasoning
½ teaspoon paprika
Sea salt, freshly ground black pepper, to taste
¼ cup sugar-free mayonnaise
1 large egg, beaten
Avocado oil spray
Elevated Tartar Sauce, for serving

1. Cut the fish into ¾-inch-wide strips.
2. In a shallow bowl, stir together the almond flour, Old Bay seasoning, paprika, and salt and pepper to taste. In another shallow bowl, whisk together the mayonnaise and egg.
3. Dip the cod strips in the egg mixture, then the almond flour, gently pressing with your fingers to help adhere the coating.
4. Place the coated fish on a parchment paper–lined baking sheet and freeze for 30 minutes.
5. Spray the air fryer basket with oil. Set the air fryer to 400°F (205ºC). Place the fish in the basket in a single layer, and spray each piece with oil.
6. Cook for 5 minutes. Flip and spray with more oil. Cook for 4 minutes or more, until the internal temperature reaches 140°F (60ºC). Serve with the tartar sauce.

Per Serving

calories: 439 | fat: 33g | protein: 31g | carbs: 9g | net carbs: 4g | fiber: 5g

Rockfish with Avocado Cream

Prep time: 15 minutes | Cook time: 9 minutes | Serves 4

For the Fish Fillets:
1½ tablespoons balsamic vinegar
½ cup vegetable broth
⅓ teaspoon shallot powder
1 tablespoon coconut aminos
4 Rockfish fillets
1 teaspoon ground black pepper
1½ tablespoons olive oil
Fine sea salt, to taste
⅓ teaspoon garlic powder
For the Avocado Cream:
2 tablespoons Greek-style yogurt
1 clove garlic, peeled and minced
1 teaspoon ground black pepper
½ tablespoon olive oil
⅓ cup vegetable broth
1 avocado
½ teaspoon lime juice
⅓ teaspoon fine sea salt

1. In a bowl, wash and pat the fillets dry using some paper towels. Add all the seasonings. In another bowl, stir in the remaining ingredients for the fish fillets.
2. Add the seasoned fish fillets, cover and let the fillets marinate in your refrigerator for at least 3 hours.
3. Then, set your Air Fryer to cook at 325ºF (163ºC). Cook marinated rockfish fillets in the air fryer grill basket for 9 minutes.
4. In the meantime, prepare the avocado sauce by mixing all the ingredients with an immersion blender or regular blender. Serve the rockfish fillets topped with the avocado sauce. Enjoy!

Per Serving

calories: 347 | fat: 25g | protein: 3g | carbs: 7g | net carbs: 4g | fiber: 3g

Tuna with Red Onions and Herbs

Prep time: 10 minutes | Cook time: 10 minutes | Serves 4

4 tuna steaks
½ pound (227 g) red onions
4 teaspoons olive oil
1 teaspoon dried rosemary
1 teaspoon dried marjoram
1 tablespoon cayenne pepper
½ teaspoon sea salt
½ teaspoon black pepper, preferably freshly cracked
1 lemon, sliced

1. Place the tuna steaks in the lightly greased cooking basket. Top with the pearl onions, add the olive oil, rosemary, marjoram, cayenne pepper, salt, and black pepper.
2. Bake in the preheated Air Fryer at 400ºF for 9 to 10 minutes. Work in two batches.
3. Serve warm with lemon slices and enjoy!

Per Serving

calories: 487 | fat: 19g | protein: 68g | carbs: 7g | net carbs: 6g | fiber: 1g

Grilled Scallops

Prep time: 10 minutes | Cook time: 10 minutes | Serves 2

1½ tablespoons coconut aminos
1 tablespoon Mediterranean seasoning mix
⅓ cup shallots, chopped
½ tablespoon balsamic vinegar
1½ tablespoons olive oil
1 clove garlic, chopped
½ teaspoon ginger, grated
1 pound (454 g) scallops, cleaned
Belgian endive, for garnish

1. In a small-sized sauté pan that is placed over a moderate flame, simmer all ingredients, minus scallops and Belgian endive. Allow this mixture to cool down completely.
2. After that, add the scallops and let them marinate for at least 2 hours in the refrigerator.
3. Arrange the scallops in a single layer in the Air Fryer grill pan. Spritz with a cooking oil. Air-fry at 345ºfor 10 minutes, turning halfway through.
4. Serve immediately with Belgian endive. Bon appétit!

Per Serving

calories: 179 | fat: 11g | protein: 14g | carbs: 7g | net carbs: 6g | fiber: 1g

Parmesan Crumbed Fish

Prep time: 15 minutes | Cook time: 17 minutes | Serves 4

2 eggs, beaten
½ teaspoon tarragon
4 fish fillets, halved
2 tablespoons dry white wine
⅓ cup Parmesan cheese,
grated
1 teaspoon seasoned salt
⅓ teaspoon mixed peppercorns
½ teaspoon fennel seed

1. Add the Parmesan cheese, salt, peppercorns, fennel seeds, and tarragon to your food processor, blitz for about 20 seconds.
2. Drizzle fish fillets with dry white wine. Dump the egg into a shallow dish.
3. Now, coat the fish fillets with the beaten egg on all sides, then, coat them with the seasoned cracker mix.
4. Air-fry at 345ºF for about 17 minutes. Bon appétit!

Per Serving

calories: 305 | fat: 18g | protein: 27g | carbs: 6g | net carbs: 5g | fiber: 1g

Snapper with Thai Sauce

Prep time: 15 minutes | Cook time: 27 minutes | Serves 2

½ cup full-fat coconut milk
2 tablespoons lemon juice
1 teaspoon fresh ginger,
grated
2 snapper fillets
1 tablespoon olive oil
Salt and white pepper, to taste

1. Place the milk, lemon juice, and ginger in a glass bowl, add fish and let it marinate for 1 hour.
2. Removed the fish from the milk mixture and place in the Air Fryer basket. Drizzle olive oil all over the fish fillets.
3. Cook in the preheated Air Fryer at 390ºF for 15 minutes.
4. Meanwhile, heat the milk mixture over medium-high heat, bring to a rapid boil, stirring continuously. Reduce to simmer and add the salt, and pepper, continue to cook 12 minutes or more.
5. Spoon the sauce over the warm snapper fillets and serve immediately. Bon appétit!

Per Serving

calories: 420 | fat: 24g | protein: 48g | carbs: 5g | net carbs: 4g | fiber: 1g

Lobster Tails with Green Olives

Prep time: 10 minutes | Cook time: 7 minutes | Serves 5

2 pounds (907 g) fresh lobster tails, cleaned and halved, in shells
2 tablespoons butter, melted
1 teaspoon onion powder
1 teaspoon cayenne pepper
Salt and ground black pepper, to taste
2 garlic cloves, minced
1 cup green olives

1. In a plastic closeable bag, thoroughly combine all ingredients, shake to combine well.
2. Transfer the coated lobster tails to the greased cooking basket.
3. Cook in the preheated Air Fryer at 390ºfor 6 to 7 minutes, shaking the basket halfway through. Work in batches.
4. Serve with green olives and enjoy!

Per Serving
calories: 189 | fat: 7g | protein: 30g | carbs: 2g | net carbs: 1g | fiber: 1g

Crab Bun

Prep time: 15 minutes | Cook time: 20 minutes | Serves 2

5 ounces (142 g) crab meat, chopped
2 eggs, beaten
2 tablespoons coconut flour
¼ teaspoon baking powder
½ teaspoon coconut aminos
½ teaspoon ground black pepper
1 tablespoon coconut oil, softened

1. In the mixing bowl, mix crab meat with eggs, coconut flour, baking powder, coconut aminos, ground black pepper, and coconut oil.
2. Knead the smooth dough and cut it into pieces.
3. Make the buns from the crab mixture and put them in the air fryer basket.
4. Cook the crab buns at 365F (185ºC) for 20 minutes.

Per Serving
calories: 217 | fat: 13g | protein: 15g | carbs: 7g | net carbs: 4g | fiber: 3g

Creamed and Smoked White Fish

Prep time: 15 minutes | Cook time: 13 minutes | Serves 4

½ tablespoon yogurt
⅓ cup spring garlic, finely chopped
Fresh chopped chives, for garnish
3 eggs, beaten
½ teaspoon dried dill weed
1 teaspoon dried rosemary
⅓ cup scallions, chopped
⅓ cup smoked white fish, chopped
1½ tablespoons crème fraîche
1 teaspoon kosher salt
1 teaspoon dried marjoram
⅓ teaspoon ground black pepper, or more to taste
Cooking spray

1. Firstly, spritz four oven safe ramekins with cooking spray. Then, divide smoked whitefish, spring garlic, and scallions among greased ramekins.
2. Crack an egg into each ramekin, add the crème, yogurt and all seasonings.
3. Now, air-fry approximately 13 minutes at 355ºF. Taste for doneness and eat warm garnished with fresh chives. Bon appétit!

Per Serving
calories: 249 | fat: 22g | protein: 5g | carbs: 8g | net carbs: 7g | fiber: 1g

Chipotle Salmon Cakes

Prep time: 15 minutes | Cook time: 13 minutes | Serves 4

½ teaspoon chipotle powder
½ teaspoon butter, at room temperature
⅓ teaspoon smoked cayenne pepper
½ teaspoon dried parsley flakes
⅓ teaspoon ground black pepper
1 pound (454 g) salmon,
chopped into ½ inch pieces
1½ tablespoons milk
½ white onion, peeled and finely chopped
1 teaspoon fine sea salt
2 tablespoons coconut flour
2 tablespoons Parmesan cheese, grated

1. Place all ingredients in a large-sized mixing dish.
2. Shape into cakes and roll each cake over seasoned breadcrumbs. After that, refrigerate for about 2 hours.
3. Then, set your Air Fryer to cook at 395ºF for 13 minutes.
4. Serve warm with a dollop of sour cream if desired. Bon appétit!

Per Serving
calories: 401 | fat: 19g | protein: 53g | carbs: 2g | net carbs: 1g | fiber: 1g

Flounder Cutlets

Prep time: 15 minutes | Cook time: 10 minutes | Serves 2

1 egg
1 cup Pecorino Romano cheese, grated
Sea salt and white pepper, to taste
½ teaspoon cayenne pepper
1 teaspoon dried parsley flakes
2 flounder fillets

1. To make a breading station, whisk the egg until frothy.
2. In another bowl, mix Pecorino Romano cheese, and spices.
3. Dip the fish in the egg mixture and turn to coat evenly, then, dredge in the cracker crumb mixture, turning a couple of times to coat evenly.
4. Cook in the preheated Air Fryer at 390ºF (199ºC) for 5 minutes, turn them over and cook for another 5 minutes. Enjoy!

Per Serving
calories: 425 | fat: 26g | protein: 37g | carbs: 7g | net carbs: 7g | fiber: 0g

Grilled Tuna Cake

Prep time: 10 minutes | Cook time: 8 minutes | Serves 4

2 cans canned tuna fish
2 celery stalks, trimmed and finely chopped
1 egg, whisked
½ cup Parmesan cheese, grated
1 teaspoon whole-grain
mustard
½ teaspoon sea salt
¼ teaspoon freshly cracked black peppercorns
1 teaspoon paprika

1. Mix all of the above ingredients in the order listed above, mix to combine well and shape into four cakes, chill for 50 minutes.
2. Place on an Air Fryer grill pan. Spritz each cake with a non-stick cooking spray, covering all sides.
3. Grill at 360ºF (182ºC) for 5 minutes, then, pause the machine, flip the cakes over and set the timer for another 3 minutes. Serve.

Per Serving
calories: 241 | fat: 11g | protein: 30g | carbs: 2g | net carbs: 1g | fiber: 1g

Shrimp with Old Bay Seasoning

Prep time: 10 minutes | Cook time: 7 minutes | Serves 4

1 pound (454 g) medium shelled and deveined shrimp
2 tablespoons salted butter, melted
½ teaspoon Old Bay seasoning
¼ teaspoon garlic
powder
2 tablespoons sriracha
¼ teaspoon powdered erythritol
¼ cup full-fat mayonnaise
⅛ teaspoon ground black pepper

1. In a large bowl, toss shrimp in butter, Old Bay seasoning, and garlic powder. Place shrimp into the air fryer basket.
2. Adjust the temperature to 400°F (205ºC) and set the timer for 7 minutes.
3. Flip the shrimp halfway through the cooking time. Shrimp will be bright pink when fully cooked.
4. In another large bowl, mix sriracha, powdered erythritol, mayonnaise, and pepper. Toss shrimp in the spicy mixture and serve immediately.

Per Serving
calories: 143 | fat: 6g | protein: 16g | carbs: 3g | net carbs: 3g | fiber: 0g

Lemony Salmon

Prep time: 10 minutes | Cook time: 12 minutes | Serves 2

2 (4-ounce / (113 g)) salmon fillets, skin removed
2 tablespoons unsalted butter, melted
½ teaspoon garlic powder
1 medium lemon
½ teaspoon dried dill

1. Place each fillet on a 5-inch × 5-inch square of aluminum foil. Drizzle with butter and sprinkle with garlic powder.
2. Zest half of the lemon and sprinkle zest over salmon. Slice other half of the lemon and lay two slices on each piece of salmon. Sprinkle dill over salmon.
3. Gather and fold foil at the top and sides to fully close packets. Place foil packets into the air fryer basket.
4. Adjust the temperature to 400°F (205ºC) and set the timer for 12 minutes.
5. Salmon will be easily flaked and have an internal temperature of at least 145°F (63ºC) when fully cooked. Serve immediately.

Per Serving
calories: 252 | fat: 16g | protein: 20g | carbs: 2g | net carbs: 1g | fiber: 1g

Piri Piri King Prawns

Prep time: 10 minutes | Cook time: 8 minutes | Serves 2

12 king prawns, rinsed
1 tablespoon coconut oil
½ teaspoon piri piri powder
Salt and ground black pepper, to taste
1 teaspoon garlic paste
1 teaspoon onion powder
½ teaspoon cumin powder
1 teaspoon curry powder

1. In a mixing bowl, toss all ingredient until the prawns are well coated on all sides.
2. Cook in the preheated Air Fryer at 360ºF for 4 minutes. Shake the basket and cook for 4 minutes or more.
3. Serve over hot rice if desired. Bon appétit!

Per Serving

calories: 220 | fat: 10g | protein: 18g | carbs: 15g | net carbs: 14g | fiber: 1g

Salmon Patties

Prep time: 10 minutes | Cook time: 8 minutes | Serves 2

2 pouches (5-ounce / (142 g)) cooked pink salmon
1 large egg
¼ cup ground pork rinds
2 tablespoons full-fat mayonnaise
2 teaspoons sriracha
1 teaspoon chili powder

1. Mix all ingredients in a large bowl and form into four patties. Place patties into the air fryer basket.
2. Adjust the temperature to 400°F (205ºC) and set the timer for 8 minutes.
3. Carefully flip each patty halfway through the cooking time. Patties will be crispy on the outside when fully cooked.

Per Serving

calories: 319 | fat: 19g | protein: 34g | carbs: 2g | net carbs: 1g | fiber: 1g

Tuna Patties with Cheese Sauce

Prep time: 15 minutes | Cook time: 20 minutes | Serves 4

1 pound (454 g) canned tuna, drained
1 egg, whisked
1 garlic clove, minced
2 tablespoons shallots, minced
1 cup Romano cheese, grated
Sea salt and ground black pepper, to taste
1 tablespoon sesame oil
Cheese Sauce:
1 tablespoon butter
1 cup beer
2 tablespoons Colby cheese, grated

1. In a mixing bowl, thoroughly combine the tuna, egg, garlic, shallots, Romano cheese, salt, and black pepper. Shape the tuna mixture into four patties and place in your refrigerator for 2 hours.
2. Brush the patties with sesame oil on both sides. Cook in the preheated Air Fryer at 360ºF for 14 minutes.
3. In the meantime, melt the butter in a pan over a moderate heat. Add the beer and whisk until it starts bubbling.
4. Now, stir in the grated cheese and cook for 3 to 4 minutes longer or until the cheese has melted. Spoon the sauce over the fish cake burgers and serve immediately.

Per Serving

calories: 309 | fat: 15g | protein: 31g | carbs: 8g | net carbs: 7g | fiber: 1g

Duo-Cheese Hake

Prep time: 30 minutes | Cook time: 17 minutes | Serves 4

1 tablespoon avocado oil
1 pound (454 g) hake fillets
1 teaspoon garlic powder
Sea salt and ground white pepper, to taste
2 tablespoons shallots, chopped
1 bell pepper, seeded
and chopped
½ cup Cottage cheese
½ cup sour cream
1 egg, well whisked
1 teaspoon yellow mustard
1 tablespoon lime juice
½ cup Swiss cheese, shredded

1. Brush the bottom and sides of a casserole dish with avocado oil. Add the hake fillets to the casserole dish and sprinkle with garlic powder, salt, and pepper.
2. Add the chopped shallots and bell peppers.
3. In a mixing bowl, thoroughly combine the Cottage cheese, sour cream, egg, mustard, and lime juice. Pour the mixture over fish and spread evenly.
4. Cook in the preheated Air Fryer at 370ºF (188ºC) for 10 minutes.
5. Top with the Swiss cheese and cook for an additional 7 minutes. Let it rest for 10 minutes before slicing and serving. Bon appétit!

Per Serving

calories: 335 | fat: 18g | protein: 34g | carbs: 8g | net carbs: 7g | fiber: 1g

Tilapia and Parmesan Bake

Prep time: 10 minutes | Cook time: 10 minutes | Serves 6

1 cup Parmesan cheese, grated
1 teaspoon paprika
1 teaspoon dried dill weed
2 pounds (907 g) tilapia
fillets
⅓ cup mayonnaise
½ tablespoon lime juice
Salt and ground black pepper, to taste

1. Mix the mayonnaise, Parmesan, paprika, salt, black pepper, and dill weed until everything is thoroughly combined.
2. Then, drizzle tilapia fillets with the lime juice.
3. Cover each fish fillet with Parmesan/mayo mixture, roll them in Parmesan/paprika mixture. Bake at 335ºF for about 10 minutes. Eat warm and enjoy!

Per Serving
calories: 294 | fat: 16g | protein: 36g | carbs: 3g | net carbs: 2g | fiber: 1g

Fried Haddock

Prep time: 15 minutes | Cook time: 13 minutes | Serves 2

2 haddock fillets
½ cup Parmesan cheese, freshly grated
1 teaspoon dried parsley flakes
1 egg, beaten
½ teaspoon coarse sea
salt
¼ teaspoon ground black pepper
¼ teaspoon cayenne pepper
2 tablespoons olive oil

1. Start by preheating your Air Fryer to 360ºF. Pat dry the haddock fillets and set aside.
2. In a shallow bowl, thoroughly combine the Parmesan and parsley flakes. Mix until everything is well incorporated.
3. In a separate shallow bowl, whisk the egg with salt, black pepper, and cayenne pepper.
4. Dip the haddock fillets into the egg. Then, dip the fillets into the Parmesan mixture until well coated on all sides.
5. Drizzle the olive oil all over the fish fillets. Lower the coated fillets into the lightly greased Air Fryer basket. Cook for 11 to 13 minutes. Bon appétit!

Per Serving
calories: 434 | fat: 26g | protein: 43g | carbs: 4g | net carbs: 3g | fiber: 1g

Tuna Avocado Bites

Prep time: 10 minutes | Cook time: 7 minutes | Makes 12 bites

1 (10-ounce / 283-g) can tuna, drained
¼ cup full-fat mayonnaise
1 stalk celery, chopped
1 medium avocado, peeled, pitted, and
mashed
½ cup blanched finely ground almond flour, divided
2 teaspoons coconut oil

1. In a large bowl, mix tuna, mayonnaise, celery, and mashed avocado. Form the mixture into balls.
2. Roll balls in almond flour and spritz with coconut oil. Place balls into the air fryer basket.
3. Adjust the temperature to 400°F (205ºC) and set the timer for 7 minutes.
4. Gently turn tuna bites after 5 minutes. Serve warm.

Per Serving
calories: 323 | fat: 25g | protein: 17g | carbs: 6g | net carbs: 2g | fiber: 4g

Whitefish Fillet with Green Bean

Prep time: 1 hour 20 minutes | Cook time: 15 minutes | Serves 4

1 pound (454 g) whitefish fillets, minced
½ pound (227g) green beans, finely chopped
½ cup scallions, chopped
1 chili pepper, seeded and minced
1 tablespoon red curry paste
1 tablespoon fish sauce
2 tablespoons apple cider vinegar
1 teaspoon water
Sea salt flakes, to taste
½ teaspoon cracked black peppercorns
2 tablespoons butter, at room temperature
½ teaspoon lemon

1. Add all ingredients in the order listed above to the mixing dish. Mix to combine well using a spatula or your hands.
2. Form into small cakes and chill for 1 hour. Place a piece of aluminum foil over the cooking basket. Place the cakes on foil.
3. Cook at 390ºF (199ºC) for 10 minutes, pause the machine, flip each fish cake over and air-fry for additional 5 minutes. Mound a cucumber relish onto the plates, add the fish cakes and serve warm.

Per Serving
calories: 231 | fat: 12g | protein: 23g | carbs: 6g | net carbs: 4g | fiber: 2g

Almond Salmon Fillets with Pesto

Prep time: 5 minutes | Cook time: 12 minutes | Serves 2

¼ cup pesto
¼ cup sliced almonds, roughly chopped
2 (1½ -inch-thick) salmon
fillets (about 4 ounces each/ 113 g)
2 tablespoons unsalted butter, melted

1. In a small bowl, mix pesto and almonds. Set aside.
2. Place fillets into a 6-inch round baking dish.
3. Brush each fillet with butter and place half of the pesto mixture on the top of each fillet. Place dish into the air fryer basket.
4. Adjust the temperature to 390°F (199ºC) and set the timer for 12 minutes.
5. Salmon will easily flake when fully cooked and reach an internal temperature of at least 145°F (63ºC). Serve warm.

Per Serving

calories: 433 | fat: 34g | protein: 23g | carbs: 6g | net carbs: 4g | fiber: 2g

Tilapia with Pecan

Prep time: 20 minutes | Cook time: 16 minutes | Serves 5

2 tablespoons ground flaxseeds
1 teaspoon paprika
Sea salt and white pepper, to taste
1 teaspoon garlic paste
2 tablespoons extra-virgin olive oil
½ cup pecans, ground
5 tilapia fillets, slice into halves

1. Combine the ground flaxseeds, paprika, salt, white pepper, garlic paste, olive oil, and ground pecans in a Ziploc bag. Add the fish fillets and shake to coat well.
2. Spritz the Air Fryer basket with cooking spray. Cook in the preheated Air Fryer at 400ºF (205ºC) for 10 minutes, turn them over and cook for 6 minutes or more. Work in batches.
3. Serve with lemon wedges, if desired. Enjoy!

Per Serving

calories: 264 | fat: 17g | protein: 6g | carbs: 4g | net carbs: 2g | fiber: 2g

Crab Patties

Prep time: 20 minutes | Cook time: 14 minutes | Serves 3

2 eggs, beaten
1 shallot, chopped
2 garlic cloves, crushed
1 tablespoon olive oil
1 teaspoon yellow mustard
1 teaspoon fresh cilantro, chopped
10 ounces (283 g) crab meat
1 teaspoon smoked paprika
½ teaspoon ground black pepper
Sea salt, to taste
¾ cup Parmesan cheese

1. In a mixing bowl, thoroughly combine the eggs, shallot, garlic, olive oil, mustard, cilantro, crab meat, paprika, black pepper, and salt. Mix until well combined.
2. Shape the mixture into 6 patties. Roll the crab patties over grated Parmesan cheese, coating well on all sides. Place in your refrigerator for 2 hours.
3. Spritz the crab patties with cooking oil on both sides. Cook in the preheated Air Fryer at 360ºF (182ºC) for 14 minutes. Serve on dinner rolls if desired. Bon appétit!

Per Serving

calories: 279 | fat: 15g | protein: 28g | carbs: 6g | net carbs: 5g | fiber: 1g

Salmon Burgers with Asian Sauce

Prep time: 10 minutes | Cook time: 10 minutes | Serves 4

1 pound (454 g) salmon
1 egg
1 garlic clove, minced
2 green onions, minced
1 cup Parmesan cheese
Sauce:
1 teaspoon rice wine
1½ tablespoons soy sauce
A pinch of salt
1 teaspoon gochugaru (Korean red chili pepper flakes)

1. Start by preheating your Air Fryer to 380ºF. Spritz the Air Fryer basket with cooking oil.
2. Mix the salmon, egg, garlic, green onions, and Parmesan cheese in a bowl, knead with your hands until everything is well incorporated.
3. Shape the mixture into equally sized patties. Transfer your patties to the Air Fryer basket.
4. Cook the fish patties for 10 minutes, turning them over halfway through.
5. Meanwhile, make the sauce by whisking all ingredients. Serve the warm fish patties with the sauce on the side.

Per Serving

calories: 301 | fat: 15g | protein: 33g | carbs: 6g | net carbs: 5.8g | fiber: 0.2g

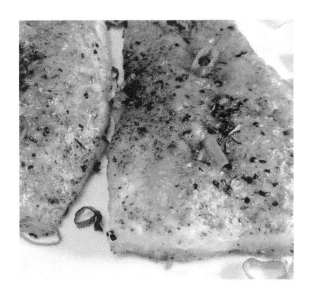

White Fish Fillets with Parmesan, page 82

Sardinas Fritas, page 82

Chipotle Salmon Cakes, page 88

Grilled Scallops, page 87

Lemony Shrimp Skewers with Vermouth

Prep time: 10 minutes | Cook time: 5 minutes | Serves 4

1½ pounds (680 g) shrimp	pepper, freshly ground
¼ cup vermouth	2 tablespoons olive oil
2 cloves garlic, crushed	8 skewers, soaked in water for 30 minutes
Kosher salt, to taste	1 lemon, cut into wedges
¼ teaspoon black	

1. Add the shrimp, vermouth, garlic, salt, black pepper, and olive oil in a ceramic bowl, let it sit for 1 hour in your refrigerator.
2. Discard the marinade and toss the shrimp with flour. Thread on to skewers and transfer to the lightly greased cooking basket.
3. Cook at 400ºF for 5 minutes, tossing halfway through. Serve with lemon wedges. Bon appétit!

Per Serving

calories: 228 | fat: 7g | protein: 26g | carbs: 5g | net carbs: 4g | fiber: 1g

Lemon Cod

Prep time: 20 minutes | Cook time: 10 minutes | Serves 2

2 medium-sized cod fillets	grain mustard
½ tablespoon fresh lemon juice	Sea salt and ground black pepper, to taste
1 ½ tablespoons olive oil	½ cup coconut flour
½ tablespoon whole-	2 eggs

1. Set your Air Fryer to cook at 355ºF (181ºC). Thoroughly combine olive oil and coconut flour in a shallow bowl.
2. In another shallow bowl, whisk the egg. Drizzle each cod fillet with lemon juice and spread with mustard. Then, sprinkle each fillet with salt and ground black pepper.
3. Dip each fish fillet into the whisked egg, now, roll it in the olive oil mixture.
4. Place in a single layer in the Air Fryer cooking basket. Cook for 10 minutes, working in batches, turning once or twice. Serve.

Per Serving

calories: 501 | fat: 35g | protein: 30g | carbs: 32g | net carbs: 31g | fiber: 1g

French Sea Bass

Prep time: 15 minutes | Cook time: 10 minutes | Serves 2

1 tablespoon olive oil	1 tablespoon gherkins, drained and chopped
2 sea bass fillets	2 tablespoons scallions, finely chopped
Sauce:	
½ cup mayonnaise	2 tablespoons lemon juice
1 tablespoon capers, drained and chopped	

1. Start by preheating your Air Fryer to 395ºF. Drizzle olive oil all over the fish fillets.
2. Cook the sea bass in the preheated Air Fryer for 10 minutes, flipping them halfway through the cooking time.
3. Meanwhile, make the sauce by whisking the remaining ingredients until everything is well incorporated. Place in the refrigerator until ready to serve. Bon appétit!

Per Serving

calories: 384 | fat: 29g | protein: 28g | carbs: 4g | net carbs: 3g | fiber: 1g

Japanese Flounder Fillets

Prep time: 15 minutes | Cook time: 12 minutes | Serves 4

4 flounder fillets	¼ cup soy sauce
Sea salt and freshly cracked mixed peppercorns, to taste	1 tablespoon grated lemon rind
1½ tablespoons dark sesame oil	2 garlic cloves, minced
2 tablespoons sake	2 tablespoons chopped chives, to serve

1. Place all the ingredients, without the chives, in a large-sized mixing dish. Cover and allow it to marinate for about 2 hours in your fridge.
2. Remove the fish from the marinade and cook in the Air Fryer cooking basket at 360ºF for 10 to 12 minutes, flip once during cooking.
3. Pour the remaining marinade into a pan that is preheated over a medium-low heat, let it simmer, stirring continuously, until it has thickened.
4. Pour the prepared glaze over flounder and serve garnished with fresh chives.

Per Serving

calories: 288 | fat: 18.3g | carbs: 5.1g | protein: 193.8g | sugar: 0.2g | fiber: 0.4g

Cod Fillet with Turmeric

Prep time: 10 minutes | Cook time: 7 minutes | Serves 2

12 ounces (340 g) cod fillet
1 teaspoon ground turmeric

1 teaspoon chili flakes
1 tablespoon coconut oil, melted
½ teaspoon salt

1. Mix coconut oil with ground turmeric, chili flakes, and salt.
2. Then mix cod fillet with ground turmeric and put in the air fryer basket.
3. Cook the cod at 385F (196ºC) for 7 minutes.

Per Serving
calories: 199 | fat: 8g | protein: 30g | carbs: 2g | net carbs: 1g | fiber: 1g

Savory Shrimp

Prep time: 5 minutes | Cook time: 8 to 10 minutes | Serves 4

1 pound (454 g) fresh large shrimp, peeled and deveined
1 tablespoon avocado oil
2 teaspoons minced garlic, divided
½ teaspoon red pepper flakes

Sea salt and freshly ground black pepper, to taste
2 tablespoons unsalted butter, melted
2 tablespoons chopped fresh parsley

1. Place the shrimp in a large bowl and toss with the avocado oil, 1 teaspoon of minced garlic, and red pepper flakes. Season with salt and pepper.
2. Set the air fryer to 350°F (180ºC). Arrange the shrimp in a single layer in the air fryer basket, working in batches if necessary. Cook for 6 minutes. Flip the shrimp and cook for 2 to 4 minutes or more, until the internal temperature of the shrimp reaches 120°F (49ºC). (The time it takes to cook will depend on the size of the shrimp.)
3. While the shrimp are cooking, melt the butter in a small saucepan over medium heat and stir in the remaining 1 teaspoon of garlic.
4. Transfer the cooked shrimp to a large bowl, add the garlic butter, and toss well. Top with the parsley and serve warm.

Per Serving
calories: 220 | fat: 11g | protein: 28g | carbs: 2g | net carbs: 1g | fiber: 1g

Tilapia Fingers

Prep time: 15 minutes | Cook time: 9 minutes | Serves 4

1 pound (454 g) tilapia fillet
½ cup coconut flour
2 eggs, beaten

½ teaspoon ground paprika
1 teaspoon dried oregano
1 teaspoon avocado oil

1. Cut the tilapia fillets into fingers and sprinkle with ground paprika and dried oregano.
2. Then dip the tilapia fingers in eggs and coat in the coconut flour.
3. Sprinkle fish fingers with avocado oil and cook in the air fryer at 370F (188ºC) for 9 minutes.

Per Serving
calories: 188 | fat: 5g | protein: 26g | carbs: 9g | net carbs: 4g | fiber: 5g

Roast Swordfish Steak

Prep time: 30 minutes | Cook time: 20 minutes | Serves 3

3 bell peppers
3 swordfish steaks
1 tablespoon butter, melted
2 garlic cloves, minced
Sea salt and freshly

ground black pepper, to taste
½ teaspoon cayenne pepper
½ teaspoon ginger powder

1. Start by preheating your Air Fryer to 400ºF (205ºC). Brush the Air Fryer basket lightly with cooking oil.
2. Then, roast the bell peppers for 5 minutes. Give the peppers a half turn, place them back in the cooking basket and roast for another 5 minutes.
3. Turn them one more time and roast until the skin is charred and soft or 5 more minutes. Peel the peppers and set aside.
4. Then, add the swordfish steaks to the lightly greased cooking basket and cook at 400ºF (205ºC) for 10 minutes.
5. Meanwhile, melt the butter in a small saucepan. Cook the garlic until fragrant and add the salt, pepper, cayenne pepper, and ginger powder. Cook until everything is thoroughly heated.
6. Plate the peeled peppers and the roasted swordfish, spoon the sauce over them and serve warm.

Per Serving
calories: 460 | fat: 17g | protein: 66g | carbs: 5g | net carbs: 4g | fiber: 1g

Mackerel with Spinach

Prep time: 15 minutes | Cook time: 20 minutes | Serves 5

pound (454 g) mackerel, trimmed
1 bell pepper, chopped
½ cup spinach, chopped
1 tablespoon avocado oil
1 teaspoon ground black pepper
1 teaspoon keto tomato paste

1. In the mixing bowl, mix bell pepper with spinach, ground black pepper, and tomato paste.
2. Fill the mackerel with spinach mixture.
3. Then brush the fish with avocado oil and put it in the air fryer.
4. Cook the fish at 365F (185ºC) for 20 minutes.

Per Serving
calories: 252 | fat: 16g | protein: 22g | carbs: 2g | net carbs: 1g | fiber: 1g

Lemony Salmon Steak

Prep time: 20 minutes | Cook time: 12 minutes | Serves 2

2 salmon steaks
Coarse sea salt, to taste
¼ teaspoon freshly ground black pepper, or more to taste
1 tablespoon sesame oil
Zest of 1 lemon
1 tablespoon fresh lemon juice
1 teaspoon garlic, minced
½ teaspoon smoked cayenne pepper
½ teaspoon dried dill

1. Preheat your Air Fryer to 380ºF (193ºC). Pat dry the salmon steaks with a kitchen towel.
2. In a ceramic dish, combine the remaining ingredients until everything is well whisked.
3. Add the salmon steaks to the ceramic dish and let them sit in the refrigerator for 1 hour. Now, place the salmon steaks in the cooking basket. Reserve the marinade.
4. Cook for 12 minutes, flipping halfway through the cooking time.
5. Meanwhile, cook the marinade in a small sauté pan over a moderate flame. Cook until the sauce has thickened.
6. Pour the sauce over the steaks and serve. Bon appétit!

Per Serving
calories: 476 | fat: 16g | protein: 47g | carbs: 3g | net carbs: 2g | fiber: 1g

Herbed Halibut Steaks with Vermouth

Prep time: 10 minutes | Cook time: 10 minutes | Serves 4

1 pound (454 g) halibut steaks
Salt and pepper, to your liking
1 teaspoon dried basil
2 tablespoons honey
¼ cup vegetable oil
2 ½ tablespoons
Worcester sauce
1 tablespoon freshly squeezed lemon juice
2 tablespoons vermouth
1 tablespoon fresh parsley leaves, coarsely chopped

1. Place all the ingredients in a large-sized mixing dish. Gently stir to coat the fish evenly.
2. Set your Air Fryer to cook at 390ºF, roast for 5 minutes. Pause the machine and flip the fish over.
3. Then, cook for another 5 minutes, check for doneness and cook for a few more minutes as needed. Bon appétit!

Per Serving
calories: 304 | fat: 21g | protein: 22g | carbs: 9g | net carbs: 8g | fiber: 1g

Beer Marinated Scallops

Prep time: 5 minutes | Cook time: 7 minutes | Serves 4

2 pounds (907 g) sea scallops
½ cup beer
4 tablespoons butter
2 sprigs rosemary, only
leaves
Sea salt and freshly cracked black pepper, to taste

1. In a ceramic dish, mix the sea scallops with beer, let it marinate for 1 hour.
2. Meanwhile, preheat your Air Fryer to 400ºF. Melt the butter and add the rosemary leaves. Stir for a few minutes.
3. Discard the marinade and transfer the sea scallops to the Air Fryer basket. Season with salt and black pepper.
4. Cook the scallops in the preheated Air Fryer for 7 minutes, shaking the basket halfway through the cooking time. Work in batches.
5. Bon appétit!

Per Serving
calories: 471 | fat: 27g | protein: 54g | carbs: 2g | net carbs: 1.9g | fiber: 0.1g

Salmon Fritters with Zucchini

Prep time: 15 minutes | Cook time: 12 minutes | Serves 4

2 tablespoons almond flour
1 zucchini, grated
1 egg, beaten
6 ounces (170 g) salmon
fillet, diced
1 teaspoon avocado oil
½ teaspoon ground black pepper

1. Mix almond flour with zucchini, egg, salmon, and ground black pepper.
2. Then make the fritters from the salmon mixture.
3. Sprinkle the air fryer basket with avocado oil and put the fritters inside.
4. Cook the fritters at 375F (190ºC) for 6 minutes per side.

Per Serving
calories: 103 | fat: 5g | protein: 11g | carbs: 3g | net carbs: 2g | fiber: 1g

Shrimp with Basil

Prep time: 15 minutes | Cook time: 5 minutes | Serves 4

½ tablespoon fresh basil leaves, chopped
1½ pounds (680 g) shrimp, shelled and deveined
1½ tablespoons olive oil
3 cloves garlic, minced
1 teaspoon smoked cayenne pepper
½ teaspoon fresh mint, roughly chopped
½ teaspoon ginger, freshly grated
1 teaspoon sea salt

1. Firstly, set your Air Fryer to cook at 395ºF.
2. In a mixing dish, combine all of the above items, toss until everything is well combined and let it stand for about 28 minutes.
3. Air-fry for 3 to 4 minutes. Bon appétit!

Per Serving
calories: 261 | fat: 10g | protein: 4g | carbs: 1g | net carbs: 0.8g | fiber: 0.2g

Baked Monkfish with Olives

Prep time: 20 minutes | Cook time: 12 minutes | Serves 2

2 teaspoons olive oil
1 cup celery, sliced
2 bell peppers, sliced
1 teaspoon dried thyme
½ teaspoon dried marjoram
½ teaspoon dried rosemary
2 monkfish fillets
1 tablespoon coconut aminos
2 tablespoons lime juice
Coarse salt and ground black pepper, to taste
1 teaspoon cayenne pepper
½ cup Kalamata olives, pitted and sliced

1. In a nonstick skillet, heat the olive oil for 1 minute. Once hot, sauté the celery and peppers until tender, for about 4 minutes. Sprinkle with thyme, marjoram, and rosemary and set aside.
2. Toss the fish fillets with the coconut aminos, lime juice, salt, black pepper, and cayenne pepper. Place the fish fillets in a lightly greased cooking basket and bake at 390ºF (199ºC) for 8 minutes.
3. Turn them over, add the olives, and cook for an additional 4 minutes. Serve with the sautéed vegetables on the side. Bon appétit!

Per Serving
calories: 292 | fat: 19g | protein: 22g | carbs: 9g | net carbs: 6g | fiber: 3g

Curried Halibut

Prep time: 10 minutes | Cook time: 10 minutes | Serves 4

2 medium-sized halibut fillets
1 teaspoon curry powder
½ teaspoon ground coriander
Kosher salt and freshly cracked mixed peppercorns, to taste
1½ tablespoons olive oil
½ cup Parmesan cheese, grated
2 eggs
½ teaspoon hot paprika
A few drizzles of tabasco sauce

1. Set your Air Fryer to cook at 365ºF.
2. Then, grab two mixing bowls. In the first bowl, combine the Parmesan cheese with olive oil.
3. In another shallow bowl, thoroughly whisk the egg. Next step, evenly drizzle the halibut fillets with Tabasco sauce, add hot paprika, curry, coriander, salt, and cracked mixed peppercorns.
4. Dip each fish fillet into the whisked egg, now, roll it over the Parmesan mix.
5. Place in a single layer in the Air Fryer cooking basket. Cook for 10 minutes, working in batches. Serve over creamed salad if desired. Bon appétit!

Per Serving
calories: 237 | fat: 18g | protein: 14g | carbs: 5g | net carbs: 4g | fiber: 1g

Tilapia with Balsamic Vinegar

Prep time: 5 minutes | Cook time: 15 minutes | Serves 4

4 tilapia fillets, boneless
2 tablespoons balsamic vinegar
1 teaspoon avocado oil
1 teaspoon dried basil

1. Sprinkle the tilapia fillets with balsamic vinegar, avocado oil, and dried basil.
2. Then put the fillets in the air fryer basket and cook at 365F (185ºC) for 15 minutes.

Per Serving

calories: 96 | fat: 1g | protein: 21g | carbs: 1g | net carbs: 0g | fiber: 1g

Sweet Tilapia Fillets

Prep time: 5 minutes | Cook time: 14 minutes | Serves 4

2 tablespoons erythritol
1 tablespoon apple cider vinegar
4 tilapia fillets, boneless
1 teaspoon olive oil

1. Mix apple cider vinegar with olive oil and erythritol.
2. Then rub the tilapia fillets with the sweet mixture and put in the air fryer basket in one layer.
3. Cook the fish at 360F (182ºC) for 7 minutes per side.

Per Serving

calories: 101 | fat: 2g | protein: 20g | carbs: 0g | net carbs: 0g | fiber: 0g

Salmon with Endives

Prep time: 5 minutes | Cook time: 20 minutes | Serves 4

2 endives, shredded
1 pound (454 g) salmon fillet, chopped
1 tablespoon ghee
1 teaspoon ground coriander
¼ cup coconut cream

1. Put all ingredients in the air fryer and shake gently.
2. Close the lid and cook the meal ay 360F (182ºC) for 20 minutes. Shake the fish every 5 minutes.

Per Serving

calories: 223 | fat: 13g | protein: 23g | carbs: 3g | net carbs: 1g | fiber: 2g

Lobster Tail with Lime

Prep time: 10 minutes | Cook time: 6 minutes | Serves 4

4 lobster tails, peeled
2 tablespoons lime juice
½ teaspoon dried basil
½ teaspoon coconut oil, melted

1. Mix lobster tails with lime juice, dried basil, and coconut oil.
2. Put the lobster tails in the air fryer and cook at 380F (193ºC) for 6 minutes.

Per Serving

calories: 83 | fat: 1g | protein: 16g | carbs: 1g | net carbs: 1g | fiber: 0g

Tuna Steak

Prep time: 10 minutes | Cook time: 12 minutes | Serves 4

pound (454-g) tuna steaks, boneless and cubed
1 tablespoon mustard
1 tablespoon avocado oil
1 tablespoon apple cider vinegar

1. Mix avocado oil with mustard and apple cider vinegar.
2. Then brush tuna steaks with mustard mixture and put in the air fryer basket.
3. Cook the fish at 360F (182ºC) for 6 minutes per side.

Per Serving

calories: 227 | fat: 8g | protein: 34g | carbs: 2g | net carbs: 1g | fiber: 1g

Air Fried Sardines

Prep time: 15 minutes | Cook time: 10 minutes | Serves 5

12 ounces (340 g) sardines, trimmed, cleaned
1 cup coconut flour
1 tablespoon coconut oil
1 teaspoon salt

1. Sprinkle the sardines with salt and coat in the coconut flour.
2. Then grease the air fryer basket with coconut oil and put the sardines inside.
3. Cook them at 385F (196ºC) for 10 minutes.

Per Serving

calories: 165 | fat: 10g | protein: 17g | carbs: 1g | net carbs: 1g | fiber: 0g

Savory Tilapia

Prep time: 5 minutes | Cook time: 20 minutes | Serves 4

4 tilapia fillets, boneless
1 teaspoon chili flakes
1 teaspoon dried oregano

1 tablespoon avocado oil
1 teaspoon mustard

1. Rub the tilapia fillets with chili flakes, dried oregano, avocado oil, and mustard and put in the air fryer.
2. Cook it for 10 minutes per side at 360F (182ºC).

Per Serving
calories: 103 | fat: 1g | protein: 21g | carbs: 1g | net carbs: 0g | fiber: 1g

Air Fried Mussels

Prep time: 10 minutes | Cook time: 2 minutes | Serves 5

pounds (907-g) mussels, cleaned, peeled
1 teaspoon onion powder
1 teaspoon ground cumin

1 tablespoon avocado oil
¼ cup apple cider vinegar

1. Mix mussels with onion powder, ground cumin, avocado oil, and apple cider vinegar.
2. Put the mussels in the air fryer and cook at 395F (202ºC) for 2 minutes.

Per Serving
calories: 166 | fat: 4g | protein: 22g | carbs: 8g | net carbs: 7g | fiber: 1g

Cod Fillets with Jalapeño

Prep time: 5 minutes | Cook time: 14 minutes | Serves 4

4 cod fillets, boneless
1 jalapeño, minced
1 tablespoon avocado oil

½ teaspoon minced garlic

1. In the shallow bowl, mix minced jalapeño, avocado oil, and minced garlic.
2. Put the cod fillets in the air fryer basket in one layer and top with minced jalapeño mixture.
3. Cook the fish at 365F (185ºC) for 7 minutes per side.

Per Serving
calories: 96 | fat: 2g | protein: 20g | carbs: 2g | net carbs: 1g | fiber: 1g

Crisp Catfish

Prep time: 10 minutes | Cook time: 12 minutes | Serves 4

pound (907-g) catfish fillet
½ cup almond flour

2 eggs, beaten
1 teaspoon salt
1 teaspoon avocado oil

1. Sprinkle the catfish fillet with salt and dip in the eggs.
2. Then coat the fish in the almond flour and put in the air fryer basket. Sprinkle the fish with avocado oil.
3. Cook the fish for 6 minutes per side at 380F (193ºC).

Per Serving
calories: 423 | fat: 26g | protein: 41g | carbs: 3g | net carbs: 1g | fiber: 2g

Delicious Scallops

Prep time: 10 minutes | Cook time: 6 minutes | Serves 4

12 ounces scallops
1 tablespoon dried rosemary

½ teaspoon Pink salt
1 tablespoon avocado oil

1. Sprinkle scallops with dried rosemary, Pink salt, and avocado oil.
2. Then put the scallops in the air fryer basket in one layer and cook at 400F (205ºC) for 6 minutes.

Per Serving
calories: 82 | fat: 1g | protein: 14g | carbs: 3g | net carbs: 2g | fiber: 1g

Calamari with Hot Sauce

Prep time: 10 minutes | Cook time: 6 minutes | Serves 2

10 ounces calamari, trimmed
2 tablespoons keto hot

sauce
1 tablespoon avocado oil

1. Slice the calamari and sprinkle with avocado oil.
2. Put the calamari in the air fryer and cook at 400F (205ºC) for 3 minutes per side.
3. Then transfer the calamari in the serving plate and sprinkle with hot sauce.

Per Serving
calories: 36 | fat: 2g | protein: 3g | carbs: 2g | net carbs: 1g | fiber: 1g

Salmon with Coconut

Prep time: 15 minutes | Cook time: 8 minutes | Serves 4

2 pounds (907 g) salmon fillet
¼ cup coconut shred
2 eggs, beaten
1 teaspoon coconut oil
1 teaspoon Italian seasonings

1. Cut the salmon fillet into servings.
2. Then sprinkle the fish with Italian seasonings and dip in the eggs.
3. After this, coat every salmon fillet in coconut shred and put it in the air fryer.
4. Cook the fish at 375F (190ºC) for 4 minutes per side.

Per Serving
calories: 395 | fat: 22g | protein: 47g | carbs: 2g | net carbs: 1g | fiber: 1g

Basil Salmon Fillet

Prep time: 10 minutes | Cook time: 8 minutes | Serves 2

10 ounces (283 g) salmon fillet
½ teaspoon ground coriander
1 teaspoon ground cumin
1 teaspoon dried basil
1 tablespoon avocado oil

1. In the shallow bowl, mix ground coriander, ground cumin, and dried basil.
2. Then coat the salmon fillet in the spices and sprinkle with avocado oil.
3. Put the fish in the air fryer basket and cook at 395F (202ºC) for 4 minutes per side.

Per Serving
calories: 201 | fat: 9g | protein: 28g | carbs: 1g | net carbs: 0g | fiber: 1g

Cheddar Shrimp

Prep time: 15 minutes | Cook time: 5 minutes | Serves 4

14 ounces (397 g) shrimps, peeled
1 egg, beaten
½ cup of coconut milk
1 cup Cheddar cheese,
shredded
½ teaspoon coconut oil
1 teaspoon ground coriander

1. In the mixing bowl, mix shrimps with egg, coconut
milk, Cheddar cheese, coconut oil, and ground coriander.
2. Then put the mixture in the baking ramekins and put in the air fryer.
3. Cook the shrimps at 400F (205ºC) for 5 minutes.

Per Serving
calories: 321 | fat: 19g | protein: 32g | carbs: 4g | net carbs: 3g | fiber: 1g

Salmon with Cauliflower

Prep time: 10 minutes | Cook time: 25 minutes | Serves 4

1 pound (454 g) salmon fillet, diced
1 cup cauliflower, shredded
1 tablespoon dried cilantro
1 tablespoon coconut oil, melted
1 teaspoon ground turmeric
¼ cup coconut cream

1. Mix salmon with cauliflower, dried cilantro, ground turmeric, coconut cream, and coconut oil.
2. Transfer the salmon mixture in the air fryer and cook the meal at 350F (180ºC) for 25 minutes. Stir the meal every 5 minutes to avoid the burning.

Per Serving
calories: 222 | fat: 14g | protein: 23g | carbs: 3g | net carbs: 2g | fiber: 1g

Shrimp with Swiss Chard

Prep time: 10 minutes | Cook time: 10 minutes | Serves 4

pound (454-g) shrimp, peeled and deveined
½ teaspoon smoked paprika
½ cup Swiss chard,
chopped
2 tablespoons apple cider vinegar
1 tablespoon coconut oil
¼ cup heavy cream

1. Mix shrimps with smoked paprika and apple cider vinegar.
2. Put the shrimps in the air fryer and add coconut oil.
3. Cook the shrimps at 350F (180ºC) for 10 minutes.
4. Then mix cooked shrimps with remaining ingredients and carefully mix.

Per Serving
calories: 193 | fat: 8g | protein: 26g | carbs: 2g | net carbs: 1g | fiber: 1g

Creamy Haddock

Prep time: 10 minutes | Cook time: 8 minutes | Serves 4

pound (454-g) haddock fillet
1 teaspoon cayenne pepper
1 teaspoon salt
1 teaspoon coconut oil
½ cup heavy cream

1. Grease the baking pan with coconut oil.
2. Then put haddock fillet inside and sprinkle it with cayenne pepper, salt, and heavy cream.
3. Put the baking pan in the air fryer basket and cook at 375F (190ºC) for 8 minutes.

Per Serving
calories: 190 | fat: 7g | protein: 28g | carbs: 2g | net carbs: 1g | fiber: 1g

Cod with Tomatillos

Prep time: 10 minutes | Cook time: 15 minutes | Serves 4

2 ounces (57 g) tomatillos, chopped
pound (454-g) cod fillet, roughly chopped
1 tablespoon avocado oil
1 tablespoon lemon juice
1 teaspoon keto tomato paste

1. Mix avocado oil with lemon juice and tomato paste.
2. Then mix cod fillet with tomato mixture and put in the air fryer.
3. Add lemon juice and tomatillos.
4. Cook the cod at 370F (188ºC) for 15 minutes.

Per Serving
calories: 102 | fat: 2g | protein: 20g | carbs: 2g | net carbs: 1g | fiber: 1g

Crispy Flounder

Prep time: 10 minutes | Cook time: 12 minutes | Serves 2

2 flounder fillets
1 egg
½ teaspoon Worcestershire sauce
¼ cup coconut flour
¼ cup almond flour
½ teaspoon lemon pepper
½ teaspoon coarse sea salt
¼ teaspoon chili powder

1. Rinse and pat dry the flounder fillets.
2. Whisk the egg and Worcestershire sauce in a shallow bowl. In a separate bowl, mix the coconut flour, almond flour, lemon pepper, salt, and chili powder.
3. Then, dip the fillets into the egg mixture. Lastly, coat the fish fillets with the coconut flour mixture until they are coated on all sides.
4. Spritz with cooking spray and transfer to the Air Fryer basket. Cook at 390ºfor 7 minutes.
5. Turn them over, spritz with cooking spray on the other side, and cook another 5 minutes. Bon appétit!

Per Serving
calories: 325 | fat: 18.3g | carbs: 6.1g | protein:34.4g | sugar: 2.2g | fiber: 1.7g

Bacon Halibut Steak

Prep time: 15 minutes | Cook time: 10 minutes | Serves 4

24 ounces (680 g) halibut steaks (6-ounce / 170-g each fillet)
1 teaspoon avocado oil
1 teaspoon ground black pepper
4 ounces (113 g) bacon, sliced

1. Sprinkle the halibut steaks with avocado oil and ground black pepper.
2. Then wrap the fish in the bacon slices and put in the air fryer.
3. Cook the fish at 390F (199ºC) for 5 minutes per side.

Per Serving
calories: 266 | fat: 14g | protein: 33g | carbs: 2g | net carbs: 1g | fiber: 1g

Rosemary Shrimp Skewers

Prep time: 10 minutes | Cook time: 5 minutes | Serves 5

pounds (1.8-kg) shrimps, peeled
1 tablespoon dried rosemary
1 tablespoon avocado oil
1 teaspoon apple cider vinegar

1. Mix the shrimps with dried rosemary, avocado oil, and apple cider vinegar.
2. Then sting the shrimps into skewers and put in the air fryer.
3. Cook the shrimps at 400F (205ºC) for 5 minutes.

Per Serving
calories: 437 | fat: 6g | protein: 83g | carbs: 6g | net carbs: 5g | fiber: 1g

Snapper with Shallot and Tomato

Prep time: 20 minutes | Cook time: 15 minutes | Serves 2

2 snapper fillets
1 shallot, peeled and sliced
2 garlic cloves, halved
1 bell pepper, sliced
1 small-sized serrano pepper, sliced

1 tomato, sliced
1 tablespoon olive oil
¼ teaspoon freshly ground black pepper
½ teaspoon paprika
Sea salt, to taste
2 bay leaves

1. Place two parchment sheets on a working surface. Place the fish in the center of one side of the parchment paper.
2. Top with the shallot, garlic, peppers, and tomato. Drizzle olive oil over the fish and vegetables. Season with black pepper, paprika, and salt. Add the bay leaves.
3. Fold over the other half of the parchment. Now, fold the paper around the edges tightly and create a half moon shape, sealing the fish inside.
4. Cook in the preheated Air Fryer at 390ºF (199ºC) for 15 minutes. Serve warm.

Per Serving
calories: 329 | fat: 9g | protein: 47g | carbs: 13g | net carbs: 12g | fiber: 1g

Creamy Tuna Pork Casserole

Prep time: 15 minutes | Cook time: 15 minutes | Serves 4

2 tablespoons salted butter
¼ cup diced white onion
¼ cup chopped white mushrooms
2 stalks celery, finely chopped
½ cup heavy cream
½ cup vegetable broth
2 tablespoons full-fat

mayonnaise
¼ teaspoon xanthan gum
½ teaspoon red pepper flakes
2 medium zucchini, spiralized
2 cans (5-ounce / (142-g)) albacore tuna
1 ounce (28 g) pork rinds, finely ground

1. In a large saucepan over medium heat, melt butter. Add onion, mushrooms, and celery and sauté until fragrant, about 3 to 5 minutes.
2. Pour in heavy cream, vegetable broth, mayonnaise, and xanthan gum. Reduce heat and continue cooking for an additional 3 minutes, until the mixture begins to thicken.
3. Add red pepper flakes, zucchini, and tuna. Turn off

heat and stir until zucchini noodles are coated.
4. Pour into 4-cup round baking dish. Top with ground pork rinds and cover the top of the dish with foil. Place into the air fryer basket.
5. Adjust the temperature to 370°F (188ºC) and set the timer for 15 minutes.
6. When there is 3 minutes remaining, remove the foil to brown the top of the casserole. Serve warm.

Per Serving
calories: 339 | fat: 25g | protein: 20g | carbs: 6g | net carbs: 4g | fiber: 2g

Creamy Mackerel

Prep time: 10 minutes | Cook time: 6 minutes | Serves 4

pound (907-g) mackerel fillet
1 cup coconut cream
1 teaspoon ground

coriander
1 teaspoon cumin seeds
1 garlic clove, peeled, chopped

1. Chop the mackerel roughly and sprinkle it with coconut cream, ground coriander, cumin seeds, and garlic.
2. Then put the fish in the air fryer and cook at 400F (205ºC) for 6 minutes.

Per Serving
calories: 735 | fat: 54g | protein: 55g | carbs: 4g | net carbs: 2g | fiber: 2g

Tilapia with Fennel Seeds

Prep time: 15 minutes | Cook time: 10 minutes | Serves 4

pound (907-g) tilapia fillet
1 teaspoon fennel seeds
1 tablespoon avocado oil
½ teaspoon lime zest,

grated
1 tablespoon coconut aminos

1. In the shallow bowl, mix fennel seeds with avocado oil, lime zest, and coconut aminos.
2. Then brush the tilapia fillet with fennel seeds and put in the air fryer.
3. Cook the fish at 380F (193ºC) for 10 minutes.

Per Serving
calories: 194 | fat: 2g | protein: 42g | carbs: 1g | net carbs: 0g | fiber: 1g

Tuna Casserole

Prep time: 15 minutes | Cook time: 16 minutes | Serves 4

5 eggs, beaten
½ chili pepper, deveined and finely minced
1½ tablespoons sour cream
⅓ teaspoon dried oregano
½ tablespoon sesame oil

⅓ cup yellow onions, chopped
2 cups canned tuna
½ bell pepper, deveined and chopped
⅓ teaspoon dried basil
Fine sea salt and ground black pepper, to taste

1. Warm sesame oil in a nonstick skillet that is preheated over a moderate flame. Then, sweat the onions and peppers for 4 minutes, or until they are just fragrant.
2. Add chopped canned tuna and stir until heated through.
3. Meanwhile, lightly grease a baking dish with a pan spray. Throw in sautéed tuna/pepper mix. Add the remaining ingredients in the order listed above.
4. Bake for 12 minutes at 325ºF. Eat warm garnished with Tabasco sauce if desired.

Per Serving

calories: 268 | fat: 16g | protein: 28g | carbs: 3g | net carbs: 2g | fiber: 1g

Cod Fillets with Avocado and Cabbage

Prep time: 10 minutes | Cook time: 10 minutes | Serves 2

1 cup shredded cabbage
¼ cup full-fat sour cream
2 tablespoons full-fat mayonnaise
¼ cup chopped pickled jalapeños
2 (3-ounce / (85-g)) cod fillets

1 teaspoon chili powder
1 teaspoon cumin
½ teaspoon paprika
¼ teaspoon garlic powder
1 medium avocado, peeled, pitted, and sliced
½ medium lime

1. In a large bowl, place cabbage, sour cream, mayonnaise, and jalapeños. Mix until fully coated. Let it sit for 20 minutes in the refrigerator.
2. Sprinkle cod fillets with chili powder, cumin, paprika, and garlic powder. Place each fillet into the air fryer basket.
3. Adjust the temperature to 370°F (188ºC) and set the timer for 10 minutes.
4. Flip the fillets halfway through the cooking time.

When fully cooked, fish should have an internal temperature of at least 145°F (63ºC).

5. To serve, divide slaw mixture into two serving bowls, break cod fillets into pieces and spread over the bowls, and top with avocado. Squeeze lime juice over each bowl. Serve immediately.

Per Serving

calories: 342 | fat: 25g | protein: 16g | carbs: 12g | net carbs: 6g | fiber: 6g

Salmon with Provolone Cheese

Prep time: 5 minutes | Cook time: 15 minutes | Serves 4

1 pound (454 g) salmon fillet, chopped
2 ounces (57 g) Provolone cheese,

grated
1 teaspoon avocado oil
¼ teaspoon ground paprika

1. Sprinkle the salmon fillets with avocado oil and put in the air fryer.
2. Then sprinkle the fish with ground paprika and top with Provolone cheese.
3. Cook the fish at 360F (182ºC) for 15 minutes.

Per Serving

calories: 202 | fat: 10g | protein: 26g | carbs: 1g | net carbs: 0g | fiber: 1g

Italian Salmon with Olives

Prep time: 15 minutes | Cook time: 15 minutes | Serves 4

1 pound (454 g) salmon fillet
4 kalamata olives, sliced
1 teaspoon avocado oil

1 teaspoon Italian seasonings
2 ounces (57 g) Mozzarella, shredded

1. Make the cut in the salmon in the shape of the pocket.
2. The fill the salmon cut with olives and Mozzarella.
3. Secure the cut with the help of the toothpick and sprinkle the salmon with Italian seasonings and avocado oil.
4. Cook the salmon in the air fryer basket and cook it at 380F (193ºC) for 15 minutes.

Per Serving

calories: 200 | fat: 10g | protein: 26g | carbs: 2g | net carbs: 1g | fiber: 1g

Parmesan Mackerel

Prep time: 10 minutes | Cook time: 7 minutes | Serves 2

12 ounces (340 g) mackerel fillet
2 ounces (57 g) Parmesan, grated

1 teaspoon ground coriander
1 tablespoon olive oil

1. Sprinkle the mackerel fillet with olive oil and put it in the air fryer basket.
2. Top the fish with ground coriander and Parmesan.
3. Cook the fish at 390F (199ºC) for 7 minutes.

Per Serving
calories: 597 | fat: 43g | protein: 50g | carbs: 1g | net carbs: 1g | fiber: 0g

Golden Shrimp

Prep time: 20 minutes | Cook time: 7 minutes | Serves 4

2 egg whites
½ cup coconut flour
1 cup Parmigiano-Reggiano, grated
½ teaspoon celery seeds
½ teaspoon porcini powder
½ teaspoon onion powder

1 teaspoon garlic powder
½ teaspoon dried rosemary
½ teaspoon sea salt
½ teaspoon ground black pepper
1½ pounds (680g) shrimp, deveined

1. Whisk the egg with coconut flour and Parmigiano-Reggiano. Add in seasonings and mix to combine well.
2. Dip your shrimp in the batter. Roll until they are covered on all sides.
3. Cook in the preheated Air Fryer at 390ºF (199ºC) for 5 to 7 minutes or until golden brown. Work in batches. Serve with lemon wedges if desired.

Per Serving
calories: 300 | fat: 11g | protein: 44g | carbs: 7g | net carbs: 6g | fiber: 1g

Fijan Coconut Tilapia

Prep time: 15 minutes | Cook time: 12 minutes | Serves 2

1 cup coconut milk
2 tablespoons lime juice
2 tablespoons Shoyu sauce
Salt and white pepper, to taste
1 teaspoon turmeric powder

½ teaspoon ginger powder
½ Thai Bird's Eye chili, seeded and finely chopped
1 pound (454 g) tilapia
2 tablespoons olive oil

1. In a mixing bowl, thoroughly combine the coconut milk with the lime juice, Shoyu sauce, salt, pepper, turmeric, ginger, and chili pepper. Add tilapia and let it marinate for 1 hour.
2. Brush the Air Fryer basket with olive oil. Discard the marinade and place the tilapia fillets in the Air Fryer basket.
3. Cook the tilapia in the preheated Air Fryer at 400ºF for 6 minutes, turn them over and cook for 6 minutes or more. Work in batches.
4. Serve with some extra lime wedges if desired. Enjoy!

Per Serving
calories: 426 | fat: 22g | protein: 50g | carbs: 9g | net carbs: 6g | fiber: 3g

Chapter 7 Vegetarian Mains

Zucchini and Bell Pepper Kabobs

Prep time: 15 minutes | Cook time: 15 minutes | Serves 4

1 medium-sized zucchini, cut into 1-inch pieces
2 red bell peppers, cut into 1-inch pieces
1 green bell pepper, cut into 1-Inch pleces
1 red onion, cut into 1-inch pieces

2 tablespoons olive oil
Sea salt, to taste
½ teaspoon black pepper, preferably freshly cracked
½ teaspoon red pepper flakes

1. Soak the wooden skewers in water for 15 minutes.
2. Thread the vegetables on skewers, drizzle olive oil all over the vegetable skewers, sprinkle with spices.
3. Cook in the preheated Air Fryer at 400ºF for 13 minutes. Serve warm and enjoy!

Per Serving
calories: 86 | fat: 6.9g | protein: 1.1g | total carbs: 5.9g | fiber: 1.1g

Mexican Cauliflower Fritters

Prep time: 15 minutes | Cook time: 14 minutes | Serves 6

2 teaspoons chili powder
1½ teaspoons kosher salt
1 teaspoon dried marjoram, crushed
2 ½ cups cauliflower, broken into florets

1 ⅓ cups tortilla chip crumbs
½ teaspoon crushed red pepper flakes
3 eggs, whisked
1½ cups Queso cotija cheese, crumbled

1. Blitz the cauliflower florets in your food processor until they're crumbled (it is the size of rice). Then, combine the cauliflower "rice" with the other items.
2. Now, roll the cauliflower mixture into small balls, refrigerate for 30 minutes.
3. Preheat your Air Fryer to 345ºand set the timer for 14 minutes, cook until the balls are browned and serve right away.

Per Serving
calories: 190 | fat: 14.1g | protein: 11.5g | total carbs: 4.7g | fiber: 1.3g

Balsamic Green Beans

Prep time: 10 minutes | Cook time: 10 minutes | Serves 4

¾ pound (340 g) green beans, cleaned
1 tablespoon balsamic vinegar
¼ teaspoon kosher salt
½ teaspoon mixed

peppercorns, freshly cracked
1 tablespoon butter
2 tablespoons toasted sesame seeds, to serve

1. Set your Air Fryer to cook at 390ºF.
2. Mix the green beans with all of the above ingredients, apart from the sesame seeds. Set the timer for 10 minutes.
3. Meanwhile, toast the sesame seeds in a small-sized nonstick skillet, make sure to stir continuously.
4. Serve sautéed green beans on a nice serving platter sprinkled with toasted sesame seeds. Bon appétit!

Per Serving
calories: 73 | fat: 3.0g | protein: 1.6g | total carbs: 6.1g | fiber: 2.1g

Herbed Broccoli and Celery Root

Prep time: 15 minutes | Cook time: 15 minutes | Serves 2

½ pound (227 g) broccoli florets
1 celery root, peeled and cut into 1-inch pieces
1 onion, cut into wedges
2 tablespoons unsalted

butter, melted
½ cup chicken broth
¼ cup tomato sauce
1 teaspoon parsley
1 teaspoon rosemary
1 teaspoon thyme

1. Start by preheating your Air Fryer to 380ºF. Place all ingredients in a lightly greased casserole dish. Stir to combine well.
2. Bake in the preheated Air Fryer for 10 minutes. Gently stir the vegetables with a large spoon and cook for 5 minutes or more.
3. Serve in individual bowls with a few drizzles of lemon juice. Bon appétit!

Per Serving
calories: 141 | fat: 11.3g | protein: 2.5g | total carbs: 8.1g | fiber: 2.6g

Super Cheese Cauliflower Fritters

Prep time: 15 minutes | Cook time: 10 minutes | Serves 8

2 pounds (907 g) cauliflower florets
½ cup scallions, finely chopped
½ teaspoon freshly ground black pepper, or more to taste

1 tablespoon fine sea salt
½ teaspoon hot paprika
2 cups Colby cheese, shredded
1 cup Parmesan cheese, grated
¼ cup olive oil

1. Firstly, boil the cauliflower until fork tender. Drain, peel and mash your cauliflower.
2. Thoroughly mix the mashed cauliflower with scallions, pepper, salt, paprika, and Colby cheese. Then, shape the balls using your hands. Now, flatten the balls to make the patties.
3. Roll the patties over grated Parmesan cheese. Drizzle olive oil over them.
4. Next, cook your patties at 360ºF (182ºC) approximately 10 minutes, working in batches. Serve with tabasco mayo if desired. Bon appétit!

Per Serving
calories: 282 | fat: 22g | protein: 13g | carbs: 8g | net carbs: 6g | fiber: 2g

Tofu with Chili-Galirc Sauce

Prep time: 10 minutes | Cook time: 20 minutes | Serves 4

1 (16-ounce / 454-g) block extra-firm tofu
2 tablespoons coconut aminos
1 tablespoon toasted sesame oil

1 tablespoon olive oil
1 tablespoon chili-garlic sauce
1½ teaspoons black sesame seeds
1 scallion, thinly sliced

1. Press the tofu for at least 15 minutes by wrapping it in paper towels and setting a heavy pan on top so that the moisture drains.
2. Slice the tofu into bite-size cubes and transfer to a bowl. Drizzle with the coconut aminos, sesame oil, olive oil, and chili-garlic sauce. Cover and refrigerate for 1 hour or up to overnight.
3. Preheat the air fryer to 400°F (205ºC).
4. Arrange the tofu in a single layer in the air fryer basket. Pausing to shake the pan halfway through the cooking time, air fry for 15 to 20 minutes until crisp. Serve with any juices that accumulate in the bottom of the air fryer, sprinkled with the sesame seeds and

sliced scallion.

Per Serving
calories: 180 | fat: 13g | protein: 11g | carbs: 5g | net carbs: 4g | fiber: 1g

Fauxtato Casserole

Prep time: 15 minutes | Cook time: 55 minutes | Serves 6

2 cups cauliflower florets
1 cup chicken broth or water
1 cup canned pumpkin puree
⅓ cup unsalted butter, melted, plus more for the pan
¼ cup Swerve confectioners-style sweetener
¼ cup unsweetened, unflavored almond milk
2 large eggs, beaten

1 teaspoon fine sea salt
1 teaspoon vanilla extract
Topping:
1 cup chopped pecans
½ cup blanched almond flour or pecan meal
½ cup Swerve confectioners-style sweetener
⅓ cup unsalted butter, melted
Chopped fresh parsley leaves, for garnish (optional)

1. Preheat the air fryer to 350°F.
2. Place the cauliflower florets in a 6-inch pie pan or a casserole dish that will fit in your air fryer. Add the broth to the pie pan. Cook in the air fryer for 20 minutes, or until the cauliflower is very tender.
3. Drain the cauliflower and transfer it to a food processor. Set the pie pan aside, you'll use it in the next step. Blend the cauliflower until very smooth. Add the pumpkin, butter, sweetener, almond milk, eggs, salt, and vanilla and puree until smooth.
4. Grease the pie pan that you cooked the cauliflower in with butter. Pour the cauliflower-pumpkin mixture into the pan. Set aside.
5. Make the topping: In a large bowl, mix together all the ingredients for the topping until well combined. Crumble the topping over the cauliflower-pumpkin mixture.
6. Cook in the air fryer for 30 to 35 minutes, until cooked through and golden brown on top. Garnish with fresh parsley before serving, if desired.
7. Store leftovers in an airtight container in the fridge for up to 4 days or in the freezer for up to a month. Reheat in a preheated 350°F air fryer for 6 minutes, or until heated through.

Per Serving
calories: 421 | fat: 40g | protein: 8g | total carbs: 10g | fiber: 5g

Zucchini and Mushroom Kebab

Prep time: 40 minutes | Cook time: 8 minutes | Makes 8 skewers

1 medium zucchini, trimmed and cut into ½-inch slices
½ medium yellow onion, peeled and cut into 1-inch squares
1 medium red bell pepper, seeded and cut
into 1-inch squares
16 whole cremini mushrooms
⅓ cup basil pesto
½ teaspoon salt
¼ teaspoon ground black pepper

1. Divide zucchini slices, onion, and bell pepper into eight even portions. Place on 6-inch skewers for a total of eight kebabs. Add 2 mushrooms to each skewer and brush kebabs generously with pesto.
2. Sprinkle each kebab with salt and black pepper on all sides, then place into ungreased air fryer basket. Adjust the temperature to 375°F (190ºC) and set the timer for 8 minutes, turning kebabs halfway through cooking. Vegetables will be browned at the edges and tender-crisp when done. Serve warm.

Per Serving
calories: 107 | fat: 7g | protein: 4g | carbs: 10g | net carbs: 8g | fiber: 2g

Tempura Bowl

Prep time: 20 minutes | Cook time: 10 minutes | Serves 3

7 tablespoons whey protein isolate
1 teaspoon baking powder
Kosher salt and ground black pepper, to taste
½ teaspoon paprika
1 teaspoon dashi granules
2 eggs
1 tablespoon mirin
3 tablespoons soda water
1 cup Parmesan cheese, grated
1 onion, cut into rings
1 bell pepper
1 zucchini, cut into slices
3 asparagus spears
2 tablespoons olive oil

1. In a shallow bowl, mix the whey protein isolate, baking powder, salt, black pepper, paprika, dashi granules, eggs, mirin, and soda water.
2. In another shallow bowl, place grated Parmesan cheese.
3. Dip the vegetables in tempura batter, lastly, roll over Parmesan cheese to coat evenly. Drizzle each piece with olive oil.
4. Cook in the preheated Air Fryer at 400ºF for 10

minutes, shaking the basket halfway through the cooking time. Work in batches until the vegetables are crispy and golden brown. Bon appétit!

Per Serving
calories: 324 | fat: 19.2g | protein: 11.6g | total carbs: 19.5g | fiber: 2g

Eggplant Lasagna

Prep time: 15 minutes | Cook time: 36 minutes | Serves 4

1 small eggplant (about ¾ pound / 340 g), sliced into rounds
2 teaspoons salt
1 tablespoon olive oil
1 cup shredded Mozzarella, divided
1 cup ricotta cheese
1 large egg
¼ cup grated Parmesan cheese
½ teaspoon dried oregano
1½ cups no-sugar-added marinara
1 tablespoon chopped fresh parsley

1. Preheat the air fryer to 350°F (180ºC). Coat a 6-cup casserole dish that fits in your air fryer with olive oil, set aside.
2. Arrange the eggplant slices in a single layer on a baking sheet and sprinkle with the salt. Let sit for 10 minutes. Use a paper towel to remove the excess moisture and salt.
3. Working in batches if necessary, brush the eggplant with the olive oil and arrange in a single layer in the air fryer basket. Pausing halfway through the cooking time to turn the eggplant, air fry for 6 minutes until softened. Transfer the eggplant back to the baking sheet and let it cool.
4. In a small bowl, combine ½ cup of the Mozzarella with the ricotta, egg, Parmesan, and oregano. To assemble the lasagna, spread a spoonful of marinara in the bottom of the casserole dish, followed by a layer of eggplant, a layer of the cheese mixture, and a layer of marinara. Repeat the layers until all of the ingredients are used, ending with the remaining ½ cup of Mozzarella. Scatter the parsley on top. Cover the baking dish with foil.
5. Increase the air fryer to 370°F (188ºC) and air fry for 30 minutes. Uncover the dish and continue baking for 10 minutes longer until the cheese begins to brown. Let the casserole sit for at least 10 minutes before serving.

Per Serving
calories: 350 | fat: 22g | protein: 20g | carbs: 17g | net carbs: 12g | fiber: 5g

Greek Green Salad

Prep time: 15 minutes | Cook time: 6 minutes | Serves 4

1 red onion, sliced
1 pound (454 g) cherry tomatoes
½ pound (227 g) asparagus
1 cucumber, sliced
2 cups baby spinach
2 tablespoons white vinegar
¼ cup extra-virgin olive oil
2 tablespoons fresh parsley
Sea salt and pepper to taste
½ cup Kalamata olives, pitted and sliced

1. Begin by preheating your Air Fryer to 400ºF.
2. Place the onion, cherry tomatoes, and asparagus in the lightly greased Air Fryer basket. Bake for 5 to 6 minutes, tossing the basket occasionally.
3. Transfer to a salad bowl. Add the cucumber and baby spinach.
4. Then, whisk the vinegar, olive oil, parsley, salt, and black pepper in a small mixing bowl. Dress your salad, add Kalamata olives.
5. Toss to combine well and serve.

Per Serving

calories: 183 | fat: 15.8g | protein: 3.1g | total carbs: 9.7g | fiber: 3.7g

Cheese Stuffed Mushrooms

Prep time: 15 minutes | Cook time: 12 minutes | Serves 5

½ cup Parmesan cheese, grated
2 cloves garlic, pressed
2 tablespoons fresh coriander, chopped
⅓ teaspoon kosher salt
½ teaspoon crushed red pepper flakes
1½ tablespoons olive oil
20 medium-sized
mushrooms, cut off the stems
½ cup Gorgonzola cheese, grated
¼ cup low-fat mayonnaise
1 teaspoon prepared horseradish, well-drained
1 tablespoon fresh parsley, finely chopped

1. Mix the Parmesan cheese together with the garlic, coriander, salt, red pepper, and the olive oil, mix to combine well.
2. Stuff the mushroom caps with the cheese filling. Top with grated Gorgonzola.
3. Place the mushrooms in the Air Fryer grill pan and slide them into the machine. Grill them at 380ºF for 8 to 12 minutes or until the stuffing is warmed

through.
4. Meanwhile, prepare the horseradish sauce by mixing the mayonnaise, horseradish and parsley. Serve the horseradish sauce with the warm fried mushrooms. Enjoy!

Per Serving

calories: 180 | fat: 13.2g | protein: 1.6g | total carbs: 6.2g | fiber: 1g

Crunchy Cauliflower Mac 'n' Cheese

Prep time: 10 minutes | Cook time: 15 minutes | Serves 4

2 cups frozen chopped cauliflower, thawed
2 ounces (57 g) cream cheese (¼ cup), softened
¼ cup shredded Gruyère or Swiss cheese
¼ cup shredded sharp Cheddar cheese
2 tablespoons finely diced onions
3 tablespoons beef broth
¼ teaspoon fine sea salt
Topping:
¼ cup pork dust
¼ cup unsalted butter, melted, plus more for greasing ramekins
4 slices bacon, finely diced
For Garnish (Optional):
Chopped fresh thyme or chives

1. Preheat the air fryer to 375°F.
2. Place the cauliflower on a paper towel and pat dry. Cut any large pieces of cauliflower into ½-inch pieces.
3. In a medium-sized bowl, stir together the cream cheese, Gruyère, Cheddar, and onions. Slowly stir in the broth and combine well. Add the salt and stir to combine. Add the cauliflower and stir gently to mix the cauliflower into the cheese sauce.
4. Grease four 4-ounce (113-g) ramekins with butter. Divide the cauliflower mixture among the ramekins, filling each three-quarters full.
5. Make the topping: In a small bowl, stir together the pork dust, butter, and bacon until well combined. Divide the topping among the ramekins.
6. Place the ramekins in the air fryer (if you're using a smaller air fryer, work in batches if necessary) and cook for 15 minutes, or until the topping is browned and the bacon is crispy.
7. Garnish with fresh thyme or chives, if desired.
8. Store leftovers in the ramekins covered with foil. Reheat in a preheated 375°F air fryer for 6 minutes, or until the cauliflower is heated through and the top is crispy.

Per Serving

calories: 305 | fat: 26g | protein: 12g | total carbs: 6g | fiber: 3g

Roasted Green Beans

Prep time: 15 minutes | Cook time: 5 minutes | Serves 4

¾ pound (340 g) trimmed green beans, cut into bite-sized pieces
Salt and freshly cracked mixed pepper, to taste
1 shallot, thinly sliced
1 tablespoon lime juice
1 tablespoon champagne vinegar
¼ cup extra-virgin olive oil
½ teaspoon mustard seeds
½ teaspoon celery seeds
1 tablespoon fresh basil leaves, chopped
1 tablespoon fresh parsley leaves
1 cup goat cheese, crumbled

1. Toss the green beans with salt and pepper in a lightly greased Air Fryer basket.
2. Cook in the preheated Air Fryer at 400ºF for 5 minutes or until tender.
3. Add the shallots and gently stir to combine.
4. In a mixing bowl, whisk the lime juice, vinegar, olive oil, and spices. Dress the salad and top with the goat cheese. Serve at room temperature or chilled. Enjoy!

Per Serving
calories: 280 | fat: 23.3g | protein: 9.3g | total carbs: 18.8g | fiber: 2.4g

Tomato Bites with Parmesan-Pecan Sauce

Prep time: 15 minutes | Cook time: 15 minutes | Serves 4

For the Sauce:
½ cup Parmigiano-Reggiano cheese, grated
4 tablespoons pecans, chopped
1 teaspoon garlic puree
½ teaspoon fine sea salt
⅓ cup extra-virgin olive oil
For the Tomato Bites:
2 large-sized Roma
tomatoes, cut into thin slices and pat them dry
8 ounces (227 g) Halloumi cheese, cut into thin slices
⅓ cup onions, sliced
1 teaspoon dried basil
¼ teaspoon red pepper flakes, crushed
⅛ teaspoon sea salt

1. Start by preheating your Air Fryer to 385ºF.
2. Make the sauce by mixing all ingredients, except the extra-virgin olive oil, in your food processor.
3. While the machine is running, slowly and gradually pour in the olive oil, puree until everything is well-blended.
4. Now, spread 1 teaspoon of the sauce over the top of

each tomato slice. Place a slice of Halloumi cheese on each tomato slice. Top with onion slices. Sprinkle with basil, red pepper, and sea salt.
5. Transfer the assembled bites to the Air Fryer cooking basket. Drizzle with a nonstick cooking spray and cook for approximately 13 minutes.
6. Arrange these bites on a nice serving platter, garnish with the remaining sauce and serve at room temperature. Bon appétit!

Per Serving
calories: 428 | fat: 38.4g | protein: 8.8g | total carbs: 14.5g | fiber: 1.3g

Artichoke Tart

Prep time: 10 minutes | Cook time: 40 minutes | Serves 6

Crust:
1 cup blanched almond flour
1 cup grated Parmesan cheese
1 large egg
Filling:
4 ounces (113 g) cream cheese (½ cup), softened
1 (8-ounce / 227-g) package frozen chopped
spinach, thawed and drained
½ cup artichoke hearts, drained and chopped
⅓ cup shredded Parmesan cheese, plus more for topping
1 large egg
1 clove garlic, minced
¼ teaspoon fine sea salt

1. Preheat the air fryer to 350°F.
2. Make the crust: Place the almond flour and cheese in a large bowl and mix until well combined. Add the egg and mix until the dough is well combined and stiff.
3. Press the dough into a 6-inch pie pan. Bake for 8 to 10 minutes, until it starts to brown lightly.
4. Meanwhile, make the filling: Place the cream cheese in a large bowl and stir to break it up. Add the spinach, artichoke hearts, cheese, egg, garlic, and salt. Stir well to combine.
5. Pour the spinach mixture into the prebaked crust and sprinkle with additional Parmesan. Place in the air fryer and cook for 25 to 30 minutes, until cooked through.
6. Store leftovers in an airtight container in the fridge for up to 4 days or in the freezer for up to a month. Reheat in a preheated 350°F air fryer for 5 minutes, or until heated through.

Per Serving
calories: 228 | fat: 7g | protein: 14g | total carbs: 6g | fiber: 2g

Buddha Bowl

Prep time: 15 minutes | Cook time: 12 minutes | Serves 3

1 (1-pound / 454-g) head cauliflower, food-processed into rice-like particles
2 bell pepper, spiralized
Coarse sea salt and ground black pepper, to taste
3 cups baby spinach
2 tablespoons

champagne vinegar
4 tablespoons mayonnaise
1 teaspoon yellow mustard
4 tablespoons olive oil, divided
2 tablespoons cilantro leaves, chopped
2 tablespoons pine nuts

1. Start by preheating the Air Fryer to 400ºF.
2. Place the cauliflower florets and bell peppers in the lightly greased Air Fryer basket. Season with salt and black pepper, cook for 12 minutes, tossing halfway through the cooking time.
3. Toss with the baby spinach. Add the champagne vinegar, mayonnaise, mustard, and olive oil. Garnish with fresh cilantro and pine nuts. Bon appétit!

Per Serving
calories: 329 | fat: 32.3g | carbs: 8.6g | protein: 3.4g | sugar: 0.5g | fiber: 3g

Falafel with Mayo

Prep time: 20 minutes | Cook time: 15 minutes | Serves 2

Keto Falafel:
½ pound (227 g) cauliflower
½ onion, chopped
2 cloves garlic, minced
2 tablespoons fresh cilantro leaves, chopped
¼ cup almond meal
½ teaspoon baking powder
1 teaspoon cumin powder

A pinch of ground cardamom
Sea salt and ground black pepper, to taste
Homemade Mayonnaise:
1 egg yolk
1 tablespoon sour cream
¼ cup olive oil
¼ teaspoon salt
1 tablespoon lemon juice

1. Pulse all the falafel ingredients in your food processor.
2. Form the falafel mixture into balls and place them in the lightly greased Air Fryer basket.
3. Cook at 380ºF for about 15 minutes, shaking the basket occasionally to ensure even cooking.
4. In a mixing bowl, place egg yolk and sour cream.

Gradually and slowly, pour in your oil while whisking constantly.
5. Once you reach a thick consistency, add in the salt and lemon juice. Whisk again to combine. Serve falafel with your homemade mayonnaise and enjoy!

Per Serving
calories: 378 | fat: 36.8g | carbs: 9g | protein: 5.8g | sugar: 0.9g | fiber: 3.3g

Indian Zucchini and Kohlrabi Kofta

Prep time: 20 minutes | Cook time: 23 minutes | Serves 4

Veggie Balls:
¾ pound (340 g) zucchini, grated and well drained
¼ pound (113 g) kohlrabi, grated and well drained
2 cloves garlic, minced
1 tablespoon Garam masala
1 cup paneer, crumbled
¼ cup coconut flour
½ teaspoon chili powder
Himalayan pink salt and ground black pepper, to taste

Sauce:
1 tablespoon sesame oil
½ teaspoon cumin seeds
2 cloves garlic, roughly chopped
1 onion, chopped
1 Kashmiri chili pepper, seeded and minced
1 (1-inch) piece ginger, chopped
1 teaspoon paprika
1 teaspoon turmeric powder
2 ripe tomatoes, pureed
½ cup vegetable broth
¼ full fat coconut milk

1. Start by preheating your Air Fryer to 360ºF. Thoroughly combine the zucchini, kohlrabi, garlic, Garam masala, paneer, coconut flour, chili powder, salt and ground black pepper.
2. Shape the vegetable mixture into small balls and arrange them in the lightly greased cooking basket.
3. Cook in the preheated Air Fryer at 360ºF for 15 minutes or until thoroughly cooked and crispy. Repeat the process until you run out of ingredients.
4. Heat the sesame oil in a saucepan over medium heat and add the cumin seeds. Once the cumin seeds turn brown, add the garlic, onions, chili pepper, and ginger. Sauté for 2 to 3 minutes.
5. Add the paprika, turmeric powder, tomatoes, and broth, let it simmer, covered, for 4 to 5 minutes, stirring occasionally.
6. Add the coconut milk. Heat off, add the veggie balls and gently stir to combine. Bon appétit!

Per Serving
calories: 259 | fat: 19.1g | protein: 2.9g | total carbs: 9.1g | fiber: 3.4g

Cauliflower and Mushroom with Yogurt Tahini Sauce

Prep time: 20 minutes | Cook time: 16 minutes | Serves 4

1 pound (454 g) cauliflower florets
1 pound (454 g) button mushrooms
2 tablespoons olive oil
½ teaspoon white pepper
½ teaspoon dried dill weed
½ teaspoon cayenne pepper
½ teaspoon celery seeds
½ teaspoon mustard

seeds
Salt, to taste
Yogurt Tahini Sauce:
1 cup plain yogurt
2 heaping tablespoons tahini paste
1 tablespoon lemon juice
1 tablespoon extra-virgin olive oil
½ teaspoon Aleppo pepper, minced

1. Toss the cauliflower and mushrooms with olive oil and spices. Preheat your Air Fryer to 380ºF.
2. Add the cauliflower to the cooking basket and cook for 10 minutes.
3. Add the mushrooms, turn the temperature to 390º and cook for 6 minutes or more.
4. While the vegetables are cooking, make the sauce by whisking all ingredients. Serve the warm vegetables with the sauce on the side. Bon appétit!

Per Serving

calories: 185 | fat: 14.8g | protein: 3.9g | total carbs: 9.2g | fiber: 3.1g

Cheese-Broccoli Fritters

Prep time: 10 minutes | Cook time: 25 minutes | Serves 4

1 cup broccoli florets
1 cup shredded Mozzarella cheese
¾ cup almond flour
½ cup flaxseed meal, divided
2 teaspoons baking

powder
1 teaspoon garlic powder
Salt and freshly ground black pepper
2 eggs, lightly beaten
½ cup ranch dressing

1. Preheat the air fryer to 400°F (205ºC).
2. In a food processor fitted with a metal blade, pulse the broccoli until very finely chopped.
3. Transfer the broccoli to a large bowl and add the Mozzarella, almond flour, ¼ cup of the flaxseed meal, baking powder, and garlic powder. Stir until thoroughly combined. Season to taste with salt and black pepper. Add the eggs and stir again to form a sticky dough. Shape the dough into 1¼-inch fritters.
4. Place the remaining ¼ cup flaxseed meal in a shallow bowl and roll the fritters in the meal to form an even coating.
5. Working in batches if necessary, arrange the fritters in a single layer in the basket of the air fryer and spray generously with olive oil. Pausing halfway through the cooking time to shake the basket, air fry for 20 to 25 minutes until the fritters are golden brown and crispy. Serve with the ranch dressing for dipping.

Per Serving

calories: 450 | fat: 36g | protein: 19g | carbs: 16g | net carbs: 10g | fiber: 6g

Shepherd's Pie

Prep time: 20 minutes | Cook time: 25 minutes | Serves 5

2 tablespoons olive oil
2 bell peppers, seeded and sliced
1 celery, chopped
1 onion, chopped
2 garlic cloves, minced
1 cup cooked bacon, diced
1½ cups beef bone broth
5 ounces (142 g) green beans, drained

Sea salt and freshly ground black pepper, to taste
8 ounces (227 g) cauliflower pulsed in a food processor to a fine-crumb like consistency
½ cup milk
2 tablespoons butter, melted

1. Heat the olive oil in a saucepan over medium-high heat. Now, cook the peppers, celery, onion, and garlic until they have softened, for about 7 minutes
2. Add the bacon and broth. Bring to a boil and cook for 2 minutes or more. Stir in green beans, salt and black pepper, continue to cook until everything is heated through.
3. Transfer the mixture to the lightly greased baking pan.
4. Microwave cauliflower rice for 5 minutes.
5. In a small bowl, combine the cauliflower, milk, and melted butter. Stir until well mixed and spoon evenly over the vegetable mixture. Smooth it with a spatula and transfer to the Air Fryer cooking basket.
6. Bake in the preheated Air Fryer at 400ºF for 12 minutes. Place on a wire rack to cool slightly before slicing and serving. Bon appétit!

Per Serving

calories: 214 | fat: 18.5g | carbs: 8.5g | protein: 4.4g | sugar: 0.9g | fiber: 2.2g

Fried Cauliflower Rice with Green Onions

Prep time: 5 minutes | Cook time: 8 minutes | Serves 4

2 cups cauliflower florets
⅓ cup sliced green onions, plus more for garnish
3 tablespoons wheat-free tamari or coconut aminos
1 clove garlic, smashed to a paste or minced

1 teaspoon grated fresh ginger
1 teaspoon fish sauce or fine sea salt
1 teaspoon lime juice
⅛ teaspoon ground black pepper

1. Preheat the air fryer to 375°F.
2. Place the cauliflower in a food processor and pulse until it resembles grains of rice.
3. Place all the ingredients, including the riced cauliflower, in a large bowl and stir well to combine.
4. Transfer the cauliflower mixture to a 6-inch pie pan or a casserole dish that will fit in your air fryer. Cook for 8 minutes, or until soft, shaking halfway through. Garnish with sliced green onions before serving.
5. Store leftovers in an airtight container in the fridge for up to 4 days. Reheat in a preheated 375°F air fryer for 4 minutes, or until heated through.

Per Serving

calories: 30 | fat: 0g | protein: 3g | total carbs: 4g | fiber: 1g

Oyster Mushroom Omelet

Prep time: 20 minutes | Cook time: 35 minutes | Serves 2

3 king oyster mushrooms, thinly sliced
1 lemongrass, chopped
½ teaspoon dried marjoram
5 eggs
⅓ cup Swiss cheese, grated
2 tablespoons sour cream
1½ teaspoon dried rosemary
2 teaspoons red pepper

flakes, crushed
2 tablespoons butter, melted
½ red onion, peeled and sliced into thin rounds
½ teaspoon garlic powder
1 teaspoon dried dill weed
Fine sea salt and ground black pepper, to your liking

1. Melt the margarine in a skillet that is placed over a medium flame. Then, sweat the onion, mushrooms, and lemongrass until they have softened, reserve.

2. Then, preheat the Air Fryer to 325ºF. Then, crack the eggs into a mixing bowl and whisk them well. Then, fold in the sour cream and give it a good stir.
3. Now, stir in the salt, black pepper, red pepper, rosemary, garlic powder, marjoram, and dill.
4. Next step, grease the inside of an Air Fryer baking dish with a thin layer of a cooking spray. Pour the egg/seasoning mixture into the baking dish, throw in the reserved mixture. Top with the Swiss cheese.
5. Set the timer for 35 minutes, cook until a knife inserted in the center comes out clean and dry.

Per Serving

calories: 362 | fat: 29g | protein: 1.5g | total carbs: 7.2g | fiber: 1.4g

Cauliflower with Cheese

Prep time: 15 minutes | Cook time: 30 minutes | Serves 4

5 cups cauliflower florets
⅔ cup almond flour
½ teaspoon salt
¼ cup unsalted butter,

melted
¼ cup grated Parmesan cheese

1. In a food processor fitted with a metal blade, pulse the cauliflower until finely chopped. Transfer the cauliflower to a large microwave-safe bowl and cover it with a paper towel. Microwave for 5 minutes. Spread the cauliflower on a towel to cool.
2. When cool enough to handle, draw up the sides of the towel and squeeze tightly over a sink to remove the excess moisture. Return the cauliflower to the food processor and whirl until creamy. Sprinkle the flour and salt and pulse until a sticky dough comes together.
3. Transfer the dough to a workspace lightly floured with almond flour. Shape the dough into a ball and divide into 4 equal sections. Roll each section into a rope 1-inch thick. Slice the dough into squares with a sharp knife.
4. Preheat the air fryer to 400°F (205ºC).
5. Working in batches if necessary, place the gnocchi in a single layer in the basket of the air fryer and spray generously with olive oil. Pausing halfway through the cooking time to turn the gnocchi, air fry for 25 to 30 minutes until golden brown and crispy on the edges. Transfer to a large bowl and toss with the melted butter and Parmesan cheese.

Per Serving

calories: 360 | fat: 20g | protein: 9g | carbs: 14g | net carbs: 10g | fiber: 4g

Eggplant with Tomato and Cheese

Prep time: 35 minutes | Cook time: 5 minutes | Serves 4

1 eggplant, peeled and sliced	1 teaspoon dried oregano
2 bell peppers, seeded and sliced	1 teaspoon smoked paprika
1 red onion, sliced	Salt and ground black pepper, to taste
1 teaspoon fresh garlic, minced	1 tomato, sliced
4 tablespoons olive oil	6 ounces (170 g) halloumi cheese, sliced lengthways
1 teaspoon mustard	

1. Start by preheating your Air Fryer to 370ºF (188ºC). Spritz a baking pan with nonstick cooking spray.
2. Place the eggplant, peppers, onion, and garlic on the bottom of the baking pan. Add the olive oil, mustard, and spices. Transfer to the cooking basket and cook for 14 minutes.
3. Top with the tomatoes and cheese, increase the temperature to 390ºF (199ºC) and cook for 5 minutes or more until bubbling. Let it sit on a cooling rack for 10 minutes before serving.
4. Bon appétit!

Per Serving

calories: 306 | fat: 16.1g | protein: 39.6g | carbs: 8.8g | net carbs: 7g | fiber: 1.8g

Coriander and Cheddar Balls

Prep time: 15 minutes | Cook time: 10 minutes | Serves 6

1 cup almond flour	minced
¼ cup flaxseed meal	¼ teaspoon cumin powder
A pinch of salt	
½ cup canola oil	1 teaspoon dried parsley flakes
1 cup Cheddar cheese, cubed	Water
½ cup green coriander,	

1. Firstly, make the dough by mixing the flour, salt, and canola oil, add water and knead it into dough. Let it stay for about 20 minutes.
2. Divide the dough into equal size balls. Sprinkle cheese cubes with green coriander, cumin powder, and parsley.
3. Now, press the cheese cubes down into the center of the dough balls. Then, pinch the edges securely to form a ball. Repeat with the rest of the dough.
4. Lay the balls in the Air Fryer's cooking basket, spritz

each ball with a cooking spray, coating on all sides. After that, cook for 8 to 10 minutes, shaking the basket once during the cooking time.

5. Serve with your favorite sauce for dipping. Bon appétit!

Per Serving

calories: 380 | fat: 36.5g | carbs: 5.8g | protein: 9.9g | sugar: 0.8g | fiber: 3.9g

Zucchini Cheese Tart

Prep time: 15 minutes | Cook time: 50 minutes | Serves 6

½ cup grated Parmesan cheese, divided	1 zucchini, thinly sliced (about 2 cups)
1½ cups almond flour	1 cup ricotta cheese
1 tablespoon coconut flour	3 eggs
½ teaspoon garlic powder	2 tablespoons heavy cream
¾ teaspoon salt, divided	2 cloves garlic, minced
¼ cup unsalted butter, melted	½ teaspoon dried tarragon

1. Preheat the air fryer to 330°F (166ºC). Coat a round 6-cup pan with olive oil and set aside.
2. In a large bowl, whisk ¼ cup of the Parmesan with the almond flour, coconut flour, garlic powder, and ¼ teaspoon of the salt. Stir in the melted butter until the dough resembles coarse crumbs. Press the dough firmly into the bottom and up the sides of the prepared pan. Air fry for 12 to 15 minutes until the crust begins to brown. Let it cool to room temperature.
3. Meanwhile, place the zucchini in a colander and sprinkle with the remaining ½ teaspoon salt. Toss gently to distribute the salt and let it sit for 30 minutes. Use paper towels to pat the zucchini dry.
4. In a large bowl, whisk together the ricotta, eggs, heavy cream, garlic, and tarragon. Gently stir in the zucchini slices. Pour the cheese mixture into the cooled crust and sprinkle with the remaining ¼ cup Parmesan.
5. Increase the air fryer to 350°F (180ºC). Place the pan in the air fryer basket and air fry for 45 to 50 minutes, or until set and a tester inserted into the center of the tart comes out clean. Serve warm or at room temperature.

Per Serving

calories: 390 | fat: 30g | protein: 19g | carbs: 14g | net carbs: 12g | fiber: 2g

Artichoke Tart, page 110

Crunchy Cauliflower Mac 'n' Cheese, page 109

Tomato Bites with Parmesan-Pecan Sauce,
page 110

Zucchini with Spinach, page 122

Baked Rainbow Vegetables

Prep time: 20 minutes | Cook time: 50 minutes | Serves 4

1 pound (454 g) cauliflower, chopped into small florets
2 tablespoons olive oil
½ teaspoon red pepper flakes, crushed
½ teaspoon freshly ground black pepper
Salt, to taste
3 bell peppers, thinly sliced
1 serrano pepper, thinly sliced
2 medium-sized tomatoes, sliced
1 leek, thinly sliced
2 garlic cloves, minced
1 cup Monterey cheese, shredded

1. Start by preheating your Air Fryer to 350ºF. Spritz a casserole dish with cooking oil.
2. Place the cauliflower in the casserole dish in an even layer, drizzle 1 tablespoon of olive oil over the top. Then, add the red pepper, black pepper, and salt.
3. Add 2 bell peppers and ½ of the leeks. Add the tomatoes and the remaining 1 tablespoon of olive oil.
4. Add the remaining peppers, leeks, and minced garlic. Top with the cheese.
5. Cover the casserole with foil and bake for 32 minutes. Remove the foil and increase the temperature to 400ºF, bake an additional 16 minutes. Bon appétit!

Per Serving
calories: 233 | fat: 17.2g | protein: 1.1g | total carbs: 9.7g | fiber: 3.2g

Mushroom with Artichoke and Spinach

Prep time: 10 minutes | Cook time: 14 minutes | Serves 4

2 tablespoons olive oil
4 large portobello mushrooms, stems removed and gills scraped out
½ teaspoon salt
¼ teaspoon freshly ground pepper
4 ounces (113 g) goat cheese, crumbled
½ cup chopped marinated artichoke hearts
1 cup frozen spinach, thawed and squeezed dry
½ cup grated Parmesan cheese
2 tablespoons chopped fresh parsley

1. Preheat the air fryer to 400°F (205ºC).
2. Rub the olive oil over the portobello mushrooms until thoroughly coated. Sprinkle both sides with the salt and black pepper. Place top-side down on a clean work surface.
3. In a small bowl, combine the goat cheese, artichoke hearts, and spinach. Mash with the back of a fork until thoroughly combined. Divide the cheese mixture among the mushrooms and sprinkle with the Parmesan cheese.
4. Air fry for 10 to 14 minutes until the mushrooms are tender and the cheese has begun to brown. Top with the fresh parsley just before serving.

Per Serving
calories: 270 | fat: 23g | protein: 8g | carbs: 11g | net carbs: 7g | fiber: 4g

Cauliflower Steak with Gremolata

Prep time: 15 minutes | Cook time: 25 minutes | Serves 4

2 tablespoons olive oil
1 tablespoon Italian seasoning
1 large head cauliflower, outer leaves removed and sliced lengthwise through the core into thick "steaks"
Salt and freshly ground black pepper
¼ cup Parmesan cheese
Gremolata:
1 bunch Italian parsley (about 1 cup packed)
2 cloves garlic
Zest of 1 small lemon, plus 1–2 teaspoons lemon juice
½ cup olive oil
Salt and pepper to taste

1. Preheat the air fryer to 400°F (205ºC).
2. In a small bowl, combine the olive oil and Italian seasoning. Brush both sides of each cauliflower "steak" generously with the oil. Season to taste with salt and black pepper.
3. Working in batches if necessary, arrange the cauliflower in a single layer in the air fryer basket. Pausing halfway through the cooking time to turn the "steaks," air fry for 15 to 20 minutes until the cauliflower is tender and the edges begin to brown. Sprinkle with the Parmesan and air fry for 5 minutes or longer.
4. To make the gremolata: In a food processor fitted with a metal blade, combine the parsley, garlic, and lemon zest and juice. With the motor running, add the olive oil in a steady stream until the mixture forms a bright green sauce. Season to taste with salt and black pepper. Serve the cauliflower steaks with the gremolata spooned over the top.

Per Serving
calories: 390 | fat: 36g | protein: 7g | carbs: 14g | net carbs: 8g | fiber: 6g

Fried Yellow Beans

Prep time: 10 minutes | Cook time: 8 minutes | Serves 3

¾ pound (340 g) wax yellow beans, cleaned
2 tablespoons peanut oil
4 tablespoons Romano cheese, grated
Sea salt and ground black pepper, to taste
½ teaspoon red pepper flakes, crushed
2 tablespoons pecans, sliced
⅓ cup blue cheese, crumbled

1. Toss the wax beans with the peanut oil, Romano cheese, salt, black pepper, and red pepper.
2. Place the wax beans in the lightly greased cooking basket.
3. Cook in the preheated Air Fryer at 400ºF for 5 minutes. Shake the basket once or twice.
4. Add the pecans and cook for 3 minutes or more or until lightly toasted. Serve topped with blue cheese and enjoy!

Per Serving

calories: 236 | fat: 21g | protein: 2.5g | total carbs: 7.9g | fiber: 0.6g

Zucchini and Cauliflower Fritters

Prep time: 15 minutes | Cook time: 12 minutes | Serves 2

1 zucchini, grated and squeezed
1 cup cauliflower florets, boiled
4 tablespoons Romano cheese, grated
2 tablespoons fresh shallots, minced
1 teaspoon fresh garlic, minced
1 tablespoon peanut oil
Sea salt and ground black pepper, to taste
1 teaspoon cayenne pepper

1. In a mixing bowl, thoroughly combine all ingredients until everything is well incorporated.
2. Shape the mixture into patties. Spritz the Air Fryer basket with cooking spray.
3. Cook in the preheated Air Fryer at 365ºF for 6 minutes. Turn them over and cook for a further 6 minutes
4. Serve immediately and enjoy!

Per Serving

calories: 172 | fat: 13.4g | protein: 2.5g | total carbs: 7.6g | fiber: 1.5g

Spinach Cheese Casserole

Prep time: 15 minutes | Cook time: 15 minutes | Serves 4

1 tablespoon salted butter, melted
¼ cup diced yellow onion
8 ounces (227 g) full-fat cream cheese, softened
⅓ cup full-fat mayonnaise
⅓ cup full-fat sour cream
¼ cup chopped pickled
jalapeños
2 cups fresh spinach, chopped
2 cups cauliflower florets, chopped
1 cup artichoke hearts, chopped

1. In a large bowl, mix butter, onion, cream cheese, mayonnaise, and sour cream. Fold in jalapeños, spinach, cauliflower, and artichokes.
2. Pour the mixture into a 4-cup round baking dish. Cover with foil and place into the air fryer basket.
3. Adjust the temperature to 370°F (188ºC) and set the timer for 15 minutes.
4. In the last 2 minutes of cooking, remove the foil to brown the top. Serve warm.

Per Serving

calories: 423 | fat: 36.3g | protein: 6.7g | carbs: 12.1g | net carbs: 6.8g | fiber: 5.3g

Fried Mushrooms with Parmesan

Prep time: 10 minutes | Cook time: 6 minutes | Serves 4

1 pound (454 g) button mushrooms
1½ cups pork rinds
1 cup Parmesan cheese, grated
2 eggs, whisked
½ teaspoon salt
2 tablespoons fresh parsley leaves, roughly chopped

1. Pat the mushrooms dry with a paper towel.
2. To begin, set up your "breading" station. Mix the pork rinds and Parmesan cheese in a shallow dish. In a separate dish, whisk the eggs.
3. Start by dipping the mushrooms into the eggs. Press your mushrooms into the parm/pork rind mixture, coating evenly.
4. Spritz the Air Fryer basket with cooking oil. Add the mushrooms and cook at 400ºF for 6 minutes, flipping them halfway through the cooking time.
5. Sprinkle with the salt. Serve garnished with fresh parsley leaves. Bon appétit!

Per Serving

calories: 338 | fat: 22.3g | protein: 2.1g | total carbs: 8g | fiber: 1.2g

Cauliflower and Broccoli Meal

Prep time: 10 minutes | Cook time: 16 minutes | Serves 6

1 pound (454 g) cauliflower florets
1 pound (454 g) broccoli florets
2 ½ tablespoons sesame oil
½ teaspoon smoked
cayenne pepper
¾ teaspoon sea salt flakes
1 tablespoon lemon zest, grated
½ cup Colby cheese, shredded

1. Prepare the cauliflower and broccoli using your favorite steaming method. Then, drain them well, add the sesame oil, cayenne pepper, and salt flakes.
2. Air-fry at 390ºF for approximately 16 minutes, make sure to check the vegetables halfway through the cooking time.
3. Afterwards, stir in the lemon zest and Colby cheese, toss to coat well and serve immediately!

Per Serving

calories: 133 | fat: 9.0g | protein: 5g | total carbs: 9.5g | fiber: 3.6g

Shirataki Noodles with Fennel Bulb

Prep time: 15 minutes | Cook time: 15 minutes | Serves 3

1 fennel bulb, quartered
Salt and white pepper, to taste
1 clove garlic, finely chopped
1 green onion, thinly sliced
1 cup Chinese cabbage, shredded
2 tablespoons rice wine vinegar
2 tablespoons sesame oil
1 teaspoon ginger, freshly grated
1 tablespoon soy sauce
1⅓ cups Shirataki noodles, boiled

1. Start by preheating your Air Fryer to 370ºF.
2. Now, cook the fennel bulb in the lightly greased cooking basket for 15 minutes, shaking the basket once or twice.
3. Let it cool completely and toss with the remaining ingredients. Serve well chilled.

Per Serving

calories: 208 | fat: 10.2g | carbs: 9.7g | protein: 1.7g | sugar: 0.7g | fiber: 3.9g

Cheese Stuffed Zucchini

Prep time: 20 minutes | Cook time: 8 minutes | Serves 4

1 large zucchini, cut into four pieces
2 tablespoons olive oil
1 cup Ricotta cheese, room temperature
2 tablespoons scallions, chopped
1 heaping tablespoon fresh parsley, roughly
chopped
1 heaping tablespoon coriander, minced
2 ounces (57 g) Cheddar cheese, preferably freshly grated
1 teaspoon celery seeds
½ teaspoon salt
½ teaspoon garlic pepper

1. Cook your zucchini in the Air Fryer cooking basket for approximately 10 minutes at 350ºF (180ºC). Check for doneness and cook for 2-3 minutes longer if needed.
2. Meanwhile, make the stuffing by mixing the other items.
3. When your zucchini is thoroughly cooked, open them up. Divide the stuffing among all zucchini pieces and bake for an additional 5 minutes.

Per Serving

calories: 199 | fat: 16.4g | protein: 9.2g | carbs: 4.5g | net carbs: 4g | fiber: 0.5g

Peperonata Siciliana

Prep time: 15 minutes | Cook time: 20 minutes | Serves 4

4 tablespoons olive oil
4 bell peppers, seeded and sliced
1 serrano pepper, seeded and sliced
½ cup onion, peeled and sliced
2 garlic cloves, crushed
1 large tomato, pureed
Sea salt and black pepper
1 teaspoon cayenne pepper
4 fresh basil leaves
8 Sicilian olives green, pitted and sliced

1. Brush the sides and bottom of the cooking basket with 1 tablespoon of olive oil. Add the peppers, onions, and garlic to the cooking basket. Cook for 5 minutes or until tender.
2. Add the tomatoes, salt, black pepper, and cayenne pepper, add the remaining tablespoon of olive oil and cook in the preheated Air Fryer at 380ºF for 15 minutes, stirring occasionally.
3. Divide between individual bowls and garnish with basil leaves and olives. Bon appétit!

Per Serving

calories: 165 | fat: 14.4g | carbs: 8.8g | protein: 1.7g | sugar: 0.3g | fiber: 1.8g

Cheese Stuffed Pepper

Prep time: 20 minutes | Cook time: 15 minutes | Serves 2

1 red bell pepper, top and seeds removed
1 yellow bell pepper, top and seeds removed
Salt and pepper, to taste
1 cup Cottage cheese
4 tablespoons mayonnaise
2 pickles, chopped

1. Arrange the peppers in the lightly greased cooking basket. Cook in the preheated Air Fryer at 400ºF (205ºC) for 15 minutes, turning them over halfway through the cooking time.
2. Season with salt and pepper.
3. Then, in a mixing bowl, combine the cream cheese with the mayonnaise and chopped pickles. Stuff the pepper with the cream cheese mixture and serve. Enjoy!

Per Serving

calories: 360 | fat: 27.3g | protein: 20.3g | carbs: 7.6g | net carbs: 6.4g | fiber: 1.2g

Broccoli Croquettes

Prep time: 15 minutes | Cook time: 10 minutes | Serves 4

½ pound (227 g) broccoli florets
1 tablespoon ground flaxseeds
1 yellow onion, finely chopped
1 bell pepper, seeded and chopped
2 garlic cloves, pressed
1 teaspoon turmeric
powder
½ teaspoon ground cumin
½ cup almond flour
½ cup Parmesan cheese
2 eggs, whisked
Salt and ground black pepper, to taste
2 tablespoons olive oil

1. Blanch the broccoli in salted boiling water until al-dente, for about 3 to 4 minutes. Drain well and transfer to a mixing bowl, mash the broccoli florets with the remaining ingredients.
2. Form the mixture into patties and place them in the lightly greased Air Fryer basket.
3. Cook at 400ºF for 6 minutes, turning them over halfway through the cooking time, work in batches.
4. Serve warm with mayonnaise. Enjoy!

Per Serving

calories: 219 | fat: 16.6g | carbs: 6.5g | protein: 10g | sugar: 1g | fiber: 3.2g

Hungarian Pilau with Mushrooms

Prep time: 15 minutes | Cook time: 20 minutes | Serves 4

1½ cups cauliflower rice
3 cups vegetable broth
2 tablespoons olive oil
1 pound (454 g) fresh porcini mushrooms, sliced
2 tablespoons olive oil
2 garlic cloves
1 onion, chopped
¼ cup dry vermouth
1 teaspoon dried thyme
½ teaspoon dried tarragon
1 teaspoon sweet Hungarian paprika

1. Thoroughly combine cauliflower rice with the remaining ingredients in a lightly greased baking dish.
2. Cook in the preheated Air Fryer at 370ºfor 20 minutes, checking periodically to ensure even cooking.
3. Serve in individual bowls. Bon appétit!

Per Serving

calories: 198 | fat: 15.1g | carbs: 9.8g | protein: 8.4g | sugar: 1.4g | fiber: 2.6g

Double-Cheese Cauliflower Croquettes

Prep time: 15 minutes | Cook time: 16 minutes | Serves 4

1 pound (454 g) cauliflower florets
2 eggs
1 tablespoon olive oil
2 tablespoons scallions, chopped
1 garlic clove, minced
1 cup Colby cheese,
shredded
½ cup Parmesan cheese, grated
Sea salt and ground black pepper, to taste
¼ teaspoon dried dill weed
1 teaspoon paprika

1. Blanch the cauliflower in salted boiling water for about 3 to 4 minutes until al dente. Drain well and pulse in a food processor.
2. Add the remaining ingredients, mix to combine well. Shape the cauliflower mixture into bite-sized tots.
3. Spritz the Air Fryer basket with cooking spray.
4. Cook in the preheated Air Fryer at 375ºF for 16 minutes, shaking halfway through the cooking time. Serve with your favorite sauce for dipping. Bon appétit!

Per Serving

calories: 274 | fat: 19g | protein: 6.4g | total carbs: 18.8g | fiber: 2.7g

Cheddar Green Beans

Prep time: 15 minutes | Cook time: 15 minutes | Serves 3

½ pound (227 g) green beans
9 ounces (255 g) Cheddar cheese, sliced
¼ cup tomato paste, no sugar added
1 tablespoon white vinegar
1 tablespoon mustard
¼ teaspoon ground black pepper
½ teaspoon sea salt
¼ teaspoon smoked paprika
½ teaspoon freshly grated ginger
2 cloves garlic, minced
2 tablespoons olive oil

1. Toss green beans with the tomato paste, white vinegar, mustard, black pepper, sea salt, paprika, ginger, garlic, and olive oil.
2. Cook at 390ºF for 10 minutes. Top with Cheddar cheese and cook for an additional 5 minutes or until cheese melts.
3. Serve immediately. Bon appétit!

Per Serving
calories: 454 | fat: 38g | carbs: 7.7g | protein: 22.1g | sugar: 1.1g | fiber: 2.3g

Asparagus with Broccoli

Prep time: 25 minutes | Cook time: 22 minutes | Serves 4

½ pound (227g) asparagus, cut into 1 ½-inch pieces
½ pound (227g) broccoli, cut into 1 ½-inch pieces
2 tablespoons olive oil
Some salt and white pepper, to taste
½ cup vegetable broth
2 tablespoons apple cider vinegar

1. Place the vegetables in a single layer in the lightly greased cooking basket. Drizzle the olive oil over the vegetables.
2. Sprinkle with salt and white pepper.
3. Cook at 380ºF (193ºC) for 15 minutes, shaking the basket halfway through the cooking time.
4. Add ½ cup of vegetable broth to a saucepan, bring to a rapid boil and add the vinegar. Cook for 5 to 7 minutes or until the sauce has reduced by half.
5. Spoon the sauce over the warm vegetables and serve immediately. Bon appétit!

Per Serving
calories: 181 | fat: 7g | protein: 3g | carbs: 4g | net carbs: 1g | fiber: 3g

Broccoli with Herbed Garlic Sauce

Prep time: 19 minutes | Cook time: 15 minutes | Serves 4

2 tablespoons olive oil
Kosher salt and freshly ground black pepper, to taste
1 pound (454 g) broccoli florets
For the Dipping Sauce:
2 teaspoons dried rosemary, crushed
3 garlic cloves, minced
⅓ teaspoon dried marjoram, crushed
¼ cup sour cream
⅓ cup mayonnaise

1. Lightly grease your broccoli with a thin layer of olive oil. Season with salt and ground black pepper.
2. Arrange the seasoned broccoli in an Air Fryer cooking basket. Bake at 395ºF (202ºC) for 15 minutes, shaking once or twice.
3. In the meantime, prepare the dipping sauce by mixing all the sauce ingredients. Serve warm broccoli with the dipping sauce and enjoy!

Per Serving
calories: 247 | fat: 22g | protein: 4g | carbs: 9g | net carbs: 6g | fiber: 3g

Mushroom Soufflés

Prep time: 15 minutes | Cook time: 12 minutes | Serves 4

3 large eggs, whites and yolks separated
½ cup sharp white Cheddar cheese
3 ounces (85 g) cream cheese, softened
¼ teaspoon cream of tartar
¼ teaspoon salt
¼ teaspoon ground black pepper
½ cup cremini mushrooms, sliced

1. In a large bowl, whip egg whites until stiff peaks form, for about 2 minutes. In a separate large bowl, beat Cheddar, egg yolks, cream cheese, cream of tartar, salt, and pepper together until combined.
2. Fold egg whites into cheese mixture, being careful not to stir. Fold in mushrooms, then pour mixture evenly into four ungreased 4-inch ramekins.
3. Place ramekins into air fryer basket. Adjust the temperature to 350°F (180ºC) and set the timer for 12 minutes. Eggs will be browned on the top and firm in the center when done. Serve warm.

Per Serving
calories: 185 | fat: 14g | protein: 10g | carbs: 2g | net carbs: 2g | fiber: 0g

Riced Cauliflower with Eggs

Prep time: 10 minutes | Cook time: 12 minutes | Serves 4

2 cups cauliflower, food-processed into rice-like particles
2 tablespoons peanut oil
½ cup scallions, chopped
2 bell peppers, chopped
4 eggs, beaten
Sea salt and ground black pepper, to taste
½ teaspoon granulated garlic

1. Grease a baking pan with nonstick cooking spray.
2. Add the cauliflower rice and the other ingredients to the baking pan.
3. Cook at 400ºF for 12 minutes, checking occasionally to ensure even cooking. Enjoy!

Per Serving

calories: 149 | fat: 11g | carbs: 6.1g | protein: 2.4g | sugar: 0.6g | fiber: 1.7g

Cheesy Zucchini

Prep time: 10 minutes | Cook time: 8 minutes | Serves 4

2 tablespoons salted butter
¼ cup diced white onion
½ teaspoon minced garlic
½ cup heavy whipping cream
2 ounces (57 g) full-fat cream cheese
1 cup shredded sharp Cheddar cheese
2 medium zucchini, spiralized

1. In a large saucepan over medium heat, melt butter. Add onion and sauté until it begins to soften, for 1 to 3 minutes. Add garlic and sauté for 30 seconds, then pour in cream and add cream cheese.
2. Remove the pan from heat and stir in Cheddar. Add the zucchini and toss in the sauce, then put into a 4-cup round baking dish. Cover the dish with foil and place into the air fryer basket.
3. Adjust the temperature to 370°F (188°C) and set the timer for 8 minutes.
4. After 6 minutes remove the foil and let the top brown for the remaining cooking time. Stir and serve.

Per Serving

calories: 337 | fat: 28.4g | protein: 9.6g | carbs: 5.9g | net carbs: 4.7g | fiber: 1.2g

Roasted Spaghetti Squash

Prep time: 10 minutes | Cook time: 45 minutes | Serves 6

1 (4-pound / 1.8-kg) spaghetti squash, halved and seeded
2 tablespoons coconut oil
4 tablespoons salted butter, melted
1 teaspoon garlic powder
2 teaspoons dried parsley

1. Brush shell of spaghetti squash with coconut oil. Brush inside with butter. Sprinkle inside with garlic powder and parsley.
2. Place squash skin side down into ungreased air fryer basket, working in batches if needed. Adjust the temperature to 350°F (180ºC) and set the timer for 30 minutes. When the timer beeps, flip squash and cook for an additional 15 minutes until fork-tender.
3. Use a fork to remove spaghetti strands from shell and serve warm.

Per Serving

calories: 104 | fat: 7g | protein: 1g | carbs: 9g | net carbs: 7g | fiber: 2g

Balsamic Cauliflower and Mushroom

Prep time: 15 minutes | Cook time: 12 minutes | Serves 3

½ pound (227 g) cauliflower florets
½ pound (227 g) button mushrooms, whole
1 cup pearl onions, whole
Pink Himalayan salt and ground black pepper, to taste
¼ teaspoon smoked paprika
1 teaspoon garlic powder
½ teaspoon dried thyme
½ teaspoon dried marjoram
3 tablespoons olive oil
2 tablespoons balsamic vinegar

1. Toss all ingredients in a large mixing dish.
2. Roast in the preheated Air Fryer at 400ºF for 5 minutes. Shake the basket and cook for 7 minutes or more.
3. Serve with some extra fresh herbs if desired. Bon appétit!

Per Serving

calories: 170 | fat: 14g | protein: 4.2g | total carbs: 9.7g | fiber: 2.9g

Stuffed Bell Peppers

Prep time: 10 minutes | Cook time: 15 minutes | Serves 2

2 bell peppers, tops and seeds removed
Salt and pepper, to taste
⅔ cup cream cheese
2 tablespoons mayonnaise
1 tablespoon fresh celery stalks, chopped

1. Arrange the peppers in the lightly greased cooking basket. Cook in the preheated Air Fryer at 400ºF for 15 minutes, turning them over halfway through the cooking time.
2. Season with salt and pepper.
3. Then, in a mixing bowl, combine the cream cheese with the mayonnaise and chopped celery. Stuff the pepper with the cream cheese mixture and serve.

Per Serving

calories: 378 | fat: 38g | protein: 2.5g | total carbs: 17.6g | fiber: 2.6g

Zucchini with Spinach

Prep time: 9 minutes | Cook time: 7 minutes | Serves 6

4 eggs, slightly beaten
½ cup almond flour
½ cup goat cheese, crumbled
1 teaspoon fine sea salt
4 garlic cloves, minced
1 cup baby spinach
½ cup Parmesan cheese
grated
⅓ teaspoon red pepper flakes
1 pound (454 g) zucchini, peeled and grated
⅓ teaspoon dried dill weed

1. Thoroughly combine all ingredients in a bowl. Now, roll the mixture to form small croquettes.
2. Air fry at 335ºF (168ºC) for 7 minutes or until golden. Tate, adjust for seasonings and serve warm.

Per Serving

calories: 171 | fat: 10.8g | protein: 3.1g | carbs: 15.9g | net carbs: 14.9g | fiber: 1g

Citrus Zucchini Balls

Prep time: 5 minutes | Cook time: 15 minutes | Serves 4

1 pound (454 g) zucchini, grated
1 tablespoon orange juice
½ teaspoon ground cinnamon
¼ teaspoon ground cloves
½ cup almond meal
1 teaspoon baking powder
1 cup coconut flakes

1. In a mixing bowl, thoroughly combine all ingredients, except for coconut flakes.
2. Roll the balls in the coconut flakes.
3. Bake in the preheated Air Fryer at 360ºF for 15 minutes or until thoroughly cooked and crispy.
4. Repeat the process until you run out of ingredients. Bon appétit!

Per Serving

calories: 166 | fat: 13.1g | carbs: 9.6g | protein: 6.2g | sugar: 0.1g | fiber: 4.7g

Rosemary Cauliflower Au Gratin

Prep time: 15 minutes | Cook time: 20 minutes | Serves 4

¾ pound (340 g) cauliflower, steamed
1 onion, sliced
2 garlic cloves, minced
1 bell pepper, deveined and sliced
2 eggs, beaten
1 cup sour cream
Kosher salt and ground black pepper, to taste
1 teaspoon cayenne pepper
1 tablespoon fresh rosemary

1. Place your vegetables in the lightly greased casserole dish. In a mixing dish, thoroughly combine the remaining ingredients.
2. Spoon the cream mixture on top of the vegetables.
3. Bake in the preheated Air Fryer at 325ºF for 20 minutes. Serve warm.

Per Serving

calories: 157 | fat: 10.3g | carbs: 3.7g | protein: 8.2g | sugar: 1g | fiber: 1.4g

Roast Eggplant and Zucchini Bites

Prep time: 35 minutes | Cook time: 30 minutes | Serves 8

2 teaspoons fresh mint leaves, chopped
1½ teaspoons red pepper chili flakes
2 tablespoons melted butter

1 pound (454 g) eggplant, peeled and cubed
1 pound (454 g) zucchini, peeled and cubed
3 tablespoons olive oil

1. Toss all of the above ingredients in a large-sized mixing dish.
2. Roast the eggplant and zucchini bites for 30 minutes at 325ºF (163ºC) in your Air Fryer, turning once or twice.
3. Serve with a homemade dipping sauce.

Per Serving
calories: 110 | fat: 8.3g | protein: 2.6g | carbs: 8.8g | net carbs: 6.3g | fiber: 2.5g

Ricotta and Mixed Green Omelet

Prep time: 10 minutes | Cook time: 15 minutes | Serves 2

⅓ cup Ricotta cheese
5 eggs, beaten
½ red bell pepper, seeded and sliced
1 cup mixed greens, roughly chopped

½ green bell pepper, seeded and sliced
½ teaspoon dried basil
½ chipotle pepper, finely minced
½ teaspoon dried oregano

1. Lightly coat the inside of a baking dish with a pan spray.
2. Then, throw all ingredients into the baking dish, give it a good stir.
3. Bake at 325ºF for 15 minutes.

Per Serving
calories: 409 | fat: 29.5g | protein: 2.9g | total carbs: 26.9g | fiber: 1.4g

Fried Butternut Squash Croquettes

Prep time: 10 minutes | Cook time: 17 minutes | Serves 4

⅓ cup all-purpose flour
⅓ teaspoon freshly ground black pepper, or more to taste
⅓ teaspoon dried sage
4 cloves garlic, minced

1½ tablespoons olive oil
⅓ butternut squash, peeled and grated
2 eggs, well whisked
1 teaspoon fine sea salt
A pinch of ground allspice

1. Thoroughly combine all ingredients in a mixing bowl.
2. Preheat your Air Fryer to 345º and set the timer for 17 minutes, cook until your fritters are browned, serve right away.

Per Serving
calories: 152 | fat: 10.02g | protein: 5.8g | total carbs: 9.4g | fiber: 0.4g

Chapter 8 Side Dishes

Crispy Green Beans

Prep time: 5 minutes | Cook time: 8 minutes | Serves 4

2 teaspoons olive oil
½ pound (227g) fresh green beans, ends trimmed

¼ teaspoon salt
¼ teaspoon ground black pepper

1. In a large bowl, drizzle olive oil over green beans and sprinkle with salt and pepper.
2. Place green beans into ungreased air fryer basket. Adjust the temperature to 350°F (180ºC) and set the timer for 8 minutes, shaking the basket two times during cooking. Green beans will be dark golden and crispy at the edges when done. Serve warm.

Per Serving
calories: 37 | fat: 2g | protein: 1g | carbs: 4g | net carbs: 2g | fiber: 2g

Golden Broccoli Salad

Prep time: 5 minutes | Cook time: 7 minutes | Serves 4

2 cups fresh broccoli florets, chopped
1 tablespoon olive oil
¼ teaspoon salt
⅛ teaspoon ground black pepper

¼ cup lemon juice, divided
¼ cup shredded Parmesan cheese
¼ cup sliced roasted almonds

1. In a large bowl, toss broccoli and olive oil together. Sprinkle with salt and pepper, then drizzle with 2 tablespoons of lemon juice.
2. Place broccoli into ungreased air fryer basket. Adjust the temperature to 350°F (180ºC) and set the timer for 7 minutes, shaking the basket halfway through cooking. Broccoli will be golden on the edges when done.
3. Place broccoli into a large serving bowl and drizzle with remaining lemon juice. Sprinkle with Parmesan and almonds. Serve warm.

Per Serving
calories: 102 | fat: 7g | protein: 4g | carbs: 6g | net carbs: 4g | fiber: 2g

Sweet Potato Glazed with Tamarind

Prep time: 15 minutes | Cook time: 22 minutes | Serves 4

⅓ teaspoon white pepper
1 tablespoon butter, melted
½ teaspoon turmeric powder
5 garnet sweet potatoes, peeled and diced

A few drops liquid Stevia
2 teaspoons tamarind paste
1½ tablespoons fresh lime juice
1½ teaspoons ground allspice

1. In a mixing bowl, toss all ingredients until sweet potatoes are well coated.
2. Air-fry them at 335ºF for 12 minutes.
3. Pause the Air Fryer and toss again. Increase the temperature to 390ºF and cook for an additional 10 minutes. Eat warm.

Per Serving
calories: 103 | fat: 9.1g | carbs: 4.9g | protein: 1.9g | sugar: 1.2g | fiber: 0.3g

Fried Pickles

Prep time: 15 minutes | Cook time: 15 minutes | Serves 6

⅓ cup milk
1 teaspoon garlic powder
2 medium-sized eggs
1 teaspoon fine sea salt
⅓ teaspoon chili powder

⅓ cup all-purpose flour
½ teaspoon shallot powder
2 jars sweet and sour pickle spears

1. Pat the pickle spears dry with a kitchen towel. Then, take two mixing bowls.
2. Whisk the egg and milk in a bowl. In another bowl, combine all dry ingredients.
3. Firstly, dip the pickle spears into the dry mix, then coat each pickle with the egg/milk mixture, dredge them in the flour mixture again for additional coating.
4. Air fry battered pickles for 15 minutes at 385ºF. Enjoy!

Per Serving
calories: 58 | fat: 2g | carbs: 6.8g | protein: 3.2g | sugar: 0.9g | fiber: 0.4g

Parmesan-Crusted Brussels Sprouts

Prep time: 5 minutes | Cook time: 8 minutes | Serves 4

2 cups Brussels sprouts, trimmed and halved
3 tablespoons ghee or coconut oil, melted
1 teaspoon fine sea salt or smoked salt
Dash of lime or lemon juice

Thinly sliced Parmesan cheese, for serving (optional, omit for dairy-free)
Lemon slices, for serving (optional)

1. Spray the air fryer basket with avocado oil. Preheat the air fryer to 400°F.
2. In a large bowl, toss together the Brussels sprouts, ghee, and salt. Add the lime or lemon juice.
3. Place the Brussels sprouts in the air fryer basket and cook for 8 minutes, or until crispy, shaking the basket after 5 minutes. Serve with thinly sliced Parmesan and lemon slices, if desired.
4. Best served fresh. Store leftovers in an airtight container in the fridge for up to 5 days. Reheat in a preheated 390°F air fryer for 3 minutes, or until heated through.

Per Serving

calories: 149 | fat: 12g | protein: 4g | total carbs: 10g | fiber: 4g

Turmeric Cauliflower Steaks

Prep time: 5 minutes | Cook time: 15 minutes | Serves 4

¼ cup avocado oil
¼ cup lemon juice
2 cloves garlic, minced
1 teaspoon grated fresh ginger
1 tablespoon turmeric powder
1 teaspoon fine sea salt
1 medium head

cauliflower
Full-fat sour cream, for serving (optional)
Extra-virgin olive oil, for serving (optional)
Chopped fresh cilantro leaves, for garnish (optional)

1. Preheat the air fryer to 400°F.
2. In a large shallow dish, combine the avocado oil, lemon juice, garlic, ginger, turmeric, and salt. Slice the cauliflower into ½-inch steaks and place them in the marinade. Cover and refrigerate for 20 minutes or overnight.
3. Remove the cauliflower steaks from the marinade and place them in the air fryer basket. Cook for 15 minutes, or until tender and slightly charred on the

edges.
4. Serve with sour cream and a drizzle of olive oil, and sprinkle with chopped cilantro leaves if desired.
5. Store leftovers in an airtight container in the fridge for up to 4 days or in the freezer for up to a month. Reheat in a preheated 400°F air fryer for 5 minutes, or until warm.

Per Serving

calories: 69 | fat: 4g | protein: 4g | total carbs: 8g | fiber: 4g

Tomato Provençal

Prep time: 10 minutes | Cook time: 15 minutes | Serves 4

4 small ripe tomatoes connected on the vine
¼ teaspoon fine sea salt
¼ teaspoon ground black pepper
½ cup powdered Parmesan cheese
2 tablespoons chopped fresh parsley

¼ cup minced onions
2 cloves garlic, minced
½ teaspoon chopped fresh thyme leaves
For Garnish:
Fresh parsley leaves
Ground black pepper
Sprig of fresh basil

1. Spray the air fryer basket with avocado oil. Preheat the air fryer to 350°F.
2. Slice the tops off the tomatoes without removing them from the vine. Do not discard the tops. Use a large spoon to scoop the seeds out of the tomatoes. Sprinkle the insides of the tomatoes with the salt and pepper.
3. In a medium-sized bowl, combine the cheese, parsley, onions, garlic, and thyme. Stir to combine well. Divide the mixture evenly among the tomatoes.
4. Spray avocado oil on the tomatoes and place them in the air fryer basket. Place the tomato tops in the air fryer basket next to, not on top of, the filled tomatoes. Cook for 15 minutes, or until the filling is golden and the tomatoes are soft yet still holding their shape.
5. Garnish with fresh parsley, ground black pepper, and a sprig of basil. Serve warm, with the tomato tops on the vine.
6. Store leftovers in an airtight container in the refrigerator for up to 4 days. Reheat in a preheated 350°F air fryer for about 3 minutes, until heated through.

Per Serving

calories: 68 | fat: 3g | protein: 5g | total carbs: 6g | fiber: 1g

Mushrooms with Thyme

Prep time: 5 minutes | Cook time: 10 minutes | Serves 4

3 tablespoons unsalted butter, melted
1 (8-ounce / 227-g) package button mushrooms, sliced

2 cloves garlic, minced
3 sprigs fresh thyme leaves, plus more for garnish
½ teaspoon fine sea salt

1. Spray the air fryer basket with avocado oil. Preheat the air fryer to 400°F.
2. Place all the ingredients in a medium-sized bowl. Use a spoon or your hands to coat the mushroom slices.
3. Place the mushrooms in the air fryer basket in one layer, work in batches if necessary. Cook for 10 minutes, or until slightly crispy and brown. Garnish with thyme sprigs before serving.
4. Store leftovers in an airtight container in the fridge for up to 5 days or in the freezer for up to a month. Reheat in a preheated 350°F air fryer for 5 minutes, or until heated through.

Per Serving
calories: 82 | fat: 9g | protein: 1g | total carbs: 1g | fiber: 0.2g

Breadsticks with Garlic Butter

Prep time: 10 minutes | Cook time: 12 minutes | Serves 6

Dough:
1¾ cups shredded Mozzarella cheese
2 tablespoons unsalted butter
1 large egg, beaten
¾ cup blanched almond flour
⅛ teaspoon fine sea salt
Garlic Butter:
3 tablespoons unsalted

butter, softened
2 cloves garlic, minced
Topping:
½ cup shredded Parmesan cheese
1 teaspoon dried basil leaves
1 teaspoon dried oregano leaves
For Serving (Optional):
½ cup marinara sauce

1. Preheat the air fryer to 400°F. Place a piece of parchment paper in a 6-inch square casserole dish and spray it with avocado oil.
2. Make the dough: Place the Mozzarella cheese and butter in a microwave-safe bowl and microwave for 1 to 2 minutes, until the cheese is entirely melted. Stir well. Add the egg and, using a hand mixer on low speed, combine well. Add the almond flour and salt and combine well with the hand mixer.

3. Lay a piece of parchment paper on the countertop and place the dough on it. Knead it for about 3 minutes, the dough should be thick yet pliable. (Note: If the dough is too sticky, chill it in the refrigerator for an hour or overnight.) Place the dough in the prepared casserole dish and use your hands to spread it out to fill the bottom of the casserole dish.
4. Make the garlic butter: In a small dish, stir together the butter and garlic until well combined.
5. Spread the garlic butter on top of the dough. Top with the Parmesan, basil, and oregano. Place in the air fryer and cook for 10 minutes, or until golden brown and cooked through.
6. Cut into 1-inch-wide breadsticks and serve with marinara sauce, if desired. Best served fresh, but leftovers can be stored in an airtight container in the fridge for up to 3 days. Reheat in a preheated 400°F air fryer for 3 minutes, or until the cheese is hot and bubbly.

Per Serving
calories: 301 | fat: 26g | protein: 14g | total carbs: 6g | fiber: 2g

Broccoli with Sesame Dressing

Prep time: 5 minutes | Cook time: 10 minutes | Serves 4

6 cups broccoli florets, cut into bite-size pieces
1 tablespoon olive oil
¼ teaspoon salt
2 tablespoons sesame seeds
2 tablespoons rice

vinegar
2 tablespoons coconut aminos
2 tablespoons sesame oil
½ teaspoon Swerve
¼ teaspoon red pepper flakes (optional)

1. Preheat the air fryer to 400°F (205ºC).
2. In a large bowl, toss the broccoli with the olive oil and salt until thoroughly coated.
3. Transfer the broccoli to the air fryer basket. Pausing halfway through the cooking time to shake the basket, air fry for 10 minutes until the stems are tender and the edges are beginning to crisp.
4. Meanwhile, in the same large bowl, whisk together the sesame seeds, vinegar, coconut aminos, sesame oil, Swerve, and red pepper flakes (if using).
5. Transfer the broccoli to the bowl and toss until thoroughly coated with the seasonings. Serve warm or at room temperature.

Per Serving
calories: 180 | fat: 13g | protein: 5g | carbs: 14g | net carbs: 10g | fiber: 4g

Ranch Cauliflower

Prep time: 5 minutes | Cook time: 12 minutes | Serves 4

4 cups cauliflower florets
2 tablespoons dried parsley
1 tablespoon plus 1 teaspoon onion powder
2 teaspoons garlic powder
1½ teaspoons dried dill weed
1 teaspoon dried chives
1 teaspoon fine sea salt or smoked salt
1 teaspoon ground black pepper
Ranch Dressing, for serving (optional)

1. Preheat the air fryer to 400°F.
2. Place the cauliflower in a large bowl and spray it with avocado oil.
3. Place the parsley, onion powder, garlic powder, dill weed, chives, salt, and pepper in a small bowl and stir to combine well. Sprinkle the ranch seasoning over the cauliflower.
4. Place the cauliflower in the air fryer and cook for 12 minutes, or until tender and crisp on the edges. Serve with ranch dressing for dipping, if desired.
5. Store leftovers in an airtight container in the fridge for up to 4 days or in the freezer for up to a month. Reheat in a preheated 400°F air fryer for 5 minutes, or until crisp.

Per Serving

calories: 62 | fat: 0.1g | protein: 6g | total carbs: 12g | fiber: 6g

Celery Croquettes with Chive Mayo

Prep time: 15 minutes | Cook time: 6 minutes | Serves 4

2 medium-sized celery stalks, trimmed and grated
½ cup of leek, finely chopped
1 tablespoon garlic paste
¼ teaspoon freshly cracked black pepper
1 teaspoon fine sea salt
1 tablespoon fresh dill, finely chopped
1 egg, lightly whisked
¼ cup almond flour
½ cup parmesan cheese, freshly grated
¼ teaspoon baking powder
2 tablespoons fresh chives, chopped
4 tablespoons mayonnaise

1. Place the celery on a paper towel and squeeze them to remove excess liquid.
2. Combine the vegetables with the other ingredients, except the chives and mayo. Shape the balls using 1 tablespoon of the vegetable mixture.
3. Then, gently flatten each ball with your palm or a wide spatula. Spritz the croquettes with a non-stick cooking oil.
4. Air-fry the vegetable croquettes in a single layer for 6 minutes at 360ºF.
5. Meanwhile, mix fresh chives and mayonnaise. Serve warm croquettes with chive mayo. Bon appétit!

Per Serving

calories: 214 | fat: 18g | protein: 7g | carbs: 6.8g | net carbs: 5.2g | fiber: 1.6g

Bean Mushroom Casserole

Prep time: 10 minutes | Cook time: 12 minutes | Serves 4

1 pound (454 g) fresh green beans, ends trimmed, strings removed, and chopped into 2-inch pieces
1 (8-ounce / 227-g) package sliced brown mushrooms
½ onion, sliced
1 clove garlic, minced
1 tablespoon olive oil
½ teaspoon salt
¼ teaspoon freshly ground black pepper
4 ounces (113 g) cream cheese
½ cup chicken stock
¼ teaspoon ground nutmeg
½ cup grated Cheddar cheese

1. Preheat the air fryer to 400°F (205ºC). Coat a 6-cup casserole dish with olive oil and set aside.
2. In a large bowl, combine the green beans, mushrooms, onion, garlic, olive oil, salt, and pepper. Toss until the vegetables are thoroughly coated with the oil and seasonings.
3. Transfer the mixture to the air fryer basket. Pausing halfway through the cooking time to shake the basket, air fry for 10 minutes until tender.
4. While the vegetables are cooking, in a 2-cup glass measuring cup, warm the cream cheese and chicken stock in the microwave on high for 1 to 2 minutes until the cream cheese is melted. Add the nutmeg and whisk until smooth.
5. Transfer the vegetables to the prepared casserole dish and pour the cream cheese mixture over the top. Top with the Cheddar cheese. Air fry for another 10 minutes until the cheese is melted and beginning to brown.

Per Serving

calories: 250 | fat: 19g | protein: 10g | carbs: 14g | net carbs: 10g | fiber: 4g

Brussels Sprouts and Pancetta Salad

Prep time: 15 minutes | Cook time: 15 minutes | Serves 4

⅔ pound (307 g) Brussels sprouts
1 tablespoon olive oil
Coarse sea salt and ground black pepper, to taste
2 ounces (57 g) baby arugula
1 shallot, thinly sliced

4 ounces (113 g) pancetta, chopped
Lemon Vinaigrette:
2 tablespoons extra virgin olive oil
2 tablespoons fresh lemon juice
1 tablespoon honey
1 teaspoon Dijon mustard

1. Start by preheating your Air Fryer to 380ºF.
2. Add the Brussels sprouts to the cooking basket. Brush with olive oil and cook for 15 minutes. Let it cool to room temperature for about 15 minutes.
3. Toss the Brussels sprouts with the salt, black pepper, baby arugula, and shallot.
4. Mix all ingredients for the dressing. Then, dress your salad, garnish with pancetta, and serve well chilled. Bon appétit!

Per Serving
calories: 157 | fat: 9.9g | carbs: 8.5g | protein: 3.4g | sugar: 0.3g | fiber: 3.3g

Tomato Bruschetta

Prep time: 6 minutes | Cook time: 8 minutes | Serves 6

1 small tomato, diced
2 tablespoons chopped fresh basil leaves
1 teaspoon dried oregano leaves
¼ teaspoon fine sea salt
3 tablespoons unsalted

butter, softened
1 clove garlic, minced
1 hot dog bun, cut into twelve ½-inch-thick slices
¼ cup plus 2 tablespoons shredded Parmesan cheese

1. Spray the air fryer basket with avocado oil. Preheat the air fryer to 360°F.
2. In a small bowl, stir together the tomato, basil, oregano, and salt until well combined. Set aside.
3. In another small bowl, mix together the butter and garlic. Spread the garlic butter on one side of each hot dog bun slice.
4. Place the slices in the air fryer basket buttered side down, spaced about ⅛ inch apart. Cook for 4 minutes. Remove the slices from the air fryer, flip them so that the buttered side is up, and top each slice with 1½ tablespoons of Parmesan and a dollop

of the tomato mixture.
5. Increase the air fryer temperature to 390°F and return the slices to the air fryer basket. Cook for another 2 to 4 minutes, until the bread is crispy and the cheese is melted.
6. Serve immediately. Alternatively, stop after step 3 and store the slices of bread and the tomato mixture in separate airtight containers in the fridge for up to 5 days. When you're ready to eat, cook as instructed in steps 4 and 5.

Per Serving
calories: 268 | fat: 22g | protein: 10g | total carbs: 14g | fiber: 10g

Cauliflower Tots

Prep time: 15 minutes | Cook time: 12 minutes |Makes 16 tots

1 large head cauliflower
1 cup shredded Mozzarella cheese
½ cup grated Parmesan cheese
1 large egg

¼ teaspoon garlic powder
¼ teaspoon dried parsley
⅛ teaspoon onion powder

1. On the stovetop, fill a large pot with 2 cups water and place a steamer in the pan. Bring water to a boil. Cut the cauliflower into florets and place on steamer basket. Cover pot with lid.
2. Allow the cauliflower to steam for 7 minutes until fork tender. Remove from steamer basket and place into cheesecloth or clean kitchen towel and let it cool. Squeeze over sink to remove as much excess moisture as possible. The mixture will be too soft to form into tots if not all the moisture is removed. Mash with a fork to a smooth consistency.
3. Put the cauliflower into a large mixing bowl and add Mozzarella, Parmesan, egg, garlic powder, parsley, and onion powder. Stir until fully combined. The mixture should be wet but easy to mold.
4. Take 2 tablespoons of the mixture and roll into tot shape. Repeat with remaining mixture. Place into the air fryer basket.
5. Adjust the temperature to 320°F (160ºC) and set the timer for 12 minutes.
6. Turn tots halfway through the cooking time. Cauliflower tots should be golden when fully cooked. Serve warm.

Per Serving
calories: 181 | fat: 9g | protein: 14g | carbs: 10g | net carbs: 7g | fiber: 3g

Roasted Salsa

Prep time: 5 minutes | Cook time: 30 minutes | Makes 2 cups

2 large San Marzano tomatoes, cored and cut into large chunks
½ medium white onion, peeled and large-diced
½ medium jalapeño, seeded and large-diced
2 cloves garlic, peeled and diced
½ teaspoon salt
1 tablespoon coconut oil
¼ cup fresh lime juice

1. Place tomatoes, onion, and jalapeño into an ungreased 6-inch round nonstick baking dish. Add garlic, then sprinkle with salt and drizzle with coconut oil.
2. Place dish into air fryer basket. Adjust the temperature to 300°F (150°C) and set the timer for 30 minutes. Vegetables will be dark brown around the edges and tender when done.
3. Pour mixture into a food processor or blender. Add lime juice. Process on low speed for 30 seconds until only a few chunks remain.
4. Transfer salsa to a sealable container and refrigerate for at least 1 hour. Serve chilled.

Per Serving

calories: 28 | fat: 2g | protein: 1g | carbs: 3g | net carbs: 2g | fiber: 1g

Zucchini Salad

Prep time: 5 minutes | Cook time: 7 minutes | Serves 4

2 medium zucchini, thinly sliced
5 tablespoons olive oil, divided
¼ cup chopped fresh parsley
2 tablespoons chopped fresh mint
Zest and juice of ½ lemon
1 clove garlic, minced
¼ cup crumbled feta cheese
Freshly ground black pepper

1. Preheat the air fryer to 400°F (205°C).
2. In a large bowl, toss the zucchini slices with 1 tablespoon of the olive oil.
3. Working in batches if necessary, arrange the zucchini slices in an even layer in the air fryer basket. Pausing halfway through the cooking time to shake the basket, air fry for 5 to 7 minutes until soft and lightly browned on each side.
4. Meanwhile, in a small bowl, combine the remaining 4 tablespoons olive oil, parsley, mint, lemon zest, lemon juice, and garlic.
5. Arrange the zucchini on a plate and drizzle with the dressing. Sprinkle the feta and black pepper on top. Serve warm or at room temperature.

Per Serving

calories: 195 | fat: 19g | protein: 3g | carbs: 5g | net carbs: 4g | fiber: 1g

Parmesan Flan

Prep time: 10 minutes | Cook time: 25 minutes | Serves 4

½ cup grated Parmesan cheese
1 cup heavy cream, very warm
⅛ teaspoon fine sea salt
⅛ teaspoon ground white pepper
1 large egg
1 large egg yolk

For Serving/Garnish (Optional):
2 cups arugula
1 cup heirloom cherry tomatoes, halved
4 slices Italian cured beef (omit for vegetarian)
Ground black pepper

1. Preheat the air fryer to 350°F. Grease four 4-ounce (113-g) ramekins well.
2. Place the Parmesan in a medium-sized bowl and pour in the warm cream. Stir well to combine and add the salt and pepper.
3. In a separate medium-sized bowl, beat the egg and yolk until well combined. Gradually stir in the warm Parmesan mixture.
4. Pour the egg-and-cheese mixture into the prepared ramekins, cover the ramekins with foil, and place them in a casserole dish that will fit in your air fryer.
5. Pour boiling water into the casserole dish until the water reaches halfway up the sides of the ramekins. Place the casserole dish in the air fryer and bake until the flan is just set (the mixture will jiggle slightly when moved), for about 25 minutes. Check after 20 minutes.
6. Let the flan rest for 15 minutes. Serve with arugula, halved cherry tomatoes, and slices of Italian cured beef, if desired. Garnish with ground black pepper, if desired.
7. Store leftovers in an airtight container in the fridge for up to 5 days. Reheat the flan in a ramekin in a preheated 350°F air fryer for 5 minutes, or until heated through.

Per Serving

calories: 345 | fat: 32g | protein: 14g | total carbs: 2g | fiber: 0.2g

Bok Choy with Chili-Garlic Sauce

Prep time: 10 minutes | Cook time: 10 minutes | Serves 4

2 tablespoons olive oil
2 tablespoons coconut aminos
2 teaspoons sesame oil
2 teaspoons chili-garlic sauce
2 cloves garlic, minced
1 head (about 1 pound / 454 g) bok choy, sliced lengthwise into quarters
2 teaspoons black sesame seeds

1. Preheat the air fryer to 400°F (205ºC).
2. In a large bowl, combine the olive oil, coconut aminos, sesame oil, chili-garlic sauce, and garlic. Add the bok choy and toss, massaging the leaves with your hands if necessary, until thoroughly coated.
3. Arrange the bok choy in the basket of the air fryer. Pausing about halfway through the cooking time to shake the basket, air fry for 7 to 10 minutes until the bok choy is tender and the tips of the leaves begin to crisp. Remove from the basket and let it cool for a few minutes before coarsely chopping. Serve sprinkled with the sesame seeds.

Per Serving
calories: 100 | fat: 8g | protein: 2g | carbs: 4g | net carbs: 3g | fiber: 1g

Tomato Salad with Arugula

Prep time: 10 minutes | Cook time: 10 minutes | Serves 4

4 green tomatoes
½ teaspoon salt
1 large egg, lightly beaten
½ cup peanut flour
1 tablespoon Creole seasoning
1 (5-ounce / 142-g) bag arugula
Buttermilk Dressing
1 cup mayonnaise
½ cup sour cream
2 teaspoons fresh lemon juice
2 tablespoons finely chopped fresh parsley
1 teaspoon dried dill
1 teaspoon dried chives
½ teaspoon salt
½ teaspoon garlic powder
½ teaspoon onion powder

1. Preheat the air fryer to 400°F (205ºC).
2. Slice the tomatoes into ½-inch slices and sprinkle with the salt. Let them sit for 5 to 10 minutes.
3. Place the egg in a small shallow bowl. In another small shallow bowl, combine the peanut flour and Creole seasoning. Dip each tomato slice into the egg wash, then dip into the peanut flour mixture, turning

to coat evenly.
4. Working in batches if necessary, arrange the tomato slices in a single layer in the air fryer basket and spray both sides lightly with olive oil. Air fry until browned and crisp, for 8 to 10 minutes.
5. To make the buttermilk dressing: In a small bowl, whisk together the mayonnaise, sour cream, lemon juice, parsley, dill, chives, salt, garlic powder, and onion powder.
6. Serve the tomato slices on top of a bed of the arugula with the dressing on the side.

Per Serving
calories: 560 | fat: 54g | protein: 9g | carbs: 16g | net carbs: 13g | fiber: 3g

Zucchini with Mediterranean Dipping Sauce

Prep time: 15 minutes | Cook time: 20 minutes | Serves 4

1 pound (454 g) zucchini, peeled and cubed
2 tablespoons melted butter
1 teaspoon sea salt flakes
1 sprig rosemary, leaves only, crushed
2 sprigs thyme, leaves only, crushed
½ teaspoon freshly
cracked black peppercorns
For Mediterranean Dipping Sauce:
½ cup mascarpone cheese
⅓ cup yogurt
1 tablespoon fresh dill, chopped
1 tablespoon olive oil

1. Firstly, set your Air Fryer to cook at 350ºF. Now, add the potato cubes to the bowl with cold water and soak them approximately for 35 minutes.
2. After that, dry the potato cubes using a paper towel.
3. In a mixing dish, thoroughly whisk the melted butter with sea salt flakes, rosemary, thyme, and freshly cracked peppercorns. Rub the potato cubes with this butter/spice mix.
4. Air-fry the potato cubes in the cooking basket for 18 to 20 minutes or until cooked through, make sure to shake the potatoes to cook them evenly.
5. Meanwhile, make the Mediterranean dipping sauce by mixing the remaining ingredients. Serve warm potatoes with Mediterranean sauce for dipping and enjoy!

Per Serving
calories: 184 | fat: 15.4g | carbs: 5.5g | protein: 8.1g | sugar: 1g | fiber: 1.6g

Creamed Eggs

Prep time: 15 minutes | Cook time: 18 minutes | Serves 2

1 teaspoon garlic paste
1½ tablespoons olive oil
½ cup crème fraîche
⅓ teaspoon ground black pepper, to your liking
⅓ cup Swiss cheese, crumbled
1 teaspoon cayenne

pepper
⅓ cup Swiss chard, torn into pieces
5 eggs
¼ cup yellow onions, chopped
1 teaspoon fine sea salt

1. Crack your eggs into a mixing dish, then, add the crème fraîche, salt, ground black pepper, and cayenne pepper.
2. Next, coat the inside of a baking dish with olive oil and tilt it to spread evenly. Scrape the egg/cream mixture into the baking dish. Add the other ingredients, mix to combine well.
3. Bake for 18 minutes at 292ºF. Serve immediately.

Per Serving

calories: 388 | fat: 27g | carbs: 6g | protein: 29g | sugar: 0.6g | fiber: 0.7g

Tomatoes Stuffed with Burrata Balls

Prep time: 5 minutes | Cook time: 5 minutes | Serves 4

4 medium tomatoes
½ teaspoon fine sea salt
4 (2-ounce / 57-g) Burrata balls

Fresh basil leaves, for garnish
Extra-virgin olive oil, for drizzling

1. Preheat the air fryer to 300°F.
2. Core the tomatoes and scoop out the seeds and membranes using a melon baller or spoon. Sprinkle the insides of the tomatoes with the salt.
3. Stuff each tomato with a ball of Burrata. Place in the air fryer and cook for 5 minutes, or until the cheese has softened.
4. Garnish with basil leaves and drizzle with olive oil. Serve warm.
5. Store leftovers in an airtight container in the refrigerator for up to 4 days. Reheat in a preheated 300°F air fryer for about 3 minutes, until heated through.

Per Serving

calories: 108 | fat: 7g | protein: 6g | total carbs: 5g | fiber: 2g

Curried Cauliflower

Prep time: 15 minutes | Cook time: 20 minutes | Serves 4

¼ cup olive oil
2 teaspoons curry powder
½ teaspoon salt
¼ teaspoon freshly ground black pepper

1 head cauliflower, cut into bite-size florets
½ red onion, sliced
2 tablespoons freshly chopped parsley, for garnish (optional)

1. Preheat the air fryer to 400°F (205ºC).
2. In a large bowl, combine the olive oil, curry powder, salt, and pepper. Add the cauliflower and onion. Toss gently until the vegetables are completely coated with the oil mixture. Transfer the vegetables to the basket of the air fryer.
3. Pausing about halfway through the cooking time to shake the basket, air fry for 20 minutes until the cauliflower is tender and beginning to brown. Top with the parsley, if desired, before serving.

Per Serving

calories: 165 | fat: 14g | protein: 3g | carbs: 10g | net carbs: 6g | fiber: 4g

Sesame Broccoli Florets

Prep time: 10 minutes | Cook time: 6 minutes | Serves 3

1 pound (454 g) broccoli florets
2 tablespoons sesame oil
½ teaspoon shallot powder
½ teaspoon porcini powder
1 teaspoon garlic powder

Sea salt and ground black pepper, to taste
½ teaspoon cumin powder
¼ teaspoon paprika
2 tablespoons sesame seeds

1. Start by preheating the Air Fryer to 400ºF.
2. Blanch the broccoli in salted boiling water until al dente, for about 3 to 4 minutes. Drain well and transfer to the lightly greased Air Fryer basket.
3. Add the sesame oil, shallot powder, porcini powder, garlic powder, salt, black pepper, cumin powder, paprika, and sesame seeds.
4. Cook for 6 minutes, tossing halfway through the cooking time. Bon appétit!

Per Serving

calories: 160 | fat: 13.2g | carbs: 9.7g | protein: 3.5g | sugar: 1.4g | fiber: 5g

Parmesan-Crusted Brussels Sprouts, page 126

Caramelized Broccoli, page 136

Simple Zoodles, page 137

Ranch Cauliflower, page 128

Celery Sticks

Prep time: 10 minutes | Cook time: 15 minutes | Serves 4

1 pound (454 g) celery, cut into matchsticks
2 tablespoons peanut oil
1 jalapeño, seeded and minced
¼ teaspoon dill
½ teaspoon basil
Salt and white pepper to taste

1. Start by preheating your Air Fryer to 380ºF.
2. Toss all ingredients together and place them in the Air Fryer basket.
3. Cook for 15 minutes, shaking the basket halfway through the cooking time. Transfer to a serving platter and enjoy!

Per Serving
calories: 450 | fat: 25.6g | carbs: 3.4g | protein: 50.8g | sugar: 0.3g | fiber: 1.3g

Roasted Eggplant

Prep time: 15 minutes | Cook time: 15 minutes | Serves 4

1 large eggplant
2 tablespoons olive oil
¼ teaspoon salt
½ teaspoon garlic powder

1. Remove top and bottom from eggplant. Slice eggplant into ¼-inch-thick round slices.
2. Brush slices with olive oil. Sprinkle with salt and garlic powder. Place eggplant slices into the air fryer basket.
3. Adjust the temperature to 390°F (199ºC) and set the timer for 15 minutes.
4. Serve immediately.

Per Serving
calories: 236 | fat: 13g | protein: 19g | carbs: 5g | net carbs: 5g | fiber: 0g

Pecan-Crusted Brussels Sprouts

Prep time: 10 minutes | Cook time: 30 minutes | Serves 4

½ cup pecans
1½ pounds (680g) fresh Brussels sprouts, trimmed and quartered
2 tablespoons olive oil
Salt and freshly ground black pepper
¼ cup crumbled Gorgonzola cheese

1. Spread the pecans in a single layer of the air fryer and set the heat to 350°F (180ºC). Air fry for 3 to 5 minutes until the pecans are lightly browned and fragrant. Transfer the pecans to a plate and continue preheating the air fryer, increasing the heat to 400°F (205ºC).
2. In a large bowl, toss the Brussels sprouts with the olive oil and season with salt and black pepper to taste.
3. Working in batches if necessary, arrange the Brussels sprouts in a single layer in the air fryer basket. Pausing halfway through the baking time to shake the basket, air fry for 20 to 25 minutes until the sprouts are tender and starting to brown on the edges.
4. Transfer the sprouts to a serving bowl and top with the toasted pecans and Gorgonzola. Serve warm or at room temperature.

Per Serving
calories: 250 | fat: 19g | protein: 9g | carbs: 17g | net carbs: 9g | fiber: 8g

Sausage-Stuffed Mushroom Caps

Prep time: 10 minutes | Cook time: 8 minutes | Serves 2

6 large portobello mushroom caps
½ pound (227g) Italian sausage
¼ cup chopped onion
2 tablespoons blanched
finely ground almond flour
¼ cup grated Parmesan cheese
1 teaspoon minced fresh garlic

1. Use a spoon to hollow out each mushroom cap, reserving scrapings.
2. In a medium skillet over medium heat, brown the sausage for about 10 minutes or until fully cooked and no pink remains. Drain and then add reserved mushroom scrapings, onion, almond flour, Parmesan, and garlic. Gently fold ingredients together and continue cooking for an additional minute, then remove from heat.
3. Evenly spoon the mixture into mushroom caps and place the caps into a 6-inch round pan. Place pan into the air fryer basket.
4. Adjust the temperature to 375°F (190ºC) and set the timer for 8 minutes.
5. When finished cooking, the tops will be browned and bubbling. Serve warm.

Per Serving
calories: 404 | fat: 25g | protein: 24g | carbs: 18g | net carbs: 14g | fiber: 4g

Parmesan Zucchini Crisps

Prep time: 10 minutes | Cook time: 9 minutes | Serves 4

1 pound (454 g) zucchini, peeled and sliced
1 egg, lightly beaten
1 cup Parmesan cheese, preferably freshly grated

1. Pat the zucchini dry with a kitchen towel.
2. In a mixing dish, thoroughly combine the egg and cheese. Then, coat the zucchini slices with the breadcrumb mixture.
3. Cook in the preheated Air Fryer at 400ºF for 9 minutes, shaking the basket halfway through the cooking time.
4. Work in batches until the chips is golden brown. Bon appétit!

Per Serving
calories: 157 | fat: 9.5g | carbs: 7.4g | protein: 2g | sugar: 0.4g | fiber: 1.2g

Cauliflower Rice Balls

Prep time: 10 minutes | Cook time: 8 minutes | Serves 4

1 (10-ounce / 283-g) steamer bag cauliflower rice, cooked according to package instructions
½ cup shredded Mozzarella cheese
1 large egg
2 ounces (57 g) plain pork rinds, finely crushed
¼ teaspoon salt
½ teaspoon Italian seasoning

1. Place cauliflower into a large bowl and mix with Mozzarella.
2. Whisk egg in a separate medium bowl. Place pork rinds into another large bowl with salt and Italian seasoning.
3. Separate cauliflower mixture into four equal sections and form each into a ball. Carefully dip a ball into whisked egg, then roll in pork rinds. Repeat with remaining balls.
4. Place cauliflower balls into ungreased air fryer basket. Adjust the temperature to 400°F (205ºC) and set the timer for 8 minutes. Rice balls will be golden when done.
5. Use a spatula to carefully move cauliflower balls to a large dish for serving. Serve warm.

Per Serving
calories: 158 | fat: 9g | protein: 15g | carbs: 4g | net carbs: 2g | fiber: 2g

Cauliflower Mash

Prep time: 10 minutes | Cook time: 15 minutes | Serves 6

1 (12-ounce / 340-g) steamer bag cauliflower florets, cooked according to package instructions
2 tablespoons salted butter, softened
2 ounces (57 g) cream
cheese, softened
½ cup shredded sharp Cheddar cheese
¼ cup pickled jalapeños
½ teaspoon salt
¼ teaspoon ground black pepper

1. Place cooked cauliflower into a food processor with remaining ingredients. Pulse twenty times until cauliflower is smooth and all ingredients are combined.
2. Spoon mash into an ungreased 6-inch round nonstick baking dish. Place dish into air fryer basket. Adjust the temperature to 380°F (193ºC) and set the timer for 15 minutes. The top will be golden brown when done. Serve warm.

Per Serving
calories: 117 | fat: 9g | protein: 4g | carbs: 3g | net carbs: 2g | fiber: 1g

Egg and Vegetable Salad

Prep time: 15 minutes | Cook time: 15 minutes | Serves 4

⅓ pound (151 g) Brussels sprouts
½ cup radishes, sliced
½ cup Mozzarella cheese, crumbled
1 red onion, chopped
4 eggs, hardboiled and sliced
Dressing:
¼ cup olive oil
2 tablespoons champagne vinegar
1 teaspoon Dijon mustard
Sea salt and ground black pepper, to taste

1. Start by preheating your Air Fryer to 380ºF.
2. Add the Brussels sprouts and radishes to the cooking basket. Spritz with cooking spray and cook for 15 minutes. Let it cool to room temperature for about 15 minutes.
3. Toss the vegetables with cheese and red onion.
4. Mix all ingredients for the dressing and toss to combine well. Serve topped with the hard-boiled eggs. Bon appétit!

Per Serving
calories: 298 | fat: 23.3g | carbs: 17.5g | protein: 5g | sugar: 0.6g | fiber: 2.6g

Bacon-Wrapped Asparagus

Prep time: 5 minutes | Cook time: 10 minutes | Serves 4

8 slices reduced-sodium bacon, cut in half 16 thick (about 1 pound /   454 g) asparagus spears, trimmed of woody ends

1. Preheat the air fryer to 350°F (180ºC).
2. Wrap a half piece of bacon around the center of each stalk of asparagus.
3. Working in batches, if necessary, arrange seam-side down in a single layer in the air fryer basket. Cook for 10 minutes until the bacon is crisp and the stalks are tender.

Per Serving

calories: 110 | fat: 7g | protein: 8g | carbs: 5g | net carbs: 3g | fiber: 2g

Zucchini Fritters

Prep time: 15 minutes | Cook time: 10 minutes | Serves 4

2 zucchini, grated (about 1 pound / 454 g)
1 teaspoon salt
¼ cup almond flour
¼ cup grated Parmesan cheese
1 large egg
¼ teaspoon dried thyme   ¼ teaspoon ground turmeric
¼ teaspoon freshly ground black pepper
1 tablespoon olive oil
½ lemon, sliced into wedges

1. Preheat the air fryer to 400°F (205ºC). Cut a piece of parchment paper to fit slightly smaller than the bottom of the air fryer.
2. Place the zucchini in a large colander and sprinkle with the salt. Let it sit for 5 to 10 minutes. Squeeze as much liquid as you can from the zucchini and place in a large mixing bowl. Add the almond flour, Parmesan, egg, thyme, turmeric, and black pepper. Stir gently until thoroughly combined.
3. Shape the mixture into 8 patties and arrange on the parchment paper. Brush lightly with the olive oil. Pausing halfway through the cooking time to turn the patties, air fry for 10 minutes until golden brown. Serve warm with the lemon wedges.

Per Serving

calories: 190 | fat: 16g | protein: 6g | carbs: 8g | net carbs: 6g | fiber: 2g

Caramelized Broccoli

Prep time: 5 minutes | Cook time: 8 minutes | Serves 4

4 cups broccoli florets
3 tablespoons melted ghee or butter-flavored coconut oil
1½ teaspoons fine sea   salt or smoked salt
Mayonnaise, for serving (optional, omit for egg-free)

1. Spray the air fryer basket with avocado oil. Preheat the air fryer to 400°F.
2. Place the broccoli in a large bowl. Drizzle it with the ghee, toss to coat, and sprinkle it with the salt. Transfer the broccoli to the air fryer basket and cook for 8 minutes, or until tender and crisp on the edges.
3. Store leftovers in an airtight container in the fridge for up to 4 days or in the freezer for up to a month. Reheat in a preheated 400°F air fryer for 5 minutes, or until crisp.

Per Serving

calories: 107 | fat: 9g | protein: 3g | total carbs: 6g | fiber: 2g

Cheesy Asparagus

Prep time: 10 minutes | Cook time: 18 minutes | Serves 4

½ cup heavy whipping cream
½ cup grated Parmesan cheese
2 ounces (57 g) cream cheese, softened
1 pound (454 g)   asparagus, ends trimmed, chopped into 1-inch pieces
¼ teaspoon salt
¼ teaspoon ground black pepper

1. In a medium bowl, whisk together heavy cream, Parmesan, and cream cheese until combined.
2. Place asparagus into an ungreased 6-inch round nonstick baking dish. Pour cheese mixture over top and sprinkle with salt and pepper.
3. Place dish into air fryer basket. Adjust the temperature to 350°F (180ºC) and set the timer for 18 minutes. Asparagus will be tender when done. Serve warm.

Per Serving

calories: 221 | fat: 18g | protein: 7g | carbs: 7g | net carbs: 5g | fiber: 2g

Simple Zoodles

Prep time: 5 minutes | Cook time: 8 minutes | Serves 2

1 (12-inch) zucchini

Special Equipment: Spiral slicer

1. Spray the air fryer basket with avocado oil. Preheat the air fryer to 400°F.
2. Cut the ends off the zucchini to create nice even edges. If you desire completely white noodles, peel the zucchini. Using a spiral slicer, cut the zucchini into long, thin noodles.
3. Spread out the zucchini noodles in the air fryer basket in a single layer and cook for 8 minutes, or until soft. Remove from the air fryer and serve immediately.
4. Store leftovers in an airtight container for 4 days. Reheat in a single layer in the air fryer for 3 minutes, or until heated through.

Per Serving

calories: 29 | fat: 0g | protein: 2g | total carbs: 6g | fiber: 2g

Air Fried Radishes

Prep time: 10 minutes | Cook time: 10 minutes | Serves 4

1 pound (454 g) radishes
2 tablespoons unsalted butter, melted
½ teaspoon garlic powder
½ teaspoon dried parsley
¼ teaspoon dried oregano
¼ teaspoon ground black pepper

1. Remove roots from radishes and cut into quarters.
2. In a small bowl, add butter and seasonings. Toss the radishes in the herb butter and place into the air fryer basket.
3. Adjust the temperature to 350°F (180ºC) and set the timer for 10 minutes.
4. Halfway through the cooking time, toss the radishes in the air fryer basket. Continue cooking until edges begin to turn brown.
5. Serve warm.

Per Serving

calories: 63 | fat: 5g | protein: 1g | carbs: 3g | net carbs: 2g | fiber: 1g

Tomato and Zucchini Boats

Prep time: 5 minutes | Cook time: 10 minutes | Serves 4

1 large zucchini, ends removed, halved lengthwise
6 grape tomatoes, quartered
¼ teaspoon salt
¼ cup feta cheese
1 tablespoon balsamic vinegar
1 tablespoon olive oil

1. Use a spoon to scoop out 2 tablespoons from center of each zucchini half, making just enough space to fill with tomatoes and feta.
2. Place tomatoes evenly in centers of zucchini halves and sprinkle with salt. Place into ungreased air fryer basket. Adjust the temperature to 350°F (180ºC) and set the timer for 10 minutes. When done, zucchini will be tender.
3. Transfer boats to a serving tray and sprinkle with feta, then drizzle with vinegar and olive oil. Serve warm.

Per Serving

calories: 74 | fat: 5g | protein: 2g | carbs: 4g | net carbs: 3g | fiber: 1g

Cabbage with Dijon Mustard

Prep time: 10 minutes | Cook time: 10 minutes | Serves 4

1 small head cabbage, cored and sliced into 1-inch-thick slices
2 tablespoons olive oil, divided
½ teaspoon salt
1 tablespoon Dijon mustard
1 teaspoon apple cider vinegar
1 teaspoon granular erythritol

1. Drizzle each cabbage slice with 1 tablespoon olive oil, then sprinkle with salt. Place slices into ungreased air fryer basket, working in batches if needed. Adjust the temperature to 350°F (180ºC) and set the timer for 10 minutes. Cabbage will be tender and edges will begin to brown when done.
2. In a small bowl, whisk remaining olive oil with mustard, vinegar, and erythritol. Drizzle over cabbage in a large serving dish. Serve warm.

Per Serving

calories: 111 | fat: 7g | protein: 3g | carbs: 12g | net carbs: 8g | fiber: 4g

Cripsy Broccoli with Bacon

Prep time: 10 minutes | Cook time: 10 minutes | Serves 2

3 cups fresh broccoli florets
1 tablespoon coconut oil
½ cup shredded sharp Cheddar cheese

¼ cup full-fat sour cream
4 slices sugar-free bacon, cooked and crumbled
1 scallion, sliced on the bias

1. Place broccoli into the air fryer basket and drizzle it with coconut oil.
2. Adjust the temperature to 350°F (180ºC) and set the timer for 10 minutes.
3. Toss the basket two or three times during cooking to avoid burned spots.
4. When broccoli begins to crisp at ends, remove from fryer. Top with shredded cheese, sour cream, and crumbled bacon and garnish with scallion slices.

Per Serving

calories: 361 | fat: 25g | protein: 18g | carbs: 11g | net carbs: 7g | fiber: 4g

Simple Air Fried Asparagus

Prep time: 5 minutes | Cook time: 12 minutes | Serves 4

1 tablespoon olive oil
1 pound (454 g) asparagus spears, ends trimmed
¼ teaspoon salt

¼ teaspoon ground black pepper
1 tablespoon salted butter, melted

1. In a large bowl, drizzle olive oil over asparagus spears and sprinkle with salt and pepper.
2. Place spears into ungreased air fryer basket. Adjust the temperature to 375°F (190ºC) and set the timer for 12 minutes, shaking the basket halfway through cooking. Asparagus will be lightly browned and tender when done.
3. Transfer to a large dish and drizzle with butter. Serve warm.

Per Serving

calories: 73 | fat: 6g | protein: 2g | carbs: 4g | net carbs: 2g | fiber: 2g

Bell Peppers with Sriracha Mayonnaise

Prep time: 10 minutes | Cook time: 14 minutes | Serves 2

4 bell peppers, seeded and sliced (1-inch pieces)
1 onion, sliced (1-inch pieces)
1 tablespoon olive oil
½ teaspoon dried rosemary

½ teaspoon dried basil
Kosher salt, to taste
¼ teaspoon ground black pepper
⅓ cup mayonnaise
⅓ teaspoon Sriracha

1. Toss the bell peppers and onions with the olive oil, rosemary, basil, salt, and black pepper.
2. Place the peppers and onions on an even layer in the cooking basket. Cook at 400ºF for 12 to 14 minutes.
3. Meanwhile, make the sauce by whisking the mayonnaise and Sriracha. Serve immediately.

Per Serving

calories: 346 | fat: 34.1g | carbs: 9.5g | protein: 2.3g | sugar: 0.9g | fiber: 2.1g

Brussels Sprouts with Bacon

Prep time: 5 minutes | Cook time: 12 minutes | Serves 4

2 cups trimmed and halved fresh Brussels sprouts
2 tablespoons olive oil
¼ teaspoon salt
¼ teaspoon ground black

pepper
2 tablespoons balsamic vinegar
2 slices cooked sugar-free bacon, crumbled

1. In a large bowl, toss Brussels sprouts in olive oil, then sprinkle with salt and pepper. Place into ungreased air fryer basket. Adjust the temperature to 375°F (190ºC) and set the timer for 12 minutes, shaking the basket halfway through cooking. Brussels sprouts will be tender and browned when done.
2. Place sprouts in a large serving dish and drizzle with balsamic vinegar. Sprinkle bacon over top. Serve warm.

Per Serving

calories: 112 | fat: 9g | protein: 3g | carbs: 5g | net carbs: 3g | fiber: 2g

Asparagus Fries

Prep time: 10 minutes | Cook time: 5 minutes | Serves 4

2 eggs
1 teaspoon Dijon mustard
1 cup Parmesan cheese, grated
Sea salt and ground

black pepper, to taste
18 asparagus spears, trimmed
½ cup sour cream

1. Start by preheating your Air Fryer to 400ºF.
2. In a shallow bowl, whisk the eggs and mustard. In another shallow bowl, combine the Parmesan cheese, salt, and black pepper.
3. Dip the asparagus spears in the egg mixture, then in the Parmesan mixture, press to adhere.
4. Cook for 5 minutes, work in three batches. Serve with sour cream on the side. Enjoy!

Per Serving
calories: 217 | fat: 14.4g | carbs: 7.7g | protein: 1.2g | sugar: 1.2g | fiber: 0.5g

Spinach Poppers

Prep time: 10 minutes | Cook time: 8 minutes | Makes 16 poppers

4 ounces (113 g) cream cheese, softened
1 cup chopped fresh spinach leaves
½ teaspoon garlic

powder
8 mini sweet bell peppers, tops removed, seeded, and halved lengthwise

1. In a medium bowl, mix cream cheese, spinach, and garlic powder. Place 1 tablespoon mixture into each sweet pepper half and press down to smooth.
2. Place poppers into ungreased air fryer basket. Adjust the temperature to 400°F (205ºC) and set the timer for 8 minutes. Poppers will be done when cheese is browned on top and peppers are tender-crisp. Serve warm.

Per Serving
calories: 116 | fat: 8g | protein: 3g | carbs: 5g | net carbs: 4g | fiber: 1g

Pork Onion Rings

Prep time: 10 minutes | Cook time: 5 minutes | Serves 8

1 large egg
¼ cup coconut flour
2 ounces (57 g) plain pork rinds, finely crushed

1 large white onion, peeled and sliced into 8 (¼-inch) rings

1. Whisk egg in a medium bowl. Place coconut flour and pork rinds in two separate medium bowls. Dip each onion ring into egg, then coat in coconut flour. Dip coated onion ring in egg once more, then press gently into pork rinds to cover all sides.
2. Place rings into ungreased air fryer basket. Adjust the temperature to 400°F (205ºC) and set the timer for 5 minutes, turning the onion rings halfway through cooking. Onion rings will be golden and crispy when done. Serve warm.

Per Serving
calories: 79 | fat: 3g | protein: 6g | carbs: 6g | net carbs: 4g | fiber: 2g

Cauliflower with Lime Juice

Prep time: 10 minutes | Cook time: 7 minutes | Serves 4

2 cups chopped cauliflower florets
2 tablespoons coconut oil, melted
2 teaspoons chili powder

½ teaspoon garlic powder
1 medium lime
2 tablespoons chopped cilantro

1. In a large bowl, toss cauliflower with coconut oil. Sprinkle with chili powder and garlic powder. Place seasoned cauliflower into the air fryer basket.
2. Adjust the temperature to 350°F (180ºC) and set the timer for 7 minutes.
3. Cauliflower will be tender and begin to turn golden at the edges. Place into serving bowl.
4. Cut the lime into quarters and squeeze juice over cauliflower. Garnish with cilantro.

Per Serving
calories: 73 | fat: 6g | protein: 1g | carbs: 3g | net carbs: 2g | fiber: 1g

Easy Air Fried Mushroom

Prep time: 10 minutes | Cook time: 10 minutes | Serves 4

8 ounces (227 g) cremini mushrooms, halved
2 tablespoons salted butter, melted

¼ teaspoon salt
¼ teaspoon ground black pepper

1. In a medium bowl, toss mushrooms with butter, then sprinkle with salt and pepper. Place into ungreased air fryer basket. Adjust the temperature to 400°F (205ºC) and set the timer for 10 minutes, shaking the basket halfway through cooking. Mushrooms will be tender when done. Serve warm.

Per Serving
calories: 63 | fat: 5g | protein: 1g | carbs: 3g | net carbs: 3g | fiber: 0g

Tomatoes with Feta

Prep time: 10 minutes | Cook time: 12 minutes | Serves 2

3 medium-sized tomatoes, cut into four slices, pat dry
1 teaspoon dried basil
1 teaspoon dried oregano

¼ teaspoon red pepper flakes, crushed
½ teaspoon sea salt
3 slices Feta cheese

1. Spritz the tomatoes with cooking oil and transfer them to the Air Fryer basket. Sprinkle with seasonings.
2. Cook at 350ºF for approximately 8 minutes turning them over halfway through the cooking time.
3. Top with the cheese and cook for an additional 4 minutes. Bon appétit!

Per Serving
calories: 148 | fat: 9.4g | carbs: 9.4g | protein: 2.8g | sugar: 1.2g | fiber: 0.6g

Kohlrabi Fries

Prep time: 10 minutes | Cook time: 30 minutes | Serves 4

2 pounds (907 g) kohlrabi, peeled and cut into ¼–½-inch fries

2 tablespoons olive oil
Salt and freshly ground black pepper

1. Preheat the air fryer to 400°F (205ºC).
2. In a large bowl, combine the kohlrabi and olive oil. Season to taste with salt and black pepper. Toss gently until thoroughly coated.
3. Working in batches if necessary, spread the kohlrabi in a single layer in the air fryer basket. Pausing halfway through the cooking time to shake the basket, air fry for 20 to 30 minutes until the fries are lightly browned and crunchy.

Per Serving
calories: 120 | fat: 7g | protein: 4g | carbs: 14g | net carbs: 12g | fiber: 2g

Chapter 9 Appetizers and Snacks

Brussels Sprouts Crisps

Prep time: 10 minutes | Cook time: 15 minutes | Serves 4

1 pound (454 g) Brussels sprouts, ends and yellow leaves removed and halved lengthwise
Salt and black pepper, to taste
1 tablespoon toasted sesame oil
1 teaspoon fennel seeds
Chopped fresh parsley, for garnish

1. Place the Brussels sprouts, salt, pepper, sesame oil, and fennel seeds in a resealable plastic bag. Seal the bag and shake to coat.
2. Air-fry at 380ºF for 15 minutes or until tender. Make sure to flip them over halfway through the cooking time.
3. Serve sprinkled with fresh parsley. Bon appétit!

Per Serving

calories: 174 | fat: 3.8g | carbs: 8.8g | protein: 3.4g | sugar: 1g | fiber: 3.9g

Cheesy Mini Peppers with Bacon

Prep time: 15 minutes | Cook time: 8 minutes | Serves 16 halves

8 mini sweet peppers
4 ounces (113 g) full-fat cream cheese, softened
4 slices sugar-free bacon,
cooked and crumbled
¼ cup shredded pepper jack cheese

1. Remove the tops from the peppers and slice each one in half lengthwise. Use a small knife to remove seeds and membranes.
2. In a small bowl, mix cream cheese, bacon, and pepper jack.
3. Place 3 teaspoons of the mixture into each sweet pepper and press down smooth. Place into the fryer basket.
4. Adjust the temperature to 400°F (205ºC) and set the timer for 8 minutes.
5. Serve warm.

Per Serving

calories: 176 | fat: 13g | protein: 7g | carbs: 4g | net carbs: 3g | fiber: 1g

Chicken and Cheese Dip

Prep time: 10 minutes | Cook time: 12 minutes | Serves 8

8 ounces (227 g) cream cheese, softened
2 cups chopped cooked chicken thighs
½ cup sugar-free buffalo sauce
1 cup shredded mild Cheddar cheese, divided

1. In a large bowl, combine cream cheese, chicken, buffalo sauce, and ½ cup Cheddar. Scoop dip into an ungreased 4-cup nonstick baking dish and top with remaining Cheddar.
2. Place dish into air fryer basket. Adjust the temperature to 375°F (190ºC) and set the timer for 12 minutes. Dip will be browned on top and bubbling when done. Serve warm.

Per Serving

calories: 222 | fat: 15g | protein: 14g | carbs:1g | net carbs: 1g | fiber: 0g

Bacon-Wrapped Shrimp

Prep time: 45 minutes | Cook time: 8 minutes | Serves 10

1¼ pounds (567g) shrimp, peeled and deveined
1 teaspoon paprika
½ teaspoon ground black pepper
½ teaspoon red pepper flakes, crushed
1 tablespoon salt
1 teaspoon chili powder
1 tablespoon shallot powder
¼ teaspoon cumin powder
1¼ pounds (567g) thin bacon slices

1. Toss the shrimps with all the seasoning until they are coated well.
2. Next, wrap a slice of bacon around the shrimps, securing with a toothpick, repeat with the remaining ingredients, chill for 30 minutes.
3. Air-fry them at 360ºF (182ºC) for 7 to 8 minutes, working in batches. Serve with cocktail sticks if desired. Enjoy!

Per Serving

calories: 282 | fat: 22g | protein: 19g | carbs: 2g | net carbs: 1g | fiber: 1g

Blooming Onion

Prep time: 10 minutes | Cook time: 35 minutes | Serves 8

1 extra-large onion (about 3 inches in diameter)
2 large eggs
1 tablespoon water
½ cup powdered Parmesan cheese
2 teaspoons paprika
1 teaspoon garlic powder
¼ teaspoon cayenne pepper
¼ teaspoon fine sea salt
¼ teaspoon ground black pepper

For Garnish (Optional):
Fresh parsley leaves
Powdered Parmesan cheese

For Serving (Optional):
Prepared yellow mustard
Ranch Dressing
Reduced-sugar or sugar-free ketchup

1. Spray the air fryer basket with avocado oil. Preheat the air fryer to 350°F.
2. Using a sharp knife, cut the top ½ inch off the onion and peel off the outer layer. Cut the onion into 8 equal sections, stopping 1 inch from the bottom— you want the onion to stay together at the base. Gently spread the sections, or "petals," apart.
3. Crack the eggs into a large bowl, add the water, and whisk well. Place the onion in the dish and coat it well in the egg. Use a spoon to coat the inside of the onion and all of the petals.
4. In a small bowl, combine the Parmesan, seasonings, salt, and pepper.
5. Place the onion in a 6-inch pie pan or casserole dish. Sprinkle the seasoning mixture all over the onion and use your fingers to press it into the petals. Spray the onion with avocado oil.
6. Loosely cover the onion with parchment paper and then foil. Place the dish in the air fryer. Cook for 30 minutes, then remove it from the air fryer and increase the air fryer temperature to 400°F.
7. Remove the foil and parchment and spray the onion with avocado oil again. Protecting your hands with oven-safe gloves or a tea towel, transfer the onion to the air fryer basket. Cook for an additional 3 to 5 minutes, until light brown and crispy.
8. Garnish with fresh parsley and powdered Parmesan, if desired. Serve with mustard, ranch dressing, and ketchup, if desired.
9. Store leftovers in an airtight container in the fridge for up to 4 days. Reheat in a preheated 400°F air fryer for 3 to 5 minutes, until warm and crispy.

Per Serving
calories: 51 | fat: 3g | protein: 4g | total carbs: 3g | fiber: 0.4g

Cauliflower and Prosciutto Pierogi

Prep time: 15 minutes | Cook time: 20 minutes | Makes 4 pierogies

1 cup chopped cauliflower
2 tablespoons diced onions
1 tablespoon unsalted butter (or lard or bacon fat for dairy-free), melted
pinch of fine sea salt
½ cup shredded sharp Cheddar cheese (about 2 ounces / 57 g) (or Kite Hill brand cream cheese style spread, softened, for dairy-free)
8 slices prosciutto
Fresh oregano leaves, for garnish (optional)

1. Preheat the air fryer to 350°F (180°C). Lightly grease a 7-inch pie pan or a casserole dish that will fit in your air fryer.
2. Make the filling: Place the cauliflower and onion in the pan. Drizzle with the melted butter and sprinkle with the salt. Using your hands, mix everything together, making sure the cauliflower is coated in the butter.
3. Place the cauliflower mixture in the air fryer and cook for 10 minutes, until fork-tender, stirring halfway through.
4. Transfer the cauliflower mixture to a food processor or high-powered blender. Spray the air fryer basket with avocado oil and increase the air fryer temperature to 400°F (205°C).
5. Pulse the cauliflower mixture in the food processor until smooth. Stir in the cheese.
6. Assemble the pierogi: Lay 1 slice of prosciutto on a sheet of parchment paper with a short end toward you. Lay another slice of prosciutto on top of it at a right angle, forming a cross. Spoon about 2 heaping tablespoons of the filling into the center of the cross.
7. Fold each arm of the prosciutto cross over the filling to form a square, making sure that the filling is well covered. Using your fingers, press down around the filling to even out the square shape. Repeat with the rest of the prosciutto and filling.
8. Spray the pierogi with avocado oil and place them in the air fryer basket. Cook for 10 minutes, or until crispy.
9. Garnish with oregano before serving, if desired. Store leftovers in an airtight container in the fridge for up to 4 days. Reheat in a preheated 400°F (205°C) air fryer for 3 minutes, or until heated through.

Per Serving
calories: 150 | fat: 11g | protein: 11g | carbs: 2g | net carbs: 1g | fiber: 1g

Beery Thai Prawns

Prep time: 15 minutes | Cook time: 8 minutes | Serves 4

16 prawns, cleaned and deveined
Salt and ground black pepper, to your liking
½ teaspoon cumin powder
1 teaspoon fresh lemon juice
1 medium-sized egg, whisked
⅓ cup of beer
1 teaspoon baking powder
1 tablespoon curry powder
½ teaspoon grated fresh ginger
½ cup coconut flour

1. Toss the prawns with salt, pepper, cumin powder, and lemon juice.
2. In a mixing dish, place the whisked egg, beer, baking powder, curry, and the ginger, mix to combine well.
3. In another mixing dish, place the coconut flour.
4. Now, dip the prawns in the beer mixture, roll your prawns over the coconut flour.
5. Air-fry at 360ºF for 5 minutes, turn them over, press the power button again and cook for additional 2 to 3 minutes. Bon appétit!

Per Serving
calories: 259 | fat: 15.8g | carbs: 3.4g | protein: 4.1g | sugar: 0.7g | fiber: 1.8g

Pickle Poppers Wrapped with Bacon

Prep time: 10 minutes | Cook time: 10 minutes | Serves 6

12 medium dill pickles
1 (8-ounce / 227-g) package cream cheese, softened
1 cup shredded sharp Cheddar cheese
12 slices bacon or beef bacon, sliced in half lengthwise
Ranch Dressing or Blue Cheese Dressing, for serving (optional)

1. Spray the air fryer basket with avocado oil. Preheat the air fryer to 400°F.
2. Slice the dill pickles in half lengthwise and use a spoon to scoop out the centers.
3. Place the cream cheese and Cheddar cheese in a small bowl and stir until well combined.
4. Divide the cream cheese mixture among the pickles, spooning equal amounts into the scooped-out centers. Wrap each filled pickle with a slice of bacon and secure the bacon with toothpicks.
5. Place the bacon-wrapped pickles in the air fryer basket with the bacon seam side down and cook for

8 to 10 minutes, until the bacon is crispy, flipping halfway through. Serve warm with ranch or blue cheese dressing, if desired.
6. Best served fresh. Store leftovers in an airtight container in the fridge for up to 5 days. Reheat in a preheated 400°F air fryer for 3 minutes, or until heated through.

Per Serving
calories: 87 | fat: 8g | protein: 4g | total carbs: 1g | sugar: 2g | fiber: 0.8g

Chicken Wings with Bourbon Sauce

Prep time: 10 minutes | Cook time: 32 minutes | Serves 8

2 pounds (907 g) chicken wings or drummies
½ teaspoon fine sea salt
Sauce:
½ cup chicken broth
⅓ cup Swerve confectioners-style sweetener
¼ cup tomato sauce
¼ cup wheat-free tamari
1 tablespoon apple cider vinegar
¾ teaspoon red pepper flakes
¼ teaspoon grated fresh ginger
1 clove garlic, smashed to a paste
For Garnish (Optional):
Chopped green onions
Sesame seeds

1. Spray the air fryer basket with avocado oil. Preheat the air fryer to 380°F.
2. Season the chicken wings on all sides with the salt and place them in the air fryer. Cook for 25 minutes, flipping after 15 minutes. After 25 minutes, increase the temperature to 400°F and cook for 6 to 7 minutes or more, until the skin is browned and crisp.
3. While the wings cook, make the sauce: Place all the sauce ingredients in a large sauté pan and whisk to combine. Simmer until reduced and thickened, for about 10 minutes.
4. Brush the cooked chicken wings with the sauce. Garnish with green onions and sesame seeds, if desired. Serve with extra sauce on the side for dipping.
5. Store leftovers in an airtight container in the refrigerator for up to 4 days. Reheat in a preheated 350°F air fryer for 5 minutes, then increase the temperature to 400°F and cook for 3 to 5 minutes, until warm and crispy.

Per Serving
calories: 545 | fat: 30g | protein: 42g | total carbs: 3g | fiber: 0.1g

Egg Rolls with Thousand Island Dipping Sauce

Prep time: 15 minutes | Cook time: 10 minutes | Serves 10

1 (8-ounce / 227-g) package cream cheese, softened
½ pound (227 g) cooked corned beef, chopped
½ cup drained and chopped sauerkraut
½ cup shredded Swiss cheese
20 slices prosciutto
Thousand Island Dipping Sauce:
¾ cup mayonnaise
¼ cup chopped dill pickles
¼ cup tomato sauce
2 tablespoons Swerve confectioners-style sweetener
⅛ teaspoon fine sea salt
Fresh thyme leaves, for garnish
Ground black pepper, for garnish
Sauerkraut, for serving (optional)

1. Spray the air fryer basket with avocado oil. Preheat the air fryer to 400°F.
2. Make the filling: Place the cream cheese in a medium-sized bowl and stir to break it up. Add the corned beef, sauerkraut, and Swiss cheese and stir well to combine.
3. Assemble the egg rolls: Lay 1 slice of prosciutto on a sushi mat or a sheet of parchment paper with a short end toward you. Lay another slice of prosciutto on top of it at a right angle, forming a cross. Spoon 3 to 4 tablespoons of the filling into the center of the cross.
4. Fold the sides of the top slice up and over the filling to form the ends of the roll. Tightly roll up the long piece of prosciutto, starting at the edge closest to you, into a tight egg roll shape that overlaps by an inch or so. (Note: If the prosciutto rips, it's okay. It will seal when you fry it.) Repeat with the remaining prosciutto and filling.
5. Place the egg rolls in the air fryer seam side down, leaving space between them. (If you're using a smaller air fryer, cook in batches if necessary.) Cook for 10 minutes, or until the outside is crispy.
6. While the egg rolls are cooking, make the dipping sauce: In a small bowl, combine the mayo, pickles, tomato sauce, sweetener, and salt. Stir well and garnish with thyme and ground black pepper. (The dipping sauce can be made up to 3 days ahead.)
7. Serve the egg rolls with the dipping sauce and sauerkraut if desired. Best served fresh. Store leftovers in an airtight container in the refrigerator for up to 5 days or in the freezer for up to a month. Reheat in a preheated 400°F air fryer for 4 minutes, or until heated through and crispy.

Per Serving
calories: 321 | fat: 29g | protein: 13g | total carbs: 1g | fiber: 0.1g

Guacamole Rings in Prosciutto

Prep time: 10 minutes | Cook time: 6 minutes | Serves 8

Guacamole:
2 avocados, halved, pitted, and peeled
3 tablespoons lime juice, plus more to taste
2 small plum tomatoes, diced
½ cup finely diced onions
2 small cloves garlic, smashed to a paste
3 tablespoons chopped fresh cilantro leaves
½ scant teaspoon fine sea salt
½ scant teaspoon ground cumin
2 small onions (about 1½ inches in diameter), cut into ½-inch-thick slices
8 slices prosciutto

1. Make the guacamole: Place the avocados and lime juice in a large bowl and mash with a fork until it reaches your desired consistency. Add the tomatoes, onions, garlic, cilantro, salt, and cumin and stir until well combined. Taste and add more lime juice if desired. Set aside half of the guacamole for serving. (Note: If you're making the guacamole ahead of time, place it in a large resealable plastic bag, squeeze out all the air, and seal it shut. It will keep in the refrigerator for up to 3 days when stored this way.)
2. Place a piece of parchment paper on a tray that fits in your freezer and place the onion slices on it, breaking the slices apart into 8 rings. Fill each ring with about 2 tablespoons of guacamole. Place the tray in the freezer for 2 hours.
3. Spray the air fryer basket with avocado oil. Preheat the air fryer to 400°F.
4. Remove the rings from the freezer and wrap each in a slice of prosciutto. Place them in the air fryer basket, leaving space between them (if you're using a smaller air fryer, work in batches if necessary), and cook for 6 minutes, flipping halfway through. Use a spatula to remove the rings from the air fryer. Serve with the reserved half of the guacamole.
5. Store leftovers in an airtight container in the refrigerator for up to 4 days. Reheat in a preheated 400°F air fryer for about 3 minutes, until heated through.

Per Serving
calories: 132 | fat: 9g | protein: 5g | total carbs: 10g | fiber: 4g

Crackling Bites

Prep time: 5 minutes | Cook time: 16 minutes | Serves 10

1 pound (454 g) pork rind raw, scored by the butcher	1 tablespoon sea salt 2 tablespoons smoked paprika

1. Sprinkle and rub salt on the skin side of the pork rind. Allow it to sit for 30 minutes.
2. Roast at 380ºF for 8 minutes, turn them over and cook for a further 8 minutes or until blistered.
3. Sprinkle the smoked paprika all over the pork crackling and serve. Bon appétit!

Per Serving
calories: 245 | fat: 14.1g | carbs: 2g | protein: 2.6g | sugar: 0g | fiber: 0.5g

Mozzarella Sticks with Spice Mix

Prep time: 15 minutes | Cook time: 14 minutes | Serves 12

Dough:	Spice Mix:
1¾ cups shredded Mozzarella cheese	¼ cup grated Parmesan cheese
2 tablespoons unsalted butter	3 tablespoons garlic powder
1 large egg, beaten	1 tablespoon dried oregano leaves
¾ cup blanched almond flour	1 tablespoon onion powder
⅛ teaspoon fine sea salt	**For Serving (Optional):**
24 pieces of string cheese	½ cup marinara sauce ½ cup pesto

1. Make the dough: Place the Mozzarella and butter in a large microwave-safe bowl and microwave for 1 to 2 minutes, until the cheese is entirely melted. Stir well.
2. Add the egg and, using a hand mixer on low, combine well. Add the almond flour and salt and combine well with the mixer.
3. Lay a piece of parchment paper on the countertop and place the dough on it. Knead it for about 3 minutes, the dough should be thick yet pliable. (Note: If the dough is too sticky, chill it in the refrigerator for an hour or overnight.)
4. Scoop up 3 tablespoons of the dough and flatten it into a very thin 3½ by 2-inch rectangle. Place one piece of string cheese in the center and use your hands to press the dough tightly around it. Repeat with the remaining string cheese and dough.
5. In a shallow dish, combine the spice mix ingredients. Place a wrapped piece of string cheese in the dish and roll while pressing down to form a nice crust. Repeat with the remaining pieces of string cheese. Place in the freezer for 2 hours.
6. Ten minutes before air frying, spray the air fryer basket with avocado oil and preheat the air fryer to 425°F.
7. Place the frozen Mozzarella sticks in the air fryer basket, leaving space between them, and cook for 9 to 12 minutes, until golden brown. Remove from the air fryer and serve with marinara sauce and pesto, if desired.
8. Store leftovers in an airtight container in the refrigerator for up to 3 days or in the freezer for up to a month. Reheat in a preheated 425°F air fryer for 4 minutes, or until warmed through.

Per Serving
calories: 337 | fat: 27g | protein: 23g | total carbs: 4g | fiber: 1g

Pork Belly Chips

Prep time: 5 minutes | Cook time: 12 minutes | Serves 4

1 pound (454 g) slab pork belly	Fine sea salt
½ cup apple cider vinegar	**For Serving (Optional):** Guacamole Pico de gallo

1. Slice the pork belly into ⅛-inch-thick strips and place them in a shallow dish. Pour in the vinegar and stir to coat the pork belly. Place in the fridge to marinate for 30 minutes.
2. Spray the air fryer basket with avocado oil. Preheat the air fryer to 400°F.
3. Remove the pork belly from the vinegar and place the strips in the air fryer basket in a single layer, leaving space between them. Cook in the air fryer for 10 to 12 minutes, until crispy, flipping after 5 minutes. Remove from the air fryer and sprinkle with salt. Serve with guacamole and pico de gallo, if desired.
4. Best served fresh. Store leftovers in an airtight container in the fridge for up to 5 days. Reheat in a preheated 400°F air fryer for 5 minutes, or until heated through, flipping halfway through.

Per Serving
calories: 240 | fat: 21g | protein: 13g | total carbs: 0g | fiber: 0g

Fried Leek

Prep time: 15 minutes | Cook time: 10 minutes | Serves 4

1 large-sized leek, cut into ½-inch wide rings
Salt and pepper, to taste
1 teaspoon mustard
1 cup milk
1 egg
½ cup almond flour
½ teaspoon baking powder
½ cup pork rinds, crushed

1. Toss your leeks with salt and pepper.
2. In a mixing bowl, whisk the mustard, milk and egg until frothy and pale.
3. Now, combine almond flour and baking powder in another mixing bowl. In the third bowl, place the pork rinds.
4. Coat the leek slices with the almond meal mixture. Dredge the floured leek slices into the milk/egg mixture, coating well. Finally, roll them over the pork rinds.
5. Air-fry for approximately 10 minutes at 370ºF. Bon appétit!

Per Serving
calories: 187 | fat: 13.8g | carbs: 2.8g | protein: 7.7g | sugar: 0.6g | fiber: 1.9g

Roast Chicken with Teriyaki Sauce

Prep time: 40 minutes | Cook time: 26 minutes | Serves 6

1½ pounds (680g) chicken drumettes
Sea salt and cracked black pepper, to taste
2 tablespoons fresh chives, roughly chopped
Teriyaki Sauce:
1 tablespoon sesame oil
¼ cup coconut aminos
½ cup water
½ teaspoon Five-spice powder
2 tablespoons rice wine vinegar
½ teaspoon fresh ginger, grated
2 cloves garlic, crushed

1. Start by preheating your Air Fryer to 380ºF (193ºC). Rub the chicken drumettes with salt and cracked black pepper.
2. Cook in the preheated Air Fryer approximately 15 minutes. Turn them over and cook for an additional 7 minutes.
3. While the chicken drumettes are roasting, combine the sesame oil, coconut aminos, water, Five-spice powder, vinegar, ginger, and garlic in a pan over medium heat. Cook for 5 minutes, stirring occasionally.
4. Now, reduce the heat and let it simmer until the glaze thickens.
5. After that, brush the glaze all over the chicken drumettes. Air-fry for a further 6 minutes or until the surface is crispy. Serve topped with the remaining glaze and garnished with fresh chives. Bon appétit!

Per Serving
calories: 301 | fat: 21g | protein: 22g | carbs: 4g | net carbs: 3g | fiber: 1g

Avocado Fries

Prep time: 10 minutes | Cook time: 15 minutes | Serves 6

3 firm, barely ripe avocados, halved, peeled, and pitted
2 cups pork dust
2 teaspoons fine sea salt
2 teaspoons ground black pepper
2 teaspoons ground cumin
1 teaspoon chili powder
1 teaspoon paprika
½ teaspoon garlic powder
½ teaspoon onion powder
2 large eggs
Salsa, for serving (optional)
Fresh chopped cilantro leaves, for garnish (optional)

1. Spray the air fryer basket with avocado oil. Preheat the air fryer to 400°F (205ºC).
2. Slice the avocados into thick-cut french fry shapes.
3. In a bowl, mix together the pork dust, salt, pepper, and seasonings.
4. In a separate shallow bowl, beat the eggs.
5. Dip the avocado fries into the beaten eggs and shake off any excess, then dip them into the pork dust mixture. Use your hands to press the breading into each fry.
6. Spray the fries with avocado oil and place them in the air fryer basket in a single layer, leaving space between them. If there are too many fries to fit in a single layer, work in batches. Cook in the air fryer for 13 to 15 minutes, until golden brown, flipping after 5 minutes.
7. Serve with salsa, if desired, and garnish with fresh chopped cilantro, if desired. Best served fresh.
8. Store leftovers in an airtight container in the fridge for up to 5 days. Reheat in a preheated 400°F (205ºC) air fryer for 3 minutes, or until heated through.

Per Serving
calories: 282 | fat: 22g | protein: 15g | carbs: 9g | net carbs: 2g | fiber: 7g

Kale Chips

Prep time: 5 minutes | Cook time: 10 minutes | Makes 8 cups

½ teaspoon dried chives
½ teaspoon dried dill weed
½ teaspoon dried parsley
¼ teaspoon garlic powder
¼ teaspoon onion powder
⅛ teaspoon fine sea salt
⅛ teaspoon ground black pepper
2 large bunches kale

1. Spray the air fryer basket with avocado oil. Preheat the air fryer to 360°F (182ºC).
2. Place the seasonings, salt, and pepper in a small bowl and mix well.
3. Wash the kale and pat completely dry. Use a sharp knife to carve out the thick inner stems, then spray the leaves with avocado oil and sprinkle them with the seasoning mix.
4. Place the kale leaves in the air fryer in a single layer and cook for 10 minutes, shaking and rotating the chips halfway through. Transfer the baked chips to a baking sheet to cool completely and crisp up. Repeat with the remaining kale. Sprinkle the cooled chips with salt before serving, if desired.
5. Kale chips can be stored in an airtight container at room temperature for up to 1 week, but they are best eaten within 3 days.

Per Serving
calories: 11 | fat: 1g | protein: 1g | carbs: 2g | net carbs: 1g | fiber: 1g

Cauliflower Buns

Prep time: 15 minutes | Cook time: 12 minutes | Makes 8 buns

1 (12-ounce 340-g) steamer bag cauliflower, cooked according to package instructions
½ cup shredded Mozzarella cheese
¼ cup shredded mild Cheddar cheese
¼ cup blanched finely ground almond flour
1 large egg
½ teaspoon salt

1. Let the cooked cauliflower cool about 10 minutes. Use a kitchen towel to wring out excess moisture, then place cauliflower in a food processor.
2. Add Mozzarella, Cheddar, flour, egg, and salt to the food processor and pulse twenty times until mixture is combined. It will resemble a soft, wet dough.
3. Divide mixture into eight piles. Wet your hands with water to prevent sticking, then press each pile into a flat bun shape, about ½-inch thick.
4. Cut a sheet of parchment to fit air fryer basket. Working in batches if needed, place the formed dough onto ungreased parchment in air fryer basket. Adjust the temperature to 350°F (180ºC) and set the timer for 12 minutes, turning buns halfway through cooking.
5. Let the buns cool 10 minutes before serving. Serve warm.

Per Serving
calories: 75 | fat: 5g | protein: 5g | carbs: 3g | net carbs: 2g | fiber: 1g

Bacon and Avocado Egg Bites

Prep time: 20 minutes | Cook time: 13 minutes | Serves 4

6 ounces (170 g) (about 9 slices) reduced-sodium bacon
2 hard-boiled eggs, chopped
Flesh of ½ avocado, chopped
2 tablespoons unsalted butter, softened
2 tablespoons
mayonnaise
1 jalapeño pepper, seeded and finely chopped
2 tablespoons chopped fresh cilantro
Juice of ½ lime
Salt and freshly ground black pepper

1. Arrange the bacon in a single layer in the air fryer basket (it's OK if the bacon sits a bit on the sides). Set the air fryer to 350°F (180ºC) and cook for 10 minutes. Check for crispiness and cook for 2 to 3 minutes longer if needed. Transfer the bacon to a paper towel–lined plate and let it cool completely. Reserve 2 tablespoons of bacon grease from the bottom of the air fryer basket. Finely chop the bacon and set aside in a small, shallow bowl.
2. In a large bowl, combine the eggs, avocado, butter, mayonnaise, jalapeño, cilantro, and lime juice. Mash into a smooth paste with a fork or potato smasher. Season to taste with salt and pepper.
3. Add the reserved bacon grease to the egg mixture and stir gently until thoroughly combined. Cover and refrigerate for 30 minutes, or until the mixture is firm.
4. Divide the mixture into 12 equal portions and shape into balls. Roll the balls in the chopped bacon bits until completely coated.

Per Serving
calories: 330 | fat: 31g | protein: 10g | carbs: 2g | net carbs: 2g | fiber: 0g

Broccoli Fries with Spicy Dip

Prep time: 15 minutes | Cook time: 6 minutes | Serves 4

¾ pound (340g) broccoli florets
½ teaspoon onion powder
1 teaspoon granulated garlic
½ teaspoon cayenne pepper
Sea salt and ground black pepper, to taste
2 tablespoons sesame oil

4 tablespoons Parmesan cheese, preferably freshly grated
Spicy Dip:
¼ cup mayonnaise
¼ cup Greek yogurt
¼ teaspoon Dijon mustard
1 teaspoon keto hot sauce

1. Start by preheating the Air Fryer to 400ºF (205ºC).
2. Blanch the broccoli in salted boiling water until al dente, for about 3 to 4 minutes. Drain well and transfer to the lightly greased Air Fryer basket.
3. Add the onion powder, garlic, cayenne pepper, salt, black pepper, sesame oil, and Parmesan cheese.
4. Cook for 6 minutes, tossing halfway through the cooking time.
5. Meanwhile, mix all of the spicy dip ingredients. Serve broccoli fries with chilled dipping sauce. Bon appétit!

Per Serving
calories: 219 | fat: 19g | protein: 5g | carbs: 9g | net carbs: 6g | fiber: 3g

Chicken Wings with Berbere Spice

Prep time: 5 minutes | Cook time: 32 minutes | Serves 1 dozen wings

1 dozen chicken wings or drummies
1 tablespoon coconut oil or bacon fat, melted
2 teaspoons berbere spice
1 teaspoon fine sea salt

For Serving (Omit For Egg-Free):
2 hard-boiled eggs
½ teaspoon fine sea salt
¼ teaspoon berbere spice
¼ teaspoon dried chives

1. Spray the air fryer basket with avocado oil. Preheat the air fryer to 380°F (193ºC).
2. Place the chicken wings in a large bowl. Pour the oil over them and turn to coat completely. Sprinkle the berbere and salt on all sides of the chicken.
3. Place the chicken wings in the air fryer and cook for 25 minutes, flipping after 15 minutes.
4. After 25 minutes, increase the temperature to 400°F (205ºC) and cook for 6 to 7 minutes or more, until the skin is browned and crisp.
5. While the chicken cooks, prepare the hard-boiled eggs (if using): Peel the eggs, slice them in half, and season them with the salt, berbere, and dried chives. Serve the chicken and eggs together.
6. Store leftovers in an airtight container in the fridge for up to 4 days. Reheat the chicken in a preheated 400°F (205ºC) air fryer for 5 minutes, or until heated through.

Per Serving
calories: 317 | fat: 24g | protein: 24g | carbs: 1g | net carbs: 1g | fiber: 0g

Calamari Rings

Prep time: 10 minutes | Cook time: 15 minutes | Serves 4

2 large egg yolks
1 cup powdered Parmesan cheese
¼ cup coconut flour
3 teaspoons dried oregano leaves
½ teaspoon garlic powder
½ teaspoon onion powder

1 pound (454 g) calamari, sliced into rings
Fresh oregano leaves, for garnish (optional)
1 cup no-sugar-added marinara sauce, for serving (optional)
Lemon slices, for serving (optional)

1. Spray the air fryer basket with avocado oil. Preheat the air fryer to 400°F (205ºC).
2. In a shallow dish, whisk the egg yolks. In a separate bowl, mix together the Parmesan, coconut flour, and spices.
3. Dip the calamari rings in the egg yolks, tap off any excess egg, then dip them into the cheese mixture and coat well. Use your hands to press the coating onto the calamari if necessary. Spray the coated rings with avocado oil.
4. Place the calamari rings in the air fryer, leaving space between them, and cook for 15 minutes, or until golden brown. Garnish with fresh oregano, if desired, and serve with marinara sauce for dipping and lemon slices, if desired.
5. Best served fresh. Store leftovers in an airtight container in the fridge for up to 5 days. Reheat in a preheated 400°F (205ºC) air fryer for 3 minutes, or until heated through.

Per Serving
calories: 287 | fat: 13g | protein: 28g | carbs: 11g | net carbs: 8g | fiber: 3g

Pork Egg

Prep time: 10 minutes | Cook time: 25 minutes | Makes 12 eggs

7 large eggs, divided	mayonnaise
1 ounce (28 g) plain pork rinds, finely crushed	¼ teaspoon salt
2 tablespoons	¼ teaspoon ground black pepper

1. Place 6 whole eggs into ungreased air fryer basket. Adjust the temperature to 220°F (104ºC) and set the timer for 20 minutes. When done, place eggs into a bowl of ice water to cool 5 minutes.
2. Peel cool eggs, then cut in half lengthwise. Remove yolks and place aside in a medium bowl.
3. In a separate small bowl, whisk remaining raw egg. Place pork rinds in a separate medium bowl. Dip each egg white into whisked egg, then gently coat with pork rinds. Spritz with cooking spray and place into ungreased air fryer basket. Adjust the temperature to 400°F (205ºC) and set the timer for 5 minutes, turning eggs halfway through cooking. Eggs will be golden when done.
4. Mash yolks in bowl with mayonnaise until smooth. Sprinkle with salt and pepper and mix.
5. Spoon 2 tablespoons of yolk mixture into each fried egg white. Serve warm.

Per Serving
calories: 141 | fat: 10g | protein: 10g | carbs: 1g | net carbs: 1g | fiber: 0g

Cheese Tortillas with Pork Rinds

Prep time: 10 minutes | Cook time: 5 minutes | Makes 4 tortillas

1 ounce (28 g) pork rinds	2 tablespoons full-fat cream cheese
¾ cup shredded Mozzarella cheese	1 large egg

1. Place pork rinds into food processor and pulse until finely ground.
2. Place Mozzarella into a large microwave-safe bowl. Break cream cheese into small pieces and add them to the bowl. Microwave for 30 seconds, or until both cheeses are melted and can easily be stirred together into a ball. Add ground pork rinds and egg to the cheese mixture.
3. Continue stirring until the mixture forms a ball. If it cools too much and cheese hardens, microwave for 10 more seconds.
4. Separate the dough into four small balls. Place each

ball of dough between two sheets of parchment and roll into ¼-inch flat layer.
5. Place tortillas into the air fryer basket in single layer, working in batches if necessary.
6. Adjust the temperature to 400°F (205ºC) and set the timer for 5 minutes.
7. Tortillas will be crispy and firm when fully cooked. Serve immediately.

Per Serving
calories: 145 | fat: 10g | protein: 11g | carbs: 1g | net carbs: 1g | fiber: 0g

Spinach Melts with Chilled Sauce

Prep time: 20 minutes | Cook time: 14 minutes | Serves 4

Spinach Melts:	½ teaspoon dried basil
2 cups spinach, torn into pieces	1 cup Cheddar cheese, shredded
1 ½ cups cauliflower	**Parsley Yogurt Dip:**
1 tablespoon sesame oil	½ cup Greek-Style yoghurt
½ cup scallions, chopped	
2 garlic cloves, minced	2 tablespoons mayonnaise
½ cup almond flour	
¼ cup coconut flour	2 tablespoons fresh parsley, chopped
1 teaspoon baking powder	1 tablespoon fresh lemon juice
½ teaspoon sea salt	
½ teaspoon ground black pepper	½ teaspoon garlic, smashed
¼ teaspoon dried dill	

1. Place spinach in a mixing dish, pour in hot water. Drain and rinse well.
2. Add cauliflower to the steamer basket, steam until the cauliflower is tender for about 5 minutes.
3. Mash the cauliflower, add the remaining ingredients for Spinach Melts and mix to combine well. Shape the mixture into patties and transfer them to the lightly greased cooking basket.
4. Bake at 330ºF (166ºC) for 14 minutes or until thoroughly heated.
5. Meanwhile, make your dipping sauce by whisking the remaining ingredients. Place in your refrigerator until ready to serve.
6. Serve the Spinach Melts with the chilled sauce on the side. Enjoy!

Per Serving
calories: 301 | fat: 25g | protein: 11g | carbs: 9g | net carbs: 5g | fiber: 4g

Parmesan Bell Peppers

Prep time: 20 minutes | Cook time: 7 minutes | Serves 4

1 egg, beaten
½ cup Parmesan cheese, grated
1 teaspoon sea salt
½ teaspoon red pepper

flakes, crushed
¾ pound (340g) bell peppers, seeded and cut to ¼-inch strips
2 tablespoons olive oil

1. In a mixing bowl, combine together the egg, Parmesan, salt, and red pepper flakes, mix to combine well.
2. Dip bell peppers into the batter and transfer them to the cooking basket. Brush with the olive oil.
3. Cook in the preheated Air Fryer at 390ºF (199ºC) for 4 minutes. Shake the basket and cook for a further 3 minutes. Work in batches.
4. Taste, adjust the seasonings and serve. Bon appétit!

Per Serving
calories: 163 | fat: 11g | protein: 6g | carbs: 10g | net carbs: 9g | fiber: 1g

Spinach Chips

Prep time: 20 minutes | Cook time: 10 minutes | Serves 3

3 cups fresh spinach leaves
1 tablespoon extra-virgin olive oil
1 teaspoon sea salt
½ teaspoon cayenne pepper

1 teaspoon garlic powder
Chili Yogurt Dip:
¼ cup yogurt
2 tablespoons mayonnaise
½ teaspoon chili powder

1. Toss the spinach leaves with the olive oil and seasonings.
2. Bake in the preheated Air Fryer at 350ºF (180ºC) for 10 minutes, shaking the cooking basket occasionally.
3. Bake until the edges brown, working in batches.
4. In the meantime, make the sauce by whisking all ingredients in a mixing dish. Serve immediately.

Per Serving
calories: 128 | fat: 12g | protein: 2g | carbs: 3g | net carbs: 2g | fiber: 1g

Spinach Turkey Meatball

Prep time: 10 minutes | Cook time: 10 minutes | Makes 36 meatballs

1 cup fresh spinach leaves
¼ cup peeled and diced red onion
½ cup crumbled feta cheese
1 pound (454 g) 85/15

ground turkey
½ teaspoon salt
½ teaspoon ground cumin
¼ teaspoon ground black pepper

1. Place spinach, onion, and feta in a food processor, and pulse ten times until spinach is chopped. Scoop into a large bowl.
2. Add turkey to bowl and sprinkle with salt, cumin, and pepper. Mix until fully combined. Roll mixture into thirty-six meatballs (about 1 tablespoon each).
3. Place meatballs into ungreased air fryer basket, working in batches if needed. Adjust the temperature to 350°F (180ºC) and set the timer for 10 minutes, shaking basket twice during cooking. Meatballs will be browned and have an internal temperature of at least 165°F (74ºC) when done. Serve warm.

Per Serving
calories: 115 | fat: 7g | protein: 10g | carbs: 1g | net carbs: 1g | fiber: 0g

Cabbage Bites Wrapped in Bacon

Prep time: 10 minutes | Cook time: 12 minutes | Serves 6

3 tablespoons sriracha hot chili sauce, divided
1 medium head cabbage, cored and cut into 12 bite-sized pieces
2 tablespoons coconut oil, melted

½ teaspoon salt
12 slices sugar-free bacon
½ cup mayonnaise
¼ teaspoon garlic powder

1. Evenly brush 2 tablespoons of sriracha onto cabbage pieces. Drizzle evenly with coconut oil, then sprinkle with salt.
2. Wrap each cabbage piece with bacon and secure with a toothpick. Place into ungreased air fryer basket. Adjust the temperature to 375°F (190ºC) and set the timer for 12 minutes, turning cabbage halfway through cooking. Bacon will be cooked and crispy when done.
3. In a small bowl, whisk together mayonnaise, garlic powder, and the remaining sriracha. Use as a dipping sauce for cabbage bites.

Per Serving
calories: 316 | fat: 26g | protein: 10g | carbs: 11g | net carbs: 7g | fiber: 4g

Pickle Poppers Wrapped with Bacon, page 144

Chicken Wings with Bourbon Sauce, page 144

Blooming Onion, page 143

Spiced Almond, page 158

Ranch Pickle Spears

Prep time: 40 minutes | Cook time: 10 minutes | Serves 4

4 dill pickle spears, halved lengthwise
¼ cup ranch dressing
½ cup blanched finely ground almond flour
½ cup grated Parmesan cheese
2 tablespoons dry ranch seasoning

1. Wrap spears in a kitchen towel 30 minutes to soak up excess pickle juice.
2. Pour ranch dressing into a medium bowl and add pickle spears. In a separate medium bowl, mix flour, Parmesan, and ranch seasoning.
3. Remove each spear from ranch dressing and shake off excess. Press gently into dry mixture to coat all sides. Place spears into ungreased air fryer basket. Adjust the temperature to 400°F (205ºC) and set the timer for 10 minutes, turning spears three times during cooking. Serve warm.

Per Serving

calories: 160 | fat: 11g | protein: 7g | carbs: 8g | net carbs: 6g | fiber: 2g

Beef Cheese Burger

Prep time: 20 minutes | Cook time: 15 minutes | Serves 4

1 tablespoon Dijon mustard
2 tablespoons minced scallions
1 pound (454 g) ground beef
1½ teaspoons minced
green garlic
½ teaspoon cumin
Salt and ground black pepper, to taste
12 cherry tomatoes
12 cubes Cheddar cheese

1. In a large-sized mixing dish, place the mustard, ground beef, cumin, scallions, garlic, salt, and pepper, mix with your hands or a spatula so that everything is evenly coated.
2. Form into 12 meatballs and cook them in the preheated Air Fryer for 15 minutes at 375ºF (190ºC). Air-fry until they are cooked in the middle.
3. Thread cherry tomatoes, mini burgers and cheese on cocktail sticks. Bon appétit!

Per Serving

calories: 469 | fat: 30g | protein: 3g | carbs: 4g | net carbs: 3g | fiber: 1g

Mozzarella Pizza Crust

Prep time: 5 minutes | Cook time: 10 minutes | Serves 1

½ cup shredded whole-milk Mozzarella cheese
2 tablespoons blanched finely ground almond
flour
1 tablespoon full-fat cream cheese
1 large egg white

1. Place Mozzarella, almond flour, and cream cheese in a medium microwave-safe bowl. Microwave for 30 seconds. Stir until smooth ball of dough forms. Add egg white and stir until soft round dough forms.
2. Press into a 6-inch round pizza crust.
3. Cut a piece of parchment to fit your air fryer basket and place crust on parchment. Place into the air fryer basket.
4. Adjust the temperature to 350°F (180ºC) and set the timer for 10 minutes.
5. Flip after 5 minutes and at this time place any desired toppings on the crust. Continue cooking until golden. Serve immediately.

Per Serving

calories: 314 | fat: 22g | protein: 20g | carbs: 5g | net carbs: 3g | fiber: 2g

Cauliflower with Buffalo Sauce

Prep time: 5 minutes | Cook time: 15 minutes | Serves 6

1 medium head cauliflower, leaves and core removed, cut into bite-sized pieces
4 tablespoons salted
butter, melted
¼ cup dry ranch seasoning
⅓ cup sugar-free buffalo sauce

1. Place cauliflower pieces into a large bowl. Pour butter over cauliflower and toss to coat. Sprinkle in ranch seasoning and toss to coat.
2. Place cauliflower into ungreased air fryer basket. Adjust the temperature to 350°F (180ºC) and set the timer for 12 minutes, shaking the basket three times during cooking.
3. When timer beeps, place cooked cauliflower in a clean large bowl. Toss with buffalo sauce, then return to air fryer basket to cook for another 3 minutes. Cauliflower bites will be darkened at the edges and tender when done. Serve warm.

Per Serving

calories: 112 | fat: 7g | protein: 2g | carbs: 9g | net carbs: 7g | fiber: 2g

Artichoke and Spinach Dip

Prep time: 10 minutes | Cook time: 10 minutes | Serves 6

10 ounces (283 g) frozen spinach, drained and thawed
1 (14-ounce / 397-g) can artichoke hearts, drained and chopped
¼ cup chopped pickled jalapeños
8 ounces (227 g) full-fat cream cheese, softened
¼ cup full-fat mayonnaise
¼ cup full-fat sour cream
½ teaspoon garlic powder
¼ cup grated Parmesan cheese
1 cup shredded pepper jack cheese

1. Mix all ingredients in a 4-cup baking bowl. Place into the air fryer basket.
2. Adjust the temperature to 320°F (160°C) and set the timer for 10 minutes.
3. Remove when brown and bubbling. Serve warm.

Per Serving
calories: 226 | fat: 15g | protein: 10g | carbs: 10g | net carbs: 6g | fiber: 4g

Beef Jerky

Prep time: 5 minutes | Cook time: 4 hours | Serves 10

1 pound (454 g) flat iron beef, thinly sliced
¼ cup coconut aminos
2 teaspoons Worcestershire sauce
¼ teaspoon crushed red pepper flakes
¼ teaspoon garlic powder
¼ teaspoon onion powder

1. Place all ingredients into a plastic storage bag or covered container and marinate for 2 hours in refrigerator.
2. Place each slice of jerky on the air fryer rack in a single layer.
3. Adjust the temperature to 160°F (71°C) and set the timer for 4 hours.
4. Cool and store in airtight container for up to 1 week.

Per Serving
calories: 85 | fat: 3g | protein: 10g | carbs: 1g | net carbs: 1g | fiber: 0g

Ranch Chicken with Bacon

Prep time: 10 minutes | Cook time: 15 minutes | Serves 6

2 (6-ounce / 170-g) boneless, skinless chicken breasts, cut into 1-inch cubes
1 tablespoon coconut oil
½ teaspoon salt
¼ teaspoon ground black pepper
⅓ cup ranch dressing
½ cup shredded Colby cheese
4 slices cooked sugar-free bacon, crumbled

1. Drizzle chicken with coconut oil. Sprinkle with salt and pepper, and place into an ungreased 6-inch round nonstick baking dish.
2. Place dish into air fryer basket. Adjust the temperature to 370°F (188°C) and set the timer for 10 minutes, stirring chicken halfway through cooking.
3. When timer beeps, drizzle ranch dressing over chicken and top with Colby and bacon. Adjust the temperature to 400°F (205°C) and set the timer for 5 minutes. When done, chicken will be browned and have an internal temperature of at least 165°F (74°C). Serve warm.

Per Serving
calories: 164 | fat: 9g | protein: 18g | carbs: 0g | net carbs: 0g | fiber: 0g

Chicken Wings with Parmesan Butter

Prep time: 5 minutes | Cook time: 25 minutes | Serves 4

2 pounds (907 g) raw chicken wings
1 teaspoon pink Himalayan salt
½ teaspoon garlic powder
1 tablespoon baking powder
4 tablespoons unsalted butter, melted
⅓ cup grated Parmesan cheese
¼ teaspoon dried parsley

1. In a large bowl, place chicken wings, salt, ½ teaspoon garlic powder, and baking powder, then toss. Place wings into the air fryer basket.
2. Adjust the temperature to 400°F (205°C) and set the timer for 25 minutes.
3. Toss the basket two or three times during the cooking time.
4. In a small bowl, combine butter, Parmesan, and parsley.
5. Remove wings from the fryer and place into a clean large bowl. Pour the butter mixture over the wings and toss until coated. Serve warm.

Per Serving
calories: 565 | fat: 42g | protein: 42g | carbs: 2g | net carbs: 2g | fiber: 0g

Almond Meal and Broccoli Balls

Prep time: 20 minutes | Cook time: 20 minutes | Serves 6

2 eggs, well whisked
2 cups Colby cheese, shredded
½ cup almond meal
2 tablespoons sesame seeds

Seasoned salt, to taste
¼ teaspoon ground black pepper, or more to taste
1 head broccoli, grated
1 cup Parmesan cheese, grated

1. Thoroughly combine the eggs, Colby cheese, almond meal, sesame seeds, salt, black pepper, and broccoli to make the consistency of dough.
2. Chill for 1 hour and shape into small balls, roll the patties over Parmesan cheese. Spritz them with cooking oil on all sides.
3. Cook at 360ºF (182ºC) for 10 minutes. Check for doneness and return to the Air Fryer for 8 to 10 more minutes. Serve with a sauce for dipping. Bon appétit!

Per Serving
calories: 322 | fat: 23g | protein: 19g | carbs: 9g | net carbs: 6g | fiber: 3g

Pecorino Toscano and Broccoli Fat Bombs

Prep time: 15 minutes | Cook time: 15 minutes | Serves 6

1 large-sized head of broccoli, broken into small florets
½ teaspoon sea salt
¼ teaspoon ground black pepper, or more to taste
1 tablespoon Shoyu

sauce
1 teaspoon groundnut oil
1 cup bacon bits
1 cup Pecorino Toscano, freshly grated
Paprika, to taste

1. Add the broccoli florets to boiling water, boil for approximately 4 minutes, drain well.
2. Season with salt and pepper, drizzle with Shoyu sauce and groundnut oil. Mash with a potato masher.
3. Add the bacon and cheese to the mixture, shape the mixture into bite-sized balls.
4. Air-fry at 390ºF for 10 minutes, shake the Air Fryer basket, push the power button again, and continue to cook for 5 minutes or more.
5. Toss the fried keto bombs with paprika. Bon appétit!

Per Serving
calories: 171 | fat: 12.2g | carbs: 7.7g | protein: 9.1g | sugar: 1.5g | fiber: 2g

Tomato Chips

Prep time: 15 minutes | Cook time: 10 minutes | Serves 4

4 Roma tomatoes, sliced
2 tablespoons olive oil
Sea salt and white pepper, to taste

1 teaspoon Italian seasoning mix
½ cup Parmesan cheese, grated

1. Start by preheating your Air Fryer to 350ºF (180ºC). Generously grease the Air Fryer basket with nonstick cooking oil.
2. Toss the sliced tomatoes with the remaining ingredients. Transfer them to the cooking basket without overlapping.
3. Cook in the preheated Air Fryer for 5 minutes. Shake the cooking basket and cook for an additional 5 minutes. Work in batches.
4. Serve with Mediterranean aioli for dipping, if desired. Bon appétit!

Per Serving
calories: 130 | fat: 10g | protein: 5g | carbs: 6g | net carbs: 5g | fiber: 1g

Bacon-Wrapped Jalapeños

Prep time: 10 minutes | Cook time: 12 minutes | Makes 12 poppers

3 ounces (85 g) cream cheese, softened
⅓ cup shredded mild Cheddar cheese
¼ teaspoon garlic powder
6 jalapeños

(approximately 4-inch long), tops removed, sliced in half lengthwise and seeded
12 slices sugar-free bacon

1. Place cream cheese, Cheddar, and garlic powder in a large microwave-safe bowl. Microwave 30 seconds on high, then stir. Spoon cheese mixture evenly into hollowed jalapeños.
2. Wrap 1 of slice bacon around each jalapeño half, completely covering jalapeño, and secure with a toothpick. Place jalapeños into ungreased air fryer basket. Adjust the temperature to 400°F (205ºC) and set the timer for 12 minutes, turning jalapeños halfway through cooking. Bacon will be crispy when done. Serve warm.

Per Serving
calories: 278 | fat: 21g | protein: 15g | carbs: 3g | net carbs: 2g | fiber: 1g

Pork Meatball with Romano Cheese

Prep time: 20 minutes | Cook time: 18 minutes | Serves 8

½ teaspoon fine sea salt
1 cup Romano cheese, grated
3 cloves garlic, minced
1½ pound (680g) ground pork
½ cup scallions, finely chopped
2 eggs, well whisked
⅓ teaspoon cumin powder
⅔ teaspoon ground black pepper, or more to taste
2 teaspoons basil

1. Simply combine all the ingredients in a large-sized mixing bowl.
2. Shape into bite-sized balls, cook the meatballs in the air fryer for 18 minutes at 345ºF (174ºC). Serve with some tangy sauce such as marinara sauce if desired. Bon appétit!

Per Serving
calories: 350 | fat: 25g | protein: 28g | carbs: 2g | net carbs: 1g | fiber: 1g

Salami Roll-Ups

Prep time: 5 minutes | Cook time: 4 minutes | Makes 16 roll-ups

4 ounces (113 g) cream cheese, broken into 16 equal pieces
16 (0.5-ounce / 14-g) deli slices Genoa salami

1. Place a piece of cream cheese at the edge of a slice of salami and roll to close. Secure with a toothpick. Repeat with remaining cream cheese pieces and salami.
2. Place roll-ups in an ungreased 6-inch round nonstick baking dish and place into air fryer basket. Adjust the temperature to 350ºF (180ºC) and set the timer for 4 minutes. Salami will be crispy and cream cheese will be warm when done. Let it cool 5 minutes before serving.

Per Serving
calories: 269 | fat: 22g | protein: 11g | carbs: 2g | net carbs: 2g | fiber: 0g

Chicken Nuggets

Prep time: 20 minutes | Cook time: 12 minutes | Serves 6

1 pound (454 g) chicken breasts, slice into tenders
½ teaspoon cayenne pepper
Salt and black pepper, to taste
¼ cup almond meal
1 egg, whisked
½ cup Parmesan cheese, freshly grated
¼ cup mayo
¼ cup no-sugar-added barbecue sauce

1. Pat the chicken tenders dry with a kitchen towel. Season with the cayenne pepper, salt, and black pepper.
2. Dip the chicken tenders into the almond meal, followed by the egg. Press the chicken tenders into the Parmesan cheese, coating evenly.
3. Place the chicken tenders in the lightly greased Air Fryer basket. Cook at 360ºfor 9 to 12 minutes, turning them over to cook evenly.
4. In a mixing bowl, thoroughly combine the mayonnaise with the barbecue sauce. Serve the chicken nuggets with the sauce for dipping. Bon appétit!

Per Serving
calories: 268 | fat: 18g | protein: 2g | carbs: 4g | net carbs: 3g | fiber: 1g

Zucchini Fries

Prep time: 10 minutes | Cook time: 10 minutes | Serves 8

2 medium zucchini, ends removed, quartered lengthwise, and sliced into 3-inch long fries
½ teaspoon salt
⅓ cup heavy whipping cream
½ cup blanched finely ground almond flour
¾ cup grated Parmesan cheese
1 teaspoon Italian seasoning

1. Sprinkle zucchini with salt and wrap in a kitchen towel to draw out excess moisture. Let it sit 2 hours.
2. Pour cream into a medium bowl. In a separate medium bowl, whisk together flour, Parmesan, and Italian seasoning.
3. Place each zucchini fry into cream, then gently shake off excess. Press each fry into dry mixture, coating each side, then place into ungreased air fryer basket. Adjust the temperature to 400°F (205ºC) and set the timer for 10 minutes, turning fries halfway through cooking. Fries will be golden and crispy when done. Place on clean parchment sheet to cool for 5 minutes before serving.

Per Serving
calories: 124 | fat: 10g | protein: 5g | carbs: 4g | net carbs: 3g | fiber: 1g

Pork Meatball with Brie Cheese

Prep time: 25 minutes | Cook time: 17 minutes | Serves 8

1 teaspoon cayenne pepper
2 teaspoons mustard
2 tablespoons Brie cheese, grated
5 garlic cloves, minced
2 small-sized yellow onions, peeled and chopped
1½ pounds (680g) ground pork
Sea salt and freshly ground black pepper, to taste

1. Mix all of the above ingredients until everything is well incorporated.
2. Now, form the mixture into balls (the size of golf a ball).
3. Cook for 17 minutes at 375ºF (190ºC). Serve with your favorite sauce.

Per Serving

calories: 275 | fat: 18g | protein: 3g | carbs: 3g | net carbs: 2g | fiber: 1g

Roasted Zucchini

Prep time: 20 minutes | Cook time: 18 minutes | Serves 6

1½ pounds (680g) zucchini, peeled and cut into ½-inch chunks
2 tablespoons melted coconut oil
A pinch of coarse salt
A pinch of pepper
2 tablespoons sage, finely chopped
Zest of 1 small-sized lemon
⅛ teaspoon ground allspice

1. Toss the squash chunks with the other items.
2. Roast in the Air Fryer cooking basket at 350ºF (180ºC) for 10 minutes.
3. Pause the machine, and turn the temperature to 400ºF, stir and roast for additional 8 minutes. Bon appétit!

Per Serving

calories: 270 | fat: 15g | protein: 3g | carbs: 5g | net carbs: 4g | fiber: 1g

Pork Cheese Sticks

Prep time: 20 minutes | Cook time: 10 minutes | Makes 12 sticks

6 (1-ounce / 28-g) Mozzarella string cheese sticks
½ cup grated Parmesan cheese
½ ounce (14 g) pork rinds, finely ground
1 teaspoon dried parsley
2 large eggs

1. Place Mozzarella sticks on a cutting board and cut in half. Freeze 45 minutes or until firm. If freezing overnight, remove frozen sticks after 1 hour and place into airtight zip-top storage bag and place back in freezer for future use.
2. In a large bowl, mix Parmesan, ground pork rinds, and parsley.
3. In a medium bowl, whisk eggs.
4. Dip a frozen Mozzarella stick into beaten eggs and then into Parmesan mixture to coat. Repeat with remaining sticks. Place Mozzarella sticks into the air fryer basket.
5. Adjust the temperature to 400°F (205ºC) and set the timer for 10 minutes or until golden.
6. Serve warm.

Per Serving

calories: 236 | fat: 13g | protein: 19g | carbs: 5g | net carbs: 5g | fiber: 0g

Bacon and Beef Cheese Dip

Prep time: 20 minutes | Cook time: 10 minutes | Serves 6

8 ounces (227 g) full-fat cream cheese
¼ cup full-fat mayonnaise
¼ cup full-fat sour cream
¼ cup chopped onion
1 teaspoon garlic powder
1 tablespoon Worcestershire sauce
1¼ cups shredded medium Cheddar cheese, divided
½ pound (227g) cooked 80/20 ground beef
6 slices sugar-free bacon, cooked and crumbled
2 large pickle spears, chopped

1. Place cream cheese in a large microwave-safe bowl and microwave for 45 seconds. Stir in mayonnaise, sour cream, onion, garlic powder, Worcestershire sauce, and 1 cup of Cheddar. Add cooked ground beef and bacon. Sprinkle the remaining Cheddar on top.
2. Place in 6-inch bowl and put into the air fryer basket.
3. Adjust the temperature to 400°F (205ºC) and set the timer for 10 minutes.
4. Dip is done when top is golden and bubbling. Sprinkle pickles over dish. Serve warm.

Per Serving

calories: 457 | fat: 35g | protein: 22g | carbs: 4g | net carbs: 3g | fiber: 1g

Spiced Almond

Prep time: 5 minutes | Cook time: 6 minutes | Serves 4

1 cup raw almonds
2 teaspoons coconut oil
1 teaspoon chili powder
¼ teaspoon cumin

¼ teaspoon smoked paprika
¼ teaspoon onion powder

1. In a large bowl, toss all ingredients until almonds are evenly coated with oil and spices. Place almonds into the air fryer basket.
2. Adjust the temperature to 320°F (160ºC) and set the timer for 6 minutes.
3. Toss the fryer basket halfway through the cooking time. Allow to cool completely.

Per Serving
calories: 182 | fat: 16g | protein: 6g | carbs: 7g | net carbs: 3g | fiber: 4g

Pepperoni Cheese Roll

Prep time: 5 minutes | Cook time: 8 minutes | Makes 12 rolls

2½ cups shredded Mozzarella cheese
2 ounces (57 g) cream cheese, softened
1 cup blanched finely

ground almond flour
48 slices pepperoni
2 teaspoons Italian seasoning

1. In a large microwave-safe bowl, combine Mozzarella, cream cheese, and flour. Microwave on high 90 seconds until cheese is melted.
2. Using a wooden spoon, mix melted mixture for 2 minutes until a dough forms.
3. Once dough is cool enough to work with your hands, for about 2 minutes, spread it out into a 12-inch × 4-inch rectangle on ungreased parchment paper. Line dough with pepperoni, divided into four even rows. Sprinkle Italian seasoning evenly over pepperoni.
4. Starting at the long end of the dough, roll up until a log is formed. Slice the log into twelve even pieces.
5. Place pizza rolls in an ungreased 6-inch nonstick baking dish. Adjust the temperature to 375°F (190ºC) and set the timer for 8 minutes. Rolls will be golden and firm when done. Allow cooked rolls to cool 10 minutes before serving.

Per Serving
calories: 366 | fat: 27g | protein: 20g | carbs: 7g | net carbs: 5g | fiber: 2g

Prosciutto-Wrapped Asparagus

Prep time: 10 minutes | Cook time: 10 minutes | Serves 4

1 pound (454 g) asparagus
12 (0.5-ounce 14-g) slices prosciutto
1 tablespoon coconut oil, melted
2 teaspoons lemon juice

⅛ teaspoon red pepper flakes
⅓ cup grated Parmesan cheese
2 tablespoons salted butter, melted

1. On a clean work surface, place an asparagus spear onto a slice of prosciutto.
2. Drizzle with coconut oil and lemon juice. Sprinkle red pepper flakes and Parmesan across asparagus. Roll prosciutto around asparagus spear. Place into the air fryer basket.
3. Adjust the temperature to 375°F (190ºC) and set the timer for 10 minutes.
4. Drizzle the asparagus roll with butter before serving.

Per Serving
calories: 263 | fat: 20g | protein: 14g | carbs: 7g | net carbs: 4g | fiber: 3g

Cauliflower and Bacon Skewers

Prep time: 10 minutes | Cook time: 12 minutes | Serves 4

4 slices sugar-free bacon, cut into thirds
¼ medium yellow onion, peeled and cut into 1-inch pieces
4 ounces (113 g) (about

8) cauliflower florets
1½ tablespoons olive oil
¼ teaspoon salt
¼ teaspoon garlic powder

1. Place 1 piece bacon and 2 pieces onion on a 6-inch skewer. Add a second piece bacon, and 2 cauliflower florets, followed by another piece of bacon onto skewer. Repeat with the remaining ingredients and three additional skewers to make four total skewers.
2. Drizzle skewers with olive oil, then sprinkle with salt and garlic powder. Place skewers into ungreased air fryer basket. Adjust the temperature to 375°F (190ºC) and set the timer for 12 minutes, turning the skewers halfway through cooking. When done, vegetables will be tender and bacon will be crispy. Serve warm.

Per Serving
calories: 69 | fat: 5g | protein: 5g | carbs: 2g | net carbs: 1g | fiber: 1g

Sausage and Bacon Cheese Pizza

Prep time: 5 minutes | Cook time: 5 minutes | Serves 1

½ cup shredded Mozzarella cheese
7 slices pepperoni
¼ cup cooked ground sausage
2 slices sugar-free bacon,

cooked and crumbled
1 tablespoon grated Parmesan cheese
2 tablespoons low-carb, sugar-free pizza sauce, for dipping

1. Cover the bottom of a 6-inch cake pan with Mozzarella. Place pepperoni, sausage, and bacon on top of cheese and sprinkle with Parmesan. Place pan into the air fryer basket.
2. Adjust the temperature to 400°F (205ºC) and set the timer for 5 minutes.
3. Remove when cheese is bubbling and golden. Serve warm with pizza sauce for dipping.

Per Serving

calories: 466 | fat: 34g | protein: 28g | carbs: 5g | net carbs: 4g | fiber: 1g

Jalapeño and Bacon Cheese Bread

Prep time: 10 minutes | Cook time: 15 minutes | Serves 8 sticks

2 cups shredded Mozzarella cheese
¼ cup grated Parmesan cheese
¼ cup chopped pickled

jalapeños
2 large eggs
4 slices sugar-free bacon, cooked and chopped

1. Mix all ingredients in a large bowl. Cut a piece of parchment to fit your air fryer basket.
2. Dampen your hands with a bit of water and press out the mixture into a circle. You may need to separate this into two smaller cheese breads, depending on the size of your fryer.
3. Place the parchment and cheese bread into the air fryer basket.
4. Adjust the temperature to 320°F (160ºC) and set the timer for 15 minutes.
5. Carefully flip the bread when 5 minutes remain.
6. When fully cooked, the top will be golden brown. Serve warm.

Per Serving

calories: 273 | fat: 18g | protein: 20g | carbs: 3g | net carbs: 2g | fiber: 1g

Cheese Crisps

Prep time: 10 minutes | Cook time: 12 minutes | Serves 2

½ cup shredded Cheddar cheese   1 egg white

1. Preheat the air fryer to 400°F (205ºC). Place a piece of parchment paper in the bottom of the air fryer basket.
2. In a medium bowl, combine the cheese and egg white, stirring with a fork until thoroughly combined.
3. Place small scoops of the cheese mixture in a single layer in the basket of the air fryer (about 1-inch apart). Use the fork to spread the mixture as thin as possible. Air fry for 10 to 12 minutes until the crisps are golden brown. Let it cool for a few minutes before transferring them to a plate. Store at room temperature in an airtight container for up to 3 days.

Per Serving

calories: 120 | fat: 10g | protein: 9g | carbs: 1g | net carbs: 1g | fiber: 0g

Double-Cheese Mushroom

Prep time: 10 minutes | Cook time: 8 minutes | Serves 20 mushrooms

4 ounces (113 g) cream cheese, softened
6 tablespoons shredded pepper jack cheese
2 tablespoons chopped pickled jalapeños
20 medium button

mushrooms, stems removed
2 tablespoons olive oil
¼ teaspoon salt
⅛ teaspoon ground black pepper

1. In a large bowl, mix cream cheese, pepper jack, and jalapeños together.
2. Drizzle mushrooms with olive oil, then sprinkle with salt and pepper. Spoon 2 tablespoons of cheese mixture into each mushroom and place in a single layer into ungreased air fryer basket. Adjust the temperature to 370°F (188ºC) and set the timer for 8 minutes, checking halfway through cooking to ensure even cooking, rearranging if some are darker than others. When they're golden and cheese is bubbling, mushrooms will be done. Serve warm.

Per Serving

calories: 87 | fat: 7g | protein: 3g | carbs: 2g | net carbs: 2g | fiber: 0g

Scallops and Bacon Kabobs

Prep time: 40 minutes | Cook time: 6 minutes | Serves 6

1 pound (454 g) sea scallops
½ cup coconut milk
1 tablespoon vermouth
Sea salt and ground black pepper, to taste
½ pound (227g) bacon, diced
1 shallot, diced
1 teaspoon garlic powder
1 teaspoon paprika

1. In a ceramic bowl, place the sea scallops, coconut milk, vermouth, salt, and black pepper, let it marinate for 30 minutes.
2. Assemble the skewers alternating the scallops, bacon, and shallots. Sprinkle garlic powder and paprika all over the skewers.
3. Bake in the preheated air Fryer at 400ºF (205ºC) for 6 minutes. Serve warm and enjoy!

Per Serving
calories: 228 | fat: 15g | protein: 15g | carbs: 5g | net carbs: 5g | fiber: 0g

Spanish Churros

Prep time: 10 minutes | Cook time: 6 minutes | Serves 4

¾ cup water
1 tablespoon swerve
¼ teaspoon sea salt
¼ teaspoon grated nutmeg
¼ teaspoon ground cloves
6 tablespoons butter
¾ cup almond flour
2 eggs

1. To make the dough, boil the water in a pan over medium-high heat, now, add the swerve, salt, nutmeg, and cloves, cook until dissolved.
2. Add the butter and turn the heat to low. Gradually stir in the almond flour, whisking continuously, until the mixture forms a ball.
3. Remove from the heat, fold in the eggs one at a time, stirring to combine well.
4. Pour the mixture into a piping bag with a large star tip. Squeeze 4-inch strips of dough into the greased Air Fryer pan.
5. Cook at 410ºF for 6 minutes, working in batches. Bon appétit!

Per Serving
calories: 321 | fat: 31.1g | carbs: 4.4g | protein: 8.4g | sugar: 1.1g | fiber: 2.3g

Air Fried Eggplant

Prep time: 45 minutes | Cook time: 13 minutes | Serves 4

1 eggplant, peeled and thinly sliced
Salt, to taste
½ cup almond meal
¼ cup olive oil
½ cup water
1 teaspoon garlic powder
½ teaspoon dried dill weed
½ teaspoon ground black pepper, to taste

1. Salt the eggplant slices and let them stay for about 30 minutes. Squeeze the eggplant slices and rinse them under cold running water.
2. Toss the eggplant slices with the other ingredients. Cook at 390ºF (199ºC) for 13 minutes, working in batches.
3. Serve with a sauce for dipping. Bon appétit!

Per Serving
calories: 241 | fat: 21g | protein: 4g | carbs: 9g | net carbs: 4g | fiber: 5g

Zucchini and Bacon Cheese Cake

Prep time: 22 minutes | Cook time: 13 minutes | Serves 4

⅓ cup Swiss cheese, grated
⅓ teaspoon fine sea salt
⅓ teaspoon baking powder
⅓ cup scallions, finely chopped
½ tablespoon fresh basil, finely chopped
1 zucchini, trimmed and grated
½ teaspoon freshly cracked black pepper
1 teaspoon Mexican oregano
1 cup bacon, chopped
¼ cup almond meal
¼ cup coconut flour
2 small eggs, lightly beaten
1 cup Cotija cheese, grated

1. Mix all ingredients, except for Cotija cheese, until everything is well combined.
2. Then, gently flatten each ball. Spritz the cakes with a nonstick cooking oil.
3. Bake your cakes for 13 minutes at 305ºF (152ºC), work with batches. Serve warm with tomato ketchup and mayonnaise.

Per Serving
calories: 311 | fat: 25g | protein: 18g | carbs: 5g | net carbs: 3g | fiber: 2g

Pepperoni Chips

Prep time: 5 minutes | Cook time: 8 minutes | Serves 2

14 slices pepperoni

1. Place pepperoni slices into ungreased air fryer basket. Adjust the temperature to 350°F (180°C) and set the timer for 8 minutes. Pepperoni will be browned and crispy when done. Let it cool 5 minutes before serving. Store in airtight container at room temperature up to 3 days.

Per Serving

calories: 69 | fat: 5g | protein: 3g | carbs: 0g | net carbs: 0g | fiber: 0g

Three Cheese Dip

Prep time: 5 minutes | Cook time: 12 minutes | Serves 8

8 ounces (227 g) cream cheese, softened	½ cup shredded sharp Cheddar cheese
½ cup mayonnaise	¼ cup shredded Monterey jack cheese
¼ cup sour cream	

1. In a large bowl, combine all ingredients. Scoop mixture into an ungreased 4-cup nonstick baking dish and place into air fryer basket.
2. Adjust the temperature to 375°F (190°C) and set the timer for 12 minutes. Dip will be browned on top and bubbling when done. Serve warm.

Per Serving

calories: 245 | fat: 23g | protein: 5g | carbs: 2g | net carbs: 2g | fiber: 0g

Bacon-Wrapped Onion Rings

Prep time: 5 minutes | Cook time: 10 minutes | Serves 8

1 large white onion, peeled and cut into 16	(¼-inch-thick) slices
	8 slices sugar-free bacon

1. Stack 2 slices onion and wrap with 1 slice bacon. Secure with a toothpick. Repeat with remaining onion slices and bacon.
2. Place onion rings into ungreased air fryer basket. Adjust the temperature to 350°F (180°C) and set the timer for 10 minutes, turning rings halfway through cooking. Bacon will be crispy when done. Serve warm.

Per Serving

calories: 84 | fat: 4g | protein: 5g | carbs: 8g | net carbs: 6g | fiber: 2g

Crispy Cauliflower Florets

Prep time: 20 minutes | Cook time: 12 minutes | Serves 2

3 cups cauliflower florets	1 teaspoon sage
2 tablespoons sesame oil	1 teaspoon rosemary
1 teaspoon onion powder	Sea salt and cracked
1 teaspoon garlic powder	black pepper, to taste
1 teaspoon thyme	1 teaspoon paprika

1. Start by preheating your Air Fryer to 400°F (205°C).
2. Toss the cauliflower with the remaining ingredients, toss to coat well.
3. Cook for 12 minutes, shaking the cooking basket halfway through the cooking time. They will crisp up as they cool. Bon appétit!

Per Serving

calories: 160 | fat: 14g | protein: 3g | carbs: 8g | net carbs: 5g | fiber: 3g

Pork Rind Chicken with Guacamole

Prep time: 5 minutes | Cook time: 5 minutes | Serves 2

1 ounce (28 g) pork rinds	¼ cup sliced pickled jalapeños
4 ounces (113 g) shredded cooked chicken	¼ cup guacamole
½ cup shredded Monterey jack cheese	¼ cup full-fat sour cream

1. Place pork rinds into 6-inch round baking pan. Cover with shredded chicken and Monterey jack cheese. Place pan into the air fryer basket.
2. Adjust the temperature to 370°F (188°C) and set the timer for 5 minutes or until cheese is melted.
3. Top with jalapeños, guacamole, and sour cream. Serve immediately.

Per Serving

calories: 395 | fat: 27g | protein: 30g | carbs: 3g | net carbs: 2g | fiber: 1g

Chapter 10 Desserts

Molton Cake

Prep time: 10 minutes | Cook time: 10 minutes | Serves 4

4 ounces (113 g) butter, melted
4 ounces (113 g) dark chocolate
2 eggs, lightly whisked
2 tablespoons monk fruit sweetener
2 tablespoons almond meal
1 teaspoon baking powder
½ teaspoon ground cinnamon
¼ teaspoon ground star anise

1. Begin by preheating your Air Fryer to 370ºF. Spritz the sides and bottom of a baking pan with nonstick cooking spray.
2. Melt the butter and dark chocolate in a microwave-safe bowl. Mix the eggs and monk fruit until frothy.
3. Pour the butter/chocolate mixture into the egg mixture. Stir in the almond meal, baking powder, cinnamon, and star anise. Mix until everything is well incorporated.
4. Scrape the batter into the prepared pan. Bake in the preheated Air Fryer for 9 to 11 minutes.
5. Let it stand for 2 minutes. Invert on a plate while warm and serve. Bon appétit!

Per Serving
calories: 408 | fat: 39.5g | carbs: 7.2g | protein: 8.1g | sugar: 0.7g | fiber: 4.1g

Almond and Chocolate Cookies

Prep time: 15 minutes | Cook time: 15 minutes | Serves 10

2 cups almond flour
½ cup coconut flour
5 ounces (142 g) swerve
5 ounces (142 g) butter, softened
1 egg, beaten
1 teaspoon vanilla
essence
4 ounces (113 g) double cream
3 ounces (85 g) bakers' chocolate, unsweetened
1 teaspoon cardamom seeds, finely crushed

1. Start by preheating your Air Fryer to 350ºF.
2. In a mixing bowl, thoroughly combine the flour, swerve, and butter. Mix until your mixture resembles breadcrumbs.
3. Gradually, add the egg and vanilla essence. Shape your dough into small balls and place in the parchment-lined Air Fryer basket.
4. Bake in the preheated Air Fryer for 10 minutes. Rotate the pan and bake for another 5 minutes. Transfer the freshly baked cookies to a cooling rack.
5. As the biscuits are cooling, melt the double cream and bakers' chocolate in the Air Fryer safe bowl at 350ºF. Add the cardamom seeds and stir well.
6. Spread the filling over the cooled biscuits and sandwich together. Bon appétit!

Per Serving
calories: 303 | fat: 29.6g | carbs: 8.5g | protein: 6.5g | sugar: 1.6g | fiber: 4.3g

Blueberry and Chocolate Cupcakes

Prep time: 15 minutes | Cook time: 15 minutes | Serves 6

3 teaspoons cocoa powder, unsweetened
½ cup blueberries
1¼ cups almond flour
½ cup milk
1 stick butter, room temperature
3 eggs
¾ cup granulated erythritol
1 teaspoon pure rum extract
½ teaspoon baking soda
1 teaspoon baking powder
¼ teaspoon grated nutmeg
½ teaspoon ground cinnamon
⅛ teaspoon salt

1. Grab two mixing bowls. In the first bowl, thoroughly combine the erythritol, almond flour, baking soda, baking powder, salt, nutmeg, cinnamon and cocoa powder.
2. Take the second bowl and cream the butter, egg, rum extract, and milk, whisk to combine well. Now, add the wet mixture to the dry mixture. Fold in blueberries.
3. Press the prepared batter mixture into a lightly greased muffin tin. Bake at 345ºfor 15 minutes. Use a toothpick to check if your cupcakes are baked. Bon appétit!

Per Serving
calories: 303 | fat: 28g | carbs: 7.7g | protein: 8.1g | sugar: 0.2g | fiber: 3g

Orange Custard

Prep time: 15 minutes | Cook time: 40 minutes | Serves 6

6 eggs
7 ounces (198 g) cream cheese, at room temperature
2 ½ cans condensed milk, sweetened
½ cup swerve

½ teaspoon orange rind, grated
1½ cardamom pods, bruised
2 teaspoons vanilla paste
¼ cup fresh orange juice

1. In a saucepan, melt swerve over a moderate flame, it takes about 10 to 12 minutes. Immediately but carefully pour the melted sugar into six ramekins, tilting to coat their bottoms, allow them to cool slightly.
2. In a mixing dish, beat the cheese until smooth, now, fold in the eggs, one at a time, and continue to beat until pale and creamy.
3. Add the orange rind, cardamom, vanilla, orange juice, and the milk, mix again. Pour the mixture over the caramelized sugar. Air-fry, covered, at 325ºF for 28 minutes or until it has thickened.
4. Refrigerate overnight, garnish with berries or other fruits and serve.

Per Serving

calories: 247 | fat: 18.8g | carbs: 7.8g | protein: 10.7g | sugar: 0.4g | fiber: 0g

Whiskey Chocolate Brownies

Prep time: 15 minutes | Cook time: 35 minutes | Serves 10

3 tablespoons whiskey
8 ounces (227 g) white chocolate
¾ cup almond flour
¼ cup coconut flakes
½ cup coconut oil
2 eggs plus an egg yolk, whisked

¾ cup monk fruit
2 tablespoons cocoa powder, unsweetened
¼ teaspoon ground cardamom
1 teaspoon pure rum extract

1. Microwave white chocolate and coconut oil until everything's melted, allow the mixture to cool at room temperature.
2. After that, thoroughly whisk the eggs, monk fruit, rum extract, cocoa powder and cardamom.
3. Next step, add the rum/egg mixture to the chocolate mixture. Stir in the flour and coconut flakes, mix to combine.

4. Mix cranberries with whiskey and let them soak for 15 minutes. Fold them into the batter. Press the batter into a lightly buttered cake pan.
5. Air-fry for 35 minutes at 340ºF. Allow them to cool slightly on a wire rack before slicing and serving.

Per Serving

calories: 303 | fat: 28g | carbs: 9.1g | protein: 5.5g | sugar: 0.7g | fiber: 5.2g

Raspberry and Chocolate Cake

Prep time: 15 minutes | Cook time: 27 minutes | Serves 4

⅓ cup monk fruit
¼ cup unsalted butter, room temperature
1 egg plus 1 egg white, lightly whisked
3 ounces (85 g) almond flour
2 tablespoons Dutch-process cocoa powder
½ teaspoon ground

cinnamon
1 tablespoon candied ginger
⅛ teaspoon table salt
For the Filling:
2 ounces (57 g) fresh raspberries
⅓ cup monk fruit
1 teaspoon fresh lime juice

1. Firstly, set your Air Fryer to cook at 315ºF. Then, spritz the inside of two cake pans with the butter-flavored cooking spray.
2. In a mixing bowl, beat the monk fruit and butter until creamy and uniform. Then, stir in the whisked eggs. Stir in the almond flour, cocoa powder, cinnamon, ginger and salt.
3. Press the batter into the cake pans, use a wide spatula to level the surface of the batter. Bake for 20 minutes or until a wooden stick inserted in the center of the cake comes out completely dry.
4. While your cake is baking, stir together all of the ingredients for the filling in a medium saucepan. Cook over high heat, stirring frequently and mashing with the back of a spoon, bring to a boil and decrease the temperature.
5. Continue to cook, stirring until the mixture thickens, for another 7 minutes. Let the filling cool to room temperature.
6. Spread ½ of raspberry filling over the first crust. Top with another crust, spread remaining filling over top. Spread frosting over top and sides of your cake.
7. Enjoy!

Per Serving

calories: 217 | fat: 18.8g | carbs: 8.6g | protein: 7.5g | sugar: 0.7g | fiber: 4.6g

Chocolate Chip Cookie

Prep time: 20 minutes | Cook time: 11 minutes | Serves 8

1 stick butter, at room temperature
1¼ cups Swerve
¼ cup chunky peanut butter
1 teaspoon vanilla paste
1 fine almond flour
⅔ cup coconut flour
⅓ cup cocoa powder,
unsweetened
1 ½ teaspoons baking powder
¼ teaspoon ground cinnamon
¼ teaspoon ginger
½ cup chocolate chips, unsweetened

1. In a mixing dish, beat the butter and Swerve until creamy and uniform. Stir in the peanut butter and vanilla.
2. In another mixing dish, thoroughly combine the flour, cocoa powder, baking powder, cinnamon, and ginger.
3. Add the flour mixture to the peanut butter mixture, mix to combine well. Afterwards, fold in the chocolate chips.
4. Drop by large spoonfuls onto a parchment-lined Air Fryer basket. Bake at 365ºF (185ºC) for 11 minutes or until golden brown on the top. Bon appétit!

Per Serving
calories: 303 | fat: 28g | protein: 6g | carbs: 10g | net carbs: 5g | fiber: 5g

Baked Cheesecake

Prep time: 40 minutes | Cook time: 35 minutes | Serves 6

½ cup almond flour
1½ tablespoons unsalted butter, melted
2 tablespoons erythritol
1 (8-ounce / 227-g) package cream cheese, softened
¼ cup powdered erythritol
½ teaspoon vanilla paste
1 egg, at room temperature
Topping:
1½ cups sour cream
3 tablespoons powdered erythritol
1 teaspoon vanilla extract

1. Thoroughly combine the almond flour, butter, and 2 tablespoons of erythritol in a mixing bowl. Press the mixture into the bottom of lightly greased custard cups.
2. Then, mix the cream cheese, ¼ cup of powdered erythritol, vanilla, and egg using an electric mixer on low speed. Pour the batter into the pan, covering the crust.

3. Bake in the preheated Air Fryer at 330ºF (166ºC) for 35 minutes until edges are puffed and the surface is firm.
4. Mix the sour cream, 3 tablespoons of powdered erythritol, and vanilla for the topping, spread over the crust and allow it to cool to room temperature.
5. Transfer to your refrigerator for 6 to 8 hours. Serve well chilled.

Per Serving
calories: 306 | fat: 27g | protein: 8g | carbs: 9g | net carbs: 7g | fiber: 2g

Cranberry Butter Cake

Prep time: 30 minutes | Cook time: 20 minutes | Serves 8

1 cup almond flour
⅓ teaspoon baking soda
⅓ teaspoon baking powder
¾ cup erythritol
½ teaspoon ground cloves
⅓ teaspoon ground cinnamon
½ teaspoon cardamom
1 stick butter
½ teaspoon vanilla paste
2 eggs plus 1 egg yolk,
beaten
½ cup cranberries, fresh or thawed
1 tablespoon browned butter
For Ricotta Frosting:
½ stick butter
½ cup firm Ricotta cheese
1 cup powdered erythritol
¼ teaspoon salt
Zest of ½ lemon

1. Start by preheating your Air Fryer to 355ºF (181ºC).
2. In a mixing bowl, combine the flour with baking soda, baking powder, erythritol, ground cloves, cinnamon, and cardamom.
3. In a separate bowl, whisk 1 stick butter with vanilla paste, mix in the eggs until light and fluffy. Add the flour/sugar mixture to the butter/egg mixture. Fold in the cranberries and browned butter.
4. Scrape the mixture into the greased cake pan. Then, bake in the preheated Air Fryer for about 20 minutes.
5. Meanwhile, in a food processor, whip ½ stick of the butter and Ricotta cheese until there are no lumps.
6. Slowly add the powdered erythritol and salt until your mixture has reached a thick consistency. Stir in the lemon zest, mix to combine and chill completely before using.
7. Frost the cake and enjoy!

Per Serving
calories: 286 | fat: 27g | protein: 8g | carbs: 10g | net carbs: 5g | fiber: 5g

Pecan and Coconut Cookies

Prep time: 15 minutes | Cook time: 25 minutes | Serves 10

¾ cup coconut oil, room temperature
1½ cups coconut flour
1 cup pecan nuts, unsalted and roughly chopped
3 eggs plus an egg yolk, whisked
1½ cups extra-fine almond flour
¾ cup monk fruit
¼ teaspoon freshly

grated nutmeg
⅓ teaspoon ground cloves
½ teaspoon baking powder
⅓ teaspoon baking soda
½ teaspoon pure vanilla extract
½ teaspoon pure coconut extract
⅛ teaspoon fine sea salt

1. In a bowl, combine both types of flour, baking soda and baking powder. In a separate bowl, beat the eggs with coconut oil. Combine egg mixture with the flour mixture.
2. Throw in the other ingredients, mixing well. Shape the mixture into cookies.
3. Bake at 370ºF for about 25 minutes. Bon appétit!

Per Serving
calories: 354 | fat: 36g | carbs: 6.3g | protein: 5.9g | sugar: 0.8g | fiber: 3.7g

Chocolate Butter Cake

Prep time: 20 minutes | Cook time: 11 minutes | Serves 4

4 ounces (113 g) butter, melted
4 ounces (113 g) dark chocolate
2 eggs, lightly whisked
2 tablespoons monk fruit
2 tablespoons almond

meal
1 teaspoon baking powder
½ teaspoon ground cinnamon
¼ teaspoon ground star anise

1. Begin by preheating your Air Fryer to 370ºF (188ºC). Spritz the sides and bottom of a baking pan with nonstick cooking spray.
2. Melt the butter and dark chocolate in a microwave-safe bowl. Mix the eggs and monk fruit until frothy.
3. Pour the butter/chocolate mixture into the egg mixture. Stir in the almond meal, baking powder, cinnamon, and star anise. Mix until everything is well incorporated.
4. Scrape the batter into the prepared pan. Bake in the preheated Air Fryer for 9 to 11 minutes.

5. Let it stand for 2 minutes. Invert on a plate while warm and serve. Bon appétit!

Per Serving
calories: 408 | fat: 39g | protein: 8g | carbs: 7g | net carbs: 3g | fiber: 4g

Swiss Orange Roll

Prep time: 20 minutes | Cook time: 12 minutes | Serves 6

½ cup milk
¼ cup swerve
1 tablespoon yeast
½ stick butter, at room temperature
1 egg, at room temperature
¼ teaspoon salt
1 cup almond flour
1 cup coconut flour
2 tablespoons fresh

orange juice
Filling:
2 tablespoons butter
4 tablespoons swerve
1 teaspoon ground star anise
¼ teaspoon ground cinnamon
1 teaspoon vanilla paste
½ cup confectioners' swerve

1. Heat the milk in a microwave safe bowl and transfer the warm milk to the bowl of a stand electric mixer. Add the ¼ cup of swerve and yeast, and mix to combine well. Cover and let it sit until the yeast is foamy.
2. Then, beat the butter on low speed. Fold in the egg and mix again. Add salt and flour. Add the orange juice and mix on medium speed until a soft dough forms.
3. Knead the dough on a lightly floured surface. Cover it loosely and let it sit in a warm place for about 1 hour or until doubled in size. Then, spritz the bottom and sides of a baking pan with cooking oil (butter flavored).
4. Roll your dough out into a rectangle.
5. Spread 2 tablespoons of butter all over the dough. In a mixing dish, combine 4 tablespoons of swerve, ground star anise, cinnamon, and vanilla, sprinkle evenly over the dough.
6. Then, roll up your dough to form a log. Cut into 6 equal rolls and place them in the parchment-lined Air Fryer basket.
7. Bake at 350ºfor 12 minutes, turning them halfway through the cooking time. Dust with confectioners' swerve and enjoy!

Per Serving
calories: 275 | fat: 25.3g | carbs: 7.9g | protein: 6.3g | sugar: 1.1g| fiber: 3.5

Blackberry Muffins

Prep time: 15 minutes | Cook time: 12 minutes | Serves 8

1½ cups almond flour
½ teaspoon baking soda
1 teaspoon baking powder
¼ teaspoon kosher salt
½ cup swerve

2 eggs, whisked
½ cup milk
¼ cup coconut oil, melted
½ teaspoon vanilla paste
½ cup fresh blackberries

1. In a mixing bowl, combine the almond flour, baking soda, baking powder, swerve, and salt. Whisk to combine well.
2. In another mixing bowl, mix the eggs, milk, coconut oil, and vanilla.
3. Now, add the wet egg mixture to dry the flour mixture. Then, carefully fold in the fresh blackberries, gently stir to combine.
4. Scrape the batter mixture into the muffin cups. Bake your muffins at 350ºF for 12 minutes or until the tops are golden brown.
5. Sprinkle some extra icing sugar over the top of each muffin if desired. Serve and enjoy!

Per Serving
calories: 192 | fat: 17.3g | carbs: 5.5g | protein: 5.7g | sugar: 1g | fiber: 2.7g

Blueberry Cream Flan

Prep time: 30 minutes | Cook time: 25 minutes | Serves 6

¾ cup extra-fine almond flour
1 cup fresh blueberries
½ cup coconut cream
¾ cup coconut milk
3 eggs, whisked
½ cup Swerve
½ teaspoon baking soda

½ teaspoon baking powder
⅓ teaspoon ground cinnamon
½ teaspoon ginger
¼ teaspoon grated nutmeg

1. Lightly grease 2 mini pie pans using a nonstick cooking spray. Lay the blueberries on the bottom of the pie pans.
2. In a saucepan that is preheated over a moderate flame, warm the cream along with coconut milk until thoroughly heated.
3. Remove the pan from the heat, mix in the flour along with baking soda and baking powder.
4. In a medium-sized mixing bowl, whip the eggs, Swerve, and spices, whip until the mixture is creamy.

5. Add the creamy milk mixture. Carefully spread this mixture over the fruits.
6. Bake at 320º(160ºC) for about 25 minutes. Serve.

Per Serving
calories: 250 | fat: 22g | protein: 7g | carbs: 9g | net carbs: 6g | fiber: 3g

Chocolate Brownies

Prep time: 40 minutes | Cook time: 35 minutes | Serves 8

5 ounces (142 g) unsweetened chocolate, chopped into chunks
2 tablespoons instant espresso powder
1 tablespoon cocoa powder, unsweetened
½ cup almond butter
½ cup almond meal
¾ cup Swerve
1 teaspoon pure coffee extract
½ teaspoon lime peel zest
¼ cup coconut flour
2 eggs plus 1 egg yolk
½ teaspoon baking soda
½ teaspoon baking

powder
½ teaspoon ground cinnamon
⅓ teaspoon ancho chile powder
For the Chocolate Mascarpone Frosting:
4 ounces (113 g) mascarpone cheese, at room temperature
1½ ounces (43 g) unsweetened chocolate chips
1½ cups Swerve
¼ cup unsalted butter, at room temperature
1 teaspoon vanilla paste
A pinch of fine sea salt

1. First of all, microwave the chocolate and almond butter until completely melted, allow the mixture to cool at room temperature.
2. Then, whisk the eggs, Swerve, cinnamon, espresso powder, coffee extract, ancho chile powder, and lime zest.
3. Next step, add the vanilla/egg mixture to the chocolate/butter mixture. Stir in the almond meal and coconut flour along with baking soda, baking powder and cocoa powder.
4. Finally, press the batter into a lightly buttered cake pan. Air-fry for 35 minutes at 345ºF (174ºC).
5. In the meantime, make the frosting. Beat the butter and mascarpone cheese until creamy. Add in the melted chocolate chips and vanilla paste.
6. Gradually, stir in the Swerve and salt, beat until everything's well combined. Lastly, frost the brownies and serve.

Per Serving
calories: 363 | fat: 33g | protein: 7g | carbs: 10g | net carbs: 5g | fiber: 5g

Strawberry Pecan Pie

Prep time: 15 minutes | Cook time: 10 minutes | Serves 6

1½ cups whole shelled pecans
1 tablespoon unsalted butter, softened
1 cup heavy whipping cream
12 medium fresh strawberries, hulled
2 tablespoons sour cream

1. Place pecans and butter into a food processor and pulse ten times until a dough forms. Press dough into the bottom of an ungreased 6-inch round nonstick baking dish.
2. Place dish into air fryer basket. Adjust the temperature to 320°F (160ºC) and set the timer for 10 minutes. Crust will be firm and golden when done. Let it cool 20 minutes.
3. In a large bowl, whisk cream until fluffy and doubled in size, for about 2 minutes.
4. In a separate large bowl, mash strawberries until mostly liquid. Fold strawberries and sour cream into whipped cream.
5. Spoon mixture into cooled crust, cover, and place into refrigerator for at least 30 minutes to set. Serve chilled.

Per Serving

calories: 340 | fat: 33g | protein: 3g | carbs: 7g | net carbs: 4g | fiber: 3g

Chocolate Chips Soufflés

Prep time: 5 minutes | Cook time: 15 minutes | Serves 2

2 large eggs, whites and yolks separated
1 teaspoon vanilla extract
2 ounces (57 g) low-carb
chocolate chips
2 teaspoons coconut oil, melted

1. In a medium bowl, beat egg whites until stiff peaks form, for about 2 minutes. Set aside. In a separate medium bowl, whisk egg yolks and vanilla together. Set aside.
2. In a separate medium microwave-safe bowl, place chocolate chips and drizzle with coconut oil. Microwave on high 20 seconds, then stir and continue cooking in 10-second increments until melted, being careful not to overheat chocolate. Let it cool 1 minute.
3. Slowly pour melted chocolate into egg yolks and whisk until smooth. Then, slowly begin adding egg white mixture to chocolate mixture, about ¼ cup at a time, folding in gently.
4. Pour mixture into two 4-inch ramekins greased with cooking spray. Place ramekins into air fryer basket. Adjust the temperature to 400°F (205ºC) and set the timer for 15 minutes. Soufflés will puff up while cooking and deflate a little once cooled. The center will be set when done. Let it cool 10 minutes, then serve warm.

Per Serving

calories: 217 | fat: 18g | protein: 8g | carbs: 19g | net carbs: 11g | fiber: 8g

Butter Cheesecake

Prep time: 20 minutes | Cook time: 35 minutes | Serves 6

½ cup blanched finely ground almond flour
1 cup powdered erythritol, divided
2 tablespoons unsweetened cocoa powder
½ teaspoon baking powder
¼ cup unsalted butter,
softened
2 large eggs, divided
8 ounces (227 g) full-fat cream cheese, softened
¼ cup heavy whipping cream
1 teaspoon vanilla extract
2 tablespoons no-sugar-added peanut butter

1. In a large bowl, mix almond flour, ½ cup erythritol, cocoa powder, and baking powder. Stir in butter and one egg.
2. Scoop mixture into 6-inch round baking pan. Place pan into the air fryer basket.
3. Adjust the temperature to 300°F (150ºC) and set the timer for 20 minutes.
4. When fully cooked a toothpick inserted in center will come out clean. Allow it to fully cool and firm up for 20 minutes.
5. In a large bowl, beat cream cheese, remaining ½ cup erythritol, heavy cream, vanilla, peanut butter, and remaining egg until fluffy.
6. Pour mixture over cooled brownies. Place pan back into the air fryer basket.
7. Adjust the temperature to 300°F (150ºC) and set the timer for 15 minutes.
8. Cheesecake will be slightly browned and mostly firm with a slight jiggle when done. Allow to cool, then refrigerate 2 hours before serving.

Per Serving

calories: 347 | fat: 30g | protein: 8g | carbs: 30g | net carbs: 28g | fiber: 2g

Mixed Berry Pots

Prep time: 15 minutes | Cook time: 35 minutes | Serves 6

2 ounces (57 g) unsweetened mixed berries
½ cup granulated swerve
2 tablespoons golden flaxseed meal
¼ teaspoon ground star anise
½ teaspoon ground cinnamon

1 teaspoon xanthan gum
⅔ cup almond flour
1 cup powdered swerve
½ teaspoon baking powder
⅓ cup unsweetened coconut, finely shredded
½ stick butter, cut into small pieces

1. Toss the mixed berries with the granulated swerve, golden flaxseed meal, star anise, cinnamon, and xanthan gum. Divide between six custard cups coated with cooking spray.
2. In a mixing dish, thoroughly combine the remaining ingredients. Sprinkle over the berry mixture.
3. Bake in the preheated Air Fryer at 330ºF for 35 minutes. Work in batches if needed. Bon appétit!

Per Serving

calories: 155 | fat: 14.3g | carbs: 5.1g | protein: 3.1g | sugar: 0.8g | fiber: 2.6g

Crusted Mini Cheesecake

Prep time: 30 minutes | Cook time: 18 minutes | Serves 8

For the Crust:
⅓ teaspoon grated nutmeg
1½ tablespoons erythritol
1½ cups almond meal
8 tablespoons melted butter
1 teaspoon ground cinnamon
A pinch of kosher salt, to taste

For the Cheesecake:
2 eggs
½ cups unsweetened chocolate chips
1½ tablespoons sour cream
4 ounces (113 g) soft cheese
½ cup Swerve
½ teaspoon vanilla essence

1. Firstly, line eight cups of mini muffin pan with paper liners.
2. To make the crust, mix the almond meal together with erythritol, cinnamon, nutmeg, and kosher salt.
3. Now, add melted butter and stir well to moisten the crumb mixture.
4. Divide the crust mixture among the muffin cups and press gently to make even layers.

5. In another bowl, whip together the soft cheese, sour cream and Swerve until uniform and smooth. Fold in the eggs and the vanilla essence.
6. Then, divide chocolate chips among the prepared muffin cups. Then, add the cheese mix to each muffin cup.
7. Bake for about 18 minutes at 345ºF (174ºC). Bake in batches if needed. To finish, transfer the mini cheesecakes to a cooling rack, store in the fridge.

Per Serving

calories: 314 | fat: 29g | protein: 7g | carbs: 7g | net carbs: 4g | fiber: 3g

Golden Cheese Cookie

Prep time: 10 minutes | Cook time: 7 minutes | Serves 6

½ cup blanched finely ground almond flour
½ cup powdered erythritol, divided
2 tablespoons butter, softened
1 large egg
½ teaspoon unflavored gelatin
½ teaspoon baking powder
½ teaspoon vanilla

extract
½ teaspoon pumpkin pie spice
2 tablespoons pure pumpkin purée
½ teaspoon ground cinnamon, divided
¼ cup low-carb, sugar-free chocolate chips
3 ounces (85 g) full-fat cream cheese, softened

1. In a large bowl, mix almond flour and ¼ cup erythritol. Stir in butter, egg, and gelatin until combined.
2. Stir in baking powder, vanilla, pumpkin pie spice, pumpkin purée, and ¼ teaspoon cinnamon, then fold in chocolate chips.
3. Pour batter into 6-inch round baking pan. Place pan into the air fryer basket.
4. Adjust the temperature to 300°F (150ºC) and set the timer for 7 minutes.
5. When fully cooked, the top will be golden brown and a toothpick inserted in center will come out clean. Let it cool at least 20 minutes.
6. To make the frosting: mix cream cheese, remaining ¼ teaspoon cinnamon, and remaining ¼ cup erythritol in a large bowl. Using an electric mixer, beat until it becomes fluffy. Spread onto the cooled cookie. Garnish with additional cinnamon if desired.

Per Serving

calories: 199 | fat: 16g | protein: 5g | carbs: 22g | net carbs: 20g | fiber: 2g

Buttery Hazelnut Cookie

Prep time: 1 hour | Cook time: 20 minutes | Serves 10

4 tablespoons liquid monk fruit
½ cup hazelnuts, ground
1 stick butter, room temperature
2 cups almond flour

1 cup coconut flour
2 ounces (57 g) granulated Swerve
2 teaspoons ground cinnamon

1. Firstly, cream liquid monk fruit with butter until the mixture becomes fluffy. Sift in both types of flour.
2. Now, stir in the hazelnuts. Now, knead the mixture to form a dough, place in the refrigerator for about 35 minutes.
3. To finish, shape the prepared dough into the bite-sized balls, arrange them on a baking dish, flatten the balls using the back of a spoon.
4. Mix granulated Swerve with ground cinnamon. Press your cookies in the cinnamon mixture until they are completely covered.
5. Bake the cookies for 20 minutes at 310ºF (154ºC).
6. Leave them to cool for about 10 minutes before transferring them to a wire rack. Bon appétit!

Per Serving

calories: 246 | fat: 23g | protein: 5g | carbs: 7g | net carbs: 3g | fiber: 4g

Mozzarella Pretzels

Prep time: 10 minutes | Cook time: 10 minutes | Serves 6

1½ cups shredded Mozzarella cheese
1 cup blanched finely ground almond flour
2 tablespoons salted

butter, melted, divided
¼ cup granular erythritol, divided
1 teaspoon ground cinnamon

1. Place Mozzarella, flour, 1 tablespoon of butter, and 2 tablespoons of erythritol in a large microwave-safe bowl. Microwave on high 45 seconds, then stir with a fork until a smooth dough ball forms.
2. Separate dough into six equal sections. Gently roll each section into a 12-inch rope, then fold into a pretzel shape.
3. Place pretzels into ungreased air fryer basket. Adjust the temperature to 370°F (188ºC) and set the timer for 8 minutes, turning pretzels halfway through cooking.
4. In a small bowl, combine remaining butter, remaining erythritol, and cinnamon. Brush ½ mixture on both sides of pretzels.
5. Place pretzels back into air fryer and cook for an additional 2 minutes at 370°F (188ºC).
6. Transfer pretzels to a large plate. Brush on both sides with remaining butter mixture, then let it cool 5 minutes before serving.

Per Serving

calories: 223 | fat: 19g | protein: 11g | carbs: 13g | net carbs: 11g | fiber: 2g

Creamy Cheese Cake

Prep time: 1 hour | Cook time: 37 minutes | Serves 8

1½ cups almond flour
3 ounces (85 g) Swerve
½ stick butter, melted
20 ounces (567 g) full-fat cream cheese
½ cup heavy cream
1¼ cups granulated

Swerve
3 eggs, at room temperature
1 tablespoon vanilla essence
1 teaspoon grated lemon zest

1. Coat the sides and bottom of a baking pan with a little flour.
2. In a mixing bowl, combine the almond flour and Swerve. Add the melted butter and mix until your mixture looks like bread crumbs.
3. Press the mixture into the bottom of the prepared pan to form an even layer. Bake at 330ºF (166ºC) for 7 minutes until golden brown. Allow it to cool completely on a wire rack.
4. Meanwhile, in a mixer fitted with the paddle attachment, prepare the filling by mixing the soft cheese, heavy cream, and granulated Swerve, beat until creamy and fluffy.
5. Crack the eggs into the mixing bowl, one at a time, add the vanilla and lemon zest and continue to mix until fully combined.
6. Pour the prepared topping over the cooled crust and spread evenly.
7. Bake in the preheated Air Fryer at 330ºF (166ºC) for 25 to 30 minutes, leave it in the Air Fryer to keep warm for another 30 minutes.
8. Cover your cheesecake with plastic wrap. Place in your refrigerator and allow it to cool for at least 6 hours or overnight. Serve well chilled.

Per Serving

calories: 245 | fat: 21g | protein: 8g | carbs: 7g | net carbs: 5g | fiber: 2g

Coconut and Chocolate Cake, page 175

Orange and Coconut Cake, page 175

White Chocolate Cookies, page 176

Swiss Orange Roll, page 166

Pecan Bar

Prep time: 5 minutes | Cook time: 40 minutes | Serves 12

2 cups coconut flour
5 tablespoons erythritol
4 tablespoons coconut oil, softened

½ cup heavy cream
1 egg, beaten
4 pecans, chopped

1. Mix coconut flour, erythritol, coconut oil, heavy cream, and egg.
2. Pour the batter in the air fryer basket and flatten well.
3. Top the mixture with pecans and cook the meal at 350F (180ºC) for 40 minutes.
4. Cut the cooked meal into the bars.

Per Serving
calories: 174 | fat: 12g | protein: 4g | carbs: 14g | net carbs: 5g | fiber: 9g

Cream Puffs

Prep time: 15 minutes | Cook time: 6 minutes | Makes 8 puffs

½ cup blanched finely ground almond flour
½ cup low-carb vanilla protein powder
½ cup granular erythritol
½ teaspoon baking powder
1 large egg
5 tablespoons unsalted butter, melted

2 ounces (57 g) full-fat cream cheese
¼ cup powdered erythritol
¼ teaspoon ground cinnamon
2 tablespoons heavy whipping cream
½ teaspoon vanilla extract

1. Mix almond flour, protein powder, granular erythritol, baking powder, egg, and butter in a large bowl until a soft dough forms.
2. Place the dough in the freezer for 20 minutes. Wet your hands with water and roll the dough into eight balls.
3. Cut a piece of parchment to fit your air fryer basket. Working in batches as necessary, place the dough balls into the air fryer basket on top of parchment.
4. Adjust the temperature to 380°F (193ºC) and set the timer for 6 minutes.
5. Flip cream puffs halfway through the cooking time.
6. When the timer beeps, remove the puffs and allow them to cool.
7. In a medium bowl, beat the cream cheese, powdered erythritol, cinnamon, cream, and vanilla until fluffy.

8. Place the mixture into a pastry bag or a storage bag with the end snipped. Cut a small hole in the bottom of each puff and fill with some of the cream mixture.
9. Store in an airtight container up to 2 days in the refrigerator.

Per Serving
calories: 178 | fat: 12g | protein: 15g | carbs: 22g | net carbs: 21g | fiber: 1g

Monkey Bread

Prep time: 15 minutes | Cook time: 12 minutes | Serves 6

½ cup blanched finely ground almond flour
½ cup low-carb vanilla protein powder
¾ cup granular erythritol, divided
½ teaspoon baking powder
8 tablespoons salted

butter, melted and divided
1 ounce (28 g) full-fat cream cheese, softened
1 large egg
¼ cup heavy whipping cream
½ teaspoon vanilla extract

1. In a large bowl, combine almond flour, protein powder, ½ cup erythritol, baking powder, 5 tablespoons of butter, cream cheese, and egg. A soft, sticky dough will form.
2. Place the dough in the freezer for 20 minutes. It will be firm enough to roll into balls. Wet your hands with warm water and roll into twelve balls. Place the balls into a 6-inch round baking dish.
3. In a medium skillet over medium heat, melt remaining butter with remaining erythritol. Lower the heat and continue stirring until mixture turns golden, then add cream and vanilla. Remove from heat and allow it to thicken for a few minutes while you continue to stir.
4. While the mixture cools, place baking dish into the air fryer basket.
5. Adjust the temperature to 320°F (160ºC) and set the timer for 6 minutes.
6. When the timer beeps, flip the monkey bread over onto a plate and slide it back into the baking pan. cook for an additional 4 minutes until all the tops are brown.
7. Pour the caramel sauce over the monkey bread and cook for an additional 2 minutes. Let it cool completely before serving.

Per Serving
calories: 322 | fat: 24g | protein: 20g | carbs: 34g | net carbs: 32g | fiber: 2g

Coconut Tart with Walnuts

Prep time: 15 minutes | Cook time: 13 minutes | Serves 6

1 cup coconut milk
2 eggs
½ stick butter, at room temperature
1 teaspoon vanilla essence
¼ teaspoon ground
cardamom
¼ teaspoon ground cloves
½ cup walnuts, ground
½ cup swerve
½ cup almond flour

1. Begin by preheating your Air Fryer to 360ºF. Spritz the sides and bottom of a baking pan with nonstick cooking spray.
2. Mix all ingredients until well combined. Scrape the batter into the prepared baking pan.
3. Bake approximately 13 minutes, use a toothpick to test for doneness. Bon appétit!

Per Serving

calories: 227 | fat: 20.4g | carbs: 5g | protein: 7.1g | sugar: 0.9g | fiber: 1.5g

Macadamia Bar

Prep time: 15 minutes | Cook time: 30 minutes | Serves 10

3 tablespoons butter, softened
1 teaspoon baking powder
1 teaspoon apple cider vinegar
1.5 cups coconut flour
3 tablespoons Swerve
1 teaspoon vanilla extract
2 eggs, beaten
2 ounces macadamia nuts, chopped
Cooking spray

1. Spray the air fryer basket with cooking spray.
2. Then mix all remaining ingredients in the mixing bowl and stir until you get a homogenous mixture.
3. Pour the mixture in the air fryer basket and cook at 345F (174ºC) for 30 minutes.
4. When the mixture is cooked, cut it into bars and transfer in the serving plates.

Per Serving

calories: 158 | fat: 10g | protein: 4g | carbs: 13g | net carbs: 5g | fiber: 8g

Hazelnut Cookies

Prep time: 20 minutes | Cook time: 10 minutes | Serves 6

1 cup almond flour
½ cup coconut flour
1 teaspoon baking soda
1 teaspoon fine sea salt
1 stick butter
1 cup Swerve
2 teaspoons vanilla
2 eggs, at room temperature
1 cup hazelnuts, coarsely chopped

1. Begin by preheating your Air Fryer to 350ºF (180ºC).
2. Mix the flour with the baking soda, and sea salt.
3. In the bowl of an electric mixer, beat the butter, Swerve, and vanilla until creamy. Fold in the eggs, one at a time, and mix until well combined.
4. Slowly and gradually, stir in the flour mixture. Finally, fold in the coarsely chopped hazelnuts.
5. Divide the dough into small balls using a large cookie scoop, drop onto the prepared cookie sheets. Bake for 10 minutes or until golden brown, rotating the pan once or twice through the cooking time.
6. Work in batches and cool for a couple of minutes before removing to wire racks. Enjoy!

Per Serving

calories: 328 | fat: 32g | protein: 7g | carbs: 5g | net carbs: 3g | fiber: 2g

Pecan Butter Cookie

Prep time: 5 minutes | Cook time: 24 minutes | Makes 12 cookies

1 cup chopped pecans
½ cup salted butter, melted
½ cup coconut flour
¾ cup erythritol, divided
1 teaspoon vanilla extract

1. In a food processor, blend together pecans, butter, flour, ½ cup erythritol, and vanilla for 1 minute until a dough forms.
2. Form dough into twelve individual cookie balls, about 1 tablespoon each.
3. Cut three pieces of parchment to fit air fryer basket. Place four cookies on each ungreased parchment and place one piece parchment with cookies into air fryer basket. Adjust air fryer temperature to 325°F (163ºC) and set the timer for 8 minutes. Repeat cooking with remaining batches.
4. When the timer goes off, allow cookies to cool for 5 minutes on a large serving plate until cool enough to handle. While still warm, dust cookies with remaining erythritol. Allow to cool completely, about for 15 minutes, before serving.

Per Serving

calories: 151 | fat: 14g | protein: 2g | carbs: 13g | net carbs: 10g | fiber: 3g

Pecan and Mixed Berries Streusel

Prep time: 15 minutes | Cook time: 17 minutes | Serves 3

3 tablespoons pecans, chopped
3 tablespoons almonds, slivered
2 tablespoons walnuts, chopped
3 tablespoons granulated swerve
½ teaspoon ground cinnamon
1 egg
2 tablespoons cold salted butter, cut into pieces
½ cup mixed berries

1. Mix your nuts, swerve, cinnamon, egg, and butter until well combined.
2. Place mixed berries on the bottom of a lightly greased Air Fryer-safe dish. Top with the prepared topping.
3. Bake at 340ºF for 17 minutes. Serve at room temperature. Bon appétit!

Per Serving
calories: 255 | fat: 22.8g | carbs: 9.1g | protein: 7.3g | sugar: 0.6g | fiber: 4g

Chocolate Cake with Pecan

Prep time: 30 minutes | Cook time: 22 minutes | Serves 6

½ cup butter, melted
½ cup Swerve
1 teaspoon vanilla essence
1 egg
½ cup almond flour
½ teaspoon baking powder
¼ cup cocoa powder
½ teaspoon ground cinnamon
¼ teaspoon fine sea salt
1 ounce (28 g) bakers' chocolate, unsweetened
¼ cup pecans, finely chopped

1. Start by preheating your Air Fryer to 350ºF (180ºC). Now, lightly grease six silicone molds.
2. In a mixing dish, beat the melted butter with the Swerve until fluffy. Next, stir in the vanilla and egg and beat again.
3. After that, add the almond flour, baking powder, cocoa powder, cinnamon, and salt. Mix until everything is well combined.
4. Fold in the chocolate and pecans, mix to combine. Bake in the preheated Air Fryer for 20 to 22 minutes. Enjoy!

Per Serving
calories: 253 | fat: 25g | protein: 4g | carbs: 6g | net carbs: 3g | fiber: 3g

Berry Compote with Coconut Chips

Prep time: 15 minutes | Cook time: 20 minutes | Serves 6

1 tablespoon butter
12 ounces (340 g) mixed berries
⅓ cup granulated swerve
¼ teaspoon grated nutmeg
¼ teaspoon ground cloves
½ teaspoon ground cinnamon
1 teaspoon pure vanilla extract
½ cup coconut chips

1. Start by preheating your Air Fryer to 330ºF. Grease a baking pan with butter.
2. Place all ingredients, except for the coconut chips, in a baking pan. Bake in the preheated Air Fryer for 20 minutes.
3. Serve in individual bowls, garnished with coconut chips. Bon appétit!

Per Serving
calories: 176 | fat: 14.3g | carbs: 9.5g | protein: 0.6g | sugar: 1.1g | fiber: 2.1g

Almond Fruit Cookie

Prep time: 50 minutes | Cook time: 13 minutes | Serves 8

½ cup slivered almonds
1 stick butter, room temperature
4 ounces (113 g) monk fruit
⅔ cup blanched almond flour
⅓ cup coconut flour
⅓ teaspoon ground cloves
1 tablespoon ginger powder
¾ teaspoon pure vanilla extract

1. In a mixing dish, beat the monk fruit, butter, vanilla extract, ground cloves, and ginger until light and fluffy. Then, throw in the coconut flour, almond flour, and slivered almonds.
2. Continue mixing until it forms a soft dough. Cover and place in the refrigerator for 35 minutes. Meanwhile, preheat the Air Fryer to 315ºF (157ºC).
3. Roll dough into small cookies and place them on the Air Fryer cake pan, gently press each cookie using the back of a spoon.
4. Bake these butter cookies for 13 minutes. Bon appétit!

Per Serving
calories: 199 | fat: 19g | protein: 3g | carbs: 4g | net carbs: 2g | fiber: 2g

Mascarpone Chocolate Cake

Prep time: 15 minutes | Cook time: 18 minutes | Serves 6

2 tablespoons stevia
½ cup coconut flour
½ cup butter
1 cup mascarpone cheese, at room temperature

4 ounces (113 g) baker's chocolate, unsweetened
1 teaspoon vanilla extract
2 drops peppermint extract

1. Beat the sugar, coconut flour, and butter in a mixing bowl. Press the mixture into the bottom of a lightly greased baking pan.
2. Bake at 350ºF for 18 minutes. Place it in your freezer for 20 minutes.
3. Then, make the cheesecake topping by mixing the remaining ingredients. Place this topping over the crust and allow it to cool in your freezer for a further 15 minutes. Serve well chilled.

Per Serving

calories: 313 | fat: 31.1g | carbs: 7.8g | protein: 7.9g | sugar: 0.7g | fiber: 3.6g

Coconut and Chocolate Cake

Prep time: 10 minutes | Cook time: 15 minutes | Serves 6

½ stick butter, at room temperature
½ cup chocolate, unsweetened and chopped
1 tablespoon liquid stevia

1½ cups coconut flour
A pinch of fine sea salt
2 eggs, whisked
½ teaspoon vanilla extract

1. Begin by preheating your Air Fryer to 330ºF.
2. In a microwave-safe bowl, melt the butter, chocolate, and stevia.
3. Add the other ingredients to the cooled chocolate mixture, stir to combine well. Scrape the batter into a lightly greased baking pan.
4. Bake in the preheated Air Fryer for 15 minutes or until the center is springy and a toothpick comes out dry. Enjoy!

Per Serving

calories: 206 | fat: 20.5g | carbs: 6.7g | protein: 3.7g | sugar: 1.3g | fiber: 3.6g

Orange and Coconut Cake

Prep time: 15 minutes | Cook time: 17 minutes | Serves 6

¾ cup coconut flour
⅓ cup coconut milk
2 tablespoons orange jam, unsweetened
1 stick butter
¾ cup granulated swerve
2 eggs

1¼ cups almond flour
½ teaspoon baking powder
⅓ teaspoon grated nutmeg
¼ teaspoon salt

1. Set the Air Fryer to cook at 355ºF. Spritz the inside of a cake pan with the cooking spray. Then, beat the butter with granulated swerve until fluffy.
2. Fold in the eggs, continue mixing until smooth. Throw in the coconut flour, salt, and nutmeg, then, slowly and carefully pour in the coconut milk.
3. Finally, add almond flour, baking powder and orange jam, mix thoroughly to create the cake batter.
4. Then, press the batter into the cake pan. Bake for 17 minutes and transfer your cake to a cooling rack. Frost the cake and serve chilled. Enjoy!

Per Serving

calories: 339 | fat: 33.1g | carbs: 7.2g | protein: 6.8g | sugar: 0.4g | fiber: 3.7g

Monk Fruit Cookie

Prep time: 25 minutes | Cook time: 20 minutes | Serves 4

8 ounces (227 g) almond meal
2 tablespoons flaxseed meal
1 ounce (28 g) monk fruit
1 teaspoon baking powder

A pinch of grated nutmeg
A pinch of coarse salt
1 large egg, room temperature.
1 stick butter, room temperature
1 teaspoon vanilla extract

1. Mix the almond meal, flaxseed meal, monk fruit, baking powder, grated nutmeg, and salt in a bowl.
2. In a separate bowl, whisk the egg, butter, and vanilla extract.
3. Stir the egg mixture into dry mixture, mix to combine well or until it forms a nice, soft dough.
4. Roll your dough out and cut out with a cookie cutter of your choice.
5. Bake in the preheated Air Fryer at 350ºF (180ºC) for 10 minutes. Decrease the temperature to 330ºF (166ºC) and cook for 10 minutes longer. Bon appétit!

Per Serving

calories: 388 | fat: 38g | protein: 8g | carbs: 7g | net carbs: 4g | fiber: 3g

White Chocolate Cookies

Prep time: 15 minutes | Cook time: 11 minutes | Serves 10

¾ cup butter
1 ⅔ cups almond flour
½ cup coconut flour
2 tablespoons coconut oil
¾ cup granulated swerve
⅓ teaspoon ground anise star
⅓ teaspoon ground

allspice
⅓ teaspoon grated nutmeg
¼ teaspoon fine sea salt
8 ounces (227 g) white chocolate, unsweetened
2 eggs, well beaten

1. Put all of the above ingredients, minus 1 egg, into a mixing dish. Then, knead with hand until a soft dough is formed. Place in the refrigerator for 20 minutes.
2. Roll the chilled dough into small balls, flatten your balls and preheat the Air Fryer r to 350ºF.
3. Make an egg wash by using the remaining egg. Then, glaze the cookies with the egg wash, bake about 11 minutes. Bon appétit!

Per Serving
calories: 389 | fat: 36.3g | carbs: 9.7g | protein: 7g | sugar: 1.1g | fiber: 5.7g

Classic Raspberry Muffins

Prep time: 15 minutes | Cook time: 15 minutes | Serves 6

½ cup raspberries
¾ cup swerve
½ cup coconut oil
1 cup sour cream
1¼ teaspoons baking powder
2 cups almond flour
2 eggs

⅓ teaspoon ground allspice
⅓ teaspoon ground anise star
½ teaspoon grated lemon zest
¼ teaspoon salt

1. Grab two mixing bowls. In the first bowl, thoroughly combine the almond flour, baking powder, swerve, salt, anise, allspice and lemon zest.
2. Take the second bowl, whisk coconut oil, sour cream, and eggs, whisk to combine well. Now, add the wet mixture to the dry mixture. Fold in the raspberries.
3. Press the batter mixture into a lightly greased muffin tin. Bake at 345ºfor 15 minutes. Use a toothpick to check if your muffins are baked. Bon appétit!

Per Serving
calories: 440 | fat: 42g | carbs: 9.2g | protein: 9.4g | sugar: 0.9g | fiber: 4.6g

Vanilla Scones

Prep time: 20 minutes | Cook time: 10 minutes | Serves 6

4 ounce coconut flour
½ teaspoon baking powder
1 teaspoon apple cider vinegar

2 teaspoons mascarpone
¼ cup heavy cream
1 teaspoon vanilla extract
1 tablespoon erythritol
Cooking spray

1. In the mixing bowl, mix coconut flour with baking powder, apple cider vinegar, mascarpone, heavy cream, vanilla extract, and erythritol.
2. Knead the dough and cut into scones.
3. Then put them in the air fryer basket and sprinkle with cooking spray.
4. Cook the vanilla scones at 365F (185ºC) for 10 minutes.

Per Serving
calories: 104 | fat: 4g | protein: 3g | carbs: 14g | net carbs: 6g | fiber: 8g

Ginger and Almond Cookies

Prep time: 15 minutes | Cook time: 13 minutes | Serves 8

½ cup slivered almonds
1 stick butter, room temperature
4 ounces (113 g) monk fruit
⅔ cup blanched almond flour

⅓ cup coconut flour
⅓ teaspoon ground cloves
1 tablespoon ginger powder
¾ teaspoon pure vanilla extract

1. In a mixing dish, beat the monk fruit, butter, vanilla extract, ground cloves, and ginger until light and fluffy. Then, throw in the coconut flour, almond flour, and slivered almonds.
2. Continue mixing until it forms a soft dough. Cover and place in the refrigerator for 35 minutes. Meanwhile, preheat the Air Fryer to 315ºF.
3. Roll dough into small cookies and place them on the Air Fryer cake pan, gently press each cookie using the back of a spoon.
4. Bake these butter cookies for 13 minutes. Bon appétit!

Per Serving
calories: 199 | fat: 19.2g | carbs: 3.8g | protein: 3.3g | sugar: 0.7g | fiber: 2.2g

Coconut and Chocolate Pudding

Prep time: 15 minutes | Cook time: 15 minutes | Serves 10

1 stick butter
1¼ cups bakers' chocolate, unsweetened
1 teaspoon liquid stevia
2 tablespoons full fat coconut milk
2 eggs, beaten
⅓ cup coconut, shredded

1. Begin by preheating your Air Fryer to 330ºF.
2. In a microwave-safe bowl, melt the butter, chocolate, and stevia. Allow it to cool to room temperature.
3. Add the remaining ingredients to the chocolate mixture, stir to combine well. Scrape the batter into a lightly greased baking pan.
4. Bake in the preheated Air Fryer for 15 minutes or until a toothpick comes out dry and clean. Enjoy!

Per Serving

calories: 229 | fat: 21.3g | carbs: 5.4g | protein: 4.4g | sugar: 0.5g | fiber: 3g

Pecan Chocolate Brownies

Prep time: 10 minutes | Cook time: 20 minutes | Serves 6

½ cup blanched finely ground almond flour
½ cup powdered erythritol
2 tablespoons unsweetened cocoa powder
½ teaspoon baking
powder
¼ cup unsalted butter, softened
1 large egg
¼ cup chopped pecans
¼ cup low-carb, sugar-free chocolate chips

1. In a large bowl, mix almond flour, erythritol, cocoa powder, and baking powder. Stir in butter and egg.
2. Fold in pecans and chocolate chips. Scoop mixture into 6-inch round baking pan. Place pan into the air fryer basket.
3. Adjust the temperature to 300°F (150ºC) and set the timer for 20 minutes.
4. When fully cooked a toothpick inserted in center will come out clean. Allow it to fully cool and firm up for 20 minutes.

Per Serving

calories: 215 | fat: 18g | protein: 4g | carbs: 22g | net carbs: 19g | fiber: 3g

Provolone Cheese Balls

Prep time: 15 minutes | Cook time: 4 minutes | Serves 10

2 eggs, beaten
1 teaspoon coconut oil, melted
9 ounces (255 g) coconut flour
5 ounces (142 g) provolone cheese,
shredded
2 tablespoons erythritol
1 teaspoon baking powder
¼ teaspoon ground coriander
Cooking spray

1. Mix eggs with coconut oil, coconut flour, Provolone cheese, erythritol, baking powder, and ground cinnamon.
2. Make the balls and put them in the air fryer basket.
3. Sprinkle the balls with cooking spray and cook at 400F (205ºC) for 4 minutes.

Per Serving

calories: 176 | fat: 7g | protein: 8g | carbs: 19g | net carbs: 8g | fiber: 11g

Golden Doughnut Holes

Prep time: 10 minutes | Cook time: 6 minutes | Makes 20 doughnut holes

1 cup blanched finely ground almond flour
½ cup low-carb vanilla protein powder
½ cup granular erythritol
¼ cup unsweetened
cocoa powder
½ teaspoon baking powder
2 large eggs, whisked
½ teaspoon vanilla extract

1. Mix all ingredients in a large bowl until a soft dough forms. Separate and roll dough into twenty balls, about 2 tablespoons each.
2. Cut a piece of parchment to fit your air fryer basket. Working in batches if needed, place doughnut holes into air fryer basket on ungreased parchment. Adjust the temperature to 380°F (193ºC) and set the timer for 6 minutes, flipping doughnut holes halfway through cooking. Doughnut holes will be golden and firm when done. Let it cool completely before serving, for about 10 minutes.

Per Serving

calories: 103 | fat: 7g | protein: 8g | carbs: 13g | net carbs: 11g | fiber: 2g

Coconut Muffin

Prep time: 5 minutes | Cook time: 25 minutes | Serves 5

½ cup coconut flour
2 tablespoons cocoa powder
3 tablespoons erythritol
1 teaspoon baking powder
2 tablespoons coconut oil
2 eggs, beaten
½ cup coconut shred

1. In the mixing bowl, mix all ingredients.
2. Then pour the mixture in the molds of the muffin and transfer in the air fryer basket.
3. Cook the muffins at 350F (180ºC) for 25 minutes.

Per Serving
calories: 206 | fat: 16g | protein: 4g | carbs: 13g | net carbs: 6g | fiber: 7g

Poppy Seed Muffin

Prep time: 10 minutes | Cook time: 10 minutes | Serves 5

5 tablespoons coconut oil, softened
1 egg, beaten
1 teaspoon vanilla extract
1 tablespoon poppy seeds
1 teaspoon baking powder
2 tablespoons erythritol
1 cup coconut flour

1. In the mixing bowl, mix coconut oil with egg, vanilla extract, poppy seeds, baking powder, erythritol, and coconut flour.
2. When the mixture is homogenous, pour it in the muffin molds and transfer it in the air fryer basket.
3. Cook the muffins for 10 minutes at 365F (185ºC).

Per Serving
calories: 239 | fat: 17g | protein: 5g | carbs: 17g | net carbs: 7g | fiber: 10g

Lime Bar

Prep time: 10 minutes | Cook time: 35 minutes | Serves 10

3 tablespoons coconut oil, melted
3 tablespoons Splenda
1½ cup coconut flour
3 eggs, beaten
1 teaspoon lime zest, grated
3 tablespoons lime juice

1. Cover the air fryer basket bottom with baking paper.
2. Then in the mixing bowl, mix Splenda with coconut flour, eggs, lime zest, and lime juice.
3. Pour the mixture in the air fryer basket and flatten gently.
4. Cook the meal at 350F (180ºC) for 35 minutes.
5. Then cool the cooked meal little and cut into bars.

Per Serving
calories: 144 | fat: 7g | protein: 4g | carbs: 16g | net carbs: 8g | fiber: 7g

Mint Pie

Prep time: 15 minutes | Cook time: 25 minutes | Serves 2

1 tablespoon instant coffee
2 tablespoons almond butter, softened
2 tablespoons erythritol
1 teaspoon dried mint
3 eggs, beaten
1 teaspoon spearmint, dried
4 teaspoons coconut flour
Cooking spray

1. Spray the air fryer basket with cooking spray.
2. Then mix all ingredients in the mixer bowl.
3. When you get a smooth mixture, transfer it in the air fryer basket. Flatten it gently.
4. Cook the pie at 365F (185ºC) for 25 minutes.

Per Serving
calories: 313 | fat: 19g | protein: 16g | carbs: 20g | net carbs: 8g | fiber: 12g

Toasted Coconut Flakes

Prep time: 5 minutes | Cook time: 3 minutes | Serves 4

1 cup unsweetened coconut flakes
2 teaspoons coconut oil
¼ cup granular erythritol
⅛ teaspoon salt

1. Toss coconut flakes and oil in a large bowl until coated. Sprinkle with erythritol and salt.
2. Place coconut flakes into the air fryer basket.
3. Adjust the temperature to 300°F (150ºC) and set the timer for 3 minutes.
4. Toss the flakes when 1 minute remains. Add an extra minute if you would like a more golden coconut flake.
5. Store in an airtight container up to 3 days.

Per Serving
calories: 165 | fat: 15g | protein: 1g | carbs: 20g | net carbs: 17g | fiber: 3g

Zucchini Bread

Prep time: 10 minutes | Cook time: 40 minutes | Serves 12

2 cups coconut flour	vinegar
2 teaspoons baking powder	1 teaspoon vanilla extract
¾ cup erythritol	3 eggs, beaten
½ cup coconut oil, melted	1 zucchini, grated
1 teaspoon apple cider	1 teaspoon ground cinnamon

1. In the mixing bowl, mix coconut flour with baking powder, erythritol, coconut oil, apple cider vinegar, vanilla extract, eggs, zucchini, and ground cinnamon.
2. Transfer the mixture in the air fryer basket and flatten it in the shape of the bread.
3. Cook the bread at 350F (180ºC) for 40 minutes.

Per Serving

calories: 179 | fat: 12g | protein: 4g | carbs: 15g | net carbs: 7g | fiber: 8g

Chocolate Chip Cookie Cake

Prep time: 5 minutes | Cook time: 15 minutes | Serves 8

4 tablespoons salted butter, melted	1 cup blanched finely ground almond flour
⅓ cup granular brown erythritol	½ teaspoon baking powder
1 large egg	¼ cup low-carb chocolate chips
½ teaspoon vanilla extract	

1. In a large bowl, whisk together butter, erythritol, egg, and vanilla. Add flour and baking powder, and stir until combined.
2. Fold in chocolate chips, then spoon batter into an ungreased 6-inch round nonstick baking dish.
3. Place dish into air fryer basket. Adjust the temperature to 300°F (150ºC) and set the timer for 15 minutes. When edges are browned, cookie cake will be done.
4. Slice and serve warm.

Per Serving

calories: 170 | fat: 16g | protein: 4g | carbs: 15g | net carbs: 11g | fiber: 4g

Walnut Butter Cookie

Prep time: 40 minutes | Cook time: 15 minutes | Serves 8

½ cup walnuts, ground	2 tablespoons rum
½ cup coconut flour	½ teaspoon pure vanilla extract
1 cup almond flour	½ teaspoon pure almond extract
¾ cup Swerve	
1 stick butter, room temperature	

1. In a mixing dish, beat the butter with Swerve, vanilla, and almond extract until light and fluffy. Then, throw in the flour and ground walnuts, add in rum.
2. Continue mixing until it forms a soft dough. Cover and place in the refrigerator for 20 minutes. In the meantime, preheat the Air Fryer to 330ºF (166ºC).
3. Roll the dough into small cookies and place them on the Air Fryer cake pan, gently press each cookie using a spoon.
4. Bake butter cookies for 15 minutes in the preheated Air Fryer. Bon appétit!

Per Serving

calories: 228 | fat: 22g | protein: 4g | carbs: 4g | net carbs: 2g | fiber: 2g

Appendix 1: Measurement Conversion Chart

Volume Equivalents (Dry)	
US STANDARD	METRIC (APPROXIMATE)
1/8 teaspoon	0.5 mL
1/4 teaspoon	1 mL
1/2 teaspoon	2 mL
3/4 teaspoon	4 mL
1 teaspoon	5 mL
1 tablespoon	15 mL
1/4 cup	59 mL
1/2 cup	118 mL
3/4 cup	177 mL
1 cup	235 mL
2 cups	475 mL
3 cups	700 mL
4 cups	1 L

Temperatures Equivalents	
FAHRENHEIT (F)	CELSIUS(C) (APPROXIMATE)
225 °F	107 °C
250 °F	120 °C
275 °F	135 °C
300 °F	150 °C
325 °F	160 °C
350 °F	180 °C
375 °F	190 °C
400 °F	205 °C
425 °F	220 °C
450 °F	235 °C
475 °F	245 °C
500 °F	260 °C

Volume Equivalents (Liquid)		
US STANDARD	US STANDARD (OUNCES)	METRIC (APPROXIMATE)
2 tablespoons	1 fl.oz.	30 mL
1/4 cup	2 fl.oz.	60 mL
1/2 cup	4 fl.oz.	120 mL
1 cup	8 fl.oz.	240 mL
1 1/2 cup	12 fl.oz.	355 mL
2 cups or 1 pint	16 fl.oz.	475 mL
4 cups or 1 quart	32 fl.oz.	1 L
1 gallon	128 fl.oz.	4 L

Weight Equivalents	
US STANDARD	METRIC (APPROXIMATE)
1 ounce	28 g
2 ounces	57 g
5 ounces	142 g
10 ounces	284 g
15 ounces	425 g
16 ounces (1 pound)	455 g
1.5 pounds	680 g
2 pounds	907 g

Appendix 2: The Dirty Dozen and Clean Fifteen

The Environmental Working Group (EWG) is a widely known organization that has an eminent guide to pesticides and produce. More specifically, the group takes in data from tests conducted by the US Department of Agriculture (USDA) and then categorizes produce into a list titled "Dirty Dozen," which ranks the twelve top produce items that contain the most pesticide residues, or alternatively the "Clean Fifteen," which ranks fifteen produce items that are contaminated with the least amount of pesticide residues.

The EWG has recently released their 2021 Dirty Dozen list, and this year strawberries, spinach and kale – with a few other produces which will be revealed shortly – are listed at the top of the list. This year's ranking is similar to the 2020 Dirty Dozen list, with the few differences being that collards and mustard greens have joined kale at number three on the list. Other changes include peaches and cherries, which having been listed subsequently as seventh and eighth on the 2020 list, have now been flipped; the introduction – which the EWG has said is the first time ever – of bell and hot peppers into the 2021 list; and the departure of potatoes from the twelfth spot.

DIRTY DOZEN LIST

* Strawberries
* Spinach
* Kale, collards and mustard greens
* Nectarines
* Apples
* Grapes
* Cherries
* Peaches
* Pears
* Bell and hot peppers
* Celery
* Tomatoes

CLEAN FIFTEEN LIST

* Avocados
* Sweet corn
* Pineapple
* Onions
* Papaya
* Sweet peas (frozen)
* Eggplant
* Asparagus
* Broccoli
* Cabbage
* Kiwi
* Cauliflower
* Mushrooms
* Honeydew melon
* Cantaloupe

These lists are created to help keep the public informed on their potential exposures to pesticides, which then allows for better and healthier food choices to be made.

This is the advice that ASEQ-EHAQ also recommends. Stay clear of the dirty dozen by opting for their organic versions, and always be mindful of what you are eating and how it was grown. Try to eat organic as much as possible – whether it is on the list, or not.

Appendix 3: Recipes Index

Made in the USA
Monee, IL
05 April 2022